NEW LEGAL FOUNDATIONS
FOR
GLOBAL SURVIVAL

Security Through the Security Council

By

Benjamin B. Ferencz

Introduction By
Professor Louis B. Sohn

Bibliography Compiled by
Britt S.M. Kjölstad

NOTE: The paperback edition does not
contain the bibliography or the index.

D1157302

Library of Congress Catalog in Publication Data

Ferencz, Benjamin B.
    New Legal Foundations for Global Survival: Security Through
    the Security Council

ISBN: 0-379-21207-2   1994

ABOUT THE AUTHOR:

Benjamin B. Ferencz, born in Transylvania and raised in New York, was graduated from the Harvard Law School in 1943. He saw military service in World War II where, as a war crimes investigator, he joined in the liberation of several German concentration camps. At the age of 27, he was designated the Chief Prosecutor for the United States in the Nuremberg war crimes trial against SS extermination squads responsible for the genocidal murder of over a million innocent people. His abhorrence of all crimes against humanity stimulated his determination to dedicate himself to seeking a world order where all could live in peace and dignity regardless of their race or creed.

Dr. Ferencz helped to fashion and implement German laws to compensate victims of Nazi persecution and directed a worldwide legal-aid network to assist survivors with their claims. He represented leading churches and charities helping the oppressed in many lands. He was elected a Vice-President of the American Society of International Law and was active in many peace and international law organizations. He became an Adjunct Professor at Pace Law School where he founded a Peace Center and taught "The International Law of Peace." He is an accredited non-governmental observer at the United Nations and is a frequent lecturer. He is married, has four grown children and lives in New Rochelle, New York.

OTHER BOOKS BY BENJAMIN B. FERENCZ

Defining International Aggression - The Search for World Peace (2 vols., Oceana, 1975).

Less Than Slaves: Jewish Forced Labor and the Quest for Compensation (Harvard, 1979). [German edition, *Lohn des Grauens, Campus Verlag;* 1981 Made into a TV Documentary. Japanese edition, Gaifu Sha, 1993]

An International Criminal Court - A Step Toward World Peace (2 vols., Oceana, 1980).

Enforcing International Law - A Way to World Peace, (2 vols., Oceana, 1983).

A Common Sense Guide to World Peace (Oceana, 1985). German edition, *Wege zum Weltfrieden,* Campus Verlag, 1980.

Planethood (With Ken Keyes Jr.) (Vision Books, 1988, revised ed. 1991).[French edition, *Planethood ou les Citoyens du Monde, Les Editions Universelle du Verseau,* 1989]

World Security for the 21st Century, Editor, a Colloquium (Oceana 1991).

Benjamin B. Ferencz

ABOUT THE BOOK

This book is a thoughtful, practical and above all, timely examination of how to promote peace and security in the world. It advances the proposition - once at the core of American foreign policy - that increasing the salience of international law can help to regulate and mitigate violence in the world. And it is our own best interests. It should be read by those who despair of finding any useful steps forward from a world of anarchy and ethnic turmoil.

Daniel Patrick Moynihan
Senior Senator from New York

This creative book proposes constructive legal and moral ways by which the United Nations can be effective in the world after the Cold War.

This volume is essential reading for every person who desires to be a moral architect of the new world based on the rule of law and human dignity.

Prof. Robert F. Drinan, S.J.
Georgetown University Law Center

Benjamin Ferencz's book stands out as one that is impressive, not only because of the depth of the analysis, or because of the daring of the proposals, but because the combination of both is so rare...It is required reading for anyone seriously interested in the policy implications of the end of the cold war.

Peter Hansen
The (Stockholm) Commission on Global Governance

In this book, Ben Ferencz continues his search for a new world order under law, offering novel but practical insights on everything from the meaning of sovereignty to overhauling the U.N. Charter. It is a book that no one interested in the future of the world order should be without.

Stephen C. McCaffrey,
Professor of Law, McGeorge School of Law
Graduate & International Studies

I hope this book will be widely read, not only by legal scholars, but by thoughtful citizens in every field. In this book Ben Ferencz demonstrates that he is not only a scholar and visionary, but also a skilled architect of a peaceful future. The task remains to build upon his blueprint.

David Krieger
President
Nuclear Age Peace Foundation

A visionary scholar, Ben Ferencz presents a carefully crafted blueprint for global survival. Thoroughly researched, eloquently written with an historic context, the book is a crystallization of the author's idealistic -- and pragmatic - prescriptions for global peace and security with justice as its foundation. I consider it a masterpiece!

Prof. Ved P. Nanda
Director, International Legal Studies Program
University of Denver

APPRECIATION

May I express my appreciation to all those dedicated persons who have taken the time to give me the benefit of their wisdom, guidance or assistance. This is not to suggest that any of them shares all, or any, of the views expressed herein.

At the United Nations, I am particularly indebted to Senior Legal Officer Roy Lee, Jacqueline Dauchy, Director of the Codification Division, and her staff members Manuel Rama-Montaldo and Virginia Morris. Retired Director of the UN Office of Legal Counsel Paul Szasz, Dr. Abdel-Kader Abbadi of the Office of Political Affairs, Political Affairs Officer B. G. Ramcharan, Mr. Iqbal Riza, Assistant Secretary-General for Peace-keeping Operations and Colonel Gerard Gambiez, Chief of Stand-By Forces, provided helpful insights as did Miss Norma Chan, Political Affairs Officer of the Security Council Secretariat. Robert Rosenstock, Counsellor to the U. S. Mission to the UN and a member of the International Law Commission frequently gave me the benefit of his views.

Members of the Max Planck Institute in Heidelberg have always been helpful and I am particularly indebted to the Directors Rudolf Bernhardt, Jochen Abr. Frowein, Rüdiger Wulfram, and Library Director Joachim Schwietzke, and his assistants Dr. Harald Mueller and Irmgard Bühler. Without the help of good librarians I would be lost, and I am grateful to UN Legal Librarian Britt Kjölstad and UN Security Council Librarian and helpful Researcher Solange Habib. *bad mistake!*

Erika Schlager, Staff Assistant of the Commission on Security and Cooperation in Europe sent interesting materials, as did Professor Joseph Weiler of the Harvard Law School. My publisher, Philip F. Cohen, has always been encouraging. Among the Oceana staff I particularly appreciate the efforts of M.C. Susan DeMaio, Nicholas Brandi and John Downey. Needless to say, I am indebted to the many named, and unnamed, authors whose works on behalf of peace have inspired my own efforts to move toward our common goals. Last, but certainly very far from least, I am very deeply grateful to my good wife, Gertrude, for her understanding, patience, encouragement and constant help in an infinite variety of ways that eased the burdens of this difficult journey.

I hope that no blame will come to me for this essay, particularly if it should appear that it is neither chimerical nor injurious to anyone, and that, on the contrary, it may inspire some pen more capable than my own in judging and advancing this design...I can see no alternative so advantageous as this one for the peace and happiness of this part of the world.

William Penn (1693).[1]

---

1   I am grateful to Anne C. Kjelling, Librarian of the Nobel Peace Institute in Oslo for providing me with a copy of the original French text of William Penn's *Essai d'un Projet Pour Rendre La Paix de L'Europe Solide & Durable* (1693?) from which I have translated the cited text.

TABLE OF CONTENTS

INTRODUCTION

Professor Ferencz, a distinguished teacher and lawyer, is both an idealist and a practical person. He sets for himself -- and for mankind -- far reaching goals, and then proceeds towards them by careful steps, watching for obstacles, finding ways of getting around them, and devising the necessary machinery that would bring him and mankind -- faster to the most desirable objective -- peace with justice for all.

In his major previous books he collected the raw materials, which he now skillfully molds into a comprehensive structure for a new, a better, world. While he was writing those volumes, the world did not stand still. In fact, in the last few years the international picture started changing drastically, and the things that seemed impossible in the 1980s have become feasible in the 1990s. This book is arriving at the right moment when mankind is starting to develop a new "Agenda for Peace", and may soon be ready for dynamic changes.

The author's basic premise is that the United Nations Charter is a feasible instrument which, like the United States Constitution, can be adapted to changing circumstances, while amendments to the Charter are difficult, much can be accomplished by "innovative interpretation of that global constitution. One of the early interpretations which enabled the Security Council to function more effectively was the practice to consider a voluntary abstention from a vote by a permanent member of the council as a "concurring" vote satisfying the requirement of Article 27 of the Charter, rather than a "veto". When South Africa raised an objection to this practice, the International Court of Justice in the Case had before it a statement of the Secretary-General pointing out that the Security Council had accepted this interpretation 105 times; and the Court concurred with this view (1971 ICJ Reports; para. 22). The Court rejected the South African objection on the ground that

> "the proceedings of the Security Council extending over a long period supply abundant evidence that presidential rulings and the positions taken by members of the Council, in particular its permanent members, have consistently and uniformly interpreted the practice of voluntary abstention by a permanent member as not constituting a bar to the adoption of resolutions. By abstaining, a member does not signify its objection to the approval of what is being proposed: in order to prevent the adoption of a resolution requiring unanimity of the permanent members, a permanent member has only to cast a negative vote. This procedure followed by the Security Council, which has continued unchanged after the amendment in 1965 of Article 27 of the Charter, has been generally accepted by Members of the United Nations and evidences a general practice of that Organization."

Similarly, the International Court of Justice is likely to approve the United Nations practice of consensus, i.e. approval of a decision by the General Assembly or the Security Council without an actual vote, regardless of express voting rules in Articles 18 and 27 of the Charter. In the Security Council such decisions are announced by the President of the Council at a public meeting of the Council, after agreeing upon them in private consultations, and no vote is required. In the General Assembly, the presiding officer simply announces that the decision under discussion has been approved by "consensus" or "without vote".

Encouraged by recent events, and taking into account the various precedents established by the Security Council in the last few years, the author boldly contends that this Council can solve also the main problems of today by strengthening the laws, courts and enforcement mechanisms on which world security depends. As it has done in a number of cases, the Council can adopt a series of clarifying resolutions implementing Article I of the Charter, which commands the United Nations "to take effective collective measures for the prevention and removal of threats to the peace and for the suppression of acts of aggression and other breaches of the peace"; to bring about by peaceful means, and in conformity with the principles of justice and international law, adjustment or settlement of international disputes or situations which might lead to breaches of the peace"; "to take other appropriate measures to strengthen universal peace"; and to harmonize "the actions of nations in the attainment of these common ends".

In uniting their strength "to maintain peace and international security", the Members of the United Nations also agreed in the Charter's Preamble "to ensure, by acceptance of the principles and the institution of methods, that armed force shall not be used, save in the common interest"; and "to establish 'conditions under which justice and respect for the obligations arising from treaties and other sources of international law can be maintained." With this kind of a mandate, and with some creative thinking, there are few limits on what the Security Council can do to ensure peace and justice throughout the world. It should be remembered that the authors of the United States Constitution, in similar broad terms described the purposes of their union: to "establish justice, insure domestic tranquility, provide for common defense, promote the general welfare, and secure the blessings of liberty" to themselves and their posterity. Inspired by these words, and with the help of such interpreter's as Chief Justice Marshall, the succeeding generations during the next 200 years developed the laws and the institutions that build the mighty United States of today, of the kind, size and power that could not have been foreseen by their predecessors. Professor Ferencz exhorts the Security Council to use a similar authority that is implied in the words of the Charter, to build a United Nations worthy of the hope of those who in the aftermath of a great war were determined "to save succeeding generations from the scourge of war", and "to promote social progress and better standards of life in larger freedom."

Like America's Founding Fathers, the Member States of the United Nations need to authorize their representatives in the Security Council to prepare, in consultation with properly authorized delegates of the General Assembly, a set of basic decisions that would bring new life to the Charter and enable various United Nations institutions to deal more effectively and efficiently with the problems facing mankind. Professor Ferencz provides tentative blueprints for the Council's work in the form of twelve draft resolutions to be adopted by the Security Council.

In proposing five basic "law of peace" resolutions, the author starts with mandatory peaceful settlement of disputes, applicable not only to states, but also to individuals and groups. Anyone who tries to use force for settling a dispute would be subject to individual criminal punishment which will be meted out to all persons responsible - leaders, organizers, instigators and accomplices. No excuse will be permitted, not even self-defense. Only the Security Council would be allowed to authorize the use of force to restore peace and to punish the violator. Another rule would be to define aggression, plugging the loopholes of the General Assembly's 1974 resolution on the subject. The third resolution would prohibit and punish crimes against humanity (such as genocide, terrorism and apartheid), whenever they constitute a threat to the peace. More novel is the resolution designed to end the arms race. It would limit states to those non-nuclear armaments, forces and facilities considered by the Council to be necessary to maintain a state's internal order and protect the personal security of its citizens. In addition, the states would be obliged to train additional reserve forces in order to be able to provide "manpower for a United Nations Peace Force when called for by the Security Council." Disarmament would be carried out in stages, under strict international control that would ensure compliance, would prevent any state gaining a military advantage, and would punish violators. At the same time, measures would be taken to minimize "possible economic hardship to persons and industries affected by the transformation." The fifth law-making resolution takes into account the growing link between peace and social justice, due to the growing interdependence between on the one hand, international security, and on the other hand, economic, social and ecological factors. Consequently, this law deals with the duty of states to cooperate in promoting: a steady expansion and liberalization of world trade; an improvement in the well being and living standards of all peoples, especially those of developing countries; and the protection, preservation and enhancement of the environment. The Security Council would have the duty to protect these rights whenever it determines that their violation poses a threat to the peace.

All these resolutions build on norms that have been widely acclaimed as necessary and the Security Council would change them into clear legal obligations. The second group of three resolutions is designed to strengthen "courts for peace." They are needed to decide disputes between states, but also they must protect the integrity of international institutions. Granting more power to the United Nations requires a safeguard against arbitrary decisions. International courts are necessary as ultimate arbiters of institutional legitimacy.

One draft resolution would require states to submit a legal dispute to the International Court of Justice, whenever the Council shall determine that the continuance of such dispute is likely to endanger the maintenance of international peace and security. If the Council should determine that a party's failure to comply with a decision of the Court would pose a threat to the peace, the Council would have the duty to "use all necessary means" to ensure that the decisions would be enforced.

The second resolution would establish the International Criminal Court, the statute of which the International Law Commission of the United Nations is now preparing. The jurisdiction of the court, according to Professor Ferencz should be a broad one, including all the crimes that the Security Council determines constitute a threat to the peace, breach of the peace or act of aggression, including violation of the five "law of Peace" resolutions mentioned in the previous paragraphs, or of the Security Council's mandate to submit a legal dispute to the International Court of Justice, or its mandate to comply with the decision of that Court. The Council would also have the duty to use "all necessary means" to ensure the enforcement of the decisions of the International Criminal Court. A separate World Tribunal for Social Justice would be established by the third peace courts resolution to protect individuals against gross violations of their rights and handle other social justice and environmental issues. In particular, the Tribunal would have jurisdiction to decide all legal questions concerning the interpretation of the resolution establishing the law for enhancing social justice, but only when the Security Council has determined that a particular issue constitutes a threat to the peace. The Tribunal's decisions would also be enforced by the Security Council whenever the Council decides that such enforcement is necessary to maintain world peace and security. The draft leaves it to the Security Council to decide how the cases will be submitted to the Tribunal and whether, in particular, private individuals would have direct access to it in some situations.

Finally, the Ferencz proposal contains four resolutions to strengthen "peace enforcement" through the establishment of appropriate executive agencies able to enforce quickly and effectively the laws of peace, especially those that provide for universal disarmament, economic sanctions, United Nations police action, or enhanced social justice. The first resolution would create a United Nations Disarmament Enforcement Agency. Its task would be: to conduct an arms census; to halt the production of new weapons and the establishment of new military installations; to destroy existing military capabilities, starting with nuclear weapons and other weapons of mass destruction; to verify that there are no evasions; to convert military plants to more useful forms of production and to retrain displaced scientists, engineers and workers. A United Nations Sanctions Agency would have the task of ensuring: that the sanctions against a transgressor are comprehensive and interrupt all economic and diplomatic relations and all means of transport and communication; that the sanctions are directed against the main guilty persons and spare the innocent civilian population; that the burden will be equitably shared by all countries and that assistance be given to countries especially affected by participating in the sanctions; and that the sanctions should target vital resources. Echoing the recent proposal of the Secretary-General of the United Nations in his Agenda for Peace (1992): Professor Ferencz proposes the creation of a United Nations Police Agency that would carry out all measures by using peacekeeping forces and other forces placed at the disposal of the Security Council or recruited directly by the United Nations for a particular situation. In addition to stand-by and reserve forces, the Agency might have available rapid deployment forces that can move quickly to put out a brush fire before it becomes a conflagration. A system of checks-and-balances must be devised to ensure that any large United Nations military force does not become a dictatorial power capable of threatening a largely disarmed world. Finally, the proposals include a United Nations Social Justice Agency able to deal with such violations of fundamental human rights that pose a threat to peace. It would monitor the global human rights situation and alert the Security Council to dangerous social injustices and oppression that might rise to the levels of a threat to peace. It should try to take preventive action when an outbreak of violence is threatening. Its other main task would be to coordinate humanitarian assistance in situations caused by natural disaster, war or civil strife, and to watch over other economic, social and environmental activities which may lead to crises that may threaten world security. If a state falls to follow the recommendations of the Agency, the Council should "use all available means" to enforce these recommendations, whenever the Council decides that failure to do so would constitute a threat to the peace.

As evidenced by this survey of the main suggestions presented in this book, there are many new ideas that deserve careful considerations. The author has read widely and each suggestion is supported by precedents and collateral thoughts gleaned from many important books and essays on the subjects. What is especially attractive is the way the author has made a most convincing case for the Security Council becoming the creator of the new international order, much better than suggested by many eminent persons. It is clearly a step in the right direction and -- unlike many other proposals -- it can be accomplished without a revision of the United Nations Charter. Perhaps not all the innovations suggested in this book can be put into effect without any difficulty. It is likely that some vested interests will oppose ideas that may affect them, and that some readers might think the project too top-heavy, requiring tremendous effort by the Security Council. Others, however, will find in this book a relatively simple solution to many problems which for too long nobody has been desiring to tackle. This book should be read eagerly both by those who want to improve the United

Nations, and by those who need to become acquainted with the wide variety of thoughts on this subject, which the author has carefully collected and analyzed.

Louis B. Sohn
Washington, DC, November 1993.
Distinguished Research Professor of Law
National Law Center, George Washington University

AUTHOR'S PREFACE
What This Book is All About

Yesterday's legal institutions can hardly cope with today's world problems; they are hopelessly inadequate for the problems of tomorrow. The purpose of this book is to demonstrate that it is feasible to organize planet earth in such a way that all who dwell upon it may live in peace and dignity. To be sure, the goal of replacing the prevailing international anarchy, strife and suffering by a more humane and tranquil world order can not be attained quickly or easily. Quite the contrary. It will take patience, determination and great effort. It will probably not be accomplished without bloodshed and torment. But it must be done and it can be done.

Two days before his death, Albert Einstein approved the text of an appeal, drafted by Lord Bertrand Russell, which was signed by nine Nobel prize winning scientists. The Russell-Einstein Declaration was made public on July 9, 1955. It pointed to the perils of nuclear war and called upon all governments to find peaceful means to settle their disputes:

> We are speaking on this occasion, not as members of this or that nation, continent or creed, but as human beings, members of the species man, whose continued existence is in doubt...We have to learn to think in a new way...We appeal, as human beings, to human beings: Remember your humanity and forget the rest. If you can do so, the way lies open to a new paradise; if you cannot, there lies before you the risk of universal death.[1]

This book seeks to guide the reader to think in a new way - as a human being - in an effort to avoid the risk of universal death. In a sense, this is a "How To" book; showing by specific legal formulations how to get from here to a more peaceful world. It is the culmination of over 20 years of intensive study and builds on ten volumes I have already written. It does not purport to regulate human or national behavior generally. It is based on the premise that nations, peoples and individuals must be free to pursue their own destinies in whatever way they may see fit - providing it does not jeopardize or destroy the fundamental human rights of others to live in peace and dignity.

Its focus is thus on those minimum norms and institutions required to cope effectively with a few major world problems that seriously endanger peace and which can only be resolved by global cooperation. Of course, it does not purport to be the last word on the subject. The drafts of legal

---

1   The Declaration and related correspondence is *reproduced in* O.NATHAN & H. NORDEN, Eds., EINSTEIN ON PEACE (1960) pp. 624-637; The Declaration appeared in the N.Y. Times, July 10, 1955.

instruments and institutions which shall point the way to needed solutions
are intended to be illustrative rather than definitive. They are designed to
show that, with sufficient determination, inherent difficulties can be overcome. The objective is to persuade the reader that the problems are NOT
insurmountable and that the necessary mechanisms can be understood and
must be supported by all concerned citizens.

Admittedly, some of the difficulties have been oversimplified. That is
deliberate. There is no need to drown in a morass of details or to search for
new problems to rebut every proposed solution. Law is constantly changing
to meet new demands of a society in ferment. Fine-tuning and improvements can be worked out as required. The fact that present practices or
proposals may be less than perfect should not discourage the reader. Hope
is the motor that drives human endeavor and without it there would be no
energy to do the myriad things that must be done if greater progress is to
be made. The goal is too important to be abandoned because of minor
imperfections in proposed solutions.

The biggest obstacle to the creation of a more rational world order has
been the absence of political will on the part of decisionmakers. Those with
the power to bring about change have had little incentive for doing so. Those
without such power have, too often, been brushed aside or ignored. The
public has been lulled into apathy or despair by the false impression that
the problems were either insurmountable or so complicated that they had
better be left to political leaders. Hopefully, this book will demonstrate that
such fears are unfounded and that every thoughtful individual has a role to
play in preserving peace. Improvements in the social order are not only
necessary but also possible and indeed inevitable if humankind is to survive.

Let me at the outset explain the fundamental concepts which form the
basis for the principles and programs here expounded. I begin with the
assumption - as established in hundreds of thousands of precedents - that
every orderly society is based on three foundations:

1- *Laws* to define minimum standards of behavior;

2- *Courts* to serve as a forum for the peaceful settlement of
disputes and to determine if the agreed laws have been
violated;

3- A system of effective law *enforcement*.

To the extent that these three conditions prevail, there is relative tranquility;
to the extent that they are absent, there is turmoil.

In the international arena, the three conditions exist only in their most
primitive condition. There are very few "laws" that are universally respected, the World Court lacks compulsory jurisdiction and enforcement
against sovereign states is more honored in the breach than in the obser-

vance. The result is that we live in a period of international "wild-west". What is needed for a peaceful future is international law and order. We must replace the law of force by the force of law.

Today, *enforcement* of international law is probably the weakest leg of the wobbly tripod on which world security rests. Effective enforcement requires :

(A) Some independent managing or executive agency - such as the United Nations - to deal more effectively with those world problems that can only be managed globally.

(B) International control or elimination of all weapons of mass destruction;

(C) A system of effective sanctions - economic or military;

(D) Enhanced social justice - a more equitable sharing of the earth's resources - so that justified causes of conflict are diminished. As Nobel Laureate Willi Brandt said: "He who wants to ban war must also ban poverty."[2] The steps needed to create a more peaceful world are spelled out in greater detail in some of my earlier books.[3]

Before considering changes and improvements, it is necessary to start with an understanding of what is right and what is wrong with the present world order. Part I of the book is therefore devoted to an analysis of the origins and practices of the prevailing international legal systems. Only major issues affecting international peace and security will be considered and the focus throughout remains on the vital components: *laws, courts* and *enforcement*. The progress is noted as well as the shortcomings. The conclusion is inescapable that the present world legal order is far from satisfactory and that certain indicated changes are necessary.

Part II reconsiders the current system of global management. It challenges the validity of many firmly entrenched notions on which the present legal system relies. The growth of regional organizations is examined to see if they can serve as a useful model for future world development. The UN Charter is analyzed to plumb its real intention and meaning and many options are surveyed to determine what can best be done to make the

---

2   Cited in *Common Responsibility in the 1990's,*"The Stockholm Initiative on Global Security and Governance at 6.

3   B.FERENCZ, DEFINING INTERNATIONAL AGGRESSION, 2 vols. (1975); AN INTERNATIONAL CRIMINAL COURT, 2 vols.(1980);ENFORCING INTERNATIONAL LAW, 2 vols. (1983); A COMMON SENSE GUIDE TO WORLD PEACE (1985); WORLD SECURITY FOR THE 21ST CENTURY (1991) - all published by Oceana Publications, Dobbs Ferry, NY.

Charter more effective in preventing war: whether it must be scrapped as an out-dated prototype or whether it can be modified or otherwise salvaged to achieve its fundamental purpose of avoiding "the scourge of war."

In the concluding Part III, specific proposals are made to improve the working of the world legal order. In the codification of new international *laws* for peace, the prevailing and inadequate definition of aggression is reformulated to eliminate ambiguities deliberately inserted by those who did not want to be bound by clear rules. Crimes Against Humanity is clarified to eliminate major threats to international peace and security. In dealing with *courts*, new methods are suggested for enhancing the jurisdiction and authority of the World Court. The creation of a new International Criminal Court is urged. In *enforcing* peace, the adequacy of current legal foundation and practices is reviewed and specific major alterations called for if peace is to be maintained.

Effective methods for eliminating weapons of mass destructions and ending the arms race are outlined. Legal means for making non-military sanctions more effective are spelled out. Where sanctions fail, enforcement by UN police forces is unavoidable. Methods for creating enhanced economic and social equality and more equitable sharing of the earth's resources are also addressed by specific new instruments and institutions.

To avoid an exercise in futility, the new proposals try not to be so far ahead of the times as to lose touch with contemporary reality. The objective is to improve the system and make it work - not to tear it down. The role of the Security Council will be analyzed to show that - with appropriate new procedures designed to avoid tyranny - it holds the key to effective action in the foreseeable future. Twelve Security Council resolutions are drafted to strengthen the laws of peace, buttress the authority of courts for peace and improve the methods of enforcing peace. One omnibus resolution combines the dozen and holds forth the promise of a more rational world order than now exists.

Finally, the decisive question: "How do we get from here to there?" Re-educating people to replace the prevailing war-ethic by a new peace-ethic will be explored. In the end it will be demonstrated that everybody gains from what is here proposed.

All components of a peaceful world are interrelated and interdependent. Laws have little significance without courts; courts have no power without enforcement. There can be no peace without justice and no justice without peace. National treasure squandered on weaponry exhausts resources needed to eliminate social inequities that generate discontent and conflict. Yet, disarmament is only reasonable and possible if there is an effective international alternative to maintain the peace. Like the gears in a complicated machine, each unit depends upon, complements and reinforces the other. As long as any vital part is missing, the system remains incomplete and can not move forward as it should.

There is no reason for despair. Despite persistent and unavoidable relapses, much overall progress has already been made in the direction of a rationally managed global society. Recognizing positive trends makes it possible to build on them by constructive proposals designed to make the process more effective. When it is recognized that common goals are really attainable, the public - as well as political leaders everywhere - will see that it is in their own self-interest to build improved or new institutions as quickly as possible in order to advance the universally shared objectives of humankind.

Some years ago, a very respected international legal scholar, Professor Shabtai Rosenne, wrote a comprehensive article analyzing six volumes I had written on how to achieve world peace. Since my views were often at variance with the official position of his government, as well as my own, I was pleasantly surprised when he encouraged me to keep writing. He wrote:

> But when the political atmosphere changes, as sooner or later it
> must, Ferencz's assiduous compilations will be the quarry out
> of which the new - or renewed - structure of international law
> and international relations can be hewed.[4]

For the first time since the end of World War II, the international political atmosphere has begun to improve. The ideological cold-war between super-powers is over and - despite darkening clouds that appear from time to time - democracy seems to be expanding on a broad horizon The time to move forward is now.

In 1987, Burns H.Weston, Professor of Law at the University of Iowa, a prolific writer and staunch advocate of a more rational world, reviewed my COMMON SENSE GUIDE TO WORLD PEACE in the American Journal of International Law. He expressed appreciation for my having made the dream of world peace more credible, but he lamented that I had not provided "a map of how to get us from the crisis ridden 'here' to the common sense 'there'."[5] His criticism was justified. Ends and means go hand in hand. This book seeks to define the goal in specific legal terms and outlines the map showing the route. It offers the missing organizational blueprint to those who wish to build a more peaceful world.

---

4   Shabtai Rosenne, *Enforcing International Law - A review Article*, 14 Israel Yearbook of
     Human Rights 274 (1984) at 282; See also review by John F. Murphy in 78 AJIL 253 (1984).
5   81 AJIL 503 (1987).

It must be admitted that new legal structures can be drafted but they will have only limited value until they are put into effect. In the last analysis what will also be needed are new attitudes of heart and mind; a willingness to care and to share. There must be a greater tolerance for different points of view and different values; a willingness to compromise and to accept the "other" as a member of the same human family. [6] It will be up to the religious leaders, the teachers, the publicists and many other dedicated opinion makers to convince the public, and through them the statesmen of the world, that the time is finally ripe for fundamental change and that human intellect can and will prevail over the menacing danger of man's destructive capacity.

I hope that this book can help to persuade concerned citizens of this planet that it is possible to save the world and that it must be done soon or what's left may not be worth saving. As Lord Montbatton said, a few months before he was assassinated:

> Since the threat to humanity is the work of human beings, it is up to man to save himself from himself. [7]

To be sure, many of the new ways of thinking and new structures for peace herein proposed will be contentious - particularly among conservative international lawyers, diplomats and political leaders. In the end, the public will have to decide which values it favors - peace or power - and what it is prepared to do about it. The new legal formulations, conceptions, and proposals of this book are offered as a guiding light to those who are determined to make the future brighter than the past.

BENJAMIN B. FERENCZ
New Rochelle, New York
December 1, 1993.

---

6   I wrote about that in my popular outreach book PLANETHOOD (written with Ken Keyes Jr.). It now has nearly half-a-million copies in print and it is not copyrighted since we encourage anyone to duplicate or translate our message for peace.

7   Earl Louis Montbatton, speech on 11 May 1979, 17 Pugwash Newsletter No.4 (1980), cited in M. THEE, ARMAMENTS, ARMS CONTROL AND DISARMAMENT (1981) at 383.

PART I

THE WORLD LEGAL ORDER

What's Right and What's Wrong

However improvised and fumbling the United Nations approach may be, we have to develop it to deal with the sudden antagonisms and dangers of our world...[I]f the United Nations is to justify the hopes of its founders and of the peoples of the world, it must develop into an active and effective agency for peace and international conciliation by responding to the challenges which face it. May we have the courage, the faith, and the wisdom to make it so.

UN Secretary-General U Thant.[1]

---

1   Address to the Harvard Alumni Association, June 13, 1963, *reproduced in* L.P. BLOOMFIELD, THE POWER TO KEEP PEACE (1971) at 199.

THERE is a great deal that is right about the old world order. But there is also a great deal that needs improvement. It must be recalled that although humans have inhabited the planet for at least a million years and nations have existed for thousands of years, the effort to control the behavior of states under a rule of binding international law is barely a few hundred years old - a blink in the eye of time.

The expression "international law" first appeared toward the end of the eighteenth century and is credited to the English Jurist Jeremy Bentham. It was a time when the French political theorist Jean Jacques Rousseau and the German philosopher Immanuel Kant were also writing about ways to maintain peace among nations that seemed to be incessantly at war. [2]

In the new world of America, thirteen British colonies declared themselves independent states - bound only by their own weak Articles of Confederation and Perpetual Union. Torn by internal strife, it soon became necessary for the states to cede some of their proclaimed sovereign rights to a central authority. A Constitution of the United States of America was finally ratified in 1789. It gave the new federal government only as much authority as was necessary to enable the union to function efficiently. Thus was born a new nation that for over two hundred years has inspired people around the world with the ideal of equality and freedom for all.[3]

"We have it in our power to begin the world over again", wrote Tom Paine, pamphleteer for the American revolution.[4] The changes that have taken place in world society since Paine wrote those lines have been enormous. No one could have anticipated or believed there could be such a transformation. One need only recall the industrial revolution, the ending of colonialism, the proliferation of nation states with different cultures and ideologies, the birth of universal human rights, the expansion of international organizations, the control of disease, increased longevity, the population explosion, the speed of communications and transportation, the awesome power of nuclear energy, the efficiency of high-technology, the awareness of environmental problems and the growing recognition that we are all temporary voyagers on a small planet hurtling through a vast cosmos.

---

2   J.C. COLOMBOS, BENTHAM PLAN FOR AN UNIVERSAL AND PERPETUAL PEACE (1939) at 3; Bentham's Works in 11 volumes, Published by John Bouring (Edinburgh:Tait, 1843.); *See* FERENCZ, ENFORCING INT. L., Chap.1-3; I. KANT, *ZUM EWIGEN FRIEDEN* (1795); H. SCHLOCHAUER, *DIE IDEE DES EWIGEN FRIEDENS* (1953).

3   C.V.DOREN, THE GREAT REHEARSAL - The Story of the Making and Ratifying of the Constitution of the United States (1986).

4   T. PAINE, COMMON SENSE (1982 ed.) at 120.

How do we bring order and tranquility to this glorious new, turbulent - and frequently violent - world?

It has not yet been possible for humankind to develop the social institutions required to organize these enormous societal changes in a completely rational way. The changes have come too swiftly and improved institutions have evolved too slowly. Experiments in totalitarianism as a method of satisfying human needs have not succeeded. We have not yet been able to put in place the mechanisms needed to make the world system function as well as it should. As a consequence, we still allow millions of innocent people to die in wars, to starve to death or perish from unnecessary illness and disease, to live in squalor and in fear and to become victims of discrimination, cruelty and oppression of many kinds in many lands. This is not a tolerable situation. The present world order simply doesn't work!

Without trying to address all of the countless problems which must eventually be solved before such evils can be eliminated, let us focus our attention on the three basics of *laws, courts* and *enforcement* to see what is right and what is wrong in those three areas. Let us note the slow progress and let us consider what specific improvements are required to make the system work more effectively in providing minimum conditions of peace and dignity for all.

CHAPTER ONE
INTERNATIONAL LAWS OF PEACE

> In a very real sense the world no longer has a choice between force and law. If civilization is to survive, it must choose the rule of law.
>
> President Dwight D. Eisenhower, May 19, 1958.[1]

Laws develop in response to human needs. Like animals adapting to changed environments, humans have invented and accepted new controls when needed to prevent the destruction of the human species: Ancient Greece formulated codes to keep peace among the city-states; Roman law imposed imperial power on the far-flung empire to maintain the Pax Romana for over a hundred years; Church doctrines for the "Peace of God" were articulated to protect the interests of the Papacy; maritime trade made it necessary to outlaw piracy. The cruelties and savagery of war gave birth to "just war" principles to avoid annihilation; regulations for humane conduct of man's most inhumane activity were necessary to diminish the costs and ravages of modern combat. The development of international *law* was an evolutionary process to maintain peace.

A- International Agreements to Maintain Peace

Since Ancient days, sovereigns have formed alliances and entered into treaties designed for mutual security and protection. Such treaties were usually honored only as long as they served the interests of the signatories. For at least two centuries, nation states have been concerned about the rising costs and hazards of war and the advantages of creating a more stable and secure society. Multi-national accords for that purpose are of relatively recent vintage. Let us consider some of the leading international peace agreements to see what was right or wrong about them.

1. Hague Agreements of 1899 and 1907

What was announced as the "First International Peace Conference" in history took place in the Hague in 1899. It wasn't a peace conference at all. It was a meeting to cut back the unbearable costs of an arms race. The follow up conference had to be delayed until 1907 because some of the leading

---

1   Dept. of State Bull. 831 (1958).

participants (Russia and Japan) were already at war. Originally 26, then 44, self-styled "civilized states" drafted conventions which purported to bind the signatories to maintain peace. The Hague Convention for Pacific Settlement of International Disputes was widely acclaimed. The Hague Conventions prescribing humanitarian rules for the conduct of war were also hailed. It was the beginning of attempts to maintain peace through international law. Yet, within a decade, nations were engaged in a World War which cost the lives of ten million soldiers and ten million more civilians killed. Why?

What was fundamentally wrong was that nations which accepted the agreements never intended to be bound by strict rules. The agreements were full of loopholes. Instead of being clearly binding without equivocation, the conventions were saturated with vague escape clauses specifically designed to enable the signatories to avoid legal restraints. Thus, rather than accepting a clear legal obligation to arbitrate their disputes or have them settled in a court of law, the parties agreed only to "use their best efforts," "as far as possible," or "as far as circumstances allow." Separate reservations made it clear that nothing was considered binding if - in the opinion of the states concerned - it affected their "honor" or "vital interests."[2]

So-called Rules of war were binding - but only "as far as possible" or "as far as military requirements permit".[3] Furthermore, there was no enforcement mechanism whatsoever: no clear-cut international laws, no international courts, no international police. No wonder it didn't work!

The legal instruments so meticulously drawn might have imposed more effective restraints if the parties had skipped the evasive reservations and qualifying clauses and made provision for enforcement of their professed obligations. But it didn't happen in 1899 or in 1907. After all, it was only a beginning. U.S. Secretary of State Elihu Root - a giant in the development of international law - undoubtedly spoke for many of the participants when he said he looked forward to "continual progress toward making the practice of civilized nations conform to their peaceful professions."[4]

The Hague agreements reflected the widespread public desire for a less violent regime for resolving conflict, but the decision makers - undoubtedly

---

2   Convention for the Pacific Settlement of International Disputes is reproduced in FERENCZ, INT. CRIM.CT. vol. 1 Doc. 1. For comments and citations on the Hague Conferences see FERENCZ, ENFORCING INT. L. vol. 1, pp.36-39 and Docs. 19 and 20.

3   *See*, for example, Convention (IV) Respecting the Laws and Customs of War on Land, in ROBERTS AND GUELFF, DOCUMENTS ON THE LAWS OF WAR (1982) pp.44-59.

4   *See* FERENCZ, ENFORCING INT. L. vol.1 p.39 n. 71.

sharing the same goals - were still unable to break out of the mind-set of the past.When U.S. President Theodore Roosevelt accepted the Nobel Peace Prize in 1910, he deplored the failure of the Hague Conferences to create an executive or international police power to enforce the decisions of an arbitration court and to prevent violence between nations. All mankind, said Roosevelt, would be grateful for all time to the statesman who could bring about such a new structure of international society.[5]

2. Covenant of the League of Nations

The next major legal instrument in the evolution of the international law of peace was the Covenant of the League of Nations. When World War I ended in 1919, after four years of the bloodiest fighting ever seen on the planet, there was an enormous public outcry to prevent all future wars. To mobilize international law in the cause of peace, a League of Nations was formed in 1920. For the first time, a permanent institution was established where nations could meet to discuss problems that threatened the peace.

The principles of the Covenant included solemn obligations:

> to promote international cooperation... achieve international peace and security... not to resort to war... establish international law as the actual rule of conduct, and the maintenance of justice...[6]

The security plan of the Covenant was quite specific: the manufacture and distribution of all armaments would be placed under international controls, members were obliged to settle disputes only by arbitration or judicial settlement, aggression would be repelled by collective economic sanctions or the use of collective military might. These were important ideals and ideas about how to maintain a more peaceful world.

The records of the debates reveal that great legal minds - many from the United States - were quite capable of drafting binding legal instruments to preserve the peace. But in a voluntary society composed of sovereign powers there was no way to coerce acceptance. It was a matter of political expediency and necessity to seek consensus. That meant that the most conservative views would prevail - or there might be no progress at all.

---

5   NY Times May 6, 1910 at 4; FERENCZ, ENFORCING INT. L. vol. 1 Docs. 19 and 20.
6   Preamble to Covenant, in FERENCZ, AGGRESSION vol.1 Doc. 1.

In the end, the Covenant's provisions, instead of being binding legal obligations, were only "recommendations." Many of the terms were vague; aggression was nowhere defined. Enforcement measures could only be taken if there was *unanimous* agreement - a gap in the Covenant. Compulsory jurisdiction by an international arbitral court was not accepted. An International Criminal Court, recommended by expert jurists, was turned down by the political leaders. Without a binding method to settle disputes peacefully, no nation would disarm. An international army to enforce the rules was not accepted. The right to go to war - after some delay - was specifically preserved. In short, too many necessary parts were missing to make the professed new peace system work. The world drifted inexorably toward the next catastrophe.

The last nail in the League's coffin was the inability of the United States to become a member of the League. Although the American people clearly supported President Woodrow Wilson's inspiring vision of a peaceful and democratic world order, his aspirations were stymied by a small number of isolationist politicians in the U.S. Senate who prevented him from mustering the two-thirds vote needed for approval of the peace treaty. The weakened and inadequately structured League was unable to prevent World War II - which, before it was over, cost at least 40 million innocent lives.

No one can say for sure whether World War II could have been prevented, but it was not the League that failed the nations; the nations failed the League. Principle was made hostage to politics. A clear system of binding laws and a plausible system to preserve the peace was never given a chance.[7]

3. Kellogg-Briand Pact Renouncing War

In addition to the Covenant, there were a number of other attempts to restrict the right of states to go to war. A 1923 draft of an aborted *Treaty of Mutual Assistance* declared a war of aggression to be an international crime.[8] An equally unsuccessful Geneva Protocol of 1924 referred to the obligation "in no case to resort to war" - with certain exceptions. The League Assembly adopted a resolution saying that a war of aggression is "an international crime. A Pan-American conference declared aggression to be "a crime against the human species." [9] But aggression was nowhere defined.

7   F.P. WALTERS, A HISTORY OF THE LEAGUE OF NATIONS (1952); FERENCZ, ENFORCING INT. L. vol.1 pp.41-57.
8   League Doc. A.35. 1923. IX.

These efforts to outlaw war were a prelude to a famous treaty which was broadly accepted - the *Kellogg-Briand Pact*. Officially known as the *General Treaty for the Renunciation of War as a National Policy*, the pact was signed in Paris in 1928 to commemorate the 10th anniversary of the end of World War I. It was eventually ratified by almost all countries. In two brief sentences, the High Contracting Parties condemned recourse to war and agreed that the settlement of all disputes "of whatever nature or whatever origin" would "never be sought except by pacific means." [10] Bravo!

That sounded pretty clear and comprehensive - except for the word *"sought"* which suggested that they weren't really bound but would *try*. To make doubly sure that the treaty to renounce war would not really restrict their capacity to wage war whenever they alone saw fit, both the United States and Great Britain, as well as many other states, insisted - in separate interpretations and reservations - that their right to *self-defense* would not be limited and they alone could decide when they were going to war for that purpose.[11]

If the use of force was not characterized as "War," it might not even fall under the Paris Pact (or the League's Covenant) at all. Britain's respected Sir Arnold Duncan McNair, a noted authority, made plain his view that "it is for the Government to say whether we are at war or not."[12] What that meant in essence was that legal restraints prohibiting war could be by-passed simply by not calling a war a "war" or by arguing that it was being fought in "self-defense." It might have been foreseen that in the future armed conflicts would no longer be called "wars" and all new wars of aggression would be fought only in self-defense. Never underestimate the imagination of a good lawyer!

The Kellogg Pact illustrates the pattern of illusion and disillusion that blocked the path toward creating binding laws of peace. The one-page *General Treaty for the Renunciation of War* would have been a better legal document and might have had some deterrent effect if, instead of saying that peaceful settlement would be "sought," it had clearly stated that all

---

9   *See* H. LAUTERPACHT, OPPENHEIM'S INTERNATIONAL LAW, (1944) Sec. 52g.

10   The Treaty is *reproduced in* FERENCZ, AGGRESSION vol. 1 Doc. 7 p. 192.

11   J.T. SHOTWELL, WAR AS AN INSTRUMENT OF NATIONAL POLICY AND ITS RENUNCIATION IN THE PACT OF PARIS (1929); See FERENCZ, AGGRESSION vol.1 notes 103, 104, p.54; C.C. HYDE, INTERNATIONAL LAW vol. 2 p. 1440 n. 3 and Vol. III Sec. 596A, pp.1680-1685 (1945). The Pact is *reproduced* in Royal Inst. of Int'l Affairs, SURVEY OF INT. AFFAIRS (1918) pp.1-36.

12   A.D. McNair, LEGAL EFFECTS OF WAR (1944) at 1.

disputes would be settled *only* by peaceful means and that all violators, regardless of rank, would be held personally responsible in an international court of law! It could have been stipulated that no special "understandings" or "reservations" would be permitted. Acceptance of clearly binding obligations presumes, of course, that nations really intend to outlaw the use of military might - which obviously, at that time, was not the case.

What appeared to be a legally binding treaty to outlaw war among nations was nothing of the kind; and everybody knew it - except the general public. Although Japan and Italy signed the treaty, within the next decade, they invaded the territories of two other signatories, China and Abyssinia. The Pact of Paris, like the Hague Agreements, contained deliberate ambiguities, exculpating reservations and no system of enforcement. There was no legal way to halt the aggressors short of war. World War II, as we have indicated, left at least 40 million dead, and many more millions homeless, helpless and in utter despair. Would we never learn?

4. United Nations Charter

The United Nations Charter was the next major legal instrument in the search for world peace. The Charter, signed in 1945, tried to overcome some of the shortcomings of the Covenant of the League. To understand what's right and what's wrong with it as a constitution to bind member states, let us review the circumstances under which it came into existence.

In August 1941, with hostilities raging, Britain's Prime Minister Winston Churchill and U.S. President Franklin D. Roosevelt met on board ship and signed a declaration known as the Atlantic Charter that called for "the establishment of a wider and permanent system of general security" after the conclusion of the war. Within a few months, 24 other nations (including the Soviet Union) subscribed to it. There was thus an implied promise of the Allied powers that a new international institution would assure a more peaceful world in the future.[13]

It was the United States that took the initiative in moving to carry out the promise. A small group in the State Department began to draft a Charter for a new organization to be called "The United Nations." Roosevelt was keenly aware of the isolationist sentiments which had prevented the United States from becoming a member of the League after World War I and he had

---

13   *See* R.C. HILDEBRAND, DUMBARTON OAKS - The Origins of the UN and the Search for Postwar Security (1990) at 13.

no desire to experience Woodrow Wilson's sad rejection. It was his political judgment - no doubt correct - that following Allied victory, neither the American public nor a two-thirds majority of the Senate would be prepared to accept any international organization with authority to send U.S. troops back into battle without U.S. consent. The Soviets certainly felt the same way. If a new agency to maintain peace was to be created, it could have only limited powers. Improvements might come later. These political realities help explain some of the rather obvious shortcomings that appeared in the UN Charter.

The Charter Preamble affirms the determination of "We the Peoples"... "to save succeeding generations from the scourge of war." It speaks of "fundamental human rights," the "dignity and worth of the human person" and "better standards of life in larger freedom." These ends are to be achieved through "tolerance", united strength to maintain peace and the acceptance of principles and institutions to ensure "that armed force shall not be used, save in the common interest." The preamble expresses noble sentiments and objectives - but does not impose specific legal obligations.

The declared fundamental purpose of the United Nations, as described in its very first Article, is "to maintain international peace and security ... in conformity with the principles of justice and international law." Similar principles were enunciated in the Covenant of the ill-fated League of Nations. Experience showed that what is "just" may depend upon the eye of the beholder and "international law" may, as we have noted, also be subject to flexible interpretations.

To be sure, Article 2 set forth a number of obligations but almost all of them required explanations or clarification. For example:

Art. 2(1) says "The Organization is based on the sovereign equality of all its Members." Yet, the five Permanent Members were given a preferred position when it came to enforcement measures; some sovereigns were thus more equal than others.

Art.2(3) obliges members to "settle their disputes by peaceful means" and 2(4) requires them to "refrain"... "from the threat or use of force." Notwithstanding these restraints, Art. 51 affirms the "inherent right of individual or collective self-defence." Hundreds of thousands, perhaps millions, of innocent people have died in wars which all parties proclaimed were fought only in "self-defense" - while legal scholars argued whether Art. 2(4) was dead or alive![14]

Art.2(5) requires Members to give the UN *"every assistance"* in any action taken in accordance with the Charter and to "refrain from giving *assistance* to any state against which the UN is taking preventive or enforcement action." What constitutes "assistance" was not defined.

Art.2(6) says that the UN "shall ensure that states which are not Members" shall act in accordance with the stated UN principles of peace. A treaty normally binds only its signatories. How to enforce a treaty against states or groups that are not parties to it - and yet maintain peace - is not made clear.

Art. 2(7) contains other legal difficulties. It stipulates that the UN can not "intervene in matters which are essentially within the domestic jurisdiction of any state" - except if the Security Council is employing enforcement measures under Chapter VII. But Chapter VII enforcement can be blocked by the single veto of a Permanent Member. What about humanitarian intervention - such as to halt Genocide, apartheid or massive persecutions? Is that purely a domestic matter that bars outside intervention? When Iraq was busy killing its Kurdish citizens and others during the Gulf War of 1990, UN Secretary- General Perez de Cuellar - despite the restraints of Art. 2(7) - called for "a combination of common sense and compassion" and "a collective obligation of States to bring relief and redress in human rights emergencies".[15]

The inspiring principle of "self-determination of peoples" may run counter to the hallowed Charter principle protecting "the territorial integrity or political independence of any state." [16] Can any ethnic, religious or nationalistic group secede as an expression of its right to self-determination? How can these valid principles be reconciled when they come into conflict? Legal clarification does not appear anywhere in the UN Charter.[17]

The Charter, like earlier international agreements to preserve the peace, leaves much to be desired. The General Assembly has passed thousands of resolutions regarding Charter principles and obligations. But such resolutions, whether described as Declarations, Determinations or Agree-

---

14   *Compare* T.Franck, *Who Killed Article 2(4)?* 64 AJIL 809 (1970); L. Henkin, *The Reports of the Death of Article 2(4) are Greatly Exaggerated* 65 AJIL 544 (1971). The right of self-defense is considered hereafter in Chapter Four, Section D.

15   UN Doc. A/46/1, 6 Sept.1991 at 10. Non-interference in domestic affairs is dealt with hereafter in Chapter Four, Section B.

16   *Compare* UN Charter Art.1 (2) with Art 2 (4).

17   The right to self-determination is dealt with hereafter in Chapter Four, Section C.

ments are usually considered to be mere "recommendations" (unless they relate to budgetary matters) and their legally binding force remains controversial. As a declaration of guiding general principles, the Charter is fine; as a legal instrument to prevent sovereign states from going to war it is - as experience proves -woefully inadequate.[18]

5. *Charter of the International Military Tribunal*

About six weeks after the UN Charter was signed at San Francisco, representatives of the four allied powers (U.S., U.K., U.S.S.R. and France) met in London and completed plans for the trial at Nuremberg of major German war criminals. They agreed upon a Charter for an International Military Tribunal (IMT) that set forth the applicable laws and procedures. The Tribunal, composed of distinguished Allied jurists, would also pass judgement on the validity of the legal principles which formed the basis for the trials.

The IMT Charter listed three categories of crimes which came within the International Court's jurisdiction:

1- Crimes against Peace - planning or waging a war of aggression;

2- War Crimes - violations of the laws and customs of war;

3- Crimes against Humanity - extermination, persecutions on political, racial or religious grounds, and similar inhumane acts "whether or not in violation of the domestic law of the country where perpetrated."[19]

The articulation in the IMT Charter of the Crime against Peace and of Crimes against Humanity is particularly noteworthy. Both Prosecution and Tribunal cited the Hague Conventions which referred to "the laws of humanity and the dictates of the public conscience" - terms which seemed vague in 1907 but which were given legal significance in 1945. The Hague Conventions, the Geneva Protocols of 1924 for the Pacific Settlement of International Disputes, a Pan-American Conference condemning aggression, the Kellogg-Briand Pact as well as various resolutions of the League of Nations and others were all cited as evidence of an emerging law of peace

---

18   The UN Charter is reviewed hereafter in Chapter Five.
19   The IMT Charter is reproduced in FERENCZ, INT. CRIM. CT. vol. 1, Doc. 13. See also
       TRIALS OF WAR CRIMINALS BEFORE THE NUERNBERG MILITARY TRIBUNALS,
       (Green Series) Vol. XV (US Gov't Printing Office, 1949).

which denounced aggression as a crime. Said Chief U.S. Prosecutor Justice Robert H. Jackson (on leave from the U.S. Supreme Court):

> It is high time that we act on the juridical principles that aggressive war-making is illegal and criminal...[20]

Nineteen other nations quickly adhered to the IMT Charter. In its judgment, the Tribunal confirmed that the Charter was "not an arbitrary exercise of power on the part of the victorious nations" but was "the expression of international law existing at the time of its creation." Aggression was condemned as "the supreme international crime."[21]

The Charter, seen as articulating international law, became the model for a similar Charter for Tokyo war crimes trials against Japan's leaders. It served as the basis for a dozen subsequent trials at Nuremberg where its principles were further clarified and confirmed. It was held that Crimes against Humanity existed where atrocities were of such magnitude that they shocked the conscience of humanity and where

> the state involved, owing to indifference, impotency or complicity, has become unable or has refused to halt the crimes and punish the criminals.[22].

The principles of international law condemning aggression and crimes against humanity, confirmed in the Charter and Judgment of the Nuremberg Tribunal, were unanimously affirmed by the first General Assembly of the United Nations.[23] Past international agreements to maintain peace - imperfect by themselves - were mobilized to form a legal shield against both aggression and massive inhumanity as international law took a step forward.[24]

---

20 Jackson's Report to the President, June 6,1945, INTERNATIONAL CONFERENCE ON MILITARY TRIALS (1945) at 52. *See* T.TAYLOR, THE ANATOMY OF THE NUREMBERG TRIALS (1992).

21 *See* FERENCZ, INT. CRIM. CT. vol. 1, Doc. 15 pp.66-83.

22 TRIALS OF WAR CRIMINALS BEFORE THE NUEREMBERG MILITARY TRIBUNALS, vol. IV, p. 498, *The Einsatzgruppen Case*, B.B. Ferencz, Chief Prosecutor. Crimes against Humanity were held to violate "common international law." *Id.* Vol. III p. 979, *The Justice Case*.

23 GA Res.95 (1), 11 Dec. 1946; *reproduced in* FERENCZ, INT. CRIM. CT. vol. 2, Doc. 17 p. 127.

24 The Charter of the IMT is considered hereafter in Chapter Two, Section D.

B- Legal Declarations Concerning Peace

In addition to many international accords designed to prevent war, nations were able to agree upon a number of legal Declarations to specify rights and obligations of states in matters which might give rise to conflict. These Declarations - not legally as binding as ratified treaties - sought to reinforce the peaceful objectives prescribed in the UN Charter and earlier international legal agreements.

1. Universal Declaration of Human Rights

In 1948, the General Assembly adopted and proclaimed a Universal Declaration of Human Rights.[25] Its Preamble proclaimed the "inherent dignity" and the "equal and inalienable rights of all members of the human family" to be the "foundation of freedom, justice and peace in the world." Article 1 declared: "All human beings are born free and equal in dignity and rights. What was meant by "dignity" was not specified, but gradually the concept that human dignity was a legal right began to gain ground.[26]

The 30 articles of the Universal Declaration were reminiscent of President Franklin D. Roosevelt's rallying cry in January 1941 when he spoke of "Four Freedoms" - freedom of speech and belief and freedom from want and fear. Among other things, the Universal Declaration proclaimed: "Everyone has the right to life, liberty and security of person" (Art.3) and "the right to a standard of living adequate for the health and well-being of himself and of his family" (Art.25); "The will of the people shall be the basis of the authority of government" (Art.21).

The Universal Declaration was eventually supplemented by two International Covenants; one spelling out the Economic, Social and Cultural rights and the other the Civil and Political rights of all peoples. An Optional Protocol allowed individual complaints of violations under certain circumstances.[27] Combined, the Covenants and Protocol constituted a new "International Bill of Human Rights" which, after being adopted as binding law

---

25   GA Res. 217 A (III) 10 Dec. 1948; R. Cassin, "*La Declaration universelle et la mise en oeuvre des droits de l'homme*," RdC, Vol. 79 (1951 II) 237-367.

26   A careful juridical and philosophical analysis by Professor Jordan Paust of the University of Houston, Texas, led him to conclude: "Human dignity, as a process, is compatible with enlightened self-interest and an affirmative, optimistic involvement, a love, of self and others." J. Paust, *Human Dignity as a Constitutional Right*, 27 Howard Law J. (1983) 145 at 225.

27   GA Res. 2200 A (XXI) 16 Dec. 1966.

by the requisite number of states, entered into force in 1976. In addition to regional human rights agreements, the United Nations continued to grind out resolutions and declarations proclaiming a large variety of human rights - including freedom from various forms of discrimination and intolerance.[28]

Growing respect for individual rights was part of the evolutionary process whereby international law began to recognize and define as a legal entitlement the most fundamental needs of all human beings. What the U.S. Constitution referred to as "the pursuit of happiness" was slowly moving toward a "right to happiness" or "*le droit au bonheur* - in René Jean Dupuy's felicitous phrase.[29]

Despite repeated references to "rights," the legal instruments did not per se create binding legal obligations. Furthermore, the conventions required ratification by a given number of states before coming into force and domestic legislation was needed to put teeth into the stated objectives. The proclaimed human rights were conditional. They were - by their own terms - made subject and subordinate to such limitations as the need for "public order" and the needs of national security "in time of war or other national emergency threatening the life of the nation". Nations were not really ready to diminish their sovereign power by yielding absolute rights to their own subjects or to any international legal body.[30]

One of the most dangerous loopholes in international law is the right of nations to ignore even minimum human rights obligations in time of war or public emergency - if national leaders say it is necessary to protect the security of the state. To say that a state will respect human rights except when it decides for itself that its security is threatened, is to undermine the whole concept that the individual is entitled to protection against gross abuses by the state; it diminishes the power of law.[31]

---

28   U.N.Publ. HUMAN RIGHTS - A COMPILATION OF INTERNATIONAL INSTRUMENTS (1988); *See* B.G. RAMCHARAN, THE CONCEPT AND PRESENT STATUS OF THE INTERNATIONAL PROTECTION OF HUMAN RIGHTS: FORTY YEARS AFTER THE UNIVERSAL DECLARATION (1989).

29   R.J.DUPUY, *LA CLÔTURE DU SYSTÈME INTERNATIONAL (1989) at 28.*

30   See Universal Declaration, Art. 29(2); European Convention Art. 15; American Convention, Art. 27.

31   It has correctly been argued that the right to deviate from stated obligations must be narrowly interpreted so that derogation is legitimate only if the threat is imminent or actual, the peril extremely grave, and principles of proportionality and non-discrimination are respected at all times; J. ORAÁ, HUMAN RIGHTS IN STATES OF EMERGENCY IN INTERNATIONAL LAW (1992).

Even though the precise import of human rights declarations was not authoritatively determined, they did reflect growing concern on the part of the international community for the protection of fundamental rights for individuals everywhere.[32] The world was undergoing an evolutionary process whereby human beings were asserting their own rights independent of the interests of the nation state. The rule of law was being stimulated to meet rising human aspirations and expectations.[33]

The legal protection of human rights for all human beings was an important evolutionary movement in the right direction. What was wrong was best described in the words of Jan Martenson, past UN Under-Secretary for Human Rights, who lamented that the Universal Declaration had:

> branched out like a mighty tree into some 70 covenants, conventions and other international instruments. But without implementation, without realizing the noble undertakings as living reality for men, women and children, all over the world, these branches are reduced to dead wood.[34]

2. *Friendly Relations Declaration*

A prime example of UN efforts to clarify the Charter principles relating to world peace can be found in the Declaration of Principles of International Law Concerning Friendly Relations.[35] A UN Special Committee was appointed to clarify seven basic Charter principles including the prohibitions against the threat or use of force, the obligation to settle disputes by peaceful means, the duty not to intervene in matters within domestic jurisdiction, and the right of self-determination. These were all difficult problems which taxed the imagination and powers of the Committee representatives.

It took the Committee eight years to reach consensus. In its final sentence, the Declaration "appeals to all states to be guided by these principles." Whether the Declaration set forth binding rules of law or merely

---

32   L. Henkin, *"International Human Rights as 'Rights'"*, 1 Cardozo L. Rev. 425 (1979).

33   *See* B. Ferencz, *"The Future of Human Rights in International Jurisprudence: An Optimistic Appraisal,* 10 Hofstra Law Rev. (1982) 379; R. Bernhardt, *Schutz der Menschenrecht durch internationale Organe,* lecture at the University of Salzburg, 6 July 1990; B.G. RAMCHARAN, HUMAN RIGHTS THIRTY YEARS AFTER THE UNIVERSAL DECLARATION (1979); T. Meron, HUMAN RIGHTS IN INTERNATIONAL LAW (1984).

34   Speech at UN Conference on Human Rights in Vienna, Jan. 1993, cited in Newsletter of World Goodwill, a non-governmental organization with offices in New York, London and Geneva.

35   GA Res. 2625 (XXV) Oct. 24, 1970, 65 AJIL 243 (1971).

"recommendations," was disputed. It was another example of the evolutionary progress of law - and the obstacles.

The knowledgeable Legal Adviser to the U.S. Mission, Robert Rosenstock, a leading member of the Special Committee, described the vague
phrases and the absence of political will to accept clearly binding obligations. He concluded:

> Finally, the text is largely oriented toward the preservation and
> protection of state sovereignty rather than the development of
> new norms and new mechanisms more suited to the increas-
> ingly interdependent world of today and of the future...

> Once comparable progress is made on such matters as
> peacekeeping, dispute settlement, and economic development,
> the Friendly Relations Declaration will form an indispensable
> part of a very important whole.[36]

3. Peaceful Settlement and a Right to Peace

"Every nation and every human being, regardless of race, conscience,
language or sex, has the inherent right to life in peace," according to a 1978
UN Declaration. "A war of aggression, its planning , preparation or initia-
tion are crimes against peace and are prohibited by international law." The
same Declaration reaffirms "the right of all peoples to self-determination...[and] sovereignty...without interference or intervention in their internal affairs." [37] How to assure the right to life in peace with the right to
self-determination and non-interference with sovereignty or internal affairs
was, unfortunately, never spelled out. Various UN agencies recognized that
peace was interrelated with health, education and economic conditions, but
the best that states could come up with, when the subject of reconciling
incompatible rights was reviewed several years later, were calls for more
study, education and codification.[38]

An effort to reinforce the principle of peaceful dispute settlement
appeared in 1982 when a UN Special Committee dealing with Charter

---

36   R. Rosenstock, *"The Declaration of Principles of International Law Concerning Friendly
     Relations: A Survey*, 65 AJIL 713 (1971) at 735. See also Declaration on the Strengthening of
     International Security, GA Res. 2734 (XXV) 16 Dec. 1970.

37   Declaration on the Preparation of Societies for Life in Peace, Dec. 15, 1978, GA Res. 33/73,
     Art. 1, 2, 5.

38   Review of the Implementation of the Declaration, UN Doc.A/39/143, 1 Oct. 1984. *See* J.G.
     STARKE. THE SCIENCE OF PEACE (1986).

Reform, reached consensus on what became known as the *Manila Declaration on Peaceful Settlement of International Disputes*. It reaffirmed the Charter principle that states should settle their disputes by peaceful means and solemnly declared that

> They shall live together in peace with one another... Neither the existence of a dispute nor the failure of a procedure of peaceful settlement shall permit the use of force or threat of force...

The right to self-determination against alien domination was reaffirmed - without making clear that only peaceful means were permissible.[39]

Instead of stating clearly that nations were legally bound to honor the peace principles, the Declaration - and several others that followed - referred to what states "should" do and what they should "bear in mind" or "consider" and what was "desireable" for them to do in support of principles which states were "urged" to observe and promote. These vacillating phrases reflected the inability of all nations to agree on substance and their unwillingness to admit the truth. The longing for a more peaceful world encouraged some to overlook what was wrong and stress only what was right in the legal declarations concerning peace.

It was proclaimed as a civil right that "Every human being has the inherent right to life. This right shall be protected by law." [40] A 1984 *UN Declaration on the Right of Peoples to Peace* solemnly proclaimed that "the peoples of our planet have a sacred right to peace" and that the preservation of that right and "the promotion of its implementation" constituted "a fundamental obligation of each State." The General Assembly appealed to states and international organizations "to do their utmost to assist in implementing the right of peoples to peace...[41] No nation dared to vote against a 1984 General Assembly resolution affirming the Right of Peoples to Peace - although 34 abstained and 29 were "absent." Professor John Fried, tracing the evolution of the concept of peace as a legal right, described the Declaration as "potentially one of history's most far-reaching pronouncements." He concluded:

---

39   *Manila Declaration on the Peaceful Settlement of International Disputes*, Report of the Special Committee on the Charter, GAOR 37th Sess. Supp. No. 33 (A/37/33) (1982), *reproduced in* FERENCZ, ENFORCING INT. L. vol. 2 Doc. 75(b), *also in* 21 ILM 449 (1982). *See also* Declaration on the Enhancement of the Effectiveness of the Principle of Refraining from the Threat or Use of Force in International Relations, UN Doc. A/RES/42/22, Nov. 18, 1987, 27 ILM 1672 (1988); *Declaration on the Prevention and Removal of Disputes and Situations Which May Threaten International Peace and Security and on the Role of the United Nations in this Field*, UN Doc. A/RES/43/51, Dec.5, 1988.

40   Covenant on Civil and Political Rights, Art. 6.

41   GA Res. 39/11, 12 Nov. 1984. UN Pub. 88. XIV at 403.

The idea that "ordinary" people themselves posses an inalienable claim to live in peace, the simple proposition that peace is
due to them as their birth-right, is an idea whose time has
come.[42]

4. Declaration on the Non-Use of Force

In 1987, a Special Committee appointed by the General Assembly,
reached agreement on a *Declaration on the Enhancement of the Effectiveness of
the Principle of Refraining from the Threat or Use of Force in International
Relations.*[43] The Declaration was ten years in the making. There can be no
doubt that the improved relations between the Soviet Union and the United
States played a very important role in making consensus possible.

The Declaration, adopted without a vote, reaffirmed previous peace
declarations and "the obligation of States to settle their international disputes by peaceful means" and to maintain international peace "in conformity
with the purposes of the United Nations Charter." The language of the
Charter and the Friendly Relations Declaration was repeated with regard to
the duty of states to refrain from the threat or use of force. Failure to do so
was characterized as "a violation of international law" which "entails international responsibility" Art. (1).

An innovative Art. 2 declared that the principle of refraining from the
threat or use of force was "universal in character and is binding, regardless
of each State's political, economic, social or cultural system or relations of
alliance." The link between peace and the threat of nuclear weapons was
specifically recognized, as was the significance of human rights, terrorism,
self-determination, the arms race and the need for a new economic order.

On the other hand, most of the Declaration dealt with what states
"should" do, rather than what they were legally obliged to do. Furthermore,
the same vague clauses that had undermined earlier Declarations were also
repeated. The Charter provisions regarding self-defense were reasserted.
Exculpatory clauses tacked on at the end made doubly clear that the right
to self-determination could not be impaired and that under certain circumstances the use of force was permissible.

---

42   J. Fried, *"The United Nations Effort to Establish a Right of the Peoples to Peace,"* 2 Pace Y.B.
     Int'l L. (1990) 21 at 65.

43   GA Res. 42/22, 18 Nov. 1987; Report of the Special Committee, GAOR: Forty-Second
     Session, Supp. No. 41 (A/42/41).

Aside from its proclamations of legal obligation, the Declaration urged that the Security Council and the Secretary General be given every assistance in enhancing the effectiveness of the Charter security system. This unanimous declaration, reflected a new mood among states that had for four decades engaged in forceful political and ideological rivalry. It encouraged the Council and the Secretary-General to begin to take a more active role in maintaining peace. Despite the "constructive ambiguity" of many of its paragraphs, the Declaration was properly hailed by the Chairman of the Special Committee as a manifestation of good will and a step forward.[44]

5. New World Order

In addition to UN legal declarations concerning peace, one should not ignore the statements solemnly proclaimed by world leaders when addressing the Assembly or other major public bodies. In 1987, the United Nations began to consider "*A Comprehensive System of International Peace and Security*" put on the agenda by the Soviet Union. General Secretary Michael S. Gorbachev had written a widely-publicized article calling for a "system for a universal legal order which will ensure the primacy of international law in politics."[45]

When addressing the United Nations on 7 Dec. 1988, Mr. Gorbachev declared:

> Our ideal is a world community of States which are based on the rule of law and which subordinates their foreign policy activities to law.

His wide-ranging proposals for major reforms were received with considerable caution by the United States and its allies, some of whom were not quite convinced that the cold-war was really over. Gradually, the atmosphere began to improve. Germany's Foreign Minister, addressing the UN General Assembly on 26 Sept. 1990, said:

> Rule of law is acquiring greater significance... The task of the United Nations in this decade is to develop the international legal system further in order to ensure mankind's survival.

---

44   Statement by Mr. Tulio Treves of Italy,, Chairman of the Special Committee, introducing Report A/42/41 on 7 October 1987.

45   UN Doc. A/42/574, S/19143, 18 Sept. 1987, p.10. *See* G.I. Tunkin, *The Primacy of International Law in Politics*, in W.E.BUTLER, Ed., PERESTROIKA AND INTERNATIONAL LAW 5 (1990).

The next day, French President Mitterand declared:

> The time has come for international law to reign. We are faced
> with a choice between the law of the jungle and the rule of law.

When U.S. President Bush addressed the General Assembly four days later,
he said:

> It is in our hands...to cap a historic movement towards a new
> world order and a long era of peace. We have a vision of a new
> partnership of nations that transcends the cold war.

In his State of the Nation address on Jan. 16, 1991, President Bush reported:

> We now have before us the opportunity to forge for ourselves
> and for future generations a new world order, a world where
> the rule of law, not the law of the jungle governs the conduct of
> nations.

Many other world leaders echoed the same view. International law was
increasingly being recognized as a vital component for a peaceful world.
But there was still considerable disagreement among world leaders and
scholars about when force might legitimately be employed to maintain the
new world order that was being proclaimed.[46]

While decisionmakers spoke of a new world order, the only thing that
was visible to the naked eye was the same old disorder. More than words
would be necessary to give significance to the fine declarations concerning
peace. Oscar Arias, Nobel Prize winner and President of Costa Rica, addressing the graduating class at Harvard, urged them to take principled
risks in the struggle to build a new world. He was absolutely right when he
told his audience:

> There is a new world emerging everywhere, the results of the
> advance of freedom on all continents and within all political
> systems. We cannot betray the world freedom that wants to rise
> up. If we want to construct the future, we cannot go on staring
> at the past.[47]

---

46 *See* L.F. DAMROSCH AND D.J. SCHEFFER, LAW AND FORCE IN THE NEW
    INTERNATIONAL ORDER (1991). The use of force is considered hereafter in Chapter
    Four, Section E.

47 624 Harvard Magazine 20 (1988) at 21.

C- Codification of International Laws Affecting Peace

General declarations in favor of international law and peace are useful to point the direction in which states should move but specific details must be spelled out before law can advance from rhetoric to reality. The United Nations looks to its Sixth (Legal) Committee for developing international law to implement the objectives set forth in the Charter. The Legal Committee has been aided by the work of legal experts elected to the International Law Commission which reports its recommendations via the Sixth Committee to the General Assembly. Special Committees have been appointed from time to time to deal with particularly difficult subjects of international law.

Despite the rather elaborate mechanisms created to clarify and codify international law, ultimate decisions rest with the sovereign states that are expected to be bound by such laws. Following World War II, ideological rivalries between capitalist and socialist states tainted the approach to legal as well as political problems and hampered the speed of change toward a more peaceful world order. Newly formed African states, liberated by the decolonization process (itself a legal measure to secure world tranquility,) remained suspicious about a legal system that had kept them subjugated for so long. Persistent hostilities between Israel and its Arab neighbors added a combustible element and further impacted the search for peaceful solutions to the problems of world peace.

There remains widespread and sharp disagreement about what constitutes permissible and impermissible state behavior. Unless there are clear rules of the road which bind everyone, collision is inevitable. As Evan Luard has pointed out, peace also requires "a consensus on the principles of interaction between states.[48] But a real consensus on rules of the road for sovereign states is hard to achieve. As relations between the competing superpowers began to improve, it became possible to reach agreements on a few major legal instruments purporting to clarify or codify binding norms of international behavior that affect the peace and security of humankind - even if complete consensus was lacking.[49]

---

48   E. LUARD, CONFLICT AND PEACE IN THE MODERN INTERNATIONAL SYSTEM (1988).

49   *See* J.J. Channey, *Universal Int'l L.*, 87 AJIL 529 (1993).

1. Genocide

Shamed by the horrors perpetrated by Hitler Germany during World War II, the very first session of the General Assembly, on the unanimous recommendation of its Legal Committee, passed a resolution in 1946 affirming "that genocide is a crime under international law...for the commission of which principals and accomplices...are punishable." It invited members to enact the necessary legislation and requested that a convention outlawing genocide be drafted.[50]

By 1947, a group of impartial legal experts, recognizing that genocide could hardly be committed without the connivance of a state, drafted a convention defining the crime. A statute for an international criminal court to punish the offense was attached to the convention drafted by the UN Secretariat. It was a clear and relatively unambiguous legal document that states were urged to accept.[51] But by that time public outrage had diminished. Many states didn't like the idea of running the risk that some day their own leaders might be accused before an international tribunal. The draft that was finally accepted by the end of 1948 condemned genocide as an international crime but did not provide for any international court to deal with it.[52] In the words of French delegate Professor Chaumont:

> By rejecting the principle of international punishment, the Committee has rendered the draft convention on genocide purposeless.[53]

The situation would have been quite different if states had stipulated that the crime of genocide, like piracy, was so abhorrent that universal criminal jurisdiction applied and every state had a legal right to prosecute those responsible for the crime - regardless of their rank or station. To avoid any ambiguity it could have been stated categorically that UN Charter prohibitions against intervention in domestic affairs would not bar the UN from intervening to halt massive crimes against humanity and from punishing the perpetrators.[54] Changing or adding a few paragraphs might have saved countless lives.

---

50   GA Res. 96(1) 11 Dec. 1946. *See* FERENCZ, INT. CRIM. CT. vol. 2 Docs. 17-24 pp.5-16.

51   UN Doc. A/362, 25 Aug. 1947, reproduced in Ferencz, *supra*. **vol. 2 Doc. 19** p.131.

52   UNTS Vol. 78, p.278; *"Genocide, a Commentary on the Convention,"* 58 Yale L. Jour. 1142 (1948-1949); N. ROBINSON, THE GENOCIDE CONVENTION, A COMMENTARY (1960); L. Kuper, THE PREVENTION OF GENOCIDE (1986).

53   Meeting 10 Nov. 1948, Doc. 23, FERENCZ, INT. CRIM. CT. vol. 2, p. 162.

54   It has been agreed by UN consensus that no statutes of limitations can bar prosecution of genocide or crimes against humanity; UN GA Res. 2391 (XXIII), Nov. 26, 1968. Prohibiting crimes against humanity is dealt with hereafter in Chapter Eight, Section A.

It was right that states finally adopted a Genocide convention. What was wrong was that the law did not go far enough and the expressed determination to halt genocide was soon forgotten. Santayana's warning came true: "Those who cannot remember the past are condemned to repeat it." [55] Genocide did not disappear. It raised its ugly head in various forms in Uganda, Kamputchea, Iran, Iraq, former Yugoslavia and other parts of the globe. The International Court, with no jurisdiction over individuals and no enforcement authority, was powerless to halt the crimes. The most the Court could do was to assert its jurisdiction to interpret the Genoicde treaty and issue provisional measures calling upon all parties to prevent such crimes. The crimes continued.[56]

2. Aggression

With the beginning of détente between the Soviet Union and the United States, it became possible, in 1974, to arrive at a consensus definition of aggression - after about fifty years of indecision. Its history and an analysis of its terms need only be sketched here, having been set forth in detail elsewhere.[57]

It will be recalled that the security plan of the League was based on the assumption that aggression would be recognized and that collective measures of coercion by the non-aggressor states would force an end to the aggression and restore peace. It soon became apparent that without an agreed definition of aggression the plan couldn't work. But since major powers were not yet ready to commit their resources and military might in defense of objectives which they felt did not threaten their own vital interests, they were in no great rush to define aggression. Those who opposed any definition frequently cited Sir Austin Chamberlain's warning that it would be "a trap for the innocent and a sign-post for the guilty."[58]

---

55   G. SANTAYANA, THE LIFE OF REASON (1905) at 284.

56   ICJ Case Concerning Application of the Convention on the Prevention of the Crime of Genoicde, Order of Apr.8, 1993, *reproduced in* 87 AJIL (1993) 505; *See* ICJ Communique, unofficial order of the Court on provisional measures, 13 Sept. 1993.

57   B.FERENCZ, DEFINING INTERNATIONAL AGGRESSION (1975); A.M. Rifaat, INTERNATIONAL AGGRESSION (1979); B. Ferencz, "The United Nations Consensus Definition of Aggression - Sieve or Substance? 10 Jour. of Int'l L. and Eco. 701 (1975); T.BRUHA, DIE DEFINITION DER AGGRESSION (1980).

58   Report of the Secretary-General on the Question of Defining Aggression, UN Doc. A/2211, 3 Oct. 1952, G.A. Seventh Sess., Annexes, reproduced in FERENCZ, AGGRESSION vol. 2 p. 152. The Report contains a summary of the positions taken by different states.

The full text of the 1974 consensus definition of aggression consists of a Preamble and only eight substantive articles. The Preamble recalls the duty of states to settle disputes only by peaceful means, notes that aggression is "the most serious and dangerous form of the illegal use of force" and reaffirms principles of international law contained in the ambiguous Friendly Relations Declaration of 1970. It concludes that whether aggression had been committed has to "be considered in the light of all the circumstances of each particular case." All agreed that only the Security Council had legal authority to determine whether aggression had occurred.

The first substantive article seeks to capture the broad meaning of aggression in one declaratory sentence: "Aggression is the use of *armed* force by a State against the sovereignty, territorial integrity or political independence of any other State, or in *any other manner* inconsistent with the Charter of the United Nations, *as set out* in this definition." (Emphasis added) Each italicized word was a hotly debated compromise which was subject to varying interpretations.[59]

According to Art.2 of the definition, "The first use of armed force *in contravention of the Charter*" is "*prima facie* evidence" of aggression. The Security Council can decide "in the light of *other relevant circumstances* that an action isn't aggression after all. A number of listed acts could "qualify" as aggression (Art.3,) yet other (unlisted) acts could also constitute aggression if the Council so determined (Art.4). Art. 5 declares a war of aggression to be a crime against international peace - but makes no provision for punishment. The use of force remains permissible - if consistent with the Charter (Art.6.) The final article practically negates all the rest: Anything done in pursuit of the "right to self-determination, freedom and independence... particularly [by] peoples under colonial and racist regimes, *or other forms of alien domination*" can not be prejudiced by the definition of aggression (Art.7, emphasis added).

Thus, those most likely to commit acts that might normally be regarded as aggression are, in effect, not clearly bound by any prohibitions in the consensus definition finally reached after some fifty years of effort. Small wonder that some have criticized the definition as one where

> political reasoning prevailed over logical reasoning, which distorted the concept of aggression in favor of political expediency.[60]

---

59 FERENCZ, AGGRESSION, vol. 2 pp.19-53.
60 N. NYIRI, THE UNITED NATIONS' SEARCH FOR A DEFINITION OF AGGRESSION (1992) at 373.

It illustrated what Professor Julius Stone referred to as "an exquisite example of how conflict can be consummated in consensus.[61]

The consensus definition, with all of its built in infirmities, reflected the fears, doubts and hesitations which still plagued the international community at that time. Seen in its proper historical perspective, however, it symbolized and encouraged a determination and a direction for change which was persistent and irreversible. It demonstrated the unrelenting striving for a world society in which military aggression is outlawed. It was a small, cautious and faltering step in the direction of a more peaceful world order. What was wrong with it was - as in the case of other attempted codifications of law - that it didn't go far enough.[62]

3. Terrorism

Terroristic acts have been a bane of civilization since time immemorial. Assassination, aerial piracy, crimes against diplomats, the taking of hostages, and various other forms of terrorism still threaten the peace and security of large masses of people. Efforts to curb modern acts of terrorism by the rule of law are of fairly recent vintage.

In 1934, the peace of Europe was imperiled when King Alexander of Yugoslavia was assassinated while on a state visit to France. The murderer was a nationalist who demanded self-determination for Croatia. The assassin took refuge in a friendly country which refused to extradite him. Nations were in an uproar, with charges and counter-charges of complicity. It was reminiscent of the assassination of Archduke Ferdinand at Sarajevo in 1914 - "the shot heard round the world" that triggered World War I. The Council of the League quickly appointed a committee representing eleven nations to draft a convention that would repress "conspiracies or crimes committed with a political or terrorist purpose."[63]

By 1935, the first draft of a Convention For the Repression of Terrorism was ready. A comprehensive statute for an International Criminal Court to try such cases was attached to the terrorism convention.[64] To make a long

---

61   J. STONE, CONFLICT THROUGH CONSENSUS (1977) at 71.

62   A revised interpretation of the definition of aggression is dealt with hereafter in Chapter Eight, Section A.

63   FERENCZ, INT. CRIM. CT. vol. 1 p. 49; Doc. 7 p.270; *Report of the Committee* C.184.M. 102, 1935 V.

64   FERENCZ, INT. CRIM,. CT. vol.1, Doc. 7 pp. 296-308. It was primarily the work of a Romanian jurist, V.V. Pella, an outstanding authority who was later to form the unofficial International Association of Penal Law.

and sad story short: thirty-six states debated and amended the original and subsequent drafts. A much weakened text was ready by the end of 1937 - by which time passions had cooled. Although many states signed both the Convention for the Repression of Terrorism as well as a separate one for the establishment of an International Criminal Court, the only state that ratified the former was India and *no nation* ratified the latter. Neither convention ever went into force. Instead of closing the door on terrorism, the door was left wide open.[65]

The world's attention was again drawn to repressing terrorism when a wave of airplane hijacking began to terrorize air travelers in the 1960's. A Convention drawn up in Tokyo by the International Civil Aviation Organization in 1963 dealt with Offenses and Certain Other Acts Committed Aboard Aircraft.[66] What it failed to do was to create a legal obligation to try the offender. In fact, it stipulated that nothing in the Convention could be deemed to create an obligation to extradite. The predictable result was that hijacking became a popular means of political protest and the Tokyo Convention was unable to curb a mounting wave of aircraft piracy.

In 1970, commemorating the 25th anniversary of the UN, Secretary-General U Thant called for an international tribunal to try hijackers and declared:

> Nations and people must have the courage to resort to adequate
> new methods of international law and order.[67]

The General Assembly promptly passed a resolution condemning "without exception whatsoever all acts of aerial hijacking," and called upon states to punish perpetrators.[68] On Dec. 16, 1970, fifty nations meeting in the Hague signed a new Convention for the Suppression of Unlawful Seizure of Aircraft.[69] It improved on the Tokyo Convention in that it required states either to try the alleged offender "without exception whatsoever" or extradite him (Art.7). But there was a catch: extradition was "subject to the

---

65   For discussion and drafts of the Convention see FERENCZ, *id.* Docs. 7, 8, 9.; R. FRIEDLANDER, TERRORISM, DOCUMENTS OF INTERNATIONAL AND NATIONAL CONTROL, multi-volume series (Vol.6, 1991); J.J. Paust, "*A Survey of Possible Legal Responses to International Terrorism,*" 5 Georgia J. of Int. and Comp. L., (1975) 431-469; A. EVANS and J. MURPHY, LEGAL ASPECTS OF INTERNATIONAL TERRORISM (1978).

66   ICAO Doc. 8364, 14 Sept. 1963; UN Treaty Ser. vol. 704 No. 10106; 58 AJIL 568 (1964).

67   UN Press Release SG/SM/1333 Anv/87, Sept. 14, 1970.

68   GA Res. 2645 (XXV) Nov. 25, 1970.

69   International Civil Aviation Org., *Convention for the Suppression of Unlawful Seizures of Aircraft,* The Hague, Dec. 16, 1970, *reproduced in* 10 ILM. 133 (1971).

conditions provided for by the law of the requested States" (Art.8 (3)). That meant that hijackers could escape punishment by finding asylum in any country that was sympathetic to their goals - extradition could be refused and a local trial might be a mockery.[70]

The political climate was such that many nations refused to accept any accord that would require the trial or extradition of persons committing political offenses.[71] The shortcomings inherent in the legal instruments to stop aircraft hijacking were carried forward to other conventions dealing with other forms of terrorism.[72]

The 1973 "Convention on the Prevention and Punishment of Crimes against Internationally Protected Persons, including Diplomatic Agents" was preceded by a Preamble which recognized that the Convention

> could not in any way prejudice the exercise of the legitimate right to self-determination and independence, in accordance with the purposes and principles of the Charter...[73]

Although the Convention required extradition or trial of offenders "without exception whatsoever and without undue delay" (Art.7,) these provisions were rendered meaningless by the exculpating clause.

An International Convention against the Taking of Hostages was adopted by the General Assembly in 1979.[74] It declared hostage-taking to be an international crime but then also went on to provide that the Convention did not apply to hostage-taking

> in which people are fighting against colonial domination and alien occupation and against racist regimes in the exercise of their right of self-determination...(Art. 12).[75]

By the end of 1991, it was possible to reach consensus that:

---

70 This same fatal defect was carried forward when a new Convention for the Suppression of Unlawful Acts against the Safety of Civil Aviation was signed in Montreal in 1971; Convention dated Sept. 23, 1971, reproduced in 10 ILM 1151 (1971). *See* N. Aggarwala, M.J. Fenello, G.F. FitzGerald, *"Air Hijacking: An International Perspective"*, 585 International Conciliation 17 (1971).

71 *See* S.SCHAFER, THE POLITICAL CRIMINAL (1974); *REFLECTIONS SUR LA DEFINITION ET LA REPRESSION DU TERRORISM*, A Colloquium at the University of Brussels) (1974).

72 *See* FERENCZ, INT. CRIM. CT. vol. 2 pp. 62-100.

73 GA Res. 3166 (XXVIII), 14 Dec. 1973, *reproduced in* FERENCZ, INT. CRIM. CT. vol 2 Doc. 41(b) p.513.

74 GA Res. 34/14b (XXXIV) *reprinted in* 18 ILM 1456 (1979).

75 *See* J.L. LAMBERT, TERRORISM AND HOSTAGES IN INTERNATIONAL LAW - A COMMENTARY ON THE HOSTAGES CONVENTION 1979 (1990).

A policy of firmness and effective measures should be taken in accordance with international law in order that all acts, methods and practices of international terrorism may be brought to an end...[It condemned] as criminal and unjustifiable, all acts, methods and practices of terrorism wherever and by whomever committed, including those which jeopardize the friendly relations among States and their security.[76]

The rope tying the hands of terrorists was beginning to get tighter. But there was still no agreement on what exactly was meant by "terrorism." The last paragraph of the 1991 Preamble repeated the traditional incantation that the resolution "could in no way prejudice the right to self-determination, freedom and independence ... particularly peoples under colonial or racist regimes...or the right...to seek and receive support" in accordance with General Assembly resolutions. That left the noose sufficiently loose to permit escape. The only point on which there was real agreement was that the item should continue on the United Nations agenda - where it rests in peace.[77]

An attempt to draft an overall Convention to define terrorism and eliminate it in all its forms has not yet succeeded - despite the fact that the issues have been debated at the Legal Committee of the UN for at least the last twenty years. The convoluted title - probably the longest ever on the UN agenda - reflects the difficulties:

Measures to Prevent International Terrorism Which Endangers or Takes Innocent Human Lives or Jeopardizes Fundamental Freedoms and Study of the Underlying Causes of those Forms of Terrorism and Acts of Violence Which Lie in Misery, Frustration, Grievance and Despair and Which Cause Some People to Sacrifice Human Lives Including Their Own, In An Attempt to Effect Radical Changes.

Some considered that title itself to be an act of terrorism!

Despite the progress made and the continuing efforts to eliminate terrorism, its persistence indicates that there is still something terribly wrong with the world legal order. It has failed to resolve deep-seated hostilities or to articulate binding legal principles that make terrorism - in

---

76   GA Res. 46/51, 9 Dec. 1991, Report A/46/654, Preamble.
77   While the U.N.'s Legal Committee continued its fruitless debate on terrorism, from 11 to 14 October 1993, Haiti's Justice Minister and his bodyguards were assassinated. UN Press Release GA/L/2783, 14 October 1993.

any form - clearly unlawful and punishable. Why has it been so difficult for the world community to control acts that terrify humankind?

It is argued in defense of what is termed "terrorism" that those who resort to such unconventional violence are merely responding to injustice and it is their persecutors who should be treated as criminals. Violence in support of a justified cause - they say - should not be regarded as a criminal act. On the contrary, those who resist oppression are heroic "freedom-fighters" - regardless of the means employed. They maintain that those who lack sophisticated weapons of superpowers have no alternative other than to resort to "unconventional warfare" and to use every means and receive aid from any source and of any kind in their struggle for justice or collective self-defense. These arguments have some merit - but not much.[78]

Surely the causes of discontent must be explored and every honest effort must be made to satisfy legitimate grievances. And yet, if no agreement is possible, what then? Do the ends justify every means - including the slaughter of helpless children? Must humanity be subjected to a reign of terror in which innocent lives are put in jeopardy or kept in constant insecurity and fear because conflicting parties can not agree on what is just? A profound Professor of Philosophy at Harvard, a renowned expert on the meaning of justice, wrote:

> The aim of war is a just peace, and therefore the means employed must not destroy the possibility of peace or encourage a contempt for human life that puts the safety of ourselves and of mankind in jeopardy.[79]

The international community has not yet been able to reach agreement on when the use of force is permissible and when it is prohibited. In the nuclear age, with its uncontrollable proliferation of weapons of mass destruction, the inability to reconcile differences peacefully poses a very grave threat to human survival. The lifeblood of terrorism is fear; instead of a sense of security, a pervasive sense of anxiety and foreboding is generated everywhere. Terrorism, in all, or any, of its forms, can not be tolerated if there is to be peace and security in the world.

The Conventions made no provision for enforcement against states that did not comply; only the UN Security Council had authority to enforce the law and the Council was paralyzed by the veto power of competing Perma-

---

78   See F. MALEKIAN, INTERNATIONAL CRIMINAL LAW, 2 vols. (1991).
79   J.RAWLS, A THEORY OF JUSTICE (1971) at 379.

nent Members. The Security Council remains charged with responsibility to determine the existence of any threat to the peace and to take measures to maintain peace and security - it has failed to do so.[80]

4. A Code of Crimes against Peace and Security

The first General Assembly of the United Nations directed its newly created Committee on the Codification of International Law "to treat as a matter of primary importance" plans for the codification of offenses against the peace and security of mankind based on the principles and precedents created by the Charter and Judgment of the International Military Tribunal at Nuremberg.[81] That assignment of 1946, dealt with by the Sixth Committee, various Special Committees and also delegated to the International Law Commission, has not yet been carried out.

As long as the super-powers were gridlocked, it was not possible for significant progress to be made. Fear and distrust paralyzed action.[82] The end of the cold-war offered a new opportunity to the work of the ILC and the increase in international crimes lent a new sense of urgency to its mission. By the end of 1991, a first reading of an ILC draft code of crimes against the peace and security of mankind was being debated and it was generally regarded as an encouraging, if faltering, step in the right direction.[83] The draft articles submitted in 1992 by ILC Special Rapporteur Mr. Doudou Thiem - after about ten years of effort - remained ambivalent about which crimes should be covered by the code .The draft still had a very long way to go before it obtained the clarity needed for a penal statute.[84]

In light of outrageous atrocities such as mass rapes and "ethnic cleansing" - a euphemism for genocide - being perpetrated in the former Yugoslavia by 1991, there was a growing demand that nations that abhorred such crimes would codify them in an unequivocally binding criminal code and arrange to bring the criminals to trial.[85] The trials at Nuremberg and its

---

80   A proposed Security Council response to terrorism is considered hereafter in Chapter Four, Section C and Chapter Eight, Section A-3.

81   GA Res. 94 (I), 95 (I), 11 Dec. 1946, reproduced in FERENCZ, INT. CRIM. CT. vol. 2 Doc. 17 p.127.

82   See FERENCZ, INT. CRIM. CT. vol.2; B. Ferencz, "The Draft Code of Offenses Against the Peace and Security of Mankind" 75 AJIL 674 (1981).

83   S.C. McCaffrey, "The Forty-Second Session of the International Law Commission" 84 AJIL 930 (1990).

84   Report of the ILC, UN GAOR, 46th Sess., Supp. No. 10, UN Doc. (A/46/10) 1/46/405 (1991); U.N.Doc A/CN.4/442, 20 March 1992; See A/CN.4/449, 25 Mar. 1993; Report of the ILC, UN, GAOR, 48th Sess., Supp. No. 10 (A/48/10) covering its work from 3 May-23 July 1993.

85   See B. Ferencz, "An International Criminal Code and Court: Where They Stand and Where They're Going," 30 Col. J. Transn'l. Law (1992) 375.

aftermath awakened the public conscience to the need for clear international criminal laws to deter aggression, genocide, terrorism and other crimes against humanity. What was wrong was that sovereign states seemed more worried about preserving their powers than preserving their peoples.[86]

5. Economic Rights and Duties of States

Revolting conditions incite revolt. One of the weakest areas of codification of international laws affecting peace relates to laws to diminish the economic adversity which often gives rise to international conflict. As long as there are enormous disparities in the standards of living of different peoples, forcible efforts to correct imbalances or inequities are inevitable. People will - if they possibly can - flock or flee to those lands which offer better hope for a decent livlihood and better prospects for human dignity.

Millions of desperate refugees plead or pound at the doors of wealthier states. The danger exists that any barriers erected against them will be crushed by an uncontrollable flood of frightened humanity. It is therefore in the common interest to find legal arrangements that will enable states to cope with the problem in such humane and just manner as not to disrupt the peace of nations.

The UN Charter declares as one of its fundamental purposes "international co-operation in solving international problems of an economic, social, cultural, or humanitarian character" (Art.I). The General Assembly, acting through the Economic and Social Council (ECOSOC), is responsible for recommending and promoting cooperation and assistance in "the realization of human rights and fundamental freedoms for all" (Art.13). UN resolutions calling for economic justice and the right of peoples to sovereignty over their natural resources usually reflected a cry of anguish from the dispossessed.[87] In response, a negative vote, or silence, came from former colonial nations that had benefited from the poverty of others and who regarded the protection of their own higher standard of living as a "vested interest" to be protected at all costs. The absence of consensus meant the absence of binding legal obligations.[88]

---

86   *See* Chapter Two, Section D and Chapter Eight Section A-3 and B-2.

87   *See* GA Resolutions 1802 (XVII) 1962; 2288 (XXII) 1967; 2554 (XXIV) 1969; 2703 (XXV) 1970; 2873 (XXVI) 1971; 3116 (XXVIII) 1973.

88   *See* O. SCHACHTER, SHARING THE WORLD'S RESOURCES (1977).

In 1974, following an Assembly Declaration calling for the Establishment of a New International Economic Order (NIEO), the Assembly adopted a Charter of Economic Rights and Duties of States (CERDS) seeking

> a new system of international economic relations based on equity, sovereign equality, and interdependence of the interests of developed and developing countries.[89]

Even though serious scientists forecasted that - with proper planning and management - there would be enough food, fuel and mineral resources for everyone, the goals and principles enunciated in the Economic Charter were not universally shared.[90]

One of its 34 articles declared that each state had the right to nationalize or expropriate foreign property and it was up to the nationalizing state to decide what compensation would be paid (Art.2). It called for the transfer of modern technology to the developing countries "in accordance with procedures which are suited to their economies and their needs" (Art. 13). It enunciated a duty to achieve general and complete disarmament and to utilize the saved resources for the needs of developing countries (Art.15). The Economic Charter's angry references to "colonialism", "apartheid" and "foreign aggression, occupation and domination" reflected prevailing hostilities and tensions between North and South - the haves versus the have-nots - and doomed the document to futility.

Resolutions for a New International Economic Order have remained on the UN agenda but have made no significant progress. The problems are viewed as overwhelming. Competing needs of underdeveloped lands and the interests of private foreign capital have not been reconciled.[91] Prof. Seymour J.Rubin, long-time Executive Vice-President of the American Society of International Law, warned in 1986 that the path toward a New International Economic Order would be a tortuous one. He referred to crumbs from the tables of the rich being the traditional lot of the poor, and realistically reminded his readers: "Whether in the society of individuals or of nations, power has generally been used for the benefit of the powerful." [92]

---

89   GA Res. 3201 (S-VI) and 3202 (S-VI), 1 May 1974.

90   *See* C. FREEMAN, N. JAHODA, Eds., WORLD FUTURES - THE GREAT DEBATE (1978).

91   *See* B.H. **Weston**, *The Charter of Economic Rights and Duties of States and the Deprivation of Foreign-Owned Wealth*" 75 AJIL 437 (1981); F.C.GARCIA-AMADOR, THE EMERGING INTERNATIONAL LAW OF DEVELOPMENT (1989).

92   S.J. Rubin, *Economic and Social Human Rights and the New International Economic Order*, 67 Amer. U. Jour. of Int'l L. and Policy 67 (1986) at 87. *See* E. REUBENS, THE CHALLENGE OF THE NEW INTERNATIONAL ECONOMIC ORDER (1981).

As A.O. Adede of the UN Legal Division has pointed out, the newly elected independent states wanted to eliminate old treaties that they felt gave colonial powers unjust privileges. One dilemma was how to establish a new system that took account of disparate needs by giving added benefits to those most impoverished yet retained the traditional concept of equality of states - which was important for their pride and protection. The search for minimum standards acceptable by consensus required a careful balancing of competing interests - and the balance has not yet been found.[93]

The major industrial countries of Japan, Germany, the U.S. and U.K. were among the 20 who voted *against* the resolution for a New International Economic Order at the end of 1991.[94] The topic is scheduled for reconsideration in 1993. Without more support from the major economic powers - those expected to make the required sacrifices - any attempt to codify such an order as a legal obligation will probably not succeed. It will be recalled that General Assembly resolutions are regarded as recommendations only and have no binding legal effect.

This is not to suggest that there have been no efforts to ameliorate the economic conditions of underdeveloped areas. It is generally recognized that the world has become economically interdependent and that the failure to regulate international economic affairs is fraught with perils of many kinds. There have been a host of multi-national agreements and new institutions created to enhance economic development and to facilitate trade through the elimination of unfair practices.

The International Monetary Fund (IMF,) the International Bank for Reconstruction and Development (IBRD,) and the General Agreement on Tariffs and Trade (GATT) are illustrative. The United Nations Conference on Trade and Development (UNCTAD) has been particularly sensitive to the needs of developing countries, including those which do not have a free-market system. Thus a "Generalized System of Preferences" was accepted by GATT in 1979 to give a certain competitive advantage to the exports of underdeveloped nations.[95]

---

93   A.O. Adede, *The Minimum Standards in a World of Disparities*, in R.S.MACDONALD AND D.M. JOHNSTON, Eds., THE STRUCTURES AND PROCESS OF INTERNATIONAL LAW (1983) p.1001.

94   GA Res. 46/52, 9 Dec. 1991, Report A/46/685.

95   Tokyo Round Agreements in 1979,; GATT. Basic Instruments and selected Documents, 26th Supp. 1980, The Tokyo Round Agreement.

As the benefits of cooperation rather than competition become apparent, bi-lateral treaties are expanded to multi-national treaties and then further expanded to include larger regions like the European Community, the North Atlantic area, the Pacific Rim, the North American Free Trade Agreement (NAFTA) etc. At the same time, modest legal efforts are made to control illegal activities of transnational corporations engaged in corruption or abuse of the established legal parameters.[96]

What we are experiencing is an evolving legal system in which various international parties are slowly learning to work together for what - in the long run - is mutual advantage. Negotiations for trade benefits are a continuous process but each sovereign state thinks primarily of the immediate short-term needs or demands of its own people. Decisionmakers remain ever mindful of their own political problems back home. Creating an economic Fortress Europe to oppose an economic Fortress Asia or Fortress America may excite the spirit for the moment but is no way to maintain peace for the future. The public has yet to learn that people everywhere have the same basic needs and desires which must eventually be met - at least on a minimum standard - if there is to be tranquility in this shrinking global community.

What is still urgently required is a broader perspective that enables international law to address the basic economic needs of all persons and the elaboration of a legal system which will diminish the existing tensions that may threaten peace. Unfortunately, as Professor Louis Henkin of Columbia University correctly points out:

> There is no law and there are no legal institutions to make the economic system more just or efficient, to reduce gross inequalities, or even to create a minimal 'welfare system' that would assure the basic needs of all five billion inhabitants of the earth.[97]

A 1992 report of distinguished experts meeting under the Chairmanship of Julius K. Nyerere of Tanzania, urged the UN to assert its Charter responsibility for bringing about equitable economic reform. It deplored the exclusion of developing countries from the economic plans by the major economic powers - the G-7. It referred to the work of a small ECOSOC Expert Committee on Natural Resources (24 persons from five geographic regions) as a model for effective management of specific economic problems.[98]

---

96   S.J. Rubin, *Reflections Concerning the United Nations Commission on TNC's*, 70 AJIL 73 (1976).
97   L. Henkin, *International Law: Politics, Values and Functions*, IV *Recueil des Cours* (1989) at 347.

The idea of decentralizing specialized UN operational activities, while they remain integrated within a system of general UN control, holds great promise for the future. If such procedures can be implemented in a democratic way to be representative of varied interests - without creating a new bureaucracy - it may lead to improved global management techniques. We shall consider that further when we deal with the problems of enforcing international law.[99]

It remains a sad paradox that the world produces more than it consumes yet millions of children die and hundreds of millions of people suffer from malnutrition while over-consumption produces serious diseases in more affluent countries.[100] There is certainly something very wrong with that kind of a world order. It poses a challenge to the international legal community to find a fair and humane response that will better serve the cause of peace.

D- Evaluation

As an instrumentality for the maintenance of peace and human dignity, the promise of international law exceeds its performance. Law has not yet been able to bring order to the world. All nations pay lip service to prohibiting the use of force yet very few are prepared unconditionally to abide by their professed restraints. They are moving in the right direction but an additional impetus is needed to jolt them out of their lethargy. Whether the catalyst will be tragedy or reason remains to be seen.

Our sketch of the prevailing international laws of peace shows that - as one of the essential prerequisites for a more peaceful order - nations have been trying to formulate, define and clarify certain norms of permissible and impermissible state behavior designed to diminish, if not eliminate, the risks and hardships of war. International agreements, covenants, pacts, charters, declarations, conventions and codes, arduously drawn after years of difficult negotiation, were supposed to create a defined body of new rules for a more peaceful world governance under law - but they failed to do so.

---

98   South Centre, *Enhancing the Economic Role of the United Nations*, Oct. 1992, p. 11, 18.

99   Chapter Three, Section E; Chapter Eight, Section A-5 and C-4.

100   *See* International Conference on Nutrition sponsored by UN's World Health Organization and the Food and Agriculture Organization, in December 1992, Press Release FAO/3557, 7 Dec. 1992.

One of the reasons why the new laws proved ineffective was that they were deliberately laced with so many ambiguities, contradictions and exculpating clauses that skillful lawyers, not wishing to appear as obvious lawbreakers, could interpret them in ways that best served the national interests of their own country. Despite stated goals and accepted obligations, lawyers and diplomats found plausible interpretations to circumvent what should have been the real purposes of new legal accords.[101] As B.G. Ramcharan of the UN politely noted in his study of the workings of the International Law Commission:

> A politically influenced body is sometimes forced to depart from the position which, by applying objective criteria, it might otherwise have adopted.[102]

There was compliance with most agreements - as long as they served the interests of those who accepted them. But the continuation of massive violence on a world-wide scale proved that the new laws - loosely formulated and subject to misinterpretation - were inadequate to stem the use of force. Habits of nationalism, ethnic rivalries and warfare, prevailing for centuries, could not easily be replaced. Unable or unwilling to implement plans for "collective security," nations continued to face collective insecurity.

Despite all their infirmities, the evolving international laws of peace were not without significant legal impact. One can hardly assume that thousands of man-hours invested by legal experts from all parts of the world in drafting solemn declarations or conventions was a totally cynical and useless exercise.[103]

Rules which may begin with only moral or political force but which are frequently repeated in various forms, such as those expressed in the treaties, declarations and codes referred to above, gradually have a way of growing into binding legal obligations. Even if not accepted by consensus of *all* nations, they eventually acquire a legal force of their own. As Prof. Egon Schwelb of Yale, for many years Deputy Director of the UN Division on Human Rights, aptly wrote:

---

101 *See* D.P. FORSYTHE, THE POLITICS OF INTERNATIONAL LAW (1990); F.A. BOYLE, THE FUTURE OF INTERNATIONAL LAW AND AMERICAN FOREIGN POLICY (1989).

102 B.G. RAMCHARAN, THE INTERNATIONAL LAW COMMISSION (1977) at 206.

103 *See* HANNA BOKOR-SZEGO, THE ROLE OF THE UNITED NATIONS IN INTERNATIONAL LEGISLATION (1978); I.M. SINCLAIR, THE INTERNATIONAL LAW COMMISSION (1987).

Statements which, if approved without substantial dissent by the overwhelming majority of Governments and acquiesced in by the rest, acquire an authority which takes them out of the category of 'non-binding' pronouncements.[104]

The perceptive Prof. Rosalyn Higgins of London has confirmed that "repeated invocation of rights assists in the perception of them as normative, and assists in turn in their implementation."[105] According to Prof. Louis Sohn of Harvard, the Universal Declaration of Human Rights, was an authoritative interpretation of the UN Charter and "has over the years become a part of customary international law."[106]

During recent years, there has emerged a growing acceptance in the international community that certain international laws of peace cannot be abrogated - even by what would otherwise be considered to be binding agreements between independent states. Such norms, often described as *jus cogens* (compelling laws) have a compelling, absolute or imperative force which binds all states. It is a concept as old as law itself which has always recognized that certain interests of the community were so important for survival that no abrogation could be tolerated. Nations violate such obligatory prohibitions at their peril. They are trespassing on what is becoming a legal interest of the expanded international community as a whole. This emerging concept of obligations to the international community as a whole - which transcends even the rights of individual states - has been recognized by many modern scholars.[107]

Declarations which begin as non-binding proclamations can become binding laws in a number of ways:

(a) Norms which appear repeatedly in many UN resolutions and declarations may be seen as authoritative interpretations of the UN Charter - which is a treaty legally binding all members. They are thus on the way to becoming new obligatory legal standards.

---

104 E. SCHWELB, HUMAN RIGHTS AND THE INTERNATIONAL COMMUNITY (1964) at 74.

105 R. Higgins, *Some Thoughts on the Implementation of Human Rights* in Bulletin of Human Rights, 89/1 *Implementation of International Human Rights Instruments*, 1990 at 61.

106 L.B. SOHN, *United Nations Machinery for Implementing Human Rights*, 62 AJIL 909 (1968). For a bibliography of- writings by Professor Sohn, see T.BUERGENTHAL,Ed, CONTEMPORARY ISSUES IN INTERNATIONAL LAW,Essays in Honor of Louis B. Sohn (1984) Appendix.

107 H. Mosler, THE INTERNATIONAL SOCIETY AS A LEGAL COMMUNITY, (1980); E. Suy, "*The Concept of Jus Cogens in Public International Law,*" Carnegie Endowment Conf. on Int'l Law, Apr.1986, Papers and Proceedings, Vol. 2, p.17; J.A. Frowein,"*Die Verplichtungen erga omnes in Völkerrecht.*" in *Festschrift für H.Mosler* (1983) p. 241.

(b) The International Court of Justice is required by its statute to take into consideration "the general principles of law recognized by civilized nations" (Art. 38(1)c). How that will be interpreted may depend upon the particular facts and circumstances of the case but the World Court can not remain unmindful of evolving restraints which appear to be generally acceptable to the world community.

(c) The 1969 Vienna Convention on the Law of Treaties, prescribes that once a norm acquires the status of *jus cogens*, there may be no derogation from it in any treaty between states. An attempt to violate or subvert the accepted norms will be void. The will of the international community as a whole must be respected and given precedence over contracts between states that seek to ignore those binding international mandates.

But, there is still no universal agreement among international lawyers about exactly which norms have such universal and binding character or whether such norms exist at all.[108] According to noted British Legal Advisor and ILC member Sir Ivan M. Sinclair, "Such an international legal order is, at present, inchoate, unformed and only just discernible."[109] An excellent and comprehensive analysis by Lauri Hannikainen of Finland goes a bit further:

> The clarification of the notion of *jus cogens* in international law is advancing, but is still far from being completed.[110]

What is slowly emerging is that international norms designed to maintain peace are - according to the overwhelming majority of legal experts - increasingly acquiring a mandatory character.[111]

The prevailing trend toward strengthening the rule of law must be encouraged and strengthened.

All states - and all individuals - have an interest in a world order in which offenses against public order and security which jeopardize peace are

---

108   *See* A.D'Amato, *It's a Bird, It's a Plane, It's a Jus Cogens!* 6 Conn. J. of Int. L. 1 (1990).

109   I.M. Sinclair, THE VIENNA CONVENTION ON THE LAW OF TREATIES (1973) p.131. *See* F.A.MANN, FURTHER STUDIES IN INTERNATIONAL LAW (1990) p.102.

110   L. Hannikainen, PEREMPTORY NORMS (JUS COGENS) IN INTERNATIONAL LAW (1988) at 723.

111   A recent U.S. case held that prohibition against torture was a *jus cogens* norm which gave the court jurisdiction even where the crime was committed by a foreign state's agents against its own nationals outside the U.S. *In re Estate of Marcos Human Rights Litigation*, U.S. Ct. of Appeals, 9th Circ. Oct 21, 1992, *reproduced in* 32 ILM 106 (1993); *See* UN GA Res. 3452 (XXX) 9 Dec. 1975; GAOR, 43rd Sess., Suppl. No. 46 (A/43/46) Report of the Committee Against Torture (1988); *Filartiga v. Pena-Irala*, 630 F.2d. 876 (2d.Cir.), 19 ILM 585 (1980).

not tolerated under any circumstances. In the *Barcelona Traction* case the ICJ spoke of

> the obligations of a State towards the international community as a whole...all States can be held to have a legal interest in their protection; they are obligations *erga omnes*. Such obligations derive, for example, in contemporary international law, from the outlawing of acts of aggression, and of genocide as also from the principles and rules concerning the basic rights of the human person, including protection from slavery and racial discrimination.[112]

Yet, throughout the world, racial discrimination and poverty fester like open wounds. International laws to create economic justice among nations - an essential component of peace - have hardly begun to be written. In the long run, if there is to be peace, international laws must reflect a greater willingness to share and be fair - to consider need before greed.

We see, therefore, that there is much that is right but also much that is wrong with the international laws of peace. What is called for now is a readiness and determination by states to look beyond traditional thinking and the parochial interests of the moment and to accept clear minimum legal obligations which will help establish a more peaceful world legal order. Although we must respect and build on what has been done, we must also recognize the need for change. My esteemed professor, Roscoe Pound, wrote:

> We must go on with the legal institutions and precepts and doctrines that have come down to us until we have learned more effective instruments of social control. But we are not bound to retain them when they cease to do what they were set up to do.[113]

The General Assembly has declared the period 1990-1997 to be the UN Decade of International Law. Nations have been urged to take specific measures to enhance acceptance of the legal principles needed to maintain peace. As a promotional technique it is useful to focus attention on needed reforms. How far nations are prepared to go, remains to be seen.[114] The times demand courageous vision and a plan for moving as rapidly as possible

---

112 *Barcelona Traction Case*, ICJ Reports 1970 pp. 3, 32.

113 R. Pound, *The Task of the Law in the Atomic Age*, in S.ENGEL, Ed., LAW, STATE AND INTERNATIONAL LEGAL ORDER, Essays in Honor of Hans Kelsen 233 (1964) at 246.

114 See Report of the Secretary-General, *UN Decade of International Law*, A/48/312, 15 August 1993.

away from the shackles of past legal thinking into the new legal institutions required for a more tranquil future for coming generations.

CHAPTER TWO
INTERNATIONAL COURTS

> War is directed against those who cannot be held in check by
> judicial process.
>
> Demosthenes (ca. 341 B.C.)[1]

If we consider the present system of international courts - as well as other means of peaceful settlement - it will be quite apparent that there is considerable room for improvement. This is not to suggest that there has been no progress - quite the contrary. A brief historical review will demonstrate that we have come a very long way from the days when combat was a lawful way for nations ultimately to resolve irreconcilable differences. Change was stimulated by the enormous increases in interactions among states. The growth of international trade and travel, the development of instantaneous means of world-wide communication and the awesome threat of devastating nuclear weapons and other means of mass destruction have made it increasingly imperative to reinforce the judicial process as a means of keeping man in check in order to avoid war.

A- Peaceful Settlement Without Courts

It is logical and normal that disputes be settled by peaceful means. No one wishes to risk violence and its consequences if differences can be reconciled without combat. Yet, human history shows that armed struggle has still not been eliminated from the human experience. On the contrary, as the technology for destruction has advanced, the number of war victims has increased. Why is it that available peaceful options have proved ineffective in maintaining peace, and what cam be done about it?

1. Early Practice

According to Aristotle, "Every state is a community of some kind, and every community is established with a view to some good."[2]But reasonable men may differ about what is considered good or moral and states usually go to war because each one is convinced that it alone is in the right.

---

1   Quoted by GROTIUS, ON THE LAW OF WAR AND PEACE, (1624), (Kelsey Transl., Carnegie, 1925) *Prolegamena* Para. 25.

2   R. MCKEON, INTRODUCTION TO ARISTOTLE (1947) at 552; Compare Plato, *Politicus*, Bk. I.

Recognizing that to be so, Hugo Grotius - generally considered the father of international law - proposed three alternatives to war:

> First, war may be obviated by a conference...
> Second, war may be obviated by arbitration...
> Third, war may be obviated even by lot - the method of Solomon.

Grotius then suggested a fourth (and even better) choice: In cases where the antagonists were not ready to accept any of those three peaceful alternatives, and their "disputes would otherwise afflict whole people with very serious evils," single combat between the two sovereigns "might be accepted by their states as the lesser evil."[3]

The suggestion that kings fight it out among themselves rather than impose enormous suffering on their innocent subjects, might have been acceptable to a few heroic monarchs of that time but is not likely to appeal to many Heads of State today - unfortunately.

Scholastic theologians of the Middle Ages, such as St. Augustine and St. Thomas Aquinas, shared the Roman doctrine that no war could be "just" which was not begun in a just way. That included talking to the adversary, making your demands known and providing time for compliance. Cicero is quoted as having said

> "There are two kinds of strife - one conducted by discussion and the other by force: the one appropriate to men and the other to beasts."[4]

If disputes could not be resolved by conference with the enemy, then some form of third party intervention was the next best step.

Arbitration - referring the dispute to a third party for binding decision - was not uncommon among city-states of ancient Greece. The Pope often served as the sole arbiter in resolving conflicts among Italian nobles during the Middle Ages. Arbitration is a purely voluntary procedure and does not come into play unless parties agree to it by treaty or otherwise.

A *legal obligation* of states to settle disputes by arbitration appeared in the Jay Treaty of 1794 between Great Britain and the United States following

---

3 GROTIUS, ON THE LAW OF WAR AND PEACE, Book One: Chap. XXIII, Sec. X.

4 Cited By B. AYALA, THREE BOOKS ON THE LAWS OF WAR (1582) First Bk. Chap. II Sec.1. Ayala confirms the requirement to confer with the enemy before war can be considered "just." First Book Chap. 1. *Reproduced in* FERENCZ, ENFORCING INT. L. vol. 1 Doc. 3 p.111.

the bitter battles of the American revolution.[5]It has maintained peace between those formerly warring parties since that time and set a pattern which has often been followed. But treaties bind only the parties that agree to be bound by them and it was not uncommon to exempt from compulsory arbitration all matters affecting "honor" or "vital interests." That meant that arbitration was frequently used for commercial disputes but issues most likely to lead to war were often excluded.[6]

2. From the Hague to the League

Arbitration as a peaceful means of dispute settlement did not become institutionalized   until fairly recent times. *The Convention for the Pacific Settlement of International Disputes*, signed at the Hague in 1899 and 1907, was made subject to so many reservations - preserving the right of sovereign states to do as they wished - that it was only a modest step forward.[7] The "Pacific Settlement Convention," urging parties to have recourse to good offices or mediation before resorting to arms, contained merely *recommendations* to be followed "as far as circumstances allow." The Convention purpord to establish a Permanent Court of Arbitration. Permanent it may have been, for it still exists at the Hague today, but a Court it was not. It was nothing more than a list of arbitrators who would be available if called upon to settle disputes between states. It was a purely voluntary system which no state was obliged to accept - and very few did.[8]

Following World War I, there was a concerted effort, led by the United States, to make arbitration of international disputes mandatory. U.S. Secretary of State Elihu Root was in the forefront of the drive to create A Permanent Court of Arbitral Justice rather than the ad hoc institution which then existed and that was little used. The efforts failed when no agreement could be reached about how the judges were to be selected. The Arbitral *Court* disappeared from the agenda, to be replaced by later consideration of the Permanent Court of International Justice.[9]

---

5   Treaty of Amity, Commerce and Navigation, (1794) Cons. Treaty Series, Vol. 52, p.243, *reproduced in* FERENCZ, *Id.* vol.2 Doc. 12, p.187.

6   *See* A.M. STUYT, SURVEY OF INTERNATIONAL ARBITRATIONS 1794-1938 (1939); L. SOHN, Ed., UNITED NATIONS, SYSTEMATIC SURVEY OF TREATIES FOR THE PACIFIC SETTLEMENT OF INTERNATIONAL DISPUTES, 1928-1948 (1949).

7   PROCEEDINGS, The Conf. of 1907, Oct. 16, 1907, *Reproduced in* FERENCZ, ENFORCING INT.L. vol.1 Doc. 20 p.257.

8   Convention for the Pacific Settlement of International Disputes (1899), *reproduced in* FERENCZ, INT. CRIM. CT., vol. 1 Doc.1 p. 111; UN Reports of International Arbitral Awards.

9   Proceedings of the Hague Peace Conferences, 1907 (1920) Annex A; *reproduced in* FERENCZ, ENFORCING INT. L. vol. 1 p. 260.

The U.S. delegate to the Hague Conference noted that the American Articles of Confederation of 1777 had made provision for arbitration but

> it failed to justify its existence; lacking the essential elements of a court of justice, it was superseded within ten years of its creation by the present Supreme Court, in which controversies which might lead to war, if between sovereign states, are settled by judicial means.[10]

In 1928, the League of Nations sought to encourage the use of arbitration by making available a draft of a multilateral treaty which required compulsory conciliation and arbitration of political disputes. (*Legal* disputes were to go to the Permanent Court of Justice.) The "General Act of Geneva", as it came to be known, was widely adopted by European states.[11] The United States, Germany and the Soviet Union did not accede to it. In 1939, France, Great Britain and its Dominions announced that The General Act did not apply when war was imminent. The legal obligation to rely on arbitration was simply brushed aside. In exchange for giving up pacific settlement, what they soon got instead was World War II.[12]

3. UN Charter Options

The UN Charter mandates the "Pacific settlement of Disputes" (Chap.VI). The rationale is simple: if states must settle all disputes only by peaceful means, there will be no wars. Art. 33 directs "The parties to any dispute, the continuation of which is likely to endanger the maintenance of international peace and security" to settle the dispute by any one of eight approved peaceful methods:

1- negotiation,

2- enquiry,

3- mediation,

4- conciliation,

5- arbitration,

6- judicial settlement,

7- resort to regional agencies or arrangements, or

---

10   *Id.* at 260.

11   *General Act for the Pacific Settlement of International Disputes*, LNTS, Vol. 93, pp.344-363.

12   The UN sought to revive the General Act in 1949, but very few states were prepared to accept it. *Revised General Act*, UNTS, Vol.93, pp. 101-127.

8- other peaceful means of their own choice.

Negotiation between the parties themselves and formal or informal consultation about their differences are the obvious first steps recommended by Grotius. *Inquiry* enables parties to clarify issues by impartial fact finding that may reduce tensions or eliminate problems. *Good Offices* by third parties may facilitate a peaceful settlement. *Mediation* allows the third party to advance non-binding proposals aimed at a compromise. *Conciliation* allows both inquiry and mediation and adds the possibility of proposing a settlement to end the dispute fairly. *Arbitration* implies that the parties will be bound by the arbitral decision. *Judicial settlement* presupposes the availability of a legal tribunal with authority to render decisions that will bind the parties. *Regional Agencies or Arrangements* are available under various multilateral regional treaties. Furthermore, states are free to use any *other peaceful means* - providing it does not endanger peace and security.

In addition to prescribing at least eight peaceful options that nations must pursue in resolving controversies, the United Nations has tried to encourage peaceful settlement of disputes in a number of other ways. General Assembly and Security Council resolutions have called upon parties to a conflict to cease and desist. Conciliation Commissions and special mediators have been placed at the disposal of warring parties. UN Senior Legal Officer Prof. Roy S. Lee has pointed to another peaceful alternative that is not obvious in the UN Charter: the Secretary General may, *with the consent of the parties*, intercede in political disputes that have reached a crisis.[13]

The Secretary-General has personally intervened to resolve differences and many of his efforts at mediation, conciliation and personal diplomacy - particularly since the end of the cold-war -have been helpful in ameliorating or resolving international disputes in a peaceful way.[14] But in the usual situations of high tension or internal strife, individuals - and nations - not directly involved often stand helpless or indifferent, relying on valiant non-governmental organizations to ameliorate the human suffering.

To further facilitate peaceful settlements, UN committees formulated detailed rules for arbitration, enabling the parties to know in advance what procedures would be followed by arbiters designated by the parties them-

---

13   R.S.Lee, *A Case for Facilitation in the Settlement of Disputes* 34 German Yrbk of Int. L. 138 (1991).

14   The annual Reports of the Secretary General, UN GAOR, Suppl. No. 1, describe the work of various mediators and Conciliation Commissions, as well as the Secretary-General's role in averting or resolving crises.

selves.[15] Arbitration, less costly and less time-consuming than judicial process, continued to play a useful role in settling commercial disputes. But in matters affecting war and peace, arbitration agreements had relatively little impact.[16] After years of effort, the UN prepared a detailed commentary on the Charter options in a Handbook on the Peaceful Settlement of Disputes Between States. It was written to clarify the options and procedures and thereby to encourage states to reach agreement without resorting to war.[17]

Many states have, in fact, mandated peaceful dispute settlement in various multi-national treaties.[18] One would think that with so many peaceful options available, nations"determined to save succeeding generations from the scourge of war" would never find it necessary to turn to killing their respective citizens to resolve their differences.[19] Unfortunately, even the added Charter prohibition against "the threat or use of force" (Art.2(4)) has not put an end to massive violence between states with such different perceptions of what is right and wrong that they are willing to have their nationals kill or be killed rather than rely on peaceful settlement.[20]

Since the end of World War II, many millions have died as a direct or indirect effect of war. Herbert K. Tillema of the University of Missouri-Columbia has described no less than 265 international wars and other war-threatening armed conflicts of various sizes involving foreign overt military interventions between 1945 and the end of 1988.[21] The irony - and tragedy - is increased when it is realized, as Sydney D. Bailey has so forcefully documented, that the deliberate resort to war rarely achieves the purposes of the initiators and "war is not a very effective means of continuing a political struggle."[22] There is need for a new international mechanism or

---

15   *Draft Convention on Arbitral Procedure*, Yearbook, ILC (1953) II, pp. 208-212; ibid. (1957,1958) II, pp. 1-15.

16   *See* I.G. WETTER, THE INTERNATIONAL ARBITRAL PROCESS, PUBLIC AND PRIVATE, 5 vols. (1979).

17   *Report of the Special Committee on the Charter*, GAOR Supp. No. 33 (A/46/33) (1991) Annex; HANDBOOK ON THE PEACEFUL SETTLEMENT OF DISPUTES BETWEEN STATES (1992).

18   *See* L. Sohn, *Settlement of Disputes Relating to Interpretation and Application of Treaties*, 150 RdC, (1976 II) 195 ; UN, A SURVEY OF TREATIES FOR THE PACIFIC SETTLEMENT OF INTERNATIONAL DISPUTES (1962).

19   U.S. Congressman Ronald V. Dellums of California has called for "preventive engagement" by diplomatic, political and economic persuasion rather thaan resort to force. R.V. Dellums, Preventive Engagement, Harvard Int'l Rev. (Fall 1993) 24.

20   Sierra Leone's able Ambassador Koroma (elected to the International Court of Justice effective on 10 November 1993) proposed that a Dispute Settlement Service, subject to Security Council and Secretary-General control, be made available for early conflict resolution. Doc. A/48/398, 15 September 1993. Charles Guettel, of the Center for UN Reform, has advocated such a service for many years.

21   H.K. TILLEMA, INTERNATIONAL ARMED CONFLICT SINCE 1945 (1992).

structure with authority, power and determination to detect and tamp down smoldering fires before they burst into engulfing flames or to compel the parties to turn to law rather than war. No such agency exists.

B- A World Court

The attempt to create an international *court* with binding jurisdiction to settle controversies among states has had a checkered history. Nations have, in principle, recognized the utility of such a tribunal but, in practice, they have been reluctant to accept its strictures. It took a considerable period of time to translate the idea of a World Court into a functioning institution - even with limited authority. New means for holding men in check by judicial process are still in their infancy or only on the horizon.

1. Early Efforts

During the Second Hague Conference in 1907, U.S. delegate Joseph Choate read forth a letter from President Theodore Roosevelt supporting the idea of an "International Court of Justice." What the Americans had in mind was a court of permanent judges (rather than a list of arbitrators) based on the model of the U.S. Supreme Court,

> to make it increasingly probable that in each case that may come before them, they will decide between the nations, great or small, exactly as a judge within our own limits decides between the individuals, great or small, who come before him.[23]

Although twenty-eight states voted to consider the plan, twelve abstained and the idea died in committee.[24]

For awhile it seemed that nations would accept an international court of limited but compulsory jurisdiction to deal conclusively with disputes regarding the legality of seizing ships and cargoes as prizes of war. A convention was drafted "Relative to the Creation of an International Prize Court" that would have complete authority to resolve the type of maritime disputes that had often brought nations to the brink of war. The Convention was promptly signed by many states that agreed to be bound by the Court's decisions (Art.9).

---

22 S.D. BAILEY, HOW WARS END, vol. 2 p. ix.

23 *Proceedings of the Hague Peace Conferences*, 1907 (1920) Annex A; *reproduced in* FERENCZ, ENFORCING INT. L. vol. 1, at 261.

24 *Id.*

The Prize Court was widely hailed as "the first truly organized international court in the history of the world."[25] In his message to Congress. President Roosevelt pointed to the Court as "the great advance which the world is making towards the substitution of the rule of reason and justice in place of simple force."[26]But Great Britain, which had been one of the most ardent supporters of the Prize Court, backed down when she could not control the naval laws which the Court was to apply. Britannia may have ruled the waves but she could not get the others to waive the rules. In the end, no state ratified the Convention. They simply missed the boat.[27]

It was 1908 when the world's first international tribunal was actually created. It was limited in geographical range and legal competence. The Central American Court of Justice was established by treaty among five Central American republics.[28] Its jurisdiction allowed individual complaints but excluded matters of "vital interest" to the parties. The Court was in existence for only ten years, during which time it rendered only ten decisions. Despite the paucity of its product, its two affirmative judgments may have helped to prevent a Central American war.[29]

2. Permanent Court of International Justice

The Covenant of the League of Nations provided for the establishment of a Permanent Court of International Justice (PCIJ) that would be competent to decide "any dispute of an international character *which the parties thereto submit to it*" (Art. 14, italics added).[30] A committee of expert Jurists "chosen from among the most eminent legal authorities in the world" was assigned to plan the establishment of the PCIJ. The Jurists, of course, realized that if the Court were to be really effective it would have to be given *compulsory* jurisdiction and could not be made dependent upon the whim or wishes of one of the parties.

---

25   W.I. Hull, *Obligatory Arbitration and the Hague Conference*, 2 AJIL 731 (1908) at 742; *Report on the Draft Convention Relative to the Creation of an International Prize Court is reproduced in* FERENCZ, INT. CRIM. CT. vol 1 Doc. 2(b) p.127.

26   *Id*. Doc. 2(c) at 165.

27   *See* FERENCZ, INT. CRIM. CT. vol. 1 pp. 15-20.

28   Costa Rica, El Salvador, Guatemala, Honduras, and Nicaragua.

29   F.L. GRIEVES, SUPRANATIONALISM AND INTERNATIONAL ADJUDICATION (1969) 19-44; C.J. GUTIERREZ, *LA CORTE DE JUSTICIA CENTRO-AMERICANA* (1978); J.B. Scott, *The Central American Peace Conference of 1907*, 1 AJIL 121 (1907).

30   *Reproduced in* FERENCZ, DEFINING INT. AGGRESSION, vol. 1 Doc. 1 at 64; also ENFORCING INT. L. vol. 1 Doc. 22.

Elihu Root, who had pleaded for a court with binding jurisdiction when the matter was debated in the Hague in 1907, tried to achieve that result by arguing that mere acceptance of the Covenant (which the U.S. had not done) meant that nations were automatically bound to accept compulsory jurisdiction of the new Court. But the British voiced strong objections to such a broad, and erroneous, interpretation of Article 14. Mr. Balfour, speaking for the British Empire, explained with typical diplomatic equivocation:

> It is quite true that we are ardent supporters of the idea of an International Court of Justice. It is quite true that we desire to see the application to that Court made voluntarily and not compulsorily. This is not because we desire to discourage the movement in which we have taken part, not because we desire to check its extension to the furthest practicable fields, but because we are convinced ...that if these things are to be successful they must be allowed to grow...[31]

For the Conservative British, "the time was not yet ripe."

After a rather bitter debate, in which several delegates argued that compulsory jurisdiction was vital if the Court was to settle important disputes peacefully, a Swiss compromise (Art. 36) was accepted: every state would be given an option to stipulate in advance that it would grant the Court jurisdiction in certain types of cases - to be defined by each state. All seemed agreed that something was better than nothing; hence limited competence of the court could be accepted as an interim step. Hope was expressed that, once the court had established itself, nations could - in the future - look forward to an improved institution with broader and more compelling authority.[32]

The PCIJ was established as an independent institution which States could voluntarily join by accepting its statute, even if they were not members of the League. During its early years, the Court was instrumental in helping to resolve a number of relatively minor border disputes. These successes evoked new hopes among some scholars that "the era of self-help, a sort of state of nature era in the history of the society of states, is drawing to a close."[33] But the optimism was premature. The cases settled by the Court involved areas in which none of the major powers had a vital interest.

---

31 League of Nations, *Records of the First Assembly,* Dec. 13, 1920, *reproduced in* FERENCZ, ENFORCING INT. L. vol. 1 at 297-298.

32 *See* FERENCZ, ENFORCING INT. L. vol. 1 pp.49-52.

33 A.E. Hindmarsh, *Self-Help in Time of Peace,* 26 AJIL 315 (1932) at 323. *See* M. Hudson, *The Prospect for Int'l Law in the Twentieth Century,* X Cornell Law Q'trly (1925) No. 4.

Where important interests were threatened, major powers did not choose to turn to the so-called "World Court" for solutions.[34]

During its brief existence, the Permanent Court handled about 65 contentious cases. It rendered 21 judgments and about two dozen advisory opinions that helped to develop international law and procedures for such litigation. That, in itself, was no small achievement - even though most of those concerned realized that it did not go far enough.[35] As might have been expected, the availability of the PCIJ - with no compulsory jurisdiction - was unable to prevent World War II.

3. *International Court of Justice*

After World War II, the Permanent Court of Justice was resurrected as the International Court of Justice (ICJ). The ICJ, despite the slight change in name, continued the work of the PCIJ without major alteration. Its legal basis, structure and workings are comprehensively described in the publications of the Court itself.[36] What concerns us here is the actual functioning of the new World Court as a legal institution to help maintain peace among nations.

The organizers of the United Nations were not unmindful of the shortcomings of the PCIJ. They sought to overcome some of those failings by providing in the UN Charter that the ICJ would be "the principal judicial organ of the United Nations" (Art. 92) and that all Members of the UN would be "*ipso facto* parties to the Statute of the International Court of Justice" (Art. 93) - a provision for automatic membership which had been rejected by the League. Requiring the General Assembly "upon the recommendation of the Security Council" to deal with admission of non-UN members as parties to the ICJ Statute (Art.93) and allowing the Assembly or Council to request advisory opinions on legal matters from the ICJ (Art.95), were other new and useful ways of binding together the three limbs of the world body.

Furthermore, nations were specifically obliged to comply with ICJ decisions and if any party failed to do so, the Security Council could "decide

---

34   F.P. WALTERS, A HISTORY OF THE LEAGUE OF NATIONS (1952) pp. 152-157.

35   J.B. SCOTT, THE PROJECT OF A PERMANENT COURT OF INTERNATIONAL JUSTICE (1920); M.O. HUDSON, THE PERMANENT COURT OF INTERNATIONAL JUSTICE 1920-1942 (1943).

36   Publications of the ICJ include its official Reports of Judgments, Advisory Opinions and Orders, the Pleadings and an Annual Yearbook. Leading commentators on the work of the Court include: S. Rosenne, E. Hambro, H.J. Schlochauer and P.C. Jessup.

upon measures to be taken to give effect to the judgment" (Art.94). The legal duty to comply with ICJ judgments and the clear reference to the Security Council as an available enforcement agency were additional steps forward toward a rational rule of law.

But there are two sides to the coin. What was not made clear was whether the Security Council was under a legal *obligation* to enforce the decisions of the Court. If the non-judicial Security Council was legally bound to enforce the decisions of the ICJ, that might lower the all-important Council to merely an enforcement arm of the Court. Such a responsibility might also nullify the veto power of the Permanent Members. Obviously, these were interpretations which the politically-minded Council was not likely to accept. And it didn't.

It was left to the discretion of the Council itself to decide whether they would enforce any ICJ decision. The Security Council was not constitutionally *bound* to enforce the decisions of the UN judiciary. The ICJ was deliberately kept in the position of a court that could not know whether its decisions would be enforced or not.[37]

The ICJ suffered from other natal infirmities. We have seen that in 1920 nations were not prepared to give the PCIJ compulsory jurisdiction to adjudicate even limited types of legal disputes without the prior consent of the disputants. That was the position taken by powerful states after World War I and it remained their basic position after World War II. Sovereign states learn slowly..

Smaller nations regarded compulsory adjudication by a fair international tribunal as the best defense against domination by the big Powers. But it was not left for them to decide. For political reasons, both the United States and the Soviet Union - flushed with the pride of victory in World War II - were not prepared to accept a legal obligation empowering any third party or institution to tell them what to do. As Professor Robert Hildebrand noted:

> [T]he governments that were represented at Dumbarton Oaks had no desire to see the creation of anything too visionary...Put simply, a world of universal law and sovereign equality posed too many dangers for the Great Powers that would have to

---

37   *See* A.R.HILDEBRAND, DUMBARTON OAKS (1990) pp. 118-121.

create it; they preferred to retain enough of the old, political way of doing things to preserve their own dominance.[38]

When the Dumbarton Oaks proposals were considered at San Francisco in preparation for the signing of the new UN Charter, a Committee was appointed to draft the Charter provisions dealing with the International Court. As with the expert Jurists' opinion after World War I, a majority of the Committee favored making the Court's jurisdiction compulsory. The majority did not prevail. In order to reach agreement, the minority view had to be accepted; the ICJ, like its predecessor, became a court *without* compulsory jurisdiction.[39] The Committee concluded:

> It is confidently anticipated that the jurisdiction of this tribunal will be extended as time goes on, and past experience warrants the expectation that its exercise of this jurisdiction will command a general support...In establishing the International Court of Justice, the United Nations hold before a war-stricken world the beacons of Justice and Law and offer the possibility of substituting orderly judicial process for the vicissitudes of war and the reign of brutal force.[40]

It should be noted that the stated reason for accepting an inadequate tribunal in 1945 was similar to that given in 1920. It was hoped that the jurisdiction would be extended in the future. Aside from the inspiring rhetoric, what was actually offered was only the *"possibility"* of substituting law for force - not the legal obligation to do so.

The general public must have been further confused when, on Aug. 14, 1946, President Truman declared that the United States:

> recognizes as compulsory *ipso facto* ... the jurisdiction of the International Court of Justice... *Provided* that this declaration shall not apply to...disputes with regard to matters within the domestic jurisdiction of the United States of America *as determined by the United States of America*" (emphasis added).[41] A

---

38 A.R. HILDEBRAND, DUMBARTON OAKS (1990) at 121.

39 The United Nations Conference on International Organization, *Report of Rapporteur of Committee IV/1*, Doc. 913, June 12, 1944, *reproduced in* FERENCZ, ENFORCING INT. L. vol. 2, Doc. 41(c) at 610.

40 *Id.*

41 Declaration by the President of the United States, Aug. 14, 1946, 61 Stat. 1218, T.I.A.S. No. 1598. *See* P. Jessup, *The Development of a United States Approach to the International Court of Justice*, 5 Vanderbilt J. Transn'l L. 1 (1971). Several other states have made similar reservations. Annual Reports in the ICJ Yearbook show the latest list of reservations by different countries.

reservation that allows a state to determine unilaterally that the subject matter is domestic and hence outside the court's juris-diction is not a recognition *ipso facto* of the Court's compulsory jurisdiction at all; it is *ipso facto* a **denial** of the Courts compul-sory jurisdiction!

Furthermore, the U.S. reservation, retaining the right to decide if the ICJ has jurisdiction, is inconsistent with the Court's own Statute - approved by all members of the UN. The Statute specifically provides that jurisdiction "shall be settled by the decision of the Court" (Art. 36 (6)). The American acceptance is an illusory submission to compulsory jurisdiction, as Judge Sir Hersch Lauterpacht and others have pointed out.[42] The U.S. restriction was, in the words of Prof. Leo Gross, another great international legal scholar, "a most damaging blow at the Court. It expresses a virtually total lack of confidence in the Court.[43]

The United States was not alone in turning its back on international adjudication. Under established principles of reciprocity, other parties to a dispute could claim the same privilege; thus further undercutting the Court's authority. The Soviet Union, since the days when it was the only communist state in the world and thus felt encircled by hostile capitalists, regarded any international tribunal as inevitably biased and an unaccept-able infringement on its sovereignty.[44] Other Socialist states felt the same way. Newly formed states of Africa and Asia were distrustful and appre-hensive about laws and institutions developed without their knowledge and consent by former colonial masters who seemed primarily concerned with protecting their own patrimony.[45]

In 1985, the U.S. back-tracked even further. It petulantly withdrew its restrictive acceptance of ICJ's jurisdiction following the Court's decision against the U.S. for war-like acts, including mining the harbors of Nicara-gua.[46] Professor Richard B. Bilder of the University of Wisconsin expressed

---

42   *Case of Certain Norwegian Loans* (1957) I.C.J. Rep. 9 at 49; Preuss, *Questions Resulting from the Connolly Amendment,* #2 A.B.A.J. 660 (1946).

43   L. Gross, *The International Court of Justice, Consideration of Requirements for Enhancing Its Role in the International Legal Order,* 65 AJIL 253 (1971) at 271.

44   *See* FERENCZ, AGGRESSION, vol.1 p. 201; G.I. TUNKIN, THEORY OF INTERNATIONAL LAW (1974).

45   *See* E.McWHINNEY, THE INTERNATIONAL COURT OF JUSTICE AND THE WESTERN TRADITION OF INTERNATIONAL LAW (1987).

46   *Nicaragua v. U.S.,* Order of 10 May 1984, ICJ Judgment of 26 Nov. 1984. Distinguished American scholars had different views about how U.S. interests might best be protected against decisions of an international tribunal that some did not consider to be completely objective and which they felt had exceeded its authority. *See* A.C. AREND, Ed., THE UNITED STATES AND THE COMPULSORY JURISDICTION OF THE INTERNATIONAL COURT OF JUSTICE (1985); L.F. DAMROSCH, THE INTERNATIONAL COURT OF JUSTICE AT A CROSSROADS (1987); Note: *Alternative*

the views of many when he argued that the U.S. action was not in the national interest, and was

> based on unpersuasive reasons, and, in the way it was done, needlessly damaging to our national reputation, the Court, and the international legal system.[47]

Judges, faced with the possibility that their decisions would not be enforced, were reluctant to decide matters of substance; preferring to probe into procedural niceties or esoteric points of amorphous law in exquisite detail.[48]

Against all of these negative factors, some encouraging new developments must be weighed. As the spirit of detente began to emerge, the situation regarding the ICJ also began to change for the better. In 1987, U.S.S.R. General Secretary Gorbachev, in his widely-heralded article, wrote of the International Court of Justice:

> It's binding jurisdiction must be acknowledged by all on mutually agreed terms... We are convinced that the comprehensive system of security is at the same time a system for a universal legal order which will ensure the primacy of international law in politics.[49]

He also urged the General Assembly and the Security Council to turn to the ICJ "more frequently for advisory opinions on disputed international legal issues." [50] In 1988, the U.S. and the Soviet Union reached a provisional agreement according to which the jurisdiction of the ICJ was to be accepted should any legal dispute arise regarding six specific human rights conventions.[51]

In addition to dozens of respected decisions clarifying international law, the Court began to make use of an ad hoc procedure designed to make

---

Reservations to the Compulsory Jurisdiction of the ICJ, 72 Harv.L R. 749 (1959).

47   R.Bilder,*International Dispute Settlement and the Role of International Adjudication*, 1 Emory Jour. of Int. Dispute Res. (1987) 131, at 171.

48   *See* S.ROSENNE, THE LAW AND PRACTICE OF THE INTERNATIONAL COURT (1985).

49   M. Gorbachev, *Reality and Safeguards for a Secure World*, 16 Sept. 1987, *reproduced in* UN Doc. A/42/574, S/19143, 18 Sept. 1987.

50   *Id. See* P. Szasz, *Enhancing the Advisory Competence of the World Court*, in L. GROSS, Ed. THE FUTURE OF THE INTERNATIONAL COURT, vol.2 (1976) 499.

51   GA Doc. A/44/171, *see* 83 AJIL 457 (1989); Report of the ICJ, 1 Aug. 1988-31 July 1989, GAOR Forty-Fourth sess. Supp. No. 4 (A/44/4). For a discussion on this point and the effectiveness of the ICJ generally, *see* FERENCZ, Ed., WORLD SECURITY FOR THE 21ST CENTURY (1991) pp. 53-60.

it easier for states to accept the Court's jurisdiction with increased confidence. In 1981 (for the first time in ICJ history,) a case was sent to a five-man Chamber instead of the full fifteen-judge Court. Since the parties were consulted about the judges to be appointed, it enhanced confidence in the Court. New procedural possibilities were thus opened for more expeditious and acceptable handling of cases by the Court.[52]

In 1989, the UN created a special Trust Fund "to make available financial assistance to States where necessary so as to enable them to use the Court for the settlement of their legal differences."[53] By 1991, Governments were showing an increasing awareness of the Court's potential. What had earlier been described as "the world's most unused courthouse" began to receive more cases than ever before.[54]

In 1993, the sense of frustration and outrage at the inability of the world community to halt "ethnic cleansing" and crimes against humanity in former Yugoslavia stimulated a desperate appeal to the World Court for relief. We have briefly mentioned the suit filed by Bosnia-Herzegovina against warring Yugoslavia (Serbia and Montenegro) in which the ICJ found that it had jurisdiction to issue a provisional order directing Yugoslavia to take all measures within its power to prevent commission of the crime of genocide. The provisional decision did not deal with the merits but at least it allowed the voice of an international court to be heard in support of basic humanity.[55]

The absence of compulsory jurisdiction weighs as a very heavy anchor around the neck of the ICJ. But recent developments illustrate the growing desire for more judicial assistance to help maintain peace in the world. They are positive steps in the right direction; they should be encouraged to strengthen the power of the only World Court we have.

4. World Court for Law of the Sea

In December 1982, at Montego Bay in Jamaica, 119 delegates from 117 states signed the UN Convention on the Law of the Sea. It was an unprecedented and monumental achievement that had taken over 14 years of work

---

52 *Case Concerning Delimitation of the Maritime Boundary in the Gulf of Maine Area*, Order of 20 Jan. 1982, regarding a maritime boundary dispute between Canada and the U.S.

53 *See* 28 ILM 1589 (1989).

54 Summaries of the Judgments, Advisory opinions and Orders of the ICJ, 1948-1991 (1992) p.1.

55 ICJ Order of Provisional Measures, *Bosnia* v.*Yugoslavia*, 8 April 1993; *reproduced in* 32 ILM 888 (1993).

by representatives of more than 150 countries. Its 329 Articles and 7 Annexes, covering almost 200 pages of fine print, established a comprehensive framework for the legal regulation of all ocean space. UN Under-Secretary Bernardo Zuleta spoke of "an attempt to establish true universality in the effort to achieve a just and equitable international economic order." Secretary General Perez de Cuellar said "international law is now irrevocably transformed." Tommy Koh of Singapore, who had skillfully steered the consensus agreement to conclusion, called it the "Constitution for the Oceans" and "the victory of the rule of law and of the principle of the peaceful settlement of disputes."[56]

In addition to provisions dealing with such traditional legal issues as the limits of territorial claims to the sea, rights of commercial or military navigation and piracy, the Convention reached into the future for progressive development of the law. The sea-bed, the vast area not immediately contiguous to national boundaries, was declared to be "the common heritage of mankind" (Art. 136). Its resources were to be used for the benefit of mankind as a whole, taking into particular consideration the needs of developing states and peoples (Art.140). Rules and regulations, which states were obliged to enforce, were laid down for the protection and preservation of the marine environment (Part XII). A special Sea Bed Authority with an Assembly of all the members was created to see that the Convention was respected (Sec.4).

Disputes could be settled by any of the peaceful means described in the UN Charter (Part XV). In addition, provision was made for "Compulsory Procedures Entailing Binding Decisions" (Part XV Sec.2). If other means failed, the decision of a newly created International Tribunal for the Law of the Sea, with a Sea-Beds Disputes Chamber, would have jurisdiction to resolve the dispute (Art.288). Annex VI set forth a complete and comprehensive Statute for the International Tribunal for the Law of the Sea which - with very few exceptions (Art. 298) - would have binding jurisdiction.[57]

As in all such treaties, there were some states that would not accept some of its provisions. The United States, that had the industrial capacity to mine the sea-bed, was not inclined to accept the *diktat* or controls of any

---

56   *UN Convention on the Law of the Sea*, UN Publ. 1983, Introduction, at xix, xxix, xxxvii. Convention *reproduced in* 21 ILM 1261 (1982); *See* R.P. ANAND, ORIGIN AND DEVELOPMENT OF THE LAW OF THE SEA (1983); M.S. MCDOUGAL AND W.T. BURKE, THE PUBLIC ORDER OF THE OCEANS (1987).

57   For a comprehensive analysis of the drafting history *see* A.O. ADEDE, THE SYSTEM FOR SETTLEMENT OF DISPUTES UNDER THE UNITED NATIONS CONVENTION ON THE LAW OF THE SEA (1987).

independent Authority regarding its actions on or under the high seas.[58] Professor Louis Sohn, who played an important role in negotiating the dispute-settlement provisions of the Convention, regretted that the U.S. balked at the idea of sharing sea-bed resources. But he pointed to the fact that the dispute settlement procedures had generally been accepted by all. 90% of the treaty provisions were subject to some form of binding arbitration or decision. One of the Conventions great achievements

> was that it established a very strict method of dispute settlement for most disputes that might arise as to the interpretation and application of the Convention.[59]

Special Commissions were appointed to try to work out the final arrangements which might enable universal participation in the Convention. Ten years later, by 1992, these Special Commissions were still at work. 51 states had adhered to the Convention but a total of 60 were required before it could come into force.[60] Among those nations not ready to accept the Convention were the United States, the United Kingdom and Germany. Since Hamburg was the planned situs for the new International Tribunal, this presented some embarrassment. Nonetheless, plans for the Tribunal advanced nearly to completion with only a few relatively minor technical details of finances and logistics still to be negotiated. As of the end of 1993, it appeared that nations were on the verge of creating a new world tribunal to deal with legal problems affecting about 70% of the surface of Planet Earth. Only a last ounce of political will was required to make it a reality.

Dr. Jenks had correctly predicted in 1964:

> We are on the earliest stages of groping toward a world order based on a common law of mankind in which international adjudication takes its place with international legislation and international administration among the instruments of peace, order and good government on a world basis.[61]

---

58   *See* U.S. White House Proclamation 5030 of Mar. 10, 1983, *reproduced in* 22 ILM 461 (1983); L.Sohn, *U.S. Policy Toward Settlement of Law of the Sea Disputes*, 17 Va. J. Int. L. 9 (1976).

59   L.B. Sohn, *Symposium, The Law of the Sea Crisis*, 58 St.John's Law Rev. (1984) 237 at 264.

60   *See* UN Press Release, SEA/1327, 14 Aug. 1992; Progress Report of the Chairman of the Preparatory Commission for the International Seabed Authority and for the International Tribunal for the Law of the Sea, LOS/PCN/L. 103, 7 July, 1992,L. 107, 20 Aug. 1992.

61   C.W.JENKS, THE PROSPECTS OF INTERNATIONAL ADJUDICATION (1964) at 772-773.

C- Regional Courts

Although the "groping toward a world order based on a common law of mankind" moved forward very slowly, certain advances were possible on a regional level as new courts were created to cope with common economic and human rights problems. The study of existing regional courts - in Europe, Latin America and Africa - reflects a process of development that is still in its early or embryonic stages.

1. Court of Justice of the European Communities

It was largely due to the genius of French Statesman Jean Monnet and the cooperation of French Foreign Minister Robert Schuman that western European nations - those that had frequently gone to war over the rights to coal and steel - joined together to sign a treaty creating a common European Coal and Steel Community (ECSC). This "Treaty of Paris" entered into force in 1952 and was followed by the "Treaties of Rome" in 1957 which created the European Economic Community (EEC) and the European Atomic Energy Community (EURATOM). The new regional union was designated "The European Community" - a consolidation of a dozen sovereign nations determined to put an end to fratricidal wars and to find a common solution to common problems as part of a common future.[62]

The treaties provided for a Commission with executive powers and responsibilities, a Council composed of Ministers designated by each Member state, a Parliamentary Assembly representing the peoples of Europe (elected by universal suffrage in 1979) and finally a Court of Justice of the European Communities (CJEC), with binding authority to decide if the agreed rules had been violated.

The CJEC began its work in Luxembourg in 1952 and its practice has grown ever since. Even though its cases did not usually involve world-shaking issues, it has resolved thousands of commercial disputes and has been the most active international judicial institution ever created.[63] Community law supercedes municipal law and invalidates national legislation inconsis-

---

62 The original members, France, Germany, Italy, Belgium, Luxembourg and the Netherlands were later joined by U.K., Ireland, Northern Ireland, Denmark, Greece, Portugal and Spain. *See* speech of Jacques Delors, President of the EC Commission, reported in *Newsweek*, Oct. 31, 1988.

63 *See* Court of Justice of the European Communities, [Annual] *Reports of Cases Before the Court.*

tent with laws adopted by the EEC. The Court is accessible not merely to states but also to Community institutions and individuals. The Court, with one judge from each member, may form Chambers consisting of three or five judges to adjudicate particular categories of cases. It has exclusive jurisdiction to interpret the EEC Treaty, determine if its mandates have been violated and what remedies should apply.

The procedures of the CJEC are cumbersome. A complaint that a state has failed to live up to its legal obligations under the Treaty must first be considered by a *Commission* that gives its view in writing and allows the parties time to comply before the case is passed along to the *Court* for final decision. Under the terms of the Treaty, enforcement of CJEC decisions may be sought in the national courts of the offending state in accordance with normal domestic procedures. What is quite remarkable is that, in the end, in almost all cases, states have voluntarily complied with decisions of the Court.[64] The Court of Justice has come to play an important role in the political integration of Europe. It now offers an indispensable forum and a delicate balancing mechanism for resolving conflicts so that cooperation toward common goals can be maintained.[65]

Over the years, the functioning of the European system has gradually been improved, moving ever closer - despite occasional relapses - toward an integrated community governed by law, as part of its progress toward a democratic European Union. Despite its caution, delays and imperfections - normal for any new institution - the Court of the European Communities was a significant advance in the development of international courts as a vital legal organ of the new European political system.[66] The Court illustrated that the process of international adjudication was essential in the modern world and it encouraged the creation of a Common Court of Justice for the Andean Common Market.[67]

---

64   G. BEBR, DEVELOPMENT OF JUDICIAL CONTROL OF THE EUROPEAN COMMUNITIES (1981), lists cases and bibliography; I.N. BROWN AND F.G. JACOBS, THE COURT OF JUSTICE OF THE EUROPEAN COMMUNITIES (3rd ed. 1989).

65   A.W.GREEN, POLITICAL INTEGRATION BY JURISPRUDENCE (1969); H.RASMUSSEN, ON LAW AND POLICY IN THE EUROPEAN COURT OF JUSTICE (1986).

66   P.S.R.F.MATHIJSEN, A GUIDE TO EUROPEAN COMMUNITY LAW (1990).

67   In Jan. 1984, the Andean Group (Bolivia, Peru, Colombia, Ecuador, and Venezuela,) inaugurated a Common Court of Justice to adjudicate disputes arising in the Andean Common Market. *See* E.P. Lochridge, *The Role of the Andean Court in Consolidating Regional Integration Efforts, Georgia J. Int'l L. 381 (1980)*; F. V. Garcia Amador, *Some Legal Aspects* of the Andean Economic Integration, in ESSAYS IN TRIBUTE TO WOLFGANG FRIEDMANN (1979 p. 96; Treaty Concerning the Court of Justice of the Cartegena Agreement, May 28, 1979, *translated in* XVII ILM 1203 (1979).

To be sure, some of the reasons why the countries of western Europe were able to create such an institution was because they shared a rather similar cultural heritage, and had attained certain levels of educational and economic development. Most important: they recognized their economic interdependence and had learned through sad experience that settling disputes by war rather than law produces only bitter fruit.[68]

2. European Court of Human Rights

The European Court of Human Rights is the most important human rights court thus far developed in human history. It is a regional organization that helps to fill the void resulting from the inability of the United Nations to establish an international mechanism to enforce human rights obligations on a world-wide basis. It was a response to public demands that a more humane legal order be created in the aftermath of the barbarities of World War II.

United Nations Declarations proclaimed the universal right to life, security, and social conditions that would allow all people to live in dignity. No provisions were made for judicial determinations to ascertain whether declared rights were being violated and there was no international system established for effective enforcement of human rights obligations. Sovereign states were urged to incorporate declared social rights into their national legislation - presumably to be enforced by national courts. No doubt, many of them did - in whole or in part. But since states themselves might be the violators of the declared norms, more than exhortation was needed to offer greater protection to individuals whose rights might be jeopardized by their own government.

The UN tried to influence the behavior of sovereign states by several means:

> (1) A *Commission* on Human Rights, representing forty-three Member States, was established in 1946 by the UN's Economic and Social Council (ECOSOC) as authorized by Art. 68 of the UN Charter. It established subsidiary bodies, received reports of violations, made recommendations - but had no enforcement powers.[69]

---

68 Regionalism as a possible road to globalism in world affairs is dealt with hereafter in Chapter Five.

69 *See Official Records of the Economic and Social Council, 1991, Supp. No. 3 and later annual reports.*

(2) Pursuant to the International Covenant on Civil and Political Rights (Art.28), a Human Rights Committee, consisting of eighteen experts, was formed in 1976 with authority to hear complaints by state parties that other states were not complying with their obligations (Art.41). An ad hoc Conciliation Commission offered good offices to resolve differences (Art.42).

(3) Under an *Optional Protocol*, states could elect to have complaints from individuals also considered by the Human Rights Committee (Art.1).[70]

Other UN Agencies, such as the International Labor Organization, the UN High Commissioner for Refugees, Special Committees against apartheid and other forms of discrimination, focused on specific wrongs in specific areas and sought to eliminate abuses.[71] The United Nations and its associated agencies and non-governmental organizations were - to a certain extent - able to mobilize the power of public opinion to influence national behavior, but strict enforcement by judicial process against non-consenting sovereigns was not available. The United Nations tried its best, but its best was not good enough.[72]

Western European states took matters into their own hands. Building on the Universal Declaration, a European Convention on Human Rights (ECHR) was signed as a legally binding treaty by members of the European Community in 1950.[73] In addition to a *Commission* (for preliminary screening and attempted settlement) and a supervisory *Committee of Ministers* to which the Commission reports, there is a Human Rights *Court* with authority to render final and binding decisions. Judges are elected by the Council of Europe and almost all member states have voluntarily accepted the compulsory jurisdiction of the Court. Actions can be brought by one state against another (Art.24) or by individuals against states (Art.25), including their own.

---

70 GAOR Res. 2200 A (XXI) 16 Dec. 1966, See GAOR Supplements No. 40 (A/46/40) and annual supplements thereafter; *See* UN Dept. of Public Inf., THE UNITED NATIONS AND HUMAN RIGHTS (Periodically updated editions).

71 *See* Convention on the Elimination of All Forms of Racial Discrimination, UN GA Res. 2106 A(XX), Dec. 21, 1965; Resolution dealing with the crime of apartheid, UN GA Res. 3068 (XXVIII), 1973.

72 Alberta University Professor L.C. Green, a notorious realist, has argued that real protection of human rights is more likely to result from regional courts than any near-term efforts to gain universal support via the United Nations. L.C. Green, *Institutional Protection of Human Rights, 28 Les Cahiers de Droit* 547 (1987).

73 *The European Convention for the Protection of Human Rights and Fundamental Freedoms*, Nov. 4, 1950, UNTS, vol. 213, pp. 221-271.

The Human Rights Court, that sits in Strasbourg, is an international judicial body created on a regional basis to guard against acts of states that might be detrimental to human dignity by violating the accepted treaty. As with the Court of the European Communities, the Convention was acceptable because states shared a common desire to respect and protect certain agreed norms of behavior - up to a point.[74] The number of cases handled by the Court has been steadily increasing since the Court was founded in 1959. The opinions of the Commission and the case law of the Court have enhanced the protection of the individual and have acquired increasing respect throughout the European community.[75] The nations of western Europe were responding to the rising tide of public expectations for a more humane social order. It should not have been surprising, however that sovereign states should offer some resistance to the demand for greater legal protection against abuses by the state. Popular speeches extolling human rights was perfectly permissible; creating an independent enforcement mechanism - well that's another story.

Before a Court decision could be rendered, almost insurmountable procedural barriers, like exhausting local remedies and penetrating the screening shield put up by the Commission, had to be overcome. In the end, the system relied on good faith and "collective enforcement" by all of the members via their respective national courts. The *Committee of Ministers*, acting for the Council of Europe, was responsible for seeing that judgments are actually carried out - how that would be done was left to their discretion.

Although the Human Rights Court was not normally expected to deal with earth-shaking issues, the European Convention had its share of reservations, ambiguities and opportunities for evasion. Article 15, for example, stated:

> In time of war or other public emergency threatening the life of the nation any High Contracting Party may take measures derogating from its obligations under this Convention to the extent strictly required by the exigencies of the situation, provided that such measures are not inconsistent with its other obligations under international law.

---

74   *See* P.VAN DIJK, THEORY AND PRACTICE OF THE EUROPEAN CONVENTION ON HUMAN RIGHTS (1984).

75   *See* PUBLICATIONS OF THE EUROPEAN COURT OF HUMAN RIGHTS (Annual); EUROPEAN COMMISSION OF HUMAN RIGHTS, DECISIONS AND REPORTS (Annual).

European Human Rights Commissioner Prof. Jochen Abr.Frowein correctly concluded in 1986 that "the protection of these rights in international law is still rather weak.[76]

The reluctance of even the Strasbourg Court to enforce human rights rigorously reflects the extreme caution and conservatism of sovereign states - even in pursuit of shared goals. Although procedures can surely be streamlined, the European Court of Human Rights (like the CJEC) was an important, if hesitant step forward. The important lesson that can be drawn from the experience of the European Courts is that it is possible to create new and vibrant multi-national judicial institutions to work in conjunction with national institutions to resolve important legal differences without recourse to violence.

Nations have frequently gone to war for economic or commercial reasons or to vindicate violations of human rights. Ever since the European Community was formed, and its regional courts to resolve commercial and human rights disputes were established, there have been no more wars among its members.

It does not appear likely that the various European Community Courts will merge in the near future since they have evolved to meet different needs arising at different times and are still at different stages of development. More important than their integration, however, is the precedents they are creating for the future. According to Professor A.H. Robertson, former Council of Europe Director of Human Rights:

> Underlying the various systems which have been developed, and are developing, there is to be found a single philosophical impulse, the idea of the individual as a being of moral worth whose rights, whether in the civil or political sphere, or in the economic, social and cultural sphere, merit international protection. The promotion and protection of the rights of the individual, not just in Europe but in the world as a whole, is an idea whose time has come.[77]

---

76 J.A. Frowein, *Transnational Protection of Human Rights*, in R. Bernhardt and U. Beyerlin, Eds. REPORTS ON GERMAN PUBLIC LAW AND PUBLIC INTERNATIONAL LAW (1986) at 166.

77 A.H. ROBERTSON & J.G. MERRILLS, HUMAN RIGHTS IN EUROPE (1993) at 378-379. *See* Chapter Four, Section A on the meaning of sovereignty and the rights of the individual.

3. Other Human Rights Courts

Just as the Court of the Justice of the European Communities inspired imitation abroad, the European Court of Human Rights served as a model for similar legal institutions in other regions of the world.

(1) The Inter-American Court of Human Rights:

The 1948 Charter of the Organization of American States (OAS) was the basis for establishing a Commission and an Inter-American Court of Human Rights to help implement the American Declaration on the Rights and Duties of Man. A *Commission*, with Headquarters in Washington D.C., was approved by the OAS in 1960 to consider individual complaints and generally to promote human rights in the region. Since it began functioning in 1968, the number of *complaints* dealt with has been growing exponentially.[78]

U.S. Deputy Assistant Secretary of State for Human Rights Mark L. Schneider, addressing the American Society of International Law in 1978, said:

> When individuals disappear in the night, when dissidents are killed or tortured or committed to mental hospitals or placed behind bars for exercising fundamental civil rights, then the international community cannot remain silent.[79]

In 1979, the Inter-American *Court* of Human Rights was inaugurated in San Jose, Costa Rica as an autonomous judicial institution to interpret the 1969 American Convention on Human Rights.[80] Following the European practice, the Court can not decide a case until after it has been considered by the Commission and only if the State Parties have voluntarily accepted the Court's jurisdiction.[81] As has been noted by Prof. Thomas Buergenthal, a Judge on the Court and a great champion of human rights,

---

78   *See* Inter-American Yearbook of Human Rights; Inter-American Commission on Human Rights, Ten Years of Activities 1971-1981 (1982); *Regional Approaches to Human Rights: The Inter-American Experience*, Proc. 72 ASIL 197 (1978).

79   *Proceedings*, 72 ASIL 203 (1978).

80   American Convention on Human Rights, Nov. 23, 1969, OAS Off. Rec., OEA/Ser.K/XB4VI/1,1, *reprinted in* 9 ILM 673 (1970).

81   *See* **Inter-American Court of Human Rights, Judgments and Opinions.**

Much will still depend upon the willingness of governments to accept the Court's jurisdiction and on the willingness of the Commission to utilize the Court.[82]

Court decisions calling for monetary damages can be enforced in the national courts. Other decisions against states depend upon voluntary compliance. In the last analysis, enforcement of the Court decisions or the Commission's recommendations depends upon public opinion and "the mobilization of shame." Sometimes it is effective and often it is not.[83] Repression of human rights continues in many Latin American countries. Verbal indignation is not good enough; what is required to bring such violations of human dignity to an end is an international court with *enforcement* powers. The Commission and Court of Human Rights are moves in the right direction, but much more still needs to be done.[84]

(2) *Human Rights in Africa:*

Just as the European model stimulated the movement toward human rights protection in the American Hemisphere, it inspired nations of Africa to strive for similar goals. The record of human rights protection under colonial administration in Africa was abysmal. The 1960 UN Declaration on the Granting of Independence to Colonial Countries and Peoples gave rise to new hopes that the rule of law and respect for human dignity might finally come to the peoples of Africa.[85]

But in the vast social upheaval that was part of the decolonization process, individual and peoples rights were often sacrificed to the more immediate objectives of economic development, nation building or personal ambition. Military coups, torture, deportation and tribal wars tore the continent of many nations apart. Human rights were more honored in the breach than in the observance and there was no international legal machinery or institution that could change it.[86]

In June, 1981, the Organization of African Unity (OAU) - met in Banjul, The Gambia, with over 50 member African states. They approved the *African Charter on Human and People's Rights.*[87] It came into force in 1986 and became

---

82   *See* T. Buergenthal, *The Inter-American Court of Human Rights*, 76 AJIL 231 at 245 (1982).

83   *See* R. FISHER, IMPROVING COMPLIANCE WITH INTERNATIONAL LAW (1981).

84   *See* S. DAVIDSON, THE INTER-AMERICAN COURT OF HUMAN RIGHTS (1992).

85   UN GA Res. 1514 (XV) 1960; *See* Dr. AZIKIWE, THE FUTURE OF PAN-AFRICANISM (1961); K, BUSIA, AFRICA IN SEARCH OF DEMOCRACY (1967).

86   *See* B. Ramcharan, *Human Rights in Africa: Whither Now?*, 12 U. of Ghana L. Jour.88 (1975).

part of the Constitutions of new African countries. Former colonial powers, such as Great Britain, France, Spain, Portugal and Belgium, helped to influence the new legal regimes; but the newly developing states had their own ideas. Economic development, freedom from colonialism, entitlement to their own natural resources and self-determination also appeared in their constitutions as rights to be protected by law.[88]

The Banjul Charter, reflective of the culture of its peoples, emphasized *duties* of the family and society as well as rights (Part I). It speaks of "the right to the respect of the dignity inherent in a human being" (Art.5), and the right of all peoples "to national and international peace and security" (Art.23). Obtaining compliance with these norms is entrusted to:

(a) The African Commission on Human and People's Rights, with authority to receive, consider and report on complaints, and

(b) The Assembly of Heads of State and Government of the OAU - that has power to decide what action is appropriate.

The African Charter did not provide for enforcement by any court.[89]

Since the African Commission began functioning only in 1989, it is too early to evaluate its effectiveness. The absence of funds and national implementing legislation present formidable hurdles to be overcome. It is a further example, however, of the ongoing effort in various parts of the world, to create new judicial-type institutions to deal with the growing demand for peace and dignity for all human beings. As long as there is no court with binding authority to interpret and enforce the human rights declarations, the African Charter also illustrates the inadequacy of contemporary efforts.[90]

The sad conclusion is unavoidable that - despite progress - compliance with human rights obligations remains completely unsatisfactory and methods for judicial review and enforcement are totally inadequate. In his final Report, after ten years of service, the UN Secretary-General wrote:

---

87 Council of Ministers of the OAU,. Doc. CM/1149 (XXXVII), June 1981.

88 The Banjul Charter is *reproduced in* 21 ILM 58 (1982).

89 *See* B.H. Weston, R.A. Lukes and K.M. Hnatt, *Regional Human Rights Regimes: A Comparison and Appraisal*, 20 Vanderbilt J. of Transn. L. 585 (1987); J.A. Frowein, *The European and American Conventions on Human Rights - a Comparison* 1 Human Rights J. 44 (1980).

90 *See* THE AFRICAN CHARTER ON HUMAN AND PEOPLES' RIGHTS, U.N., (1990); U. Umozurike, *The African Charter on Human and Peoples' Rights*, 77 AJIL 902 (1983); *See* U.N. Centre for Human Rights, *African Seminar on International Human Rights Standards and the Administration of Justice* (July 1991).

Resolution of conflicts, observance of human rights and the promotion of development together weave the fabric of peace; if one of these strands is removed, the tissue will unravel...[N]o social or political dispensation can, or should endure that does not respect the dignity and worth of the human person...The promising advances of the past year in democracy and human rights should not, however, let us forget the remorseless realities of the world in which we live.[91]

It is a tragic fact that flagrant violations of human rights - economic, civil, political and social - are rampant all over the world. Governments have resisted outside scrutiny of their violations. Very few nations have been much concerned about abuses of foreign citizens by foreign governments in foreign lands - unless it reached a level to threaten their own security or political interests. The resistance of sovereign states against perceived intrusion in their internal affairs has not yet been overcome.

Despite widespread recognition that *enforcement* was vital, the world community, dependent upon the consensus of sovereign states, was unable to create any universal *court* to deal with the massive abuses of human rights that continued to plague humanity.[92] There is no international tribunal competent to monitor human rights abuses in China, India, the former Soviet Union, Middle-East and other regions where the overwhelming mass of humanity dwells. For most victims throughout the world there is still no international court to which they can turn - other than the court of public opinion.[93] When the time comes that basic individual human rights and peoples rights everywhere are protected by a universal court of law, the prospects for peace within and between nations will be immeasurably enhanced.

The ultimate test is not whether human rights are *declared* but whether they are in fact *respected*. As has been pointed out by Prof.Lung-chu Chen:

When control does not accompany decision, the protection of human rights may become mere illusion and mockery, as in some modern constitutions.[94]

---

91   J.P.DE CUELLAR, *REPORT OF THE SECRETARY GENERAL ON THE WORK OF THE ORGANIZATION* (1990) pp.25-26.

92   *See* U.N. Yearbooks on Human Rights; B. RAMCHARAN, HUMAN RIGHTS, THIRTY YEARS AFTER THE UNIVERSAL DECLARATION (1979); T. MERON, HUMAN RIGHTS IN INTERNATIONAL LAW, 2 Vols. (1984).

93   *See Report of the Commission on the Truth*, chronicling a host of human rights crimes committed in El Salvador, UN Doc. S/25500, 1 April 1993.

94   L. Chen, *Human Rights and World Public Order*, Loyala of Los Angeles, 1 Int. and Comp. Law Annual (1978) at 115.

Recognizing the close relationship, if not identity, between human rights and peace, it has repeatedly been stressed by esteemed Yale Professors Myres S. McDougal, Harold Lasswell and Professor Lung-chu Chen:

No people can be fully secure unless all people are secure.[95]

4. International Administrative Courts

There have been a host of agreements over the years providing that disputes regarding a special subject matter be resolved by a specialized international tribunal. The Paris Peace Treaty of 1856 ending the Crimean war, for example, established the European Commission of the Danube to regulate disputes regarding that river.[96] Mixed Claims Tribunals have been rather common for settling international claims. The International Labor Organization long ago created an Administrative Tribunal as an independent judicial body to resolve labor disputes between international organizations and their employees.

The International Monetary Fund, the International Bank for Reconstruction and Development, the International Civil Aviation Organization, the Food and Agricultural Organization of the UN, the World Health Organization, the International Atomic Energy Agency, the Universal Postal Union and a large number of other specialized international agencies have developed judicial-type procedures for settling disputes. Nations as far removed from each other geographically and culturally as Africa and Latin America have agreed to accept the jurisdiction of the International Centre for the Settlement of Investment Disputes and to enforce its awards immediately.[97]

All of these quasi-judicial institutions are clear illustrations that it is possible to resolve a very large range of disputes without resorting to force and that an effective way to deal with such problems is to create specialized juridical-type agencies to deal with specialized subjects in accordance with well established rules and procedures that encourage confidence among the litigants. It is all part of the evolutionary movement away from the use of

---

95 MCDOUGAL, LASSWELL AND CHEN, HUMAN RIGHTS AND WORLD PUBLIC ORDER (1980), at pp. 49, 139, 410.

96 *See* Advisory Opinion, PCIJ Series B, No. 14.

97 *See* L.B. Sohn, *The Role of International Institutions as Conflict-Adjusting Agencies*, 28 U. of Chicago L. Rev.205 (1961).

armed might and toward the rule of law for the peaceful settlement of differences.

D - International Criminal Courts

Courts to settle disputes about interpretations of treaties or other agreements and to reconcile differences between litigants are important - but another kind of tribunal is also needed. In addition to the civil courts that exist in every national society, there are also criminal courts. The same need exists in international society. To condemn crimes without providing any court to try the offenders is to mock the victims and encourage criminality.

Many of the violations of established norms of international behavior - particularly those which threaten the peace - involve the commission of international criminal offenses: aggression, genocide, grave violations of the rules of war, terrorism, apartheid and other crimes against humanity. Most, if not all of these international crimes are committed with the complicity of the state and its leaders. If those who are personally responsible for such transgressions can do so with impunity and with no risk or harm to themselves, the chances for deterring criminal behavior will be significantly diminished. Yet, the willingness of the international community to create criminal courts to discourage or punish international crimes that threaten world security has been less than impressive.

1. Historical Origins

The trial of vanquished by victors for violating rules of war has ancient historical roots.[98] Here we are concerned only with international courts to enforce the laws of peace; their provenance can be said to begin only after World War I.

In 1919, a "Commission on the Responsibility of the Authors of the War and on Enforcement of Penalties" - composed of very distinguished jurists - concluded that persons, regardless of rank or station, who had violated laws and customs of war and "the laws of humanity" were liable to criminal punishment. The laws of war had been well established at least since the

---

98   *See* R. Bierzanek, *The Prosecution of War Crimes*, in M.C. BASSIOUNI AND V. NANDA, Eds., A TREATISE ON INTERNATIONAL CRIMINAL LAW, Chap. XII(1973); T.TAYLOR, NUREMBERG AND VIETNAM, An American Tragedy (1970) Chapter 1.

Hague Conventions and no one could claim that he was unaware that atrocities against civilian populations were punishable criminal acts.

The Commission was of the opinion that a high tribunal was essential to try such criminals and that, following the Hague Convention, it should apply

> the principles of the law of nations as they result from the usages established among civilized peoples, from the laws of humanity and the dictates of public conscience[99]

Since aggression had not yet been specifically defined and no court had ever charged anyone with that crime in the past, the Commissioners felt that aggression could not yet be treated as a punishable offense by an international court of law. They recommended however that

> *for the future, penal sanctions should be provided for such grave outrages against the elementary principles of international law.*[100]

Germany and all the world was thus forewarned in 1919 that those responsible for aggression, war crimes or crimes against humanity did so at their peril and might have to answer for their deeds before a court of law.

Germany repudiated the requirement in the Treaty of Versailles that German war crimes suspects be handed over for trial before an Allied Court. Holland refused to extradite the Kaiser as long as there was no competent International Court that could act on the basis of a statute clearly defining the punishable offenses. The attempt to use criminal law to punish those responsible for World War I and its atrocities ended in a farce. [101] Allowing outrageous atrocities to go unpunished was an invitation for their repetition. The aggressions and crimes against humanity that were committed under Hitler Germany in World War II vastly exceeded in barbarity and number all of the crimes committed during World War I.

Beginning in 1941, Allied leaders repeatedly issued public warnings that Germans would be held to account and that superior orders would be no defense.[102] Many legal scholars began to lay the juridical foundation for

---

99 Preamble to the 1907 *Hague Convention Respecting the Laws and Customs of War on Land; See* A.ROBERTS AND R. GUELFF, Eds., DOCUMENTS ON THE LAWS OF WAR (982) at 45.

100 Report Presented to the Preliminary Peace Conference, Mar.29, 1919, *reproduced in* 13 AJIL Supp. (1919) also in FERENCZ, INT. CRIM. CT. vol. 1 Doc. 3 at 179, 426.

101 *See* FERENCZ, *id.* pp. 25-36; *See*, S. GLUECK, WAR CRIMINALS, THEIR PROSECUTION AND PUNISHMENT (1944).

102 *See* statements by U.S. President Franklin D. Roosevelt and British Prime Minister Winston Churchill on Oct. 25, 1941; Inter-Allied Conference at St. James Palace, London. The Declaration recalled the laws of war and warned that the Allies would seek "the

such trials by accumulating the historical record and precedents that would form the basis for future war crimes proceedings.[103] By 1943, a Convention for the Creation of an International Criminal Court was drafted by the London International Assembly - an unofficial group of expert lawyers.[104]

When World War II ended, there was an enormous and justified public outcry that those responsible for blatant aggression, genocide and crimes of such cruelty that they defied human imagination, should be brought to justice. The British were quite prepared to simply execute a batch of Nazi leaders without the delays and possible embarrassment of a trial. His Majesty's Government - noted for fair play - had reached the conclusion that "execution without trial is the preferable course."[105] It is a tribute to the United States, and particularly to its Secretary of War Henry L. Stimson, a leader of the New York Bar, that the U.S. insisted upon a fair trial in a court of law.

2. Nuremberg War Crimes Tribunals

The trials at Nuremberg of major German war criminals was not, as is sometimes believed, designed primarily to satisfy the victor's demands for vengeance. Quite the contrary; it was the result of a long historical process that culminated in the reassertion of established and emerging rules of law and the reaffirmation of the judicial process in place of the vendettas and massive reprisals which had been the practice of the past.[106]

The lawyers chosen to represent the United States and other nations, as Prosecutors or Judges, were among the most respected in the world. Robert H. Jackson was requested by President Harry Truman to take leave from the U.S. Supreme Court in order to prepare the trials and serve as U.S. Chief Prosecutor. By August 1945, a Charter for the International Military Tribunal codified the relevant international criminal laws.[107] Soon thereafter, the trial in the courthouse at Nuremberg began. Twenty-four major Nazi

---

punishment through the channel of organized justice, of those guilty of or responsible for these crimes." Jan. 13, 1942, HMSO at p.15; *See* FERENCZ INT. CRIM. CT., vol.1, Doc. 12.

103 *See* UNITED NATIONS WAR CRIMES COMMISSION, HISTORY 2 vols. (1946).

104 UNGA, ILC HISTORICAL SURVEY OF THE QUESTION OF INTERNATIONAL CRIMINAL JURISDICTION (1949) *reproduced in* FERENCZ, INT. CRIM. CT. vol. 1 Doc. 10 p. 400.

105 Aide-Memoire from the U.K. to the U.S. April 23, 1945, *reproduced in* FERENCZ, INT. CRIM.CT. vol. 1 Doc. 12 at 450.

106 *See* N. TUTOROW, WAR CRIMES, WAR CRIMINALS AND WAR CRIMES TRIALS - An Annotated Bibliography and Source Book, (1986).

107 *See* Chapter One, Section A.

criminals were accused of a conspiracy to commit Crimes against Peace, War Crimes and Crimes against Humanity.

The fundamental purpose of the trial was the advancement of law and justice. In his Opening Statement, Robert Jackson put it best:

> That four great nations, flushed with victory and stung with injury stay the hand of vengeance and voluntarily submit their captive enemies to the judgment of the law is one of the most significant tributes that Power has ever paid to Reason... To pass these defendants a poisoned chalice is to put it to our own lips as well. We must summon such detachment and intellectual integrity to our task that this trial will commend itself to posterity as fulfilling humanity's aspirations to do justice.[108]

In fact the defendants at Nuremberg were given "the kind of a trial which they, in the days of their pomp and power, never gave to anyone." [109]

The trial before the IMT was followed by twelve "Subsequent Proceedings" at Nuremberg in which Nazi leaders from many spheres of German life - doctors, judges, militarists, industrialists and Security Services - were called to account for complicity and participation in crimes described in the Charter of the IMT. These were international trials conducted by the United States pursuant to recognized international law and in accordance with authorization from the governing quadripartite Control Council for Germany. Brig. General Telford Taylor, a Harvard Law School graduate with a distinguished legal career - who later became a Professor of Law at Columbia University - was Chief of Counsel and responsible for the conduct of all twelve trials. His Final Report outlined the content of the subsequent trials and their significant contribution to the development of international laws of peace.[110]

The principles of international law recognized by both the Charter and the Judgment of the International Military Tribunal at Nuremberg were affirmed by consensus of the first General Assembly of the United Nations. They were thereby confirmed as expressions of binding international law. In addition, the Nuremberg Principles were to form the basis "for the general

---

108 R.JACKSON, THE CASE AGAINST THE NAZI WAR CRIMINALS (1946) at 3-7.

109 Closing Statement of Justice Jackson, IMT Transcript p.4333, cited by B. Ferencz, in *Nurnberg Trial Procedure and the Rights of the Accused*, 32 Jour. of Criminal L. and Criminology 144 (1948) at 151.

110 T.TAYLOR. FINAL REPORT ON THE NUERNBERG WAR CRIMES TRIALS UNDER CONTROL COUNCIL LAW NO. 10, US Gov't Printing Office (1949); *See* T. Taylor, *Nuremberg Trials; War Crimes and International Law*, Int. Conciliation (Apr.1949).

codification of offenses against the peace and security of mankind, or of an International Criminal Code." [111]

Since December 1946, nations have toyed with the idea of codifying international criminal law and creating an international court to enforce it. According to Professor Falk,

> the Nuremberg Judgment regarding the personal account-ability of leaders seems even more vital for a peaceful interna-tional society today than when it was first asserted in 1945.[112]

The public is still waiting for another Nuremberg-type tribunal.[113]

The main difficulty has been the reluctance of some powerful national leaders to subject themselves or their nationals to the rule of international law. They have refused to accept the lesson of the Nuremberg trial so aptly pointed out by Telford Taylor:

> The laws of war do not apply only to the suspected criminals of vanquished nations. There is no moral or legal basis for immu-nizing victorious nations from scrutiny. The laws of war are not a one-way street.[114]

3. Tokyo War Crimes Tribunal

While the Nuremberg proceedings were in progress, a similar war crimes trial against Japanese leaders was taking place in Tokyo. Based on a Charter similar to the IMT Charter drawn up in London, twenty-eight high-ranking Japanese Ministers, Ambassadors, Admirals and Generals had to answer to charges of aggression, war crimes and crimes against humanity. The court was composed of judges from eleven countries with which Japan had been at war.

The trial before the International Military Tribunal for the Far East (IMTFE) lasted over two-and-a-half years and was the biggest trial in recorded history. All of the defendants were convicted and seven were

---

111 GA Res.95 (I), Dec. 11, 1946, *reproduced in* FERENCZ, INT. CRIM. CT. vol. 1 Doc. 17. *See* L.S.SUNGA, INDIVIDUAL RESPONSIBILITY IN INTERNATIONAL LAW FOR SERIOUS HUMAN RIGHTS VIOLATIONS (1992).

112 R.FALK, POSITIVE PRESCRIPTIONS FOR THE NEAR FUTURE (1991) at 17; R.FALK, REVITALIZING INTERNATIONAL LAW (1989).

113 *See* B.Ferencz, *Needed: An International Criminal Court*, Vol.5, CONSTITUTION, p. 80 (Fall/1993).

114 T.TAYLOR, THE ANATOMY OF THE NUREMBERG TRIALS (1992) at 641.

sentenced to death by hanging. The verdict at the end of 1948 was not unanimous and in the dissenting opinions of some of the judges could be found some explanation of the difficulties faced by new international criminal tribunals.[115]

Dutch Judge Röling shared some of the doubts of French Judge Bernard who felt that the majority of the Court had gone too far. The dissenters would not have convicted for failure of a distant commander to halt or prevent atrocities by his troops. Röling doubted whether the existing international law really prohibited aggressive war, noting that aggression had not been precisely defined, there were no precedents for personal penal liability and the general prohibitions of the Kellogg Pact and similar declarations outlawing war all contained exculpating loopholes. Besides, Japan had not ratified the Pact. In challenging his colleagues on the bench, Röling was trying to emphasize that changes were urgently needed to improve the laws of peace. "These horrors of World War II," he said, "may compel the nations to take the legal steps to achieve the maintenance of peace. This has not been done to date."[116]

In later years, when Bert Röling, as he was known to his friends, was a Professor of International Law at the University of Gröningen, he wrote and lectured extensively on the need to develop the international law of peace and international criminal jurisdiction. He deplored the hypocrisy of nations that condemned aggressions by other states while seeking to justify their own aggressions. Echoing the sentiments expressed in the dissenting opinion of Judge Pal of India, Röling called for people to think not in terms of nationality but in "terms of humanity".[117]

Judge Pal was the most outspoken critic of the majority view at the Tokyo trial. He noted that the so-called rules of war applied "only as far as circumstances permit." He was disturbed that only victor's sat on the Court. He would have acquitted all of the defendants to show that human compassion was an integral part of justice and that it was more important to consider "world problems and humanity problems" if mankind was to "grow up quickly enough to win the race between civilization and disaster."[118]

---

115 B.V.A.RÖLING and C.F.RÜTER, Eds., THE TOKYO JUDGMENT, 3 vols. (1977); The complete transcript of the IMTFE has been compiled and edited by R.J. Pritchard and S.Z Pritchard in 27 vols. under the direction of D.C. Watt (1980). *See* S. Horwitz, *The Tokyo Trial*, International Conciliation, No. 465 (1950).

116 Judge Röling's Opinion, *extracted in* FERENCZ, INT. CRIM. CT. vol. 1 Doc. 16 at 521.

117 B.V.A. Röling, *International Law and the Maintenance of Peace*, 4 Netherlands Yearb. Int. L.(1973) 1 at 102.

Japanese Professor Onuma Yasuaki later wrote of the judges "soiled hands" as he recalled the atomic bombing of Hiroshima and Nagasaki by the United States, and the abrogation of the Japanese-Soviet Neutrality Pact by the Soviet Union as it attacked Japan as the war was about to end. He noted correctly that "The *raison d'être* of law should lie in its universal applicability." While acknowledging the aggression and crimes committed by Japan, he denounced the Tokyo trial as "sheerest hypocrisy."[119]

Debates about the validity and impact of the Nuremberg and Tokyo trials have resonated over the years. There is no doubt that these trials had a significant impact in awakening or stirring the moral consciences of peoples everywhere. The impact on governmental behavior is not so apparent.[120] Although the Nuremberg Principles were affirmed by the United Nations in 1946, and have generally been accepted as binding international law, nations have been unable to implement those laws for peace in any international criminal tribunal since that time. Whether there should be such a Court and how it is to function are issues still being considered at the United Nations.

4. *International Criminal Courts Debated*

The attempt to create an international court to deal with international crimes has had a long and sad history. It need only be sketched here since it has already been described elsewhere in considerable detail.[121]

It is ironic that the United States, which was one of the earliest exponents of such a court, should have become one of its principle challengers. Elihu Root, founder of the American Society of International law, and his able assistant U.S. Army Judge Advocate and scholar John Scott Brown, were champions of an international criminal court in the days following the First World War. Their views, and those of many other renowned international lawyers and legal associations, were as voices crying in the wind.

---

118 Judge Pal's Opinion is *extracted in* FERENCZ, INT. CRIM. CT. vol. 1 Doc. 16 at 537.

119 O. Yasuaki, *Beyond Victor's Justice*, XI Special Issue 63 (1984) abridged translation of Japanese article published in the magazine *Chuo Koron*, Aug. 1982 pp.162-189. *See* R.D. MINEAR, VICTOR'S JUSTICE - THE TOKYO WAR CRIMES TRIAL (1971).

120 *See* ASIL *Proceedings* 56-73 (1986).

121 UN HISTORICAL SURVEY OF THE QUESTION OF INTERNATIONAL CRIMINAL JURISDICTION (1949); FERENCZ, INT.CRIM. CT. 2 vols. (1980), including documents showing the Reports of the International Law Commission in 1950 and 1951, the Reports of the UN Committee on Int. Criminal Jurisdiction, 1951, 1953, 1954; J.STONE AND R.K. WOETZEL, Eds. TOWARD A FEASIBLE INTERNATIONAL CRIMINAL COURT (1970); M.C. BASSIOUNI, DRAFT STATUTE INTERNATIONAL TRIBUNAL (1993).

Proposals for an international criminal court were given scant attention after World War I. The value and importance of such tribunals was recognized after World War II. But. after their judgments were rendered, the Nuremberg and Tokyo Tribunals were dissolved. It was as if world leaders believed there would never again be such international crimes; or perhaps they didn't really dare enough or care enough. But aggression, war crimes and crimes against humanity continued on a large scale - as should have been anticipated.

By 1950, a panel of the new International Law Commission recommended that an international criminal court be created as part of the World Court or as an independent agency of the UN. The cold-war had turned into a hot war in Korea and the ILC recommendation was not well received. At the same time, the ILC was also working on drafting a code of crimes against the peace and security of mankind, which required a definition of aggression - which was nowhere in sight.

The UN appointed a Special Committee on International Criminal Jurisdiction in 1951 and within a month it had drafted statutes for a permanent international penal court based on the model of the World Court at the Hague. In the UN's Sixth Committee, the idea received the firm support of Prof. Röling, who was also a member of the International Law Commission. France was generally sympathetic, but the United Kingdom was strongly opposed to the idea and the Soviets were against independent courts in principle. The United States sat firmly on the fence.

Unable to come anywhere near consensus, the UN appointed another and larger Committee in 1953 to continue work on a criminal court and to report back in a couple of years. During that time another Special Committee would try to define aggression and draft a code of international crimes. The three efforts - defining aggression, drafting a code and creating a court - were all proceeding simultaneously on a very slow and bumpy track.

By 1954, the French war in Vietnam was escalating. That was not the best time to deal seriously with creating new legal institutions for peace. A new and expanded Committee to Define Aggression was appointed by the UN. Without a definition there could be no code of international crimes. Until there was a criminal code there was no need for a criminal court. And so the three components that had been plodding along in parallel procession were all linked and put into the deep freeze by the cold war.

It was twenty years later before aggression was defined by consensus.[122] By 1980, it was clear that the overwhelming majority of the Sixth Committee was in favor of preparing a code of international crimes; despite the skepticism of the United States, the U.K. and some others. In 1981, the subject was referred to the International Law Commission, which - to put it mildly - was not noted for its speed.[123]. Ten years later, the ILC succeeded in producing a first reading of the draft code of crimes against the peace. Despite rather severe infirmities, it was not dead on arrival at the Sixth Committee. In fact, most nations regarded the 1991 draft that took a decade to gestate as an encouraging beginning.[124]

To be sure, the international climate had changed enormously by that time. The communist bastions of Europe had crumbled. The Soviet Union was replaced by a Union of Independent States. The cold war was over. The Security Council, using its enforcement powers under Chapter VII, was beginning to function as envisaged by the Charter. The time finally seemed ripe for nations seriously to consider an International Criminal Tribunal to help maintain peace. In response to an unprecedented General Assembly directive calling for speed, by the end of 1990 it was reported by Professor Stephen McCaffrey, American member of the ILC, that there was

> broad agreement in principle, on the desirability of establishing
> a permanent international criminal court within the United
> Nations system.[125]

Subsequent events made the need for an impartial international criminal tribunal ever more pressing. Libya refused to extradite to the U.S. two of its nationals accused of bombing a Pan American plane over Lockerbie, Scotland, which resulted in hundreds of deaths on 28 December 1988. The Security Council had ordered Libya to cooperate and when it failed to comply, economic and diplomatic sanctions were imposed.[126] Libya's appeal for protection from the International Court of Justice was in vain.[127] But the sanctions did not bring about Libyan compliance. The absence of an international tribunal lent some credence to Libya's argument that, under the circumstances, the justice of an American court could not be trusted.[128]

---

122 *See* FERENCZ. AGGRESSION, 2 vols. Work on the draft code of international crimes was resumed in 1978.

123 *See* B. Ferencz, *The Draft Code of Offenses Against the Peace and Security of Mankind*, 75 AJIL 674 (1981).

124 Report of the ILC, UN GAOR, 46th Sess., Supp. No. 10, UN Doc. (A/46/10) 1991.

125 S.C. McCaffrey, *The Forty-Second Session of the International Law Commission*, 84 AJIL 930 at 933 (1990).

126 SC Res. 731 (1992) 21 Jan. 1992; SC Res. 748 (1992) 31 March 1992.

127 ICJ Order of 14 April 1992, refusing provisional measures in *Libyan Arab Jamahiriya v. U.S.A.*, 31 ILM 662 (1992).

128 On Sept.30, 1993, it was reported that Libya would not object if the men went to Scotland to stand trial - but the final decision whether to go was up to the suspects themselves! W.E. Schmidt, *Libya Says Scotland Can Try Flight 103 Suspects*, NY Times, Sept. 30, 1993 at A-12.

When war erupted in the Balkans as the former Yugoslavian Republic broke up, the new Federal Republic of Yugoslavia (Serbia and Montenegro) attacked irregular forces in Bosnia and Herzegovina. In response to a brutal process of "ethnic cleansing" directed against civilian populations, the Security Council ordered that troops be withdrawn and that attempts to change the ethnic population "cease immediately."[129]

When Serbia failed to comply, the Council ordered the imposition of a wide range of sanctions. States were called upon "to take nationally or through regional agencies or arrangements all necessary means" to assist the UN Protection Force supervising the delivery of relief supplies to suffering civilians.[130] The Council adopted a resolution warning that persons who committed grave breaches against the Geneva Conventions would be held individually responsible.[131] The American UN Representative declared: "The Governments and individuals involved must be held to account." The French delegate warned: "Those who commit these deeds will have to bear individual responsibility for them, in accordance with international law."[132] Venezuela's Mr. Arria, calling for trials of war criminals, proclaimed: "The perpetrators must not go unpunished (p. 43).

Addressing the General Assembly, the President of Bosnia and Herzgovina called for an international war crimes tribunal and the Prime Minister of Norway echoed his plea.[133] In response to growing demands for action, the Security Council called for a Commission of Experts to assemble evidence of grave violations of the rules of war.[134]

Those who spoke out so clearly for the punishment of international war criminals hardly noticed that there existed no impartial international criminal tribunal that could try the offenders. Some writers suggested that the UN Charter and the ICJ Statutes be amended to give the ICJ jurisdiction over international crimes - an idea that had been debated and discarded at the UN twenty years earlier.[135]

---

129   SC Res. 752, 15 May 1992.
130   SC Res. 757 (1992) 30 May, 1992; SC Res. 770, 771 (1992) 13 Aug. 1992.
131   SC Res. 764 (1992) 13 July 1992.
132   S/PV.3106, 13 Aug. 1992 at 39, 49.
133   GA Plenary Fifth Mtg (PM) 21 September 1992.
134   SC Res. 780, 6 October 1992.
135   B.M. YARNOLD, INTERNATIONAL FUGITIVES - A New Role for the ICJ (1991).

The United States, which had inspired the world at Nuremberg, seemed to be in no hurry to create a new international criminal court. The State Department's Legal Advisor argued at the United Nations that establishing a new tribunal was a complicated matter and since such criminals had been getting away with murder for decades, there was no reason to rush.[136] Despite American vacillation, the Legal Committee and the General Assembly asked the International Law Commission to draft the statutes for an International Criminal Court as "a matter of priority."[137]

A.N.R. Robinson, who as Prime Minister of Trinidad and Tobego had moved the UN to consider an international criminal court to try drug traffickers, was not discouraged by opposition from some of the major powers. "The path ahead will be a tortuous one," he said, addressing a world conference at the end of 1992.

> ...[W]e must succeed. And succeed we will, for we are capable of success, and we shall not have a global civilization until the rule of law is established, and fairly but firmly applied, for all of humankind.[138]

When, in 1993, a new administration assumed power in the United States, newly-elected President Bill Clinton approved a new policy. With U.S. backing, the Security Council called for the establishment of an international tribunal

> for the prosecution of persons responsible for serious violations of international humanitarian law committed in the territory of former Yugoslavia since 1991.[139]

A scant nine weeks later, the Secretary General presented the Security Council with a 48-page report including comprehensive statutes for the proposed ad hoc criminal tribunal.[140] It had been prepared by a small team of dedicated international lawyers in the Legal Division of the Secretariat.[141] Three weeks later, the Security Council took a major step forward when it

---

136 Statement by E.D. Williamson, at the UN Sixth Committee, Oct. 27, 1992, USUN Press Release #113-(92); *See* B. Ferencz , *An International Criminal Code and Court: Where They Stand and Where They're Going*, 30 Col. J. of Transn. L. 375 (1992). Compare statement of new State Dept. Legal Adviser Conrad K. Harper to Sixth Comm. on October 26, 1993.

137 GA Res. 47/33, 25 Nov. 1992; A/C.6/4.

138 A.N.R. Robinson, *An International Criminal Court: From the Design to the Construction*, an address in Syracusa, Italy on 3 Dec. 1992, reported in No. IV, *Parliamentarians for Global Action* 11 (1992).

139 SC Res. 808 (1993) 22 Feb. 1993.

140 *Report of the Secretary-General Pursuant to Paragraph 2 of Security Council Resolution 808 (1993)*, S/25704, 3 May 1993; *reprinted in* 32 ILM (1993) 1159.

141 The team included the Legal Counsel Carl-August Fleischauer. his Deputy, Ralph Zacklin, Larry Johnson, Winston Tubman, Virginia Morris and Daphna Shraga.

unanimously decided to establish the recommended international criminal tribunal to prosecute those who had violated humanitarian law in former Yugoslavia.[142] On 17 November 1993, the International War Crimes Tribunal for the former Yugoslavia held its opening session at the historic Peace Palace in the Hague. The eleven judges and the Prosecutor, Ramon- Escovar-Salom of Venezuela, began to plan their program for 1994. Despite the difficulties, it had been possible to create the tribunal in record time as a subsidiary organ of the Security Council.[143]

E - Evaluation

As we review the evolutionary development of international courts as a vital component of a rational world order - to see what's right and what's wrong - we find that considerable progress has been made and yet there remains a great deal that is lacking. Political leaders still refuse to recognize that international laws without international courts are practically meaningless and courts without compulsory jurisdiction and binding authority are not really courts at all.

Despite a large variety of peaceful options, most nations have never been ready to abandon the use of force and to rely instead upon the verdict of an international judiciary. They have ignored the 1955 warning of fifty-two Nobel Laureates:

> All nations must come to the decision to renounce force as a final resort of policy. If they are not prepared to do so, they will cease to exist.[144]

The warning should have been unnecessary. There was no shortage of rules and clear procedures requiring nations to settle disputes in a peaceful way. Nonetheless, nations and peoples continued to cope with antagonisms - not by resort to laws and courts but by using illegal military might. Why?

States chose to rely on war and violence because they were not convinced that there were any better options available to enable them to achieve

---

142 S/RES/827, 25 May 1993; *reprinted in* 32 ILM (1993) 1203. *See* T.C. Evered, *An International Criminal Court: Recent Proposals and American Concerns*, unpublished study prepared for World Federalist Organization, Washington D.C. July 1993, planned publicatiom in Pace Int. L. Rev. (1994).

143 UN Press Release SC/5745, 15 November 1993. The judges are listed in 87 AJIL (1993) at 668. See also J.C. O'Brien, *The Int'l Tribunal for Violations of Int'l Humanitarian Law in the Former Yugoslavia,* 87 AJIL 639 (1993); Comments by M.P. Scharf, 87 AJIL 604 (1993).

144 July 15, 1955 Mainau Declaration, cited in Linus Pauling, Nobel Lecture *Science and Peace*, reprinted in The Center Magazine, Nov/Dec. 1965, p.51.

their national objectives. The rules requiring peaceful settlement, although clarified, expanded and improved over the years, still lacked precision and binding authority. As long as international laws remained vague, there was no way to predict which interpretation would prevail. Parties feared to commit themselves to an outcome they could not foresee or control. Uncertain of the decision of an impartial court, and mindful of the costs and delays, disputants hesitated to subject themselves to the risk of being on the side that might be ordered to surrender something of vital importance.

Having military might available, nations weighed the risks of fighting against the risks of losing by third-party adjudication. Issues threatening the peace were often not legal but political or emotional. Stimulated by nationalistic traditions that glorified fighting for a popular cause or country, diplomats felt or feared that compromise might be viewed as weakness or cowardice. In addition, some of those who might gain from war were not eager for peace. Weighing the alternatives, those entrusted with the power of decision turned away from all of the peaceful options and chose instead to have their people fight - and die.

When states failed to honor their legal obligation, under Chapter VI of the UN Charter, to settle disputes peacefully, it was the primary responsibility of the Security Council to maintain peace by asserting its broad enforcement powers under Chapter VII. But during the first four decades of its existence the Council was frequently paralyzed by the ideological cold war and the veto-power vested in the strongest states. Parochial political considerations were allowed to subvert the clear purpose and intent of the Charter.

Sovereign states were not ready to rely on Declarations or Conventions that were ambiguous, or to accept decisions of an impartial tribunal that had no power of enforcement. The Security Council never used its authority under the Charter to enforce a decision of the World Court. With nations unable or unwilling to settle disputes by peaceful means, settlement by their own violent means became inevitable.

Faced with a vacuum in the international legal order, states of western Europe that had frequently gone to war against each other in the past, created their own regional organizations to eliminate some of the past causes of conflict. The European Economic Community created its own Court of Justice to interpret the European Treaty and to adjudicate economic disputes. The European Court of Human Rights was created to interpret the European Convention on Human Rights. It was an unbiased multi-national judiciary democratically elected to protect nations and individuals from infringements against mutually recognized legal and social obligations.

The acceptance of minimum standards of behavior is part of an evolutionary movement toward a universal culture of respect for human rights and human diversity. The European pattern of creating regional courts to determine whether the accepted economic and human rights obligations had been violated inspired the creation of a human rights tribunal for the Americas and encouraged Africa to launch a similar process. A host of administrative courts with global authority gave further evidence that there was indeed a judicial way to settle disputes of all kinds without the use of armed force.[145]

A new international court of potentially major significance now appears on the near horizon. Almost all nations of the world are ready to accept an International Tribunal for the Law of the Sea. This new international court will have binding authority to settle almost all disputes regarding the monumental Law of the Sea Treaty which controls the vast areas of the oceans. It is a brilliant ray of hope to illuminate the possibilities of international adjudication for an improved rule of law which one day may also cover the relatively small remainder of this planet.

It took the tragedies and atrocities of World War II to awaken world leaders to the need for a criminal tribunal to try those accused of aggression, war crimes and crimes against humanity. The trials at Nuremberg and Tokyo took the law a step forward as it upheld the principle that heads of state would be held personally responsible for such criminal deeds. Punishment was to be meted out only to those found guilty beyond a reasonable doubt. Innocent citizens would no longer be treated as sacrificial lambs to pay for the ambitions and illegalities of their leaders. At least that was the promise and the dream.

When the passions of the post-war period abated, powerful nations were not ready to have their own actions judged by any impartial international criminal tribunal. Failure to punish new aggressions and crimes against humanity served to encourage the repetition of such crimes. Scant attention was paid to recommendations of many legal experts and to the warning of Nobel Prize winner Sean MacBride who wrote:

> In curbing cruelty and crimes against humanity it is not sufficient to deplore them; it is essential to pass judgment and if necessary outlaw the individuals responsible.[146]

---

145 See M.W. JANIS, Ed., INTERNATIONAL COURTS FOR THE TWENTY-FIRST CENTURY (1993).

Significant progress in the use of international tribunals became possible as the cold-war came to an end. The collapse of the Soviet Union which had rejected international adjudication, and the emergence of many new states as members of the world community, opened the door to new opportunities. National leaders, who had failed to recognize that the finest exercise of sovereignty would be voluntary acceptance of binding international laws and courts, began to change their views. The growth of mutual confidence held forth great promise that a new rule of law might become acceptable. There appeared a new willingness of states that had previously isolated themselves behind a cloak of national sovereignty to accept adjudication of some important legal issues by an international tribunal.

The need for a new International Criminal Court was debated at great length at the United Nations. Despite the overwhelming majority demand for such a tribunal, no final agreement to accept a permanent criminal court has yet been reached. [147] The Security Council decision to establish an ad hoc tribunal to deal with crimes in former Yugoslavia is an encouraging movement in the direction of creating the permanent international criminal court needed to deter crimes by all who threaten peace. International law, to be worthy of the name, must apply equally to all - regardless of rank, station or nationality.

Breakaway nations and minorities, inflamed by ingrained nationalistic, religious or ethnic passions, still seek to obtain or assert their independence by every available means - including the use of armed force..Whether such violent behavior of peoples can be tamed may depend upon the ability of nations to replace the existing world disorder with an improved world legal order. Whether nationalism can be replaced by rationalism remains to be seen.[148]

One thing is clear: the absence of any impartial forum with binding authority to resolve international conflicts, and the lack of an international criminal court to punish transgressors, constitutes a fatal gap in the system of peace through law. Perhaps regional cooperation may gradually be expanded in an imaginative way until global cooperation on global prob-

---

146 8 Journal of the International Commission of Jurists (1968) at vi.

147 The divergent views of governments were heard in the Sixth Committee from 25 October to 1 November 1993.

148 Martti Koskenniemi of Finland has argued that in a world of conflicting values there can be no coherent global social life governed by one coherent scheme of global organization. M. KOSKENNIEMI, FROM APOLOGY TO UTOPIA (1989). The International Law Commission intends to complete its draft statute for a permanent International Criminal Court in 1994. See A/58/312, 25 August 1993 p. 40.

lems becomes feasible and generally acceptable. One way or the other, international courts with greater authority will be a vital component of a more peaceful world order - or there will be no peaceful world.

CHAPTER THREE
INTERNATIONAL LAW ENFORCEMENT

> Clearly, it is in our power to bring about a renaissance for a new international era... New and more enduring structures must now be built...We need a new spirit of commonality, commitment and intellectual creativity to transfer a period of hope into an era of fulfillment.
>
> UN Secretary-General Boutros Boutros-Ghali, September 1992.[1]

When Secretary-General Perez de Cuellar took office in 1982, he had warned: "We are perilously near to a new international anarchy."[2] We have noted some of the ambiguities of international laws and the limited authority of international courts which, no doubt, contributed to the former Secretary-General's melancholy appraisal. Ten years later, his successor, Mr. Boutros-Ghali, seemed more hopeful and optimistic. What seems remote today may yet be within our grasp tomorrow.

Enforcement is the weakest leg of the tripod of *law, courts* and *enforcement* on which every peaceful society depends. Before enforcement can become effective, at least five vital and buttressing components of an enforcement system must also be in place:

(1) A managing organization capable of coordinating solutions to world problems that can no longer be mastered on a national level;

(2) A system of effective control over weapons that threaten the peace of nations;

(3) Some effective method of coercion - either economic sanctions or punishment of individual lawbreakers;

(4) If sanctions fail or are inappropriate, military force may have to be used as a last resort;

(5) Finally, there must be a more just social order.

---

1   *Report on the Work of the Organization*, from the 46th to the 47th Session of the General Assembly, September 1992, at 2.

2   *Report of the Secretary-General on the Work of the Organization*, A/37/1, Sept. 1982, at 5.

Only when ALL of these legal structures (law, courts and the five components of enforcement) are firmly operational can it be anticipated that nations will recognize it to be clearly in their own self-interest to turn to law rather than to war.

We shall briefly examine each of these component parts, trace their evolutionary development, noting what is good, what went wrong and what needs improvement. We must not succumb to the temptation to abandon the child just because it was not born full grown. "Now is the time," said Boutros-Ghali, "to seize the moment for the sake of the future."[3]

A- Global Management for Global Problems

No one is suggesting that a new mammoth international bureaucracy should now be created to tell people all over the world what to do and how to behave. Quite the opposite. Experience with dictatorships has amply demonstrated that Lord Acton was right: "Absolute power corrupts absolutely." Yet, it cannot be denied that, as we approach the 21st century, the world has become so much bigger and more complicated that many of its most vital problems can not possibly be resolved on a national basis. Interdependence has become a fact of international life. Global problems can only be resolved globally.

The UN as a global management system operates through six principal organs and an intricate array of subsidiary organs, commissions, committees and specialized agencies. An indication of how complicated the world - and the UN - has become can be seen from two recent volumes outlining *Medium Term plans for the Organization for the period 1992-1997*. The UN books describe UN activities under 10 "Major Programmes" (including Maintenance of Peace and Security, Disarmament, Codification of Law, Economic and Social Development, and Human Rights) as well as 45 other "Programmes" and 250 "Subprogrammes."[4] The UN Secretariat employs over 10,000 people.[5] The Sunday Times of London quotes Boutros-Ghali to the effect that "half of them do no work."[6]How did we get to such a vast bureaucracy and why doesn't it work more efficiently?

---

3   B. Boutros-Ghali, *An Agenda for Peace*, (UN Publ. 1992) p. 48.
4   GAOR Forty-fifth Sess. Supp. No. 6 (A/45/6/Rev.1) Vol. 1 and 2 (1991); *See* J.W.MULLER, THE REFORM OF THE UNITED NATIONS, 2 vols. (1991).
5   *Report on the Work of the Organization*, Sept. 1992 Para. 21.
6   See The Earth Times, Sept. 7, 1993 at 5.

1. Early Efforts

The organization of world society along lines of the modern nation-state began with the Treaties of Westphalia that ended Europe's "Thirty Years War" around 1648. To halt the persistent feuding of competing lords and churches, Europe was realigned into a pluralistic and secular society of many independent states that were to be sovereign within their own borders. Peace was to be assured by a balance of power so that rivals, uncertain of victory, would recognize that avoiding conflict would be in their own self-interest. Unfortunately, the balance-of-power system may have balanced power but it failed to maintain peace.[7]

For centuries past, an impressive list of distinguished thinkers and philosophers had proposed new structures for international society.[8]Writers of the 17th and 18th centuries were seeking a new political system that would guarantee peace for a European continent ravaged by incessant conflict. It was proposed that European nations join together in a cooperative union - in the form of a federation, confederation or parliament - whose members would agree to respect accepted standards of peaceful state conduct. Peace would be enforced by international armies or, as Bentham and Kant suggested, simply by the power of human reason and public opinion. But European monarchs paid scant attention to philosophers, jurists or theologians. The old system of warfare continued.

A "Grand Design" came to fruition in "The New World" following the American Revolution of 1776. There, thirteen English colonies declared themselves to be independent states. They were joined together by a non-binding treaty - the Articles of Confederation. Since the Articles made no provision for a common legislature, Supreme Court or Executive to enforce the treaty, it soon proved completely unworkable. The new states, each with its own government, militia, currency and tariffs, were soon at each others throats. The solution was found after am arduous convention in the city of Philadelphia in 1787 when - "to form a more perfect Union" - the Constitution of the United States of America was signed.[9]

---

7   See L. Gross, *The Peace of Westphalia (1648-1948)* in L.GROSS, Ed., INTERNATIONAL LAW IN THE TWENTIETH CENTURY (1969).

8   *See* FERENCZ, ENFORCEMENT vol.1, Chap.2, 3; E.WYNNER AND G. LLOYD, SEARCHLIGHT ON PEACE PLANS (1949); J.G. STARKE. THE SCIENCE OF PEACE (1986).

9   A.N. HOLCOMBE, OUR MORE PERFECT UNION (1950); The Articles of Confederation and the U.S. Constitution are *extracted and reproduced in* FERENCZ, ENFORCING INT. L., vol. 1, Doc. 11.

In 1815, European nations that had defeated the Emperor in the Napoleonic Wars convened for the Congress of Vienna where all they could do to restructure their society was to barter various territories and agree to *consult* together if the peace should be threatened.[10] The Hague Conferences of 1899 and 1907 purported to be peace conferences but really did nothing to alter the organizational structure of the turbulent world which prompted the meetings.[11] Without a mechanism or agency to see that the agreed rules were carried out, it was inevitable that the rules would be ignored. Military alliances that were supposed to deter war served instead as a chain to drag in more belligerents. It would take the shock of a World War to awaken nations to the realization that a better way had to be found to manage relations among sovereign states.

2. *The League of Nations*

The "Grand Designs" that had not been taken very seriously before World War I finally attracted widespread public acclaim. Thousands of peace organizations began to clamor for a new structure of international society. President Woodrow Wilson advanced a plan for a League of Nations - an alliance of states pledged to settle all disputes by peaceful means. If any nation failed to comply, it would be confronted with a combined economic boycott and blockade by all the other members. Aggression against any member of the alliance would be repulsed by the collective armed might of the entire League.[12]

The Proposals for a League of Nations put forward on behalf of powerful Great Britain were much more conservative. Lord Phillimore's plan insisted that Britain alone could decide how to protect its vital interests.[13] A sensible French Plan would have universalized the League and created an International Court to settle legal disputes and another International Body to resolve political or other conflicts. Decisions would be enforced by sanctions, pecuniary liability of states and individual criminal responsibility of wrongdoers. Military contingents could be called up for enforcement action if needed.[14]

---

10 C.K. WEBSTER, THE CONGRESS OF VIENNA (1950).
11 *See* Chapter One, Section A-1.
12 President Wilson"s Draft of July, 1918, is *reproduced in* FERENCZ, ENFORCING INT. L., vol.1 Doc. 21 (c).
13 Sir Walter G.F. Phillimore's Proposals for a League of Nations is *reproduced in* FERENCZ, *id.* Doc, 21 (a).
14 The French Draft of June, 1918 is *reproduced in* FERENCZ, *id.* Doc. 21 (b).

What finally emerged in 1919 was a compromise that was adopted by consensus as the Covenant of the League of Nations.[15] The Covenant was a landmark in many respects:

(1) It created a permanent organization where many states could meet to discuss problems that might jeopardize peace (Art.1);

(2) It established procedures for addressing common concerns (Art.2,3,4);

(3) It recognized the need for arms control (Art.8);

(4) It outlined measures for collective action against certain forms of aggression (Art.10);

(5) It provided methods for peaceful settlement of disputes (Art.15);

(6) It prescribed a broad system of sanctions (Art.16);

(7) It recognized the League's "sacred trust" to be concerned about underdeveloped colonies and the human condition (Art.22-25).

All of these were positive steps forward, taken for the first time in human history..

Yet, for the peaceful *management* of nations, the League proved totally inadequate. What made it inadequate were the limitations and conditions placed on each of its three organizational structures: the Assembly of all members, the Council, restricted to the five Principal Allied Powers (U.S., Britain, France, Italy and Japan) plus four others selected by the Assembly and a Secretariat or administrative branch to carry on the operations of the League.

Except on purely procedural matters, the Assembly and the Council could act only by unanimous agreement (Art.5). That limitation alone would have been sufficient to doom the League to ineffectiveness. How armaments were actually to be controlled was left to the future (Art.8). The French proposals for international arms inspections and an international military force were rejected. The substitute, a Permanent Commission to advise on military matters (Art.9) was a weak and worthless compromise. War among the members was not prohibited - it simply had to be postponed for three months (Art.12). The Permanent Court of Justice could not compel parties

---

15   The Covenant of the League of Nations is *reproduced in* FERENCZ, *id.* Doc. 22.

to appear (Art.14). Even the application of sanctions (Art.16) was eventually left to the discretion of states. No one could seriously have believed that such a system would maintain peace. And it didn't!

After more than forty million people were killed in World War II, "victorious" nations were again ready to sit down at the drawing board to see whether they could agree upon a better way to manage world affairs.

3. The United Nations Organization

"If we do not want to die together in war, we must learn to live together in peace," said President Harry Truman as he opened the United Nations Conference to adopt the UN Charter in 1945.[16] We have already referred to the illusions that emerged from the Dumbarton Oaks "discussions" and the compromises that led to the acceptance of a Charter known to be inadequate.[17] Virginia University Professor Inis L. Claude, Jr. said of the agrement reached at San Francisco:

> It was to some extent an illusion fostered by the ambiguity of terms employed in the Charter, and to some extent a pretense, a posture adopted by statesmen who thought it impolitic to reject ideals that seemed to command the passionate allegiance of the greater part of humanity.[18]

Here we are concerned primarily with an examination of the effectiveness of the organization as an institution to manage relations among states. We will consider both what is right and what is wrong with this latest "Grand Design" for peace, the progress being made and what needs to be done to make it more effective in achieving its declared goal - "to save succeeding generations from the scourge of war."

(1) What's Right About the UN:

The UN Charter was a significant improvement upon the Covenant of the League.

(i) Whereas one of the criticisms of the League was that it had only limited membership and therefore could not bind the world, the membership of the United Nations Organization was substantially

---

16   DOCUMENTS ON AMERICAN FOREIGN RELATIONS, vol. 8 p. 425.
17   See Chapter One, Section A.
18   I. CLAUDE, STATES AND THE GLOBAL SYSTEM (1989) at 174-175.

enlarged and has grown to a point where it is practically universal. That is a major accomplishment of global organization for the first time in human history.

(ii) The Covenant contained a few vague provisions encouraging League members to maintain humane conditions of work, improve health and mitigate human suffering. The UN Charter (Chap.X) created a special Economic and Social Council (ECOSOC) to improve the human condition and promote "respect for, and observance of, human rights and fundamental freedoms for all" (Art.62).

(iii) Under the Covenant, no action could be taken by either the Assembly or the Council of the League without a *unanimous* vote. Under the Charter, a *majority* of the General Assembly was entitled to pass resolutions which, even if merely *"recommendations"*, could - eventually - have great significance.[19]

(iv)Under the Covenant, the Council could not act until there was a war or threat of war. The UN Security Council does not have to wait for the threat or reality of war but can investigate and urge peaceful settlement of any situation that might lead to international conflict (Art.33, 34).

(v) The Charter obliges members to make military forces available to the Security Council for enforcement action (Art.43). The Covenant had no such requirement.

(vi) Under the Charter, the right of self-defense is strictly limited. It can only be lawful if it is a temporary response to an armed attack until the Council can act (Art.51). The Covenant left self-defense open and (in a futile attempt to gain U.S. support) even authorized self-help by the U.S. to protect its interests under its self-proclaimed Monroe Doctrine (Covenant Art. 21).

Despite these important steps forward, there was still a great deal wrong with the Charter. In the next Chapters we will review the Charter in some detail to see what is needed to make it work. Here we will briefly sketch some progress and continuing shortcomings of the UN as a world management agency.

---

19   *See* B.SLOAN,UNITED NATIONS GENERAL ASSEMBLY RESOLUTIONS IN OUR CHANGING WORLD (1991).

(2) *What's Wrong With the UN:*

Trouble was built into the Charter. Among the things that were wrong at the outset may be listed:

(i) A system that has no legislative power and can only take coercive action with the consent of those to be regulated will not work in a world of competing values and interests. Consensus is not far from unanimity and a requirement of consensus among more than 180 independent states spells paralysis.

(ii) An organization that has no independent financial base, but must depend upon contributions it has no power to collect, runs the risk of becoming a helpless beggar.

(iii) During its early years, the UN was used more as a propaganda forum than an agency for maintaining peace. As UN membership increased, the pendulum of power to influence UN resolutions moved from the West to the East and to Third World countries. To many, the Assembly appeared as little more than a debating society where nations expounded their own interests to a largely inattentive audience.

(iv) The International Court, as we have seen, lacked compulsory jurisdiction.[20]

(v) The Economic and Social Council (ECOSOC), with 54 members elected by the General Assembly to deal with economic, social, and educational problems and to promote respect for "human rights and fundamental freedoms for all" (Art.62) was given only advisory functions - it could make recommendations but not take action.

(vi) Enforcement by the Security Council was dependent upon military contingents to be mustered pursuant to a future agreement - that was never reached. The Military Staff Committee, which was supposed to advise the Council, remained moribund.

(vii) Most fatal of all: the power to *act* for peace remained suspended by the power to veto enforcement action. The Permanent Members (U.S., U.K., U.S.S.R., France and China) resisted change as a challenge to the prevailing system and a threat to national or ideological inter-

---

20   *See* Chapter Two, Section B.

ests they were prepared to defend by all necessary means. Those powerful enough to risk war had the authority to block interference. Without unanimity among the "Big Five" there was no way that peace could be enforced. The "cold-war" between the U.S. and the U.S.S.R. meant that the Security Council - the agency responsible for enforcing peace - was usually disabled.

As Professor John F. Murphy of Villanova pointed out:

> There is no question that the United Nations has failed abysmally to cope satisfactorily with traditional international violence.[21]

The defects were well known to political leaders whose main justification for accepting the new system was that it seemed better than nothing. Putting the best face on the Charter, the U.S. Secretary of State reported to the President:

> What has resulted is a human document with human imperfections...an instrument by which a real beginning may be made upon the work of peace.[22]

In addition to the built-in structural defects, the UN as an operational administrative agency falls far short of expectations. The Secretariat is composed of many fine and dedicated public servants - many others merely bloat the bureaucracy. Administrative shortcomings are not without some impact on the peace-keeping capacities of the organization. An Inspection Unit, considering the three main concerns of the UN - peace, security and development - concluded that

> the outworn and obsolete nature of the institutions and their failure to adapt to the problems of the modern world are not difficult to demonstrate.[23]

An independent and efficient civil service - which the Secretariat was supposed to be - has not yet been realized.[24] The need to restructure and revitalize ECOSOC has been generally acknowledged.[25] The Secretary-Gen-

---

21   J.F. MURPHY, THE UNITED NATIONS AND THE CONTROL OF INTERNATIONAL VIOLENCE (1982) at 123.

22   *Report to the President on the Results of the San Francisco Conference,* Dept. of State Publ.2349 (1945) p.19; *See* FERENCZ, ENFORCING INT. L. vol. 2 Chap. Ten. The U.N. Charter is *reproduced in* Doc. 42.

23   Joint Inspection Unit, *Some Reflections on Reform of the United Nations,* A/40/988 (1985) at p.25; *See* Report of the Group of High Level Intergovernmental Experts to Review the Efficiency of the Administration and Financial Functioning of the United Nations, GAOR: Forty-First Sess. Supp. No. 49 (A/41/49), 15 Aug.1986; J.W. MULLER, THE REFORM OF THE UN (1991).

eral has reported a number of administrative changes but recognized that "there is still room for improvement."[26] Expensive ad hoc employments have necessitated the recruitment of retired staff or outside experts, causing concern to member states reluctant to bear the cost. [27]

In 1974, the General Assembly created a Special Committee on the Charter and the Role of the Organization. Composed of nearly fifty states, the Charter Committee has met annually to consider how the UN could be made more effective in maintaining international peace and security. The endless reaffirmation of inflexible positions confirms the observations of Maurice Bertrand that sovereign states continue to lack the political will for constructive change. Consensus declarations lacked teeth and contained the usual equivocations and loopholes.[28]

There were many other reasons why the Charter proved to be less than satisfactory. Economic and political sanctions seldom worked as intended. The Charter did not specify how the burden of sanctions was to be shared nor at which point they should be replaced by military force. There was no Charter clarification about how to reconcile the right to self-determination with the sovereignty and territorial integrity of states. The Nuremberg trials had not yet begun when the UN Charter was signed and the Charter is thus silent regarding punishment for aggression and crimes against humanity - as required by the Nuremberg judgment. The Charter did not make clear to what extent nations might intervene to halt civil wars or other acts of inhumanity committed within or outside a nations' borders. All of these shortcomings would lead to endless grief.

(3) Signs of Progress:

This is not to suggest that the UN did nothing. It did the best it could under the circumstances and often it did quite a bit. The annual reports of the Secretary-General describe not merely frustrations and failures but also a picture of persistent striving and often helping to restore or maintain peace

---

24 The new Secretary-General has pledged to reinvigorate the "international civil service" and to try to secure financial stability in a world organization whose problems are exacerbated by the sad fact that less than a third of the members pay their dues in full and on time. *Report on the Work of the Organization* (1992), Part II.

25 GA Res. 45/264, 13 May 1991, requested the Secretary General to report annually on progress in restructuring and revitalizing ECOSOC.

26 UN Doc. A/47/534, 19 Oct. 1992 at 7.

27 *See* A/48/452, 5 October 1993.

28 *See Reports of the Special Committee on the Charter*, GAOR, Supp. No. 33, (A/46/33) (1991); (A/47/33) (1992); A/48/33) (1993).

in many areas. Even with a defective Charter and inadequate administration, it was sometimes possible to have an important influence on peace.

General Assembly "Declarations" influenced the development and interpretation of international law. UN resolutions encouraged combatants to cease-fire, while investigative and mediation commissions helped to avert or diminish conflicts in such areas as Greece in 1946, Indonesia in 1947, India and Pakistan in 1949. In 1950, a multi-national army led by the United States, but nominally under the Unified Command of the UN, halted North Korean aggression.[29] But the improvised response hardly achieved the Charter's primary goal of "saving succeeding generations..." 30,000 Americans and over a million others were killed in the Korean conflict alone.[30]

In 1956, peace was restored to the Suez region by a UN Emergency Force from ten nations, which President Eisenhower described as "the first truly international peace force".[31] It should be noted that the action, directed against Permanent Members Britain and France, was authorized by an improvisation of the General *Assembly* - relying on a disputed "Uniting for Peace" resolution that asserted Assembly authority to make peace enforcement recommendations when the Council was unable to act.[32]

A civil war in the Congo in 1960 was brought to a halt with the help of a United Nations Force. The Secretary-General helped to defuse the "Cuban Missile Crisis" of 1962. Sanctions and embargoes were employed to support UN objectives in Africa and elsewhere. Wars in the Middle-East evoked UN calls for truce, mediation and UN Forces to monitor cease-fires. The UN helped monitor peace in Cyprus. These creative approaches were forerunners of even more effective UN action still to come.

Considering itself prohibited from intervening without the consent of sovereign states, the UN was unable to bring permanent peace to the Middle-East or to stop devastating wars in Vietnam or Afghanistan or between Iran and Iraq or (until recently) in Cambodia - which cost many millions of lives. But the persistent efforts of both the Assembly and the Council and the Secretary-General gave reassurance that the world organi-

---

29   Report of the Security Council to the General Assembly, GAOR: Fifth Sess., Supp. No.2 (1/1361), *reproduced in* FERENCZ, ENFORCING INT. L. vol. 2 Doc. 51 (a); SC Doc. S/3067, 26 July,1953. *reproduced in* FERENCZ, *id.* Doc. 51 (c).

30   R.LECKIE, CONFLICT, THE HISTORY OF THE KOREAN WAR, 1950-1953 (1926) at 429.

31   Dept. of State Pub. 6577 (1957) at 69.

32   GA Res. 999 (ES-1), 4 Nov. 1956, GA Res. 1000 (ES-1) 5 Nov. 1956); GA Res. 377 (V), 3 Nov.1950.

zation was not unmindful of their needs. Despite its own organizational shortcomings, the UN was determined to do the best it could under circumstances which made the task of maintaining peace quite impossible.

With the end of the cold-war, the door to possible progress was opened to the world organization. In 1989, a joint statement by the Soviet Union and the United States promised "a new beginning at the United Nations -- a new spirit of constructive cooperation."[33] New democratic states emerged in Eastern and Central Europe. Revolutionary movements in various parts of the world, that had relied on the Soviet Union for economic or military support, lost much of their momentum. Ideological divisiveness that had characterized most UN debates began to diminish. The Secretary-General was encouraged to take a more active role in the search for peace.

With UN support, a cease-fire between Iran and Iraq was negotiated; Soviet troops were withdrawn from Afghanistan; Cuban troops were removed from Angola; Namibia's independence was advanced. UN supervised free elections in that new country as well as in warring states of Central America as they moved toward reconciliation. A cease-fire went into effect in Western Sahara and a peace plan for Cambodia was worked out by UN negotiators. Unarmed UN Observers and "peace-keepers" assumed posts around the globe to monitor tense situations or serve as a buffer between warring factions. In 1988, UN Peacekeepers earned the Nobel Peace Prize.[34]

Iraq's blatant invasion and annexation of Kuwait in 1990 posed the same issue to the UN that had been faced by the League when Italy invaded Ethiopia: How to respond to clear aggression by one member against another. In contrast with the failure of the League in 1936, and the failure of the UN to respond effectively to Iraq's aggression against Iran in 1980, the UN - spurred by a U.S. poised to strike - responded immediately and effectively. 155 nations rose in the General Assembly to condemn Iraq's attack as aggression and a threat to international peace and security. A dozen rapid-fire Security Council resolutions demanded Iraq's immediate withdrawal, imposed economic sanctions, and finally authorized nations to use "all necessary means" to restore the independence of Kuwait.[35]

---

33   Press Release USUN 133-(89).

34   *See*, UN DEP'T OF PUBLIC INFORMATION, THE BLUE HELMETS, A Review of U.N. Peace-keeping (1990).

35   SC Res.678, 29 Nov. 1990; *See* J.N.MOORE, CRISIS IN THE GULF, ENFORCING THE RULE OF LAW, Documents (1992).

In response to Iraq's persistent defiance, an international coalition, led by highly automated U.S. air, ground and sea forces, pounded Iraqi troops and their home bases and routed them out of Kuwait after a hundred hours of merciless aerial bombardment. The primary objective was achieved but - as in the case of all wars - it was not exactly the type of "pacific settlement" envisioned by the Charter. The Secretary-General expressed his concern about the use of excessive and inhumane force by a coalition not under strict Security Council control. He concluded, however, that "the arrangement seemed unavoidable" and "the effectiveness of the United Nations can no longer be in doubt."[36]

4. The Means are at Hand

It is tempting to conclude that since the United Nations is becoming more effective in its ability to manage global problems relating to peace there is no need for further action or concern - "If it ain't broke, don't fix it!" That temptation disappears if one looks at the broken state of the world - despite UN improvements and recent progress.

The cost of weapons designed to kill enormous numbers of innocent human beings is still staggering. Human rights continue to be abused almost everywhere. As long as millions of people face starvation and millions more must flee their homes in terror or despair and there are violent conflicts killing large numbers of helpless people all around the globe - which is the sad reality - there remains an urgent need for better global management to resolve global problems.

During the period of nearly half a century since the prototype UN Charter was adopted, the world has endured not only many wars and great human suffering but has also undergone tremendous political, social, technological, economic, demographic and environmental change. What needs to be done now to repair the broken structure of human society?

In the 1980's, a number of unofficial Commissions composed of important world citizens called for better global management of vital problems: The "Brandt Commission" focused on human poverty; The "Palme Commission" addressed hazards posed by nuclear weaponry; The 1987 report of the "Brundtland Commission," *Our Common Future*, dealt largely with the environment; A "South Commission" headed by Julius Nyerere, former Presi-

---

36   *Report of the Secretary-General on the Work of the Organization*, A/46/1 (1991).

dent of Tanzania, urged developing nations to ensure a better future for themselves.

The most recent such Commission, "The Stockholm Commission", including many former Heads of State, called for new thinking "to build a new system for peace and security, on both a global and regional scale." Their report, *Common Responsibility in the 1990's*, declared:

> "We believe that the time is right for nations to take the great step forward, living up to their common responsibility."

Among other things, they called for:

(i) Improved UN capability to prevent conflict by anticipating it;

(ii) Global law enforcement through sanctions and military force;

(iii) Stronger and better financed UN peacekeeping;

(iv) Limiting arms trade and reduction of armed forces;

(v) Increased aid to developing countries;

(vi) Environmental protection;

(vii) Population controls;

(viii) Enhanced democracy and human rights;

(ix) Strengthening UN machinery for more effective global governance.[37]

Has the time finally come to implement the wise proposals put forth by so many courageous world leaders?

The United Nations, like the League, was designed more to protect the status quo than to reorganize the world on a rational basis. New freedoms have brought a surge of new conflicts - ethnic, national, religious and political - making the urgency for institutional change greater than ever before. New circumstances and new needs demand new approaches to resolve old as well as new problems. We shall explore the possibilities in subsequent chapters to show that solutions can be found.

---

37   For other proposals for an early warning system *see* J. MURPHY (1982) supra at 128, referring to a U.N. Peace Observation Commission set up in 1950 and described in E. LUARD, THE UNITED NATIONS (1979) at 164.

One of those who recognized the Charter deficiencies at the outset, and who fought hard and hopelessly against its most crippling provisions, was an idealistic Harvard graduate, law partner of Elihu Root and wealthy leader of the New York bar - Grenville Clark. It was primarily as a result of his determination and persistence that the framers of the Charter were persuaded to add a provision requiring the Charter to be periodically reviewed - a provision that was accepted by every member of the UN but has never been implemented. Never.[38]

Grenville Clark, co-author with Professor Louis Sohn, of the renowned treatise WORLD PEACE THROUGH WORLD LAW, knew that Charter revision would be needed and he never gave up his struggle to improve the United Nations. When he had reached the age of 85, in 1967, Grenville Clark was asked why he continued to try to prevent war. He replied:

> My dominant reason is the sense of shame at the incapacity of the human race to summon enough intelligence and will to solve this problem, when the knowledge and means to solve it are at hand.[39]

The knowledge and means to prevent war are more at hand now than ever before.

B- Disarmament

On June 26, 1945, in a beautiful city on the Pacific Ocean named after the peaceful and loving Saint Francis, the UN Charter was signed. It reaffirmed "the dignity and worth of the human person." Forty-one days later, a small fission bomb was deliberately detonated above the Japanese city of Hiroshima. Within seconds, 78,000 human beings were burned, blasted or crushed to death as a city of three hundred and forty thousand people was turned into Hell. Three days later, 40,000 more lives were annihilated the same way in Nagasaki. And - whether it was generally recognized or not - the world was changed forever.

To many, "the Bomb" was seen only as a means to end a terrible war; that it was, but there was more to it than that. We have repeatedly been

---

38   UN Charter, Article 109.

39   McCalls Magazine, *The Legacy of a Great American*, (Apr. 1967) p. 168, cited in J.P. BARATTA, GRENVILLE CLARK, WORLD FEDERALIST (1985). Institute for Global Policy Studies, Occasional Paper No. 3 (1985) at 46. In 1985, a new U.S. postage stamp was issued to honor Grenville Clark.

warned - the way nations settle their differences in the future will have to change. Human beings have mastered the capacity to destroy all life on planet earth and that carries with it the responsibility to make sure that it doesn't happen.

Albert Einstein sounded the alarm:

> The unleashed power of the atom has changed everything save our modes of thinking, and we thus drift toward unparalleled catastrophes.[40]

Former President Dwight D. Eisenhower, who led the allied forces to victory in World War II, cautioned:

> Every gun that is made, every warship launched, every rocket fired represents, in the final analysis, a theft from those who hunger and are not fed, who are cold and are not clothed.[41]

In a personal and confidential letter dated April 4, 1956, Eisenhower wrote: "The era of armaments has ended and the human race must conform its actions to this truth or die."[42] In his farewell speech as President, Eisenhower said:

> Disarmament with mutual honor and confidence is a continuing imperative. Together we must learn to compose differences, not with arms, but with intellect and decent purpose...Another war could utterly destroy this civilization.[43]

Many years later, an alarmed UN Secretary-General de Cuellar appealed to the public:

> Every person on this earth has a stake in disarmament. In the nuclear age, decisions affecting war and peace cannot be left to military strategists or even to Governments. They are indeed the responsibility of every man and woman.[44]

There is no problem more important or fundamental than the need for international disarmament. It is a global problem that cannot be solved

---

40   *See* N.Y. Times, May 25, 1946 at 13.

41   Speech by D.W. Eisenhower, April 16, 1953 to the American Society of Newspaper Editors.

42   Letter from Eisenhower to publisher Richard L. Simon of Simon and Shuster, Apr.4, 1956, cited in column by David S. Broder, The Washington Post, Sept. 7, 1983.

43   *U.S. News and World Report*, Jan. 30, 1961 at 70.

44   Special Appeal of Secretary-General de Cuellar to the General Assembly in 1984, cited in THE UNITED NATIONS AT FORTY (UN, 1985) at 89.

nationally. The proliferation of weapons that have the capacity to destroy all living things means that disarmament is more than a moral imperative; there is no choice -human survival depends on it. Yet, according to the reliable Stockholm International Peace Research Institute (SIPRI), world-wide military spending in 1990 exceeded 2 1/2 *billion* dollars *every day*. *Billions*, every *day!*[45] Until this perilous situation is changed, nations will continue to rob their citizens of the resources needed to improve the human condition and there can be no enduring peace or security on earth for anyone.

Various legal mechanisms to achieve disarmament have been considered for a long time. Some advances have been made and more progress is in the offing. On balance, however, the current picture is terrifying. Weapons of mass destruction - and the capacity to produce more of them - continue to proliferate around the globe. There exist no effective legal constraints today which would make it impossible for sovereign states to produce or sell or purchase the means to kill incredible numbers of innocent people with weapons that are genocidal, ecocidal and suicidal. It is as though the world has gone mad.

1. Early Efforts to Control Arms

What was called "The First Peace Conference" was in fact an arms-limitation conference. His Majesty; the Czar and Emperor of all the Russias, (unable to bear the burdens of an arms race,) invited over two dozen powerful states to meet in the Hague in 1899 "to seek the most effective means of ensuring to the peoples a lasting peace, and of limiting the progressive development of military armaments."[46] Instead of limiting arms, the most enduring accomplishment of the Hague Conferences of 1899 and 1907 were the Hague Rules telling armies how to kill each other in a more humane way. The implied promise that nations would limit the development of arms was never carried out. Never.

After millions of people were slaughtered in World War I, Members of the League of Nations recognized that

> the maintenance of peace requires the reduction of national
> armaments to the lowest point consistent with national safety

---

45   SIPRI Yearbok 1992.
46   J.B. SCOTT, Ed. THE PROCEEDINGS OF THE HAGUE PEACE CONFERENCES; The conference of 1899 (1920) Opening Meeting, May 18, 1899, *reproduced in* FERENCZ, ENFORCING INT. L., vol. 1, Doc. 19, at 247.

and the enforcement by common action of international obligations.[47]

There could be no increase in the agreed level of armaments without Council
consent. Members also acknowledged that "the manufacture by private
enterprise of munitions and implements of war is open to grave objections"
and they agreed to exchange "full and frank information" about the scale of
their armaments and the condition of their arms industries. Despite the
solemn undertakings by 32 "civilized states," and 13 more that acceded to
the Covenant, the obligation of Article 8 to reduce the flow of arms was never
fulfilled. Never.

In 1925, a Protocol for the Prohibition and Use in War of Asphyxiating,
Poisonous or Other Gases, and of Bacteriological Methods of Warfare was
signed by over 100 countries. Many considered its prohibitions to be part of
customary international law that would bind everyone.[48] The existence of
the legally-binding Protocol did not prevent the manufacture, stockpiling
or use of poison gas by many countries; they flouted their legal obligations
with impunity.

After the atomic bombs were dropped on Hiroshima and Nagasaki,
and the war was brought to an end, President Harry Truman, joined by
Canada and the U.K.- that had helped develop the bomb - proposed that a
United Nations Commission be created to ensure that atomic energy was
used only for peaceful purposes and "for the elimination from national
armaments of atomic weapons and of all other major weapons adaptable to
mass destruction."[49] The very first resolution of the first Assembly of the
United Nations was a unanimous call for disarmament. A Commission,
established by the General Assembly, was requested to proceed "with the
utmost dispatch," to make specific disarmament proposals, including:

> ...the elimination from national armaments of atomic weapons
> and of all other major weapons adaptable to mass destruction.[50]

A UN Atomic Energy Commission was formed and the American
proposal for the control of atomic energy was spelled out by respected

---

47   Covenant of the League, Art. 8.

48   A.ROBERTS AND R. GUELFF, DOCUMENTS ON THE LAWS OF WAR (1982) 137; US
     ARMS CONTROL AND DISARMAMENT AGENCY, ARMS CONTROL AND
     DISARMAMENT AGREEMENTS - Texts and History of Negotiations (Annual).

49   Joint Declaration by the Heads of Government, The White House, Nov. 15, 1945, *reproduced
     in* FERENCZ, ENFORCING INT. L. vol.2 Doc. 45 (a).

50   GA Res.1 (I), 24 Jan. 1946.

American elder-statesman Bernard Baruch. Under the Baruch Plan, signatories to a treaty would be legally bound to:

(1) Halt the manufacture of atomic weapons;

(2) Destroy existing atomic bombs;

(3) Ban bacteriological, chemical or other weapons of mass destruction;

(4) Allow verifiable inspection to guarantee compliance;

(5) Subject violators to criminal prosecution under the Nuremberg precedents - with no state having a right of veto.

But, the system of controls and punishment - which was the heart of the matter - would have to be in place *before* the United States would destroy its own bombs or disclose its secrets.[51] That never happened. Never.

The Soviet Union did not trust the United States and didn't like the idea of the Atomic Energy Commission prying into or trying to regulate Soviet industries. Before it would accept restraints on its own nuclear production, it first wanted to see all other nuclear states sign a convention prohibiting all atomic weapons. Thus a good idea was stymied by each of the major parties saying: "You go first." As a result, the wise Baruch Plan was left standing outside the door and went nowhere.[52]

It was, according to the UN Charter (Art.45), the responsibility of the Security Council (with the Assistance of the Military Staff Committee) to plan a system for the regulation of armaments - with the least diversion of the world's human and economic resources (Art.26). The Security Council requested the Military Staff Committee, representing the Chiefs of Staff of the permanent members (Art.47), to present a specific disarmament plan and proposals for creating the international military force that was to be made available to maintain peace.[53]

In 1947, the Military Staff Committee submitted a report showing how international armed forces could be mobilized, organized and commanded

---

51   The Baruch Plan, June 14, 1946, is *reproduced in* FERENCZ, ENFORCING INT. L. vol.2 Doc. 45 (b). Comprehensive documentation is contained in US Dept. of State, DOCUMENTS ON DISARMAMENT Vol. 1, 1945-1959.

52   *See* Statement by USSR Delegate Gromyko to the Security Council, Mar. 5, 1947, *reproduced in* FERENCZ, ENFORCING INT. L. vol.2 Doc. 45 (c).

53   SC Res.18, 13 Feb. 1947.

to maintain or restore international security. There was some disagreement regarding 16 of the 41 articles of the plan but these were mostly technical and none seemed insurmountable.[54] Yet, the agreement specifically called for by the UN Charter never materialized. Never.

At about that time, the Soviet Union, which had suffered tremendous losses in World War II, was busy trying to build a *cordon sanitaire* around its borders by installing communist governments wherever possible. In the face of perceived communist expansionism, the Truman Doctrine was proclaimed: "to support free peoples who are resisting attempted subjugation by armed minorities or outside pressures."[55] The cold-war was on; it turned former military allies into military adversaries. Both the Soviet Union and the United States continued to *talk* about arms limitations and peace but in fact they were embarked on an arms race and struggle for predominance and power.

It was difficult to distinguish proclaimed peaceful purpose from pure public propaganda. The U.S.S.R. proposed an across-the-board cut in all armaments - including nuclear weapons which they did not have. The Americans refused, holding out for an agreement on nuclear controls first - to make sure the Soviets never developed a nuclear weapons capability. France, that had suffered the direct brunt of two world wars, renewed an old call for an international arms census so that the parties - and all the world - could know what they were talking about. The powerful United States said it supported the French census and verification proposals:

> We are willing to submit ourselves to such a system of inspection and checking. We do not feel sensitive about it nor regard that it's being called for is any reflection upon our integrity or our sovereignty.[56]

But the U.S. never did what it said it was willing to do. Never.

There was much *talk*, but little arms control *action*. All states proclaimed their peaceful intentions - while the Soviet Union was beginning to test nuclear devices. New military alliances were being formed by both superpowers. The North Atlantic Treaty of 1949 and the Southeast Asia Defense

---

54   SCOR 2d Yr. Spec. Supp.No.1, Report of the Military Staff Committee, 30 Apr. 1947, *reproduced in* FERENCZ, ENFORCING INT. L. vol 2. Doc. 46 (a).

55   Message of the President to the Congress, Mar. 12, 1947, *reproduced in* FERENCZ, ENFORCING INT. L. vol.2 Doc. 665 at 666.

56   SCOR Fourth Yr. 451st Meeting, 14 Oct. 1949, *reproduced in* FERENCZ, ENFORCING INT. L. vol. 2 Doc. 46 (b) at 661.

Treaty of 1954 used identical language in pledging signatories to arm rather than disarm themselves; "to maintain and develop their individual and collective capacity to resist armed attack."[57] In response, communist countries of Eastern Europe signed the Warsaw Pact forming a Unified Command to resist attack "by all the means it considers necessary."[58]

The arms race was in full swing. The Security Council, stymied by the veto power of its feuding permanent members, was unable to discharge its primary responsibility for the maintenance of international peace. In the ensuing years, millions of people died largely because the superpowers were unwilling or unable to overcome their fears and rivalries and live up to their legal obligations under a Charter they had freely accepted and pledged to uphold. They never did. Never.

2. Plans for Complete Disarmament

In 1959, when Soviet Premier Khrushchev addressed the General Assembly, he called for a program of general and complete disarmament (GCD).[59] U.S. Ambassador Lodge indicated that the U.S. could support such a policy if other nations did the same:

> As we lay down our arms, we must be certain that effective control measures exist which ensure that all other nations will do likewise.[60]

They never did. Never.

The problem of comprehensive arms-limitation systems came under intensive study by such American scholars as Jerome Wiesner of the Massachusetts Institute of Technology, Herman Kahn at Princeton, Henry Kissinger, Thomas Schelling and Louis Sohn at Harvard and many others. There were major differences in approach; some favoring limited step-by-step arms reductions, others arguing for major transformations or total disarmament.

---

57   North Atlantic Treaty, signed at Washington, 4 April 1949, 34 UNTS 243 (1949), Art.3; Southeast Asia Collective Defense Treaty, signed at Manila, 8 Sept. 1954, 219 UNTS 28 (1955) Art.II.

58   Treaty of Friendship, Cooperation and Mutual Assistance, Warsaw, 14 May 1955, 219 UNTS 24 (1955) Art.4.

59   See GAOR Plenary, 14th Sess., Sept. 18, 1959.

60   GAOR Plenary, 14th Sess., 20 Nov. 1959 at 579.

In March, 1961, U.S. President Kennedy appointed John J. McCloy to be his Special Assistant for Disarmament. McCloy, head of the prestigious Council on Foreign Affairs, was a distinguished New York attorney and Presidential Advisor who had been the Assistant Secretary of War during World War II and then U.S. High Commissioner for Germany. McCloy was instructed to negotiate with the Soviets regarding complete disarmament possibilities. By September, McCloy had managed to reach an "Agreed Statement of Principles" with U.S.S.R. Deputy Foreign Minister Valerian Zorin.

The McCloy/Zorin "Joint Statement" consisted of eight brief articles covering about two pages. It was the most concise and sensible set of disarmament recommendations ever assembled to preserve peace. Its plan was simple:

(1) There would be general and complete disarmament, with war outlawed as a means for settling international problems.

(2) States could possess non-nuclear arms only to the extent required to maintain internal order and to provide agreed manpower for a UN peace force.

(3) Armed forces of all nations were to be disbanded - bases and military training institutions closed; arms production was to cease and existing stockpiles of weapons of mass destruction, as well as their means of delivery, were to be eliminated; no funds could be appropriated for military expenditures.

(4) The program was to be implemented within specified time-limits and in stages, with each stage being verified step by step.

(5) Disarmament was to be balanced at every stage so that equal security for all would always be ensured.

(6) From beginning to end, there would be "strict and effective international control" by a new U.N. International Disarmament Organization with unrestricted access everywhere and not subject to any veto.

(7) Institutions for maintaining peace and settling disputes by peaceful means would have to be strengthened. States would have to provide manpower for a UN peace force to deter or suppress any unlawful use of arms.

(8) Negotiations on the total program would continue without interruption until agreement was achieved.

The McCloy/Zorin Plan for General and Complete Disarmament (GCD) was submitted to the General Assembly of the UN where it was promptly hailed and unanimously recommended.[61]

President Kennedy, in a moving address to the Assembly on Sept. 25, 1961, advanced the McCloy/Zorin ideas as he challenged the Soviet Union

> not to an arms race, but to a peace race: to advance together step by step, stage by stage, until general and complete disarmament has actually been achieved.

Both the United States and the Soviet Union submitted drafts of treaties providing for general and complete disarmament.[62] Despite the Baruch Plan and the McCloy/Zorin Plan and the unanimous approval of the entire United Nations, no treaty for general and complete disarmament was ever signed. Never.

The question may well be asked: "With so many favorable recommendations from so many distinguished statesmen and the unanimous endorsement by the world organization, why wasn't such a sensible and popular plan implemented?

The formal reason why the McCloy/Zorin plan foundered appeared in the exchange of letters between Mr. McCloy and Mr. Zorin, attached to their Report. It stated that the Soviets were not ready to accept outside inspection of their *existing* military stockpiles or level of forces. They considered that an unacceptable form of international espionage. The U.S. said such verification was essential. On that quibble, which could easily have been compromised or satisfied in a number of ways, - including the designation of neutral and confidential inspectors or non-intrusive verification techniques - the agreement for comprehensive disarmament foundered and was allowed to die. The McCloy/Zorin recommendations were never mutually accepted or implemented. The publicly endorsed plans were, according to a very reliable insider, "not even negotiable."

The *truth* was that neither the Soviet Union nor the United States - despite all the resolutions and speeches to the contrary - was really ready for comprehensive disarmament. A fearful and suspicious U.S.S.R. was

---

61   Documents on Disarmament (1961); GAOR 15th Sess.(A/4879), Sept. 20, 1961; GA Res.1722 (XVI) 20 Dec. 1961.

62   *See* S. MELMEN, Ed. DISARMAMENT, ITS PROSPECTS AND ECONOMICS (1962) pp.279-331; D.G. BRENNAN, Ed., ARMS CONTROL, DISARMAMENT AND NATIONAL SECURITY (1961) pp. 228-233.

determined to safeguard its sovereignty rather than rely on the impartiality of foreign inspectors. The powerful U.S. was determined to oppose what it perceived as Soviet propaganda and to press for only such measures of limited arms control that favored the United States. Each country, with different internal political factions pulling in different directions, was immobilized. The truth was never revealed to the public.

Twenty-two years later, Robert E. Matteson, who had been Director of the Disarmament Policy Staff during 1961, and who was on loan from the Central Intelligence Agency, having been Director of the Interdepartmental White House Disarmament Staff under President Eisenhower, sent an aide-memoir to his former Chief John McCloy, which helped to explain the apparent perfidy. In his 6-page memo, Matteson stated:

> The fact was that if we had bought the Soviet GCD plan, it would have meant the eventual end of the free world; if the Soviet bought the U.S. plan, with its time phasing and verification, it would have meant not only the end of secrecy in the U.S.S.R. but the end of the Soviet system as we know it. The plans were therefore not negotiable.[63]

Instead of accepting and implementing the comprehensive system to eliminate the dreadful threat of nuclear armaments - that had been characterized by President Kennedy as a "sword of Damocles" hanging over every man, woman and child - the superpowers and their merchants of death went back to business as usual. In his Jan. 17, 1961 *"Farewell Radio and Television Address to the American People"* Eisenhower said:

> In the councils of government, we must guard against the acquisition and unwarranted influence, whether sought or unsought, by the military-industrial complex. The potential for the disastrous rise of misplaced power exists and will persist.

The President's warning went unheeded. Fear and mistrust, and possibly greed, overpowered reason.

---

63   Letter to John McCloy from Robert E. Matteson, Chairman of the Glenview Foundation, Cable, Wisconsin, 54621, dated Mar. 14, 1983; copy in Ferencz private files, with confirming letter from Matteson to Ferencz, dated Nov. 27, 1983; Further confirmed by McCloy letter to Sanford Z. Persons, 10 Oct. 1983, cited in J.P. Baratta, *Verification and Disarmament*, Monograph No. 4, Center for UN Reform Education (1988) at 50, and by Marcus Raskin who was a staff member of the National Security Council. *See* M. RASKIN, ABOLISHING THE WAR SYSTEM (1992) at 17.

3. *Slowing the Arms Race*

As the U.S. and the U.S.S.R. developed their nuclear arsenals, it became increasingly clear that weapons of mass destruction did not enhance world security - they jeopardized it. In 1961, Jerome Wiesner, Special Assistant to the President for Science and Technology, pointed out:

> There is growing realization among knowledgeable people that if the arms race is allowed to continue its accelerating pace, our country will have less security, not more, with each passing year.[64]

With the superpowers in fierce competition, thus rendering the Security Council practically helpless, major efforts to slow the arms race shifted to the General Assembly and its agencies. But the Charter authorized the Assembly only to *consider* and make *recommendations* regarding "the principles governing disarmament and the regulation of armaments" (Art.11). To help it carry out its responsibilities, the Assembly created several other organizational mechanisms to address the many facets of the disarmament problem.

The International Atomic Energy Agency (IAEA) was established in 1956 to supervise peaceful uses of atomic energy. A Ten-Nation Committee on Disarmament was expanded to become a 40-nation "Conference on Disarmament." Various UN commissions and sub-committees were formed - all without power. Several Special Sessions of the Assembly focused on disarmament. A UN Institute for Disarmament Research (UNINDIR) and a Department of Disarmament Affairs was created to disseminate disarmament information. The First Committee - the Disarmament Committee of the Assembly - kept on its agenda such topics as reduction of all types of weapons, military budgets, verification, confidence building and anything that might move nations toward "general and complete disarmament under effective international control."[65]

In addition to the mobilization of toothless UN agencies and committees to address disarmament problems, hundreds of disarmament resolutions were passed each year. The First UN Special Session on Disarmament,

---

64   DONALD C. BRENNEN, Ed., ARMS CONTROL, DISARMAMENT *AND* NATIONAL SECURITY (1961) at 14.

65   *See The United Nations and Disarmament, A Short History* (UN, 1988); *See* Final Document of the Tenth Special Session, GAOR, Supp. No.4 (A/S-10/4) 1978. The *United Nations Disarmament Yearbook* starting with 1976, reports on all facets of UN disarmament activity; J.GOLDBLAT, ARMS CONTROL AGREEMENTS Chap.7, (1993).

in 1978, called for "general and complete disarmament under effective international controls" as it repeated language from the McCloy/Zorin Agreement and the non-proliferation treaty of a decade earlier. A decade later, at the Third Special Session devoted to Disarmament, the draft comprehensive program began with the declaration:

> The States Members of the United Nations reaffirm that the ultimate goal of a comprehensive programme of disarmament is general and complete disarmament under effective international control.[66]

Despite these praiseworthy recommendations, that reflected the will of large numbers of people all around the world, it was not possible to enact effective international *laws* or to create new international *institutions* which could halt the production, sale or use of devastating military weaponry.

The best that could be achieved in the prevailing cold-war atmosphere was some limitation, rather then complete elimination, of dangerous weapons. Years of hollow rhetoric about "the will to disarm" was enough to drive such dedicated public servants as Alva Myrdal of Sweden to a feeling of near-despair as she described disarmament as "a game" - a charade that deceived the public while the arms race continued with business as usual.[67] Professor Joseph Rotblat, an emeritus professor of Physics at the University of London and the winner of the Albert Einstein Peace Prize in December 1992, said that the time had come to put the matter of arms reduction verification on the agenda of the Security Council.[68]

Despite difficulties and vacillation, several important steps forward were taken both on an international level and by multi-national or bilateral arms-limitation accords. They will illustrate that the picture is not all bleak, that it is possible to reach agreements on meaningful ways to limit the arms race and that opportunities for even more significant advances may be at hand. Only a few of the major accomplishments will be sketched here:

---

66 GAOR Fifteenth Special Session, Supp. No. 2 (A/S-15/2), 11 May 1988.
67 A. MYRDAL, THE GAME OF DISARMAMENT (1978) at xi.
68 J.Rotblat, The Feasibility of a Nuclear-Weapon-Free World, Global Security Study No. 16, Nuclear Age Peace Foundation, (Aug. 1993); *See* I.J.ROTBLAT, J.STEINBERGER & B. UDGAONKAR (Eds.) A NUCLEAR WEAPON-FREE WORLD: DERSIRABLE?, FEASIBLE? (1993).

(1) Nuclear Free Zones:

To reduce the recognized and obvious danger of the enormous destructive capacity generated by modern technology, frightened non-nuclear nations agreed that certain areas of the world should become "nuclear-free zones" where testing, use, production or even possession of nuclear weapons would be prohibited. In 1959, twelve nations (including the U.S.S.R., U.S., U.K., Japan and France) signed "The Antarctic Treaty" proclaiming that "Antarctica shall be used for peaceful purposes only."[69] An "Outer-Space Treaty" ratified by the major powers and most other nations, accorded similar protection to "Outer-Space, including the Moon and Other Celestial Bodies."[70] Latin America, with some 200 million inhabitants, sought to be protected by being declared a nuclear-free zone in 1967.[71] In 1971, it was agreed by legal treaty that the sea-bed could not be used as a base for weapons of mass destruction.[72]

In 1983, U.S. President Reagan acknowledged before the United Nations:

A Nuclear war cannot be won and must never be fought.[73]

In 1985, a *South Pacific Nuclear Free Zone Treaty* was signed, seeking to protect an area covering one-sixth of the surface of the planet.[74] A 1992 Agreement on Reconciliation between North and South Korea was followed by a Joint Declarati calling for denuclearizing the entire Korean Peninsula.[75] Africa was being considered as a potential nuclear free zone.[76] But without the

---

69   *Treaty on Antarctica*, 1 Dec. 1959, Art.1, 12 UST 794, 402 UNTS 71; *See* F.M. AUBURN, ANTARCTIC LAW AND POLITICS (1982), Treaty is at p. 298.

70   *Treaty on Principles Governing the Activities of States in the Exploration and Use of Outer Space, Including the Moon and Other Celestial Bodies*, Jan. 27, 1967, 18 UST 2410, 610 UNTS 205, *reprinted in* 6 ILM 386 (1967). *See* C.Q. CHRISTOL, THE MODERN INTERNATIONAL LAW OF OUTER SPACE (1982), Treaty is at 851, ratifications are listed at 908.

71   *Treaty of Tlateloco*, Feb. 14, 1967, 22 UST 754, 634 UNTS 281, *reprinted in* 6 ILM 521 (1967). It was hoped that the Treaty would be in force by the end of 1993. *See* Statement of Mr. Perri of Brazil in The First Committee, 18 October 1993.

72   *Treaty on the Prohibition of the Emplacement of Nuclear Weapons and Other Weapons of Mass Destruction on the Sea Bed and on the Ocean Floor and in the Subsoil Thereof*, Feb. 11, 1971, 23 UST 701, 955 UNTS 115, *reprinted in* 10 ILM 146 (1971).

73   Ronald Reagan's address to the General Assembly, 26 Sept. 1983, A/38/PV.5 26 Sept. 1983 at 3.

74   The South Pacific Nuclear Free Zone Treaty, *Treaty of Rarotonga* , August 6, 1985, *reproduced in* 24 ILM (1985) 1440.

75   Conf. on Disarmament Doc. CD/1147, 19 Feb. 1992; *Joint Declaration on the Denuclearization of the Korean Peninsula*, reproduced in Disarmament, vol. XV, No.3 (1992) at 149.

76   B.A. Adeyemi and D.A. Fischer, *Africa as a Nuclear-Weapon-Free Zone*, XIV Disarmament No.3 (1991) at 97.

participation of the U.S., U.K. and France on the Ad Hoc Committee working to make the Indian Ocean a Zone of Peace, the Committee was stymied.[77]

(2) *Limitations on Nuclear Testing:*

In 1963, an important *"Partial Test Ban Treaty"* prohibited nuclear weapons tests in the atmosphere, outer-space and under water.[78] On various occasions, some of the nuclear powers agreed to a limited moratorium on testing their nuclear weapons. Brief interludes in the perfection of nuclear arms could not bring the arms race to a halt. Attempts to reach agreement on a Comprehensive Test Ban - a necessary precursor to disarmament - although widely supported by UN bodies and private groups in many lands, were never crowned with success.[79]

(3) *Non-Proliferation Agreements:*

A *"Non-Proliferation Treaty"* of 1968, after reaffirming the goal of complete disarmament, prohibited the proliferation of nuclear weaponry. Non-nuclear states were encouraged to sign the treaty in exchange for its promise that signatories who possessed nuclear weapons would not test them, make more of them or use them. In fact, they guaranteed the security of states that agreed not to acquire their own nuclear arsenal.[80] Unfortunately, the promises of the nuclear powers not to test or manufacture nuclear weapons were not kept. Some non-nuclear states did not consider it reasonable for those who possessed such lethal weapons to claim an exclusive right to keep them while expecting non-nuclear states to remain at their mercy. Nuclear weaponry began to proliferate. Doubts were raised whether the Treaty, that was scheduled to expire in 1995, would be renewed.

(4) *Arms Limitation Agreements:*

Significant progress on a bilateral level was recorded when the U.S.S.R. and the U.S. signed a treaty in 1972, and protocol in 1974, limiting the anti-ballistic missiles that each country was permitted to have in order to defend itself against a nuclear attack.[81] In the preamble to the "ABM Treaty,"

---

77   Report of the Ad Hoc Committee on the Indian Ocean, GAOR 48th Sess. Supp. No.29 (A/48/29) 13 Aug. 1993.

78   *Treaty Banning Nuclear Weapons Tests in the Atmosphere, in Outer Space, and Under Water,* Aug. 5, 1963, 14 UST 1313, 480 UNTS 43. *Reprinted in* 2 ILM 889 (1963).

79   *See* 14 UN DISARMAMENT YEARBOOK (1989-1992).

80   *Treaty on the Non-Proliferation of Nuclear Weapons,* July 1, 1968, 21 UST 483, 729 UNTS 161, *reprinted in* 7 ILM 811 (1968).

81   *Treaty between USA and USSR on the Limitation of Anti-Ballistic Missile Systems,* Moscow, May 26, 1972, 23 UST 3435, 944 UNTS 13, *reprinted in* 11 ILM 784 (1972); Protocol dated July 3, 1974, 27 UST 1645.

both parties again declared "their intention to achieve at the earliest possible date... general and complete disarmament." The theory was that by remaining vulnerable - presumably only until general disarmament was reached - each superpower would be less inclined to attack.   To avoid disputes regarding interpretation or compliance, a Standing Consultative Commission was established (Art. XIII) - but was seldom used. War was to be deterred by "*Mutual Assured Destruction*" - a system using the very appropriate acronym - **MAD**.

In 1972 and 1979, Strategic Arms Limitation Agreements (SALT I and II) placed limitations on the number of long-range "strategic" nuclear weapons that each country might deploy.[82] These restraints were all significant but none of them was decisive and the means for verification were limited. The production of new and more powerful weapons continued unabated.

In 1988, it became possible - for the first time in history - for the U.S. and U.S.S.R. to sign "The INF Treaty" to destroy an entire category of nuclear weapons - their complete arsenals of intermediate and shorter-range missiles.[83] In a comprehensive study by qualified experts, the UN Secretary-General reported that "the quantitative growth of nuclear-weapons arsenals has been stopped"[84] But the quality and destructive power of nuclear weapons continued to be improved.

In 1991, a Strategic Arms Reduction Treaty (START 2) further reduced by some 70 per cent the number of long range nuclear warheads held by the U.S. and four republics of the former Soviet Union. It won almost unanimous Senate approval in October 1992.[85] Progress was also made in reducing conventional weapons and forces stationed in Europe.

---

82   *Interim Agreement Between the USA and USSR on Certain Measures with Respect to the Limitation of Strategic Offensive Arms,* May 26, 1972, 23 UST 3462, 94 UNTS 3, *reprinted in* 11 ILM 791 (1972); *Treaty Between the USA and USSR on the Limitation of Strategic Offensive Arms and Protocol Thereto,* June 18, 1979, S. Exec. Doc. Y, 96th Cong., 1st Sess. 37 (1979). *See* P.K. MENON, THE U.N. EFFORTS TO OUTLAW THE ARMS RACE IN OUTER SPACE (1989).

83   *Treaty Between the USA and USSR on the Elimination of their Intermediate-Range and Shorter-Range Missiles,* Dec. 8, 1987, reprinted in 27 ILM 90 (1988).

84   *General and Complete Disarmament, Comprehensive Study on Nuclear Weapons,* UN Doc. A/45/373, 18 Sept. 1990 at 5.

85   *See* N.Y. Times, Oct.2, 1992, P. A6, article by John H. Cushman; *See* M.Nash (Leich) *Contemporary Practice of the U.S.Relating to International Law, Start II Treaty ,* 87 AJIL 258 (1993).

After 20 years of negotiation, a multilateral treaty banning chemical weapons was signed by more than 120 nations meeting in Paris in January 1993. It went far beyond the Geneva Protocol of 1925. The Chemical Weapons Treaty was unique for several reasons: (a) It was global in scope; (b) it established a comprehensive verification regime by creating a new organization (Organization for the Prohibition of Chemical Weapons) to assure compliance, and (c) it provided for economic sanctions against non-signing nations.[86] Secretary-General Boutros-Ghali said:

> The Convention should go down in history as one of the most tangible signs of current progress towards a universal order.[87]

News reports spoke of the new Clinton Administration in Washington working on a broad plan of disarmament, including a worldwide ban on the production of materials for nuclear weapons. [88]

(5) Confidence Building Measures:

The superpowers agreed upon improved communications to prevent nuclear accidents or miscalculations.[89] Through the Conference on Security and Cooperation in Europe (CSCE), other confidence building measures, including notification of troop movements, were accepted. Inspections to assure compliance were also authorized.[90]

At the end of 1991, the General Assembly passed a resolution by consensus establishing a voluntary Register of Conventional Arms and calling upon states to report their imports and exports of arms.[91] Transparency in armaments was recognized as being a significant component in slowing the arms race. A Panel of Technical Experts connected with the UN Office for Disarmament Affairs began to list the tanks, armored vehicles, canons, combat aircraft warships and missiles transferred by different nations. Beginning only with the registration of trades, it was hoped that by

---

86   See A. Riding, *Signing of Chemical-Arms Pact Begins*, N.Y. Times, Int'l, Jan. 14, 1993; Text of the Convention is *reproduced in* 32 ILM 800 (1993); *Report of the Conference on Disarmament*, GAOR Forty-Seventh Sess., Supp. No. 27 (A/47/27) 1992 at 24-64; Press Release DCF/154, 9 Sept. 1992. The status of ratifications of major disarmament treaties is shown in A/47/470, 12 Oct. 1992.

87   UN Press Release SG/SM/4900, 13 Jan., 1993 at 2.

88   M.R. Gordan, *U.S. Hopes to Curb A-Arms By Restricting Fuel Output*, N.Y. Times, July 28, 1993 at A-2.

89   *The "Hot Line Modernization Agreement"*, Sept. 30, 1971, 22 UST 1598, 806 UNTS 402, *reprinted in* 10 ILM 1174 (1971).

90   See 16 UN Disarmament Yearbook (1991).

91   GA Res. 46/36 L, 9 Dec. 1991.

1996 it would be possible to register the production as well as the sale of arms.[92] As of June 1993, 58 nations, including five of the six top arms exporting countries (U.S., France, U.K., China and Germany) had submitted data.[93]

Confidence-building requires a continual process of mutual and universal disarmament. All nations must feel assured that their security is not being jeopardized by accepting restraints on their capacity to defend their interests by force of arms. But that feeling of reassurance can only come about if there is determined political will on the part of powerful states to alter past thinking and behavior and to really practice what they preach.[94] As Nabil Elaraby, Ambassador of Egypt and Chairman of the First (Disarmament) Committee said at the end of 1992:

> There is progress, it is going ahead. But I think if you want something meaningful you have to address it in a comprehensive manner and that requires two important considerations. First it has to include every facet of disarmament, not merely arms transfers, but also production and holdings. Second, it has to include weapons of mass destruction.[95]

4. Progress and Prospects

The impressive array of accomplishments toward disarmament illustrates that arms limitation agreements are not only possible, but that they are being accepted in increasing profusion. Despite all of the hesitation and some inadequacies and imperfections, the record is abundantly clear that legal instruments imposing legal obligations regarding the level of armaments *can* be drafted, negotiated, accepted, verified and enforced; if there is the will, there is a way. Destroying dangerous weapons will take many years and cost billions of dollars - as can be seen from the terms of recent arms limitation agreements. Disarmament is expensive but a constantly escalating arms race is much more expensive and can be fatal.

---

92   *See Disarmament Newsletter*, Aug-Sept. 1992 p. 8; A draft *Convention on the Monitoring, Reduction and Ultimate Abolition of the International Arms Trade* has been prepared by the World Orders Model Project, headed by Prof. Saul Mendlovitz and the Lawyers Committee on Nuclear Policy, headed by attorney Peter Weiss of New York.

93   *See Disarmament Times*, June 1993 p. 1. The item remains on the agenda for 1994. *See* A/C.1/48/L.18, 29 October 1993.

94   *See* J, DEAN, MEETING GORBACHEV'S CHALLENGE: How to Build Down the NATO-Warsaw Pact Confrontation (1992).

95   *Disarmament Times*, 18 Dec. 1992 at 4.

In 1987, Michael Gorbachev, new head of the Soviet Union, put forth a plan for comprehensive security based upon the rule of law in international affairs.

> Change has begun," he wrote, "and society cannot now turn back...We want a world free of war, without arms races, nuclear weapons and violence...It is an objective global requirement that stems from the realities of the present day.[96]

The collapse of the Soviet Union - despite the fact that it was loaded with nuclear armaments of all kinds, and probably because of it - demonstrated that weaponry can not protect a nation from dissolution. The cost and economic burden of those weapons undoubtedly emboldened the determination of people to rise in protest against their unbearable yoke. Armaments that were supposed to enhance the nation's strength actually weakened it. The cost of the arms race also significantly increased the U.S. budgetary deficit and America's ability to meet the needs of its own citizens.

On the 40th anniversary of the dropping of the atomic bomb, six distinguished political leaders met in New Delhi to express their common concerns about the continuing nuclear threat. "Nuclear war can be prevented," they said, "if our voices are joined in a universal demand in defence of our right to live." They urged people, parliaments and governments the world over to protest the fact that, worldwide, approximately one and a half million dollars were being spent *every minute* on weapons. Only then, they argued, would governments summon the necessary political will to avert the threat to the survival of humanity.[97]

What's right about the program for world disarmament is that it is moving in the right direction. What's wrong with it is that it's not moving quickly or comprehensively enough. Nations simply have not honored either the word or the spirit of their disarmament obligations.[98]

It can hardly be expected that every nation will voluntarily agree to make all needed changes in their level of armaments at the same time. The transition from an arsenal mentality will not be easy while the world is in

---

96   M. GORBACHEV, PERESTROIKA - NEW THINKING FOR OUR COUNTRY AND THE WORLD (1987) at p. 10, 11.

97   *Delhi Declaration* issued 28 Jan. 1985 by Raul Alfonsin, President of Argentina; Rajiv Gandhi, Prime Minister of India; Miguel de la Madrid, President of Mexico; Julius Nyerre, President of Tanzania, Olaf Palme, Prime Minister of Sweden and Andreas Papandreou, Prime Minister of Greece.

98   *See* S.WRIGHT, Ed., PREVENTING A BIOLOGICAL ARMS RACE (1990).

disorganized ferment and no alternative security system has been created. If human beings everywhere are to enjoy the peace and dignity to which they are entitled, comprehensive disarmament must become a part of a transformed new world order under law. Ending the arms race is sufficiently complicated and important to justify consideration of a new international institution to deal with it in a more comprehensive way - as we shall soon suggest.[99]

We must not lose sight of the fact that disarmament is only one of many changes that are required before peace can be assured. As Nobel Laureate Noel Baker pointed out:

> Lasting peace and justice will only come from the gradual accumulative inter-action of many policies and many great reforms: a conscious persistent effort to strengthen the deliberative institutions of the U.N.; the submission of all legal conflicts to the International Court; the building of international legislation and administration for the greater happiness and prosperity of mankind. But these new policies can never triumph until the arms race has been ended, and the nations have thus decided that they will finally abandon the use of force.[100]

C- Non-Military Coercion

No nation can be expected to accept any plan for complete disarmament until there exists an acceptable system, organization or institution on which it can rely for its own safety and security. Although planned and promised, no effective global security regime has ever existed in the past. It must be created now if the arms race is to be brought to an end.

To be sure, there were many methods and arrangements for peaceful resolution of conflict and there were multi-national alliances that helped to maintain peace for a relatively long period of time. But once war erupted, the normal way of restoring peace was for one party - after great losses - to surrender to the mercy of the victor.

---

99   *See* L.B. Sohn, *Adjudication and Enforcement in Arms Control*, in D.G. BRENNAN, Ed. ARMS CONTROL. DISARMAMENT AND NATIONAL SECURITY (1961) Chap. 19; CLARK AND SOHN, WORLD PEACE THROUGH WORLD LAW (1966), Annex I; M. RASKIN, ABOLISHING THE WAR SYSTEM (1992).

100   P.NOEL-BAKER, THE ARMS RACE (1958) cited by B. Urquhart, *Can the U.N. Deliver the Peace?* X *Disarmament* 79 (1987) at 81.

As weapons became more destructive, the desirability of employing non-violent forms of coercion to halt the conflict, rather than the hazardous and brutal assaults of battle, became more apparent to many people. Yet, past endeavors to establish a workable system to assure world peace by preventing war have not succeeded. Let us consider what has been done in the past, why such efforts have not yet proved effective as an acceptable substitute for war, and what improvements are needed to make it work in the future.

1. Early Sanctions

One of the earliest forms of economic coercion designed to put an end to war was to lay siege to the enemy's fortress or to blockade his ports - thereby depriving him of the means to carry on the conflict. Homer's *Iliad* wrote of the siege of Troy a thousand years before the birth of Christ. Thucydides described how, in the year 411 B.C., Athens was doomed when Sparta "cut off her food, and starved the city out."[101] Biblical Zealots found refuge on an impenetrable mountain-top at Masada near the Dead Sea and chose mass suicide rather than surrender when they were hopelessly besieged by the Romans.

Because economic sanctions could have disastrous consequences, over the years extensive rules were developed governing when the imposition of sanctions, economic reprisals or counter-measures would be lawful. The permissible limits for such methods of coercion were gradually defined by commonly accepted rules. A blockade, for example, might have an adverse impact on neutral countries or non-belligerent states desiring to enter the blockaded port or traverse the blockaded area. The right to put pressure on a state with which a nation was at war did not legally entitle it to penalize or inflict indiscriminate injury on other states.[102] The imposition of an economic blockade against a country with which one is *not* formally at war might even be regarded as an illegal act of aggression.[103] We see therefore that the application of economic sanctions - in peace or war - has international legal consequences which must be taken into account.

---

101   S.W.LIVINGSTONE, Ed., THUCYDIDES, THE HISTORY OF THE PELOPONESIAN WAR, (1943) at 388.

102   *See* H. LAUTERPACHT, Ed., OPPENHEIM'S INTERNATIONAL LAW, A Treatise by L. Oppenheim, vol.2, Part III (Eight Ed. 1955); A.E. HINDMARSH, FORCE IN PEACE, FORCE SHORT OF WAR IN INTERNATIONAL RELATIONS (1933).

103   *See* consensus definition of aggression in GA Res.3314 (XXIX) 14 Dec. 1974, Art. 3(c).

As nations grew and lost their insular character, traditional methods of siege or blockade became more difficult to apply and less effective. When methods of warfare became highly mechanized, it became increasingly apparent that a nation's entire economy was engaged in the process of waging war. It might be easier, safer and more effective to destroy the infrastructure and factories that produced supplies for the troops than to lay siege to the troops themselves. For sanctions to be most effective, the means of production would have to be crippled. Logically, that meant that civilian populations would have to be targeted as well as military. Legally that was prohibited - *unless* required by "military necessity."

As international trade grew, nations became dependent upon raw materials and commodities from many lands. Economic sanctions, to be effective, would have to acquire international scope to cut off the source of essential supplies.[104] Targeting civilians and punishing neutrals was illegal, but the justification of "military necessity" weakened the restraints of international law and increased the hazards in a world where the rule of law remained imprecise and unenforceable.[105]

2. The "Economic Weapon" of the League

The great hardships that were caused - to civilian populations in particular - by widespread economic measures of coercion during World War I gave rise to new ideas for peace-enforcement when the Covenant of the League of Nations was drafted in 1919. It should be recalled that the Covenant stipulated that peace required national armaments to be reduced and brought under international controls (Art.8), and that some alternative method of coercion against a persistent lawbreaker was recognized to be essential. As part of its comprehensive security plan, Covenant Article 16 contained what was referred to as the "economic weapon."

According to Article 16, if any nation should resort to war in disregard of its covenants, it would be deemed to have committed an act of war against all other Members of the League. All members would be obliged *immediately* to subject the aggressor to:

(1) "severance of all trade or financial relations,"

---

104 During World War I, Great Britain passed a Trading with the Enemy Act to penalize *any firm of any nationality* trading with Germany and to boycott any foreign firms violating the ban. *See* W.M. MEDLICOTT, THE ECONOMIC BLOCKADE, 2 vols. (1952, 1959).

105 *See* J.STONE, LEGAL CONTROLS OF INTERNATIONAL CONFLICT (1954).

(2) "prohibition of all intercourse between their nationals and the nationals of the covenant-breaking State" and

(3) "prevention of all financial, commercial or personal intercourse between the nationals of the covenant-breaking State and the nationals of any other State whether a Member of the League or not."

It was foreseen that financially or militarily weak states seeking to impose harsh restraints on a powerful neighbor immediately would place themselves in simultaneous economic and physical peril. Accordingly, the Covenant provided that it would be the duty of the Council to recommend to the Members what effective military, naval or air forces they would contribute to protect the covenants. Furthermore, Members were obliged to "mutually support one another ... in order to minimize the loss and inconvenience resulting" from the economic sanctions imposed on lawbreakers. In addition, any Member who violated the Covenant could be expelled from the League.[106]

Article 16 was as powerful a declaration of collective security action against an aggressor as had ever been seen anywhere. The wrongdoing State would be completely blacklisted: no commerce, no banking, no contact with any other state. The economic sanctions would be backed up by the mobilization of necessary military might, a sharing of the financial burdens caused by the sanctions and expulsion of the transgressor from the League. Prof. Oppenheim, in his famous treatise, correctly described the sanctions plan as "a fundamental feature of the Covenant and a radical innovation in International Law."[107] Why didn't it work?

The answer is clear. The most powerful Members of the League - Great Britain and France, in particular - backed out when the chips were down. They were more concerned with politics than principle. The "economic weapon" was denied the needed ammunition. The collective security plan of the Covenant was never given a chance.[108]

What actually happened was this: The First Assembly of the League appointed an International Blockade Committee to organize the machinery needed for effective international economic sanctions. The Committee

106 The Covenant of the League of Nations, League of Nations Official Journal, Feb. 1920 pp.7-8; *reproduced in* FERENCZ, DEFINING INT. AGGRESSION, vol. I, Doc. 1.

107 H. LAUTERPACHT, Ed., OPPENHEIM'S INTERNATIONAL LAW, A Treatise by L. Oppenheim, vol.2 Sec 52 (f) at 137, Sixth Ed. (1944); *See also,* Seventh Ed. Sec. 52(c) and Eight and Ninth Edition (1992).

108 *See* FERENCZ, ENFORCING INT. L., vol. 1 pp. 52-55.

quickly encountered a major policy problem - sanctions and disarmament went hand in hand. Before joining in sanctions against a powerful neighbor or trading partner, nations wanted to know in advance what economic and military help would be made available to them in case they were attacked by the state being subjected to sanctions. Conversely, states that were expected to come to the aid of others wanted to know what *their* military or economic responsibilities would be if they were called upon for a rescue operation.

As long as obligations remained unclear and the effectiveness of sanctions uncertain, no state could safely disarm. Militarists could argue that without effective international sanctions to replace the weapons of war, unilateral arms reductions might prove suicidal. International disarmament and economic blockade were thus linked and made dependent; you couldn't have one without the other.

It soon became obvious in the Blockade Committee that some states were eager to avoid the obligations spelled out in the Covenant. New rules were quietly, and unofficially, accepted that completely distorted the clear language of Article 16. Thus - according to the revised interpretation - each state could *decide for itself* whether aggression had occurred and whether sanctions should be triggered. Instead of enforcement measures starting immediately, as stipulated, the Council would recommend the starting date. Instead of breaking off *all* diplomatic relations, only *some* ties would be severed. Economic pressures would not be comprehensive but only limited.[109]

Blockade Committee Rapporteur, M. de Brouckére of Belgium, submitted a detailed and scathing report on the distortions of the Covenant. He castigated the new "interpretations" of Article 16. He also pointed out that, in order to really implement the Charter obligation, additional steps would be required:

(1) "Accurate information on the economic and financial relations between states";

(2) "A scheme for the mutual support recommended";

---

109 League of Nations, Records of the First Assembly, Meetings of the Committees, Annex 6 a, p.331-333; Records of the Second Assembly, 1921, Meeting of the Committees, Annex 5, pp.355-358, Sept. 10, 1921; *Reports and Resolutions on the Subject of Art. 16 of the Covenant*, Doc. A.14. 1927.V., p. 42. *See* D.H. MILLER, THE DRAFTING OF THE COVENANT (1928) vol. 2 p. 53.

(3) A study on the legality of blockade and national legislation to put it quickly into effect everywhere;

(4) League representatives present in areas of possible conflict to head off conflagrations, - an idea to be widely endorsed more than sixty years later under the heading of "Preventive Diplomacy"[110]

The prescient Belgian statesman warned that the "ridiculous" interpretations of Article 16, which was the supreme safeguard of peoples most exposed to aggression, would weaken the whole League. Subsequent events proved that he was right.[111]

When Italy committed blatant aggression against another member of the League - Abyssinia - in 1936, it was a clear violation of the Covenant and should have triggered immediate economic sanctions. Fifty nations condemned the Italian aggression and hosts of League committees sprang into action: lists were prepared showing which commodities and resources were vital to Italy; national legislation for export licensing and controls were already in place in most countries and were copied by others; an embargo on petroleum, iron, steel and coal was readied to cripple Italy's tanks and war-making potential. It looked like economic sanctions, rigorously applied could quickly halt Italy's aggression and restore peace to an anxious world.[112]

But France and Britain, for their own political reasons - fearing war with Italy or an Italian alliance with Hitler's illegally rearmed Germany - refused to use the "oil weapon." They reneged on their legal obligations under the Covenant - just as they had failed to intervene when Japan invaded Manchuria in 1932, and just as they would tolerate further Japanese aggression in 1937 and German aggression in 1938. Their misguided policy of appeasement in place of law was an invitation to disaster. Economic sanctions, as envisaged in the Covenant, were ready to move into position to protect international law and order. But the planned embargoes were stopped before they were started; Italy's conquest was completed, the sanctions idea was dropped and the fate of the toothless League was sealed.

---

110 *See* S/PV.3046, 31 Jan. 1992; GA Doc. A/47/277, 17 June 1992; B.G. RAMCHARAN, THE INTERNATIONAL LAW AND PRACTICE OF EARLY-WARNING AND PREVENTIVE DIPLOMACY: The Emerging Global Watch (1991).

111 League of Nations, Doc. C.740.M.279. 1926. IX, C.P.D. 1(b), Mar. 1, 1927. The De Brouckére Report is *reproduced in* FERENCZ, ENFORCING INT. L. vol.I Doc. 24.

112 *See* LAUTERPACHT *op. cit.*; F.DEAK and P. JESSUP, A COLLECTION OF NEUTRALITY LAWS, REGULATIONS AND TREATIES OF VARIOUS COUNTRIES (1939); A.E. HIGHLY, THE FIRST SANCTIONS EXPERIMENT (1939).

In 1938, a group of members of the Royal Institute of International Affairs in London, reviewing the perilous situation, confirmed that the sanctions provisions were never applied as intended by the framers of the Covenant. Their sage conclusion:

> Every failure to enforce the law or to make it wholly effective weakens the strength of the law and helps to render it eventually futile.[113]

Failure to enforce the law of sanctions rendered Article 16 futile. The path was opened for the next World War and the death and destruction that it brought to at least 40 million people.[114]

3. Sanctions under the UN Charter

The mandatory sanctions provisions of the League of Nations had been deliberately misinterpreted, watered-down and disregarded by both Britain and France. When the new UN Charter was being considered, the British Foreign Office - clinging to the same line it had taken after the first World War - wanted to keep a free hand when it came to imposing sanctions.[115] As usual, there was a compromise. UN Charter Article 41 authorizes the Security Council to

> decide what measures not involving the use of armed force are to be used to give effect to its decisions... These *may* include complete *or partial* interruption of economic relations...means of communication, and the severance of diplomatic relations (emphasis added).

If the Council should decide that Art.41 measures were inadequate, it was authorized (if it chose to do so) to take military action to restore peace.[116] But, according to Article 43, Members would make military forces available in accordance with a special agreement - that was to be worked out in the future. No such agreement was ever reached.

---

113 *International Sanctions, a Report by a Group of Members of the Royal Institute of International Affairs* (1938) at 211.

114 *See* FERENCZ, ENFORCING INT.L. vol. 2 Chap. VIII and Documents 30-35 reproducing extracts of the minutes of League meetings.

115 Since sanctions would only be applied if aggression had occurred, the British opposed any specific definition of aggression, thus keeping both the recognition of aggression and the imposition of sanctions discretionary rather than mandatory. *See* HILDEBRAND pp. 137-139, FERENCZ, DEFINING INT. AGGRESSION, vol. 2.

116 UN Charter Article 42. Sanctions imposed by, or under the direction of, the Security Council - according to Charter Art. 25, 48 and 49, - require all states to comply. *See* J.F.ROSS, NEUTRALITY AND INTERNATIONAL SANCTIONS (1990).

In short, UN Charter provisions dealing with non-military coercion were variable and optional and backed by non-existent military might. UN sanctions provisions were even weaker than those specified in the Covenant of the League of Nations. It was a legal step backward.

The fact that the Charter language was vague would not necessarily have proved fatal since there was sufficient authorization for the Security Council to do whatever was required - *if* it was prepared to act. As long as Permanent Members were engaged in an ideological Cold-War, they were unable to agree and the sanctions plan remained immobilized.

UN Resolutions recommending the imposition of economic sanctions were given scant respect by states that were trading partners or allies of the target nation. Thus, between 1961 and 1974, Western Powers did not support recommended sanctions against Portugal for suppressing its former colonies in Africa; Portugal was a member of NATO. The United Nations passed dozens of resolutions condemning *apartheid* and calling for sanctions against the racist government of South Africa. Its major trading partners, like the U.S. and U.K., voiced their opposition to racial discrimination but continued to trade with South Africa - whose capacity to impose economic counter-sanctions remained considerable.

Economic sanctions were used as weapons of the Cold War. The United States denied "Most-Favored Nation" tariff treatment to states that rejected American political, human rights or social objectives. Communist China, Cuba, Vietnam, North Korea, East Germany and the U.S.S.R. were among those nations subjected to import and export prohibitions, higher tariffs, customs duties, blocking of assets, currency, credit and travel restrictions and other economic burdens - which the target state condemned as discriminatory, unjustified or illegal.[117] Nicaragua accused the United States of illegally blockading its ports and mining its harbors, a charge upheld by the International Court of Justice.[118]

Unilateral economic sanctions, often prompted by frustration and political pressure to "do *something*" can be a slow and feeble process.[119] In protest against U.S.S.R.'s invasion of Afghanistan in 1980, for example, the U.S. imposed a grain embargo and decided to boycott the Olympics sched-

---

117 *See* S.D. Metzger, *Federal Regulation and Prohibition of Trade with Iron-Curtain Countries*, 29 Law and Contem. Problems 1000 (1964).

118 *Nicaragua v. United States of America*, ICJ Order of 10 May 1984.

119 *See* N. CHANDHOKE, THE POLITICS OF U.N. SANCTIONS (1988).

uled for Moscow in 1981. The withdrawal from the games disappointed U.S. athletes and was no more than a symbol of American disapproval of Soviet aggression. The grain embargo simply deprived American farmers of exports - the Soviets purchased grain from other countries. A 1981 U.S. embargo on shipment of parts for a Soviet pipeline across Europe sparked protests from America's allies who were partners in the Soviet project. Both embargoes were soon halted.[120] According to Prof. Elisabeth Zoller, many U.S. counter-measures did not make much sense and were ill-conceived since they usually violated rights of innocent third parties.[121]

Economic assistance can be used as both a carrot and a stick; it can be either a threat or a reward. The Soviet Union used economic coercion in a futile attempt to keep Yugoslavia within the Soviet orbit.[122] Soviet influence reached into the American hemisphere by using economic aid to gain or maintain Cuban support for Soviet political objectives.[123] The Organization of American States applied economic sanctions against Cuba and the Dominican Republic in an attempt to influence their internal behavior.[124]

Probably the most impressive use of economic sanctions was the oil embargo imposed in 1973 by the Organization of Petroleum Exporting Countries (OPEC) for the purpose of coercing Israel. Arab boycotts - without UN endorsement - were enhanced by secondary boycotts against all foreign firms doing business with Israel. Ibrahim F.I. Shihata of Kuwait argued that the "Arab oil weapon" was "an instrument for the respect and promotion of the rule of law." It was, he argued, essential as long as there was no general ban on armaments and there was no effective collective security system to serve the interests of international justice.[125]

Despite their cries of protest, almost all industrial nations dependent on Arab oil promptly complied with most Arab demands. The victim states

---

120   *See* R. Paarlberg, *Lessons of the Grain Embargo*, Foreign Affairs, Fall, 1980 p. 144; G. Ball, *The Case Against Sanctions*, N.Y. Times Mag. Sept. 12, 1982.

121   E. ZOLLER, ENFORCING INTERNATIONAL LAW THROUGH U.S. LEGISLATION (1985) at 128. *See* L. Dubois, *L'Embargo Dans La Pratique Contemporaine*, XIII *Annuaire Francais de Droit International* (1976) p.99; G. Adler-Karlsson, *Western Economic Warfare 1947-1967*, Stockholm U. Studies (1968).

122   *See* R.B. FARRELL, JUGOSLAVIA AND THE SOVIET UNION 1948-1956 (1956).

123   R.S. Walters, *Soviet Economic Aid to Cuba*, 42 International Affairs (1966) p.74.

124   *See* L. Miller, *Regional Organization and the Regulation of Internal Conflict*, 19 World Politics (1967) p.582; A. Schreiber, *Economic Coercion as an Instrument of Foreign Policy*, 25 World Politics (1973) p. 387.

125   I. Shihata, *Destination Embargo of Arab Oil: Its Legality Under International Law*, 68 AJIL 591 (1974) at 626. For a contrary view see statement by Professor John Norton Moore of the University of Virginia, who argued that without Security Council authorization secondary boycotts were an illegal violation of world order; ASIL *Proceedings*, (1977) at 180.

responded by frantic measures to decrease their vulnerability. They formed their own protective associations, lowered their consumption of oil through conservation measures and explored alternative energy sources to defend themselves against the OPEC "oil weapon." It underscored the fact that if a vital resource could be controlled under near-monopoly conditions, it could be a very potent weapon to obtain compliance with the supplier's demands. It also demonstrated the need for universal rather than unilateral action to protect the rule of international law.[126]

In most cases of unilateral or multilateral sanctions, it turned out that sovereign states were unwilling, or financially unable, to impose severe restrictions on former trading partners. Some feared reprisals from a powerful neighbor. The effect of an embargo was sometimes counter-productive since competitors were available to pick up the business and target states found new suppliers or became more cohesive and self-reliant as a consequence of imposed economic restrictions. Hardships imposed on civilian populations generated antagonism toward those responsible for the boycott and sympathy for the victims.

In short, experience showed that embargoes, boycotts and trade restraints - even by a very rich and powerful nation or a combination of states - might be a symbolic expression of abhorrence or protest that might eventually have some influence on political behavior but usually it was little more than a nuisance that caused economic distress to some but not a very effective way to restore peace.[127]

Instead of being targeted to stop specific objectionable behavior, economic sanctions usually aimed at making life intolerable for citizens of a state whose policies or deeds were objectionable to the leaders of the country imposing the sanctions. Those who suffered most were not the decision-makers responsible for the wrongdoing but innocent residents of the target country - who may even have opposed the actions of their leaders. The result was as immoral as it was ineffective. A comprehensive study of sanctions led Dr. Margaret P. Doxey to conclude that:

> except in the hypothetical case of extreme vulnerability amounting to total economic dependence on the states imposing sanctions, or of universal economic ostracism, the coercive properties of economic sanctions are limited.[128]

---

126 *See* J.PAUST, A.BLAUSTEIN AND A. HIGGINS, THE ARAB OIL WEAPON (1977).
127 *See* V. GOWLAND-DEBBAS, COLLECTIVE RESPONSES TO ILLEGAL ACTS IN INTERNATIONAL LAW (1990).
128 M.P. DOXEY, ECONOMIC SANCTIONS AND INTERNATIONAL ENFORCEMENT (1980) at 131.

As long as the cold-war was in existence, there was no realistic possibility for the Security Council to use economic sanctions to halt an illegal threat to the peace by one of the superpowers or its allies.

When the Soviet Union invaded Afghanistan, for example, it was obvious in advance that a Soviet veto would block the Security Council from taking effective counter-measures. When, in 1979, Iran seized U.S. diplomats and held them as hostages in violation of many international legal obligations, the Iranian behavior was unanimously condemned by the Security Council.[129] The condemnation was ignored by Iran. The Security Council took no enforcement action. The U.S. succeeded in obtaining a unanimous decision from the International Court of Justice saying that the hostages had to be released immediately.[130] Iran ignored the Court's decree. The Security Council still took no enforcement action. The United States, joined by some of its allies, imposed a series of economic sanctions against Iran. There was no noticeable effect in achieving the desired goal.[131]

In considering what's right and what's wrong with economic sanctions we see that the UN Charter itself offered too little support to such a system. Problems of sharing the risks and burdens of economic boycotts and of making them universal were never properly addressed or clarified. The components necessary for an effective system have never been put in place. As long as the possibility of a veto blocked Security Council action, the non-violent enforcement provisions of Chapter VII (Art. 41) remained frozen and practically useless.

Sanctions cannot work in a vacuum. Economic pressures must be coupled with many other supporting measures to be effective. Sanctions that require vastly different degrees of sacrifice by those expected to impose them will never succeed. Sanctions that penalize only the innocent while allowing those responsible for the wrongdoing to evade personal accountability will invite resentment rather than surrender. Fanatics and tyrants are seldom deterred by hardships imposed on their followers.

The Arab oil boycott demonstrated that for sanctions to achieve their objective they must restrict a vital commodity and be comprehensive

---

129   SC Res. 457 (1979) Dec. 4, 1979.
130   ICJ *Case Concerning US Diplomatic and Consular Staff in Teheran*, Provisional Order of 15 Dec. 1979 and Judgment of 24 May 1980.
131   *See Legal Responses to the Afghan/Iranian Crises*, ASIL *Proceedings* (1980) pp. 248-274.

enough to have a serious impact on the economy of the target state. They must be continued long enough to achieve the goal. These lessons should not be lost on the UN which now has new possibilities for applying the "economic weapon" under the Charter.

4. A Change in the Wind

Ironically, the most dramatic change in UN enforcement of international law by non-forceful means occurred only after the "cold-war" had ended and a new "hot-war" began. When Iraq invaded Kuwait in 1990, the Security Council - spurred by the U.S. - sprang into immediate action. Within hours of the illegal attack, the Council unanimously demanded Iraq's withdrawal.[132] Four days later, asserting its authority under Chapter VII of the Charter, the Council imposed comprehensive economic sanctions against Iraq. All states were directed to prevent all imports from Iraq. All financial or economic resources to Iraq were to be cut off. All members were under a legal obligation to "join in affording mutual assistance in carrying out the measures decided upon by the Security Council" (Art. 49). A Committee of the Security Council was designated to monitor and report on compliance.[133]

Planes carrying cargo to or from Iraq were denied landing rights and Iraqi ships were denied entry to foreign ports.[134] Following a string of escalating demands for compliance - which Iraq ignored - the Council authorized Member states "to use all necessary means" to uphold the Security Council resolutions.[135] When Iraq failed to comply by the date set, a coalition of nations - led by the United States - combined their military forces and battered Iraqi troops out of Kuwait.

Since the Council was not in command of the conduct of the Gulf War, it wasn't exactly what the Charter prescribed. But the important change was that the Security Council had used its powers under Chapter VII to authorize collective measures - a combination of non-violent sanctions ultimately backed by armed might - to enforce international law and restore peace. And it worked! Whether non-violent means alone might eventually have achieved the same goal remains speculative.

---

132   SC Res. 660, 2 Aug. 1990.
133   SC Res. 661, 6 Aug. 1990; Certain exceptions were made for strictly humanitarian or medical purposes.
134   SC Res. 670, 25 Sept. 1990.
135   SC Res. 678, 29 Nov. 1990.

As additional sanctions - to maintain peace in the future - the Security Council set the terms for the cease-fire to end the conflict. Iraq would have to surrender its territorial claims, pay compensation for damages, restitute property illegally taken, have its sale of oil controlled and destroy its chemical and biological weapons as well as its nuclear capabilities. A number of UN bodies were created to supervise, carry out or monitor compliance by Iraq.[136]

There were several hostile incidents as Iraq sought to evade, obstruct or avoid its obligations under the terms of the cease-fire. But the Council remained adamant. A UN Special Commission was set up as a subsidiary organ of the Secureity Council to supervise the sanctions aimed at the destruction of Iraq's war machine.[137] Despite relatively minor glitches and imperfections, the firm application of authority under Chapter VII turned out to be effective in severely restricting Iraq's war-making capacity.[138]

The economic embargo, prohibiting Iraq's sale of its most valued resource - oil - remained in place as long as Iraq remained defiant. To be sure, it caused hardships to the Iraqi people, but its effectiveness in modifying the Government's behavior was not apparent. After all, the top government leaders presumably were little inconvenienced personally by the hardships of the population around them.

No system was in place to prevent the blockade from being breached by individuals or states that chose for political or financial reasons to ignore it. Despite the Council's authorization for states suffering severe economic hardship to request assistance under Art. 50,[139] some neighboring states considered it more prudent to avoid the hardship by non-compliance with the trade embargo. The Secretary General recommended that the Security Council

> devise a set of measures, involving the financial institutions and other components of the United Nations system, that can be put in place to insulate States from such difficulties.

The Security Council passed the buck back to the Secretary-General by asking him to study the matter further and report back to the Council.[140] A

---

136   SC Res.687, 3 April 1991. *See* SC Res. 689, 692, 699, 700, 705, 706, 707, 712, 715 (1991).

137   SC Res. 687 (1991) Section C, 3 April 1991.

138   SC Res. 778, 2 Oct. 1992. *See* SC Res. 833, 27 May 1993. Report of the Special Commission, the IAEA and Iraq, S/26571, 12 October 1993.

139   SC Res. 669, 24 Sept. 1990.

140   S/PV.3154, 30 Dec. 1992.

Compensation Committee was appointed, but as long as it was without funds to make payments, it was unable to cope with the problem. The system of compensation envisaged by Charter Art. 50 lacked an appropriate compensation mechanism.[141]

In 1992, the Security Council imposed a series of sanctions against Libya for its refusal to renounce terrorism and its failure adequately to cooperate in the requested investigation of two suspected Libyan terrorists. The Council, exercising its authority under Chapter VII of the UN Charter, prohibited states from shipping arms to Libya and required all states to deny landing rights to Libyan aircraft.[142] Libya defied the Security Council sanctions.

It should be obvious that a more comprehensive and effective system of sanctions must be devised if force is to be diminished or replaced as a means of altering illegal state behavior. The combination of new technological possibilities to monitor imports and exports and new political developments strengthening the United Nations encourages the hope that non-forceful sanctions may play a primary peace-keeping role in the future. The appointment of a UN Special Commission as an organ of the Security Council to monitor and enforce sanctions is an important change in the wind. The search for an appropriate new legal mechanism to equalize the burdens of sanctions indicates that further changes are pending.

It is our basic theme that world peace requires many changes: clearer laws prohibiting dangerous behavior; a compulsory settlement mechanism, a tribunal to determine violations and punish violators and a system for effective international law enforcement. To manage such a system there must be an executive agency that enjoys universal respect for its impartiality and efficiency. Arms control is vital. No nation can possess weapons that threaten the survival of its neighbors. Economic sanctions must be of such type and magnitude that transgressor are physically unable to continue illegal action. Moving in the right direction produces a synergistic or snowball effect. People will be energized by awareness that changes for the better are actually taking place.

As a last resort, there must be some international military capability to deal with lawbreakers who - despite non-violent pressures - persistently

---

141   *See* D. Binder, *"Sanctions Have a $12 Billion Ripple Effect Along the Danube"*, NY Times May 22, 1993, p. 4.
142   Security Council Res. 748, 31 March 1992.

refuse to abide by international rules of law. If a criminal is to be brought to justice, and further crimes deterred, there must be a sheriff able to overpower him. Should non-forcible measures prove inadequate, it may be necessary to employ international military land, sea and air forces to restore and maintain peace. Only when all components come together within a frame that also recognizes the need for global social justice, will the new structure for a more peaceful world have been built.

D- An International Military Force

There is something ironic about the need for force to maintain peace. Yet, it cannot be denied that in every society there will always be lawbreakers ready to take the law into their own hands - regardless of economic sanctions or other methods of non-forcible coercion. Something must be done to avert the hazards arising from the melancholy fact that those who are willing to use force will almost always prevail over those who are not willing or able to do so. International force is needed as the ultimate guardian of international peace.

Unilateral national military might risks being abused for self-serving national purposes. Self-help without international controls is more likely to jeopardize world security than enhance it. An international military force, under effective UN control, is the best safeguard for world tranquility - if those who are expected to serve as the world's policemen are given the weapons and means to do the job.

1. Early Origins

The idea of collective community action against those who transgressed against communal laws can be traced back to the holy wars of Greek Amphyctyonic Councils fourteen centuries before the birth of Christ.[143] In the time of Cicero, the Fetial College of Rome was the communal body authorized to determine when force might justifiably be employed against those who had breached the peace. In the twelfth century, the Catholic Church used excommunication as a form of sanction reinforced by military Crusades to subjugate those perceived as infidels and violators of the laws of God.

---

143   *See* E.CURTIUS, HISTORY OF GREECE, Transl. by Ward, vol. 1 (1900).

Following the devastating Thirty-Years War, a new political mechanism was invented in the hope that it would curb violence and maintain peace without international armies. The Treaty of Westphalia in 1648 relied on a balance of power to avoid conflict between previously warring sovereignties. It was an agreement designed to allow nation states of Europe to continue their prerogatives within their own borders undisturbed by the debilitating and costly malignancy of armed conflict. As an arrangement to discourage wars among competing sovereigns it was a primitive system appropriate for its time. But it gave no consideration to such emerging ideas as social justice or individual human rights and therefore carried the seeds of its own collapse.

Military alliances did not put an end to wars; they merely increased the number of combatants and the numbers killed. The ideas of the French and American Revolutions began to undermine the tyranny of sovereignty. The Constitution of the United States of America was an inspiring model showing how a regime of previously independent states could organize to preserve peace and protect fundamental human freedoms.

The 1815 Congress of Vienna, convened for the purpose of preventing wars, ended with nothing more impressive than rules for administering European waterways. These evolutionary developments were not responsive enough to changing social needs to be able to displace the traditional use of military might to preserve national interests. The Hague Conventions of 1898 and 1907 laid down rules for the conduct of hostilities - not for the elimination of war.

Professor C. Van Vollenhoven of Leyden, in his historical survey of the "Law of Peace," concluded that the wise counsels and rules that leaders lauded and reiterated for maintaining peace were not observed in practice. Nation states insisted on doing as they pleased in matters affecting their vital interests; exactly what those interests were remained vague and limitless. Peace treaties that lacked a system for enforcement or punishment of violators often proved to be useless and thus the perpetuation of war was inevitable.[144]

---

144 C.VAN VOLLENHOVEN, THE LAW OF PEACE (1936).

2. After World War I

The devastation of World War I inspired the greatest organizational effort that had ever been made to change the warlike habits of past centuries. There arose an overwhelming public demand for a new structure of international society to avert another tragedy like "The Great War." At the Peace Conference in Paris, led by U.S. President Woodrow Wilson, world leaders pondered the structures required for a peaceful world.

In addition to institutions and procedures to clarify international law and facilitate peaceful resolution of future conflicts, the enforcement problem was given great consideration. There was general agreement that the imposition of political and economic sanctions was an important tool to bring about compliance. The argument was also made that if such peaceful means proved ineffective it would be necessary to use military force. Several states presented plans which included ultimate enforcement of international law by armed might under international controls.[145]

The French proposed that military sanctions be carried out by international military contingents, supplied by member States, with sufficient strength to overcome any forces opposed to the League. The League could delegate the enforcement mandate to one or more members. Military operations would be conducted by a permanent international staff answerable to the League. Failure to abide by a decision of the League or its International Court would subject the offender to sanctions, including military force.

The French Commission that drew up the plan noted specifically that public opinion among civilized nations was unanimous in recognizing that the security of states required a system of justice and equity, peaceful resolution of conflicts and, if peaceful measures failed, enforcement by international military contingents. They made it clear that they were not proposing a super-State or even a Confederation, but a reciprocal undertaking by member nations

> to use its economic, naval and military power in conjunction
> with the other Members of the League against any nation con-
> travening the Covenant...

President Woodrow Wilson also envisaged enforcement by the "collective armed might of the entire League." If blockade and other economic

---

145 *See* D.H. MILLER, THE DRAFTING OF THE COVENANT (1928) vol. 2; P.S. WILD, SANCTIONS AND TREATY ENFORCEMENT (1943) pp. 142-143.

sanctions failed, the members of the League were to use "jointly any force that may be necessary."

That great statesman, Jan Christian Smuts, referring to the immeasurable sacrifices of the world war, said the "world is ripe for the greatest step forward ever made in the government of man." He noted the need for social reforms, international law, disarmament and peaceful settlements backed by economic and political coercion. But he warned that economic sanctions alone would

> not be enough if unsupported by military and naval action... The obligation to take these measures of force should be joint and several, so that while all the members are bound to act, one or more who are better prepared for action or in greater danger than the rest may proceed ahead of the others.[146]

The proposals for an international police force were, in effect, rejected. The needed new institution to enforce peace by international military means was never created. Never.

The Covenant of the League, as adopted, reflected the political need for compromise. Instead of a system guaranteed to maintain peace, what was finally accepted was an elaborate mechanism allowing states to continue their old violent ways without outside disruption. The Council could "recommend" what military forces the Members would contribute to the League's armed forces to enforce the Covenant (Art. 16 paragraph 2), but a *recommendation* was not a legally binding *obligation*. Enforcement by Member states thus became an option rather than a duty - an option they chose not to exercise.

History soon proved that the enforcement provisions of the Covenant were too weak to prevent World War II. When the chips were down - in Manchuria, Ethiopia and elsewhere - those who held the reins of power were not willing to do what was required to uphold the rule of law and peace. The innocent public - as always - paid the price for the failure of their leaders.

3. After World War II

Despite the horrible tragedies and losses of World War II, the United Nations Charter did *not* create a new political or legal system that would

---

146 Extracts of various proposals are *Reproduced in* FERENCZ, ENFORCING INT. L., vol.1, Doc. 21.

prevent future wars. Despite the contrary public impression deliberately created - once again - leaders of powerful nations knowingly accepted an instrument that contained clear flaws instead of clear laws.

In a memorandum sent by the Secretary of State to President Roosevelt on December 29, 1943, (a year-and-a-half before the Charter was signed at San Francisco) it was proposed that if sanctions and other peaceful enforcement measures proved ineffective to restore peace, armed force should be used. But who was to provide such forces and how would they be deployed or activated? These were vital questions to which there were no ready answers.

Prof. Hildebrand has described the diplomatic discussions and manoeuvres that took place toward the end of 1944 among the Anglo-Americans and the Soviets as part of the Dumbarton Oaks "conversations." There seemed to be a general feeling among Allied political leaders that the League had failed, and World War II had been made possible, because there was no international military force in existence to prevent aggression. Views were exchanged about the nature of the new force that would be needed: the size of national military quotas, ad hoc or permanent, air contingents only or combined air, sea and ground forces. The deliberations were influenced by national pride, parochialism among different military services and practical questions of uniforms, deployment, equipment, language and command responsibilities. Strongly held views of reasonable men not only differed, but kept changing.[147]

In order to gain Congressional approval, the proposed treaty setting up the new international organization of states would require ratification by each country "in accordance with its constitutional processes" - which meant that two-thirds of the U.S. Senate would have to agree to its terms.[148] The likelihood that two-thirds of the Senate would consent to any agreement that might require U.S. "boys" to go back into battle on demand of a new international organization was remote indeed. The State Department view that was finally adopted was to postpone any definite proposal for an international military force. To avoid coming to grips with the most important issue, the decision was reached that it could be settled *after* the new international organization was created. And so a key ingredient was left out. It has not yet been found.

---

147 R.C.HILDEBRAND, DUMBARTON OAKS (1990) pp. 139-158.
148 FOREIGN RELATIONS OF THE UNITED STATES, Diplomatic Papers (1944) vol. 1; *Extracted in* FERENCZ, ENFORCING INT. L. vol. 2 Doc. 36.

The ideological war that existed between the Soviet Union and the United States, practically from the end of World War II in 1945 until the reversal of Soviet policies beginning around 1987, meant that neither universal disarmament nor an international military force could become a reality.

Article 42 of the Charter authorized the Security Council to "take such action by air, sea or land forces as may be necessary to restore international peace and security." It referred to "operations by air, sea, or land forces of Members of the United Nations." The Members undertook to make armed forces "available to the Security Council, on its call" (Art. 43). Members were obliged to "hold immediately available national air-force contingents for combined international enforcement action" (Art. 45). But the special agreements governing such details as the number and types of forces and their general location, were never reached, even though the Council was mandated to negotiate and conclude them "as soon as possible" (Art.43). The Charter mandate for a UN military force - prescribed in Articles 42 through 50 - "to maintain or restore international peace and security" have remained moribund and unimplemented since they were accepted in principle by all UN members. Is it any wonder that there has been so little peace in the world?

Both superpower rivals supported overt and covert warfare in Asia, Africa, Latin America and the Middle East during all that time - and the UN was helpless to prevent it. The Security Council, facing a possible veto by one or the other, was unable to discharge its peace enforcement responsibilities. General Assembly and Security Council resolutions calling for peace or imposing economic sanctions did not prevent or halt the conflicts that raged in Vietnam, the Middle East, Latin America, the Persian Gulf, the Falklands, and elsewhere. The inability of the UN to implement the Charter provisions for an international military force to repel aggression left a vacuum in the peace enforcement plan. It became necessary to invent new devices, or discover new interpretations, in an effort to attain the Charter objectives.

4. UN Fills an Enforcement Vacuum

In 1950, when the communist People's Democratic Republic of North Korea invaded the non-communist Republic of Korea in the South, the Security Council convened to consider the alleged aggression. As luck would have it, the U.S.S.R. had walked out of the Council in protest against the Council's refusal to seat the communist government of mainland China. With the Soviets absent, the Council passed a U.S. draft resolution determining that North Korea had committed "a breach of the peace" and calling upon all Members "to render every assistance" to the UN in forcing the North Korean communists to withdraw.[149]

In order to carry out its mandate, the Security Council adopted a loose interpretation of the Charter. Under a literal reading, the Charter made enforcement dependent upon "the concurring votes of the permanent members" (Art.27 (3)). The Soviets were absent and certainly did not join in a concurring vote. The Council ruled that absence was equivalent to concurrence! Two days later, the Council recommended that "Members furnish such assistance to the Republic of (South) Korea "as may be necessary to repel the armed attack and to restore international peace and security in the area." [150]

Based upon the imaginative Security Council authorization, an international military force, flying the UN flag alongside the flag of national units, was created. This Unified UN Command, led predominantly by air, naval and ground forces of the United States, engaged the North Koreans, and the Chinese who later joined them, in large-scale military combat.

The General Assembly, taking advantage of Soviet absence from the Council, asserted its authority to make peace enforcement recommendations on the theory that the Council was unable to discharge its primary responsibility. It overrode Soviet bloc protests and recommended an economic embargo and sanctions against the aggressors, North Korea and China.[151]

The main point to note here is that the United Nations found a way - not envisaged by the Charter yet consistent with its objectives - to create an international military force which, after heavy casualties on all sides, managed to repel aggression and bring the fighting to a halt.

Another UN military force was deployed in the Congo in 1960. The Security Council authorized Secretary-General Dag Hammarskjold to use "the requisite measure of force" if necessary to expel foreign military per-

---

149 Res.S/1501, 25 June 1950.

150 SC Res. S/1511, 27 June 1950. The Security Council report to the G.A., GAOR Fifth Sess; Supp. No. 2 (A/1361) is *reproduced in* FERENCZ, ENFORCING INT. L. vol.2 Doc. 51(a).

151 *See* R.LECKIE, CONFLICT: THE HISTORY OF THE KOREAN WAR, 1950-1953 (1962); R. HIGGINS, UNITED NATIONS PEACEKEEPING, DOCUMENTS AND COMMENTARY (1981), vol. II, Part Three; L.M. GOODRICH, KOREA, A STUDY OF US POLICY IN THE UN (1956); Many of the UN Resolutions are cited in FERENCZ, ENFORCING INT. L. vol. 2 at 451-453.

sonnel who were supporting a rebel secessionist movement in the province of Katanga. The UN Forces, supporting and acting with the consent of the lawful government, used international military muscle to return fire, repel the mercenaries and restore peace.[152]

On the basis of the Congo experience, the Secretary General concluded:

> the only way to interject an international armed force into a situation of that kind is to ensure that it is for clearly defined and restricted purposes, is fully under control of the Organization and always maintains its primary posture of arms for defence.[153]

The continuation of hostilities all over the world made it imperative for the UN to invent new ways, not foreseen by the Charter, to bring to bear more than the prestige and moral suasion of the Organization in its search for peace. If the peaceful methods of conflict resolution prescribed by Charter Chapter VI did not succeed and the enforcement measures authorized by Chapter VII could not be used by a hamstrung Security Council, something in-between (sometimes referred to as an invisible and unwritten "Chapter Six and a Half") had to be created lest the United Nations be seen as merely a toothless debating society or an overblown and helpless bureaucracy.

The term *"peace-keeping"* does not appear in the UN Charter. Yet it has come to describe a host of UN activities very closely related to maintaining peace. Peace-keeping operations are carried out by UN military personnel, volunteers from member states, sent into conflict areas but without enforcement powers and only small-arms for self defence.

Originally these "Blue Helmets" were merely observers sent in under authorization of the Security Council, or occasionally by the General Assembly, directed by the Secretary-General and always with the consent of the parties to the conflict. Later they assumed other functions such as supervising a cease-fire, patrolling an agreed-upon buffer zone, or monitoring an election. Since they could always be sent packing by the host state, they could hardly be expected to enforce peace upon a nation bent on war. Yet,

---

152 *See* R. HIGGINS, U.N. PEACEKEEPING, 1946-1967, VOL. III (1970).

153 *Report of the Secretary-General concerning the implementation of Security Council resolutions S/4387 of 14 July 1960, S/4741 of 21 Feb. 1961 and S/5002 of 24 Nov. 1961, Doc. S/5240 4 Feb.reproduced in* FERENCZ, ENFORCING INT. L. vol. II Doc. 52 (b).

they helped to fill a vacuum in the Charter. They could defuse tensions and also serve as a prototype for expanded military operations should the political climate change to allow the original Charter enforcement plan to be carried out. Despite the constraints under which they had to operate, UN Peacekeepers were so innovative that they received widespread accalim.[154]

After the cold war ended, the Security Council finally began to discharge its peace-enforcement obligations in a more responsible way than had previously proved possible. The Gulf War was the first example of how that could be done. As soon as Iraq invaded Kuwait, on August 2, 1990, the Security Council was convened. Within an hour, it unanimously demanded that Iraq withdraw immediately.[155] When Iraq refused, the Council passed a dozen resolutions in rapid succession, imposing economic sanctions and warning Iraq's leader Saddam Hussein that he would be held to account for aggression and atrocities. On November 29, 1990 the Council (Res. 660) authorized member states to use "all necessary means" to uphold the U.N. resolutions and restore peace to the area.

Faced with persistent Iraqi defiance, a coalition of nations from thirty countries (including the U.K., France, Canada, Italy, Egypt, Syria and the United Arab Emirates) blasted the Iraqi forces out of Kuwait following about 100 hours of devastating precision bombing led by the United States. A triumphant President Bush reported to the nation that the victory for Kuwait and the coalition partners was also

> a victory for the United Nations, for all mankind, for the rule of law and for what is right.[156]

In October, 1991, following UN diplomatic prodding, factions that had been at war for decades in Cambodia signed a Comprehensive Political Settlement. It invited the Security Council to establish a transitional authority in Cambodia and to supervise free election and help create conditions for a lasting peace. The UN Transitional Authority in Cambodia (UNTAC) was the largest peace-keeping operation ever undertaken by the UN.[157]

---

154 G.D. Moffett III, "Peacekeepers Win Peace Prize," *Christian Science Monitor*, Sept. 30, 1988; *See* THE BLUE HELMETS, A REVIEW OF UNITED NATIONS PEACE-KEEPING (UN Annual). Comprehensive descriptions of UN peacekeeping can be found in R. HIGGINS, U.N. PEACEKEEPING, 1946-1967, 4 VOLS. (1970); B. URQUHART, A LIFE IN PEACE AND WAR (1987); I. RIKHYE, THE THEORY AND PRACTICE OF PEACEKEEPING (1984).

155 S.C. Res.660 (1990).

156 *War in the Gulf: The White House*, N.Y. Times, Feb. 28, 1991, at A20. M. WEILER, Ed., IRAQ AND KUWAIT: THE HOSTILITIES AND THEIR AFTERMATH (1993).

157 *See* Report of the Secretary-General on Cambodia, 19 Feb. 1992; SC Res. 783 (1992) 13 Oct. 1992.

With over 20,000 military and civilian members, UNTAC was charged with a wide array of responsibilities, ranging from purely military action (including the collection of weapons) to the supervision of elections, repatriation of refugees, civil administration, rehabilitation and protection of human rights. All of these responsibilities were imposed on the Secretary-General, assisted by a Special Representative and Head of Mission aided by a military Force Commander and the troops provided by a wide array of nations.

In many other areas, such as Lebanon, Cyprus, Angola, El Salvador, former Yugoslavia, Somalia and Mozambique, international military forces under the control and direction of the UN were beginning to fill a vacuum and playing an increasingly diversified and important role in the search for world peace. In the four years following the end of the cold war, the UN fielded more peacekeeping operations than during the first forty years of its existence. It was not exactly in the form prescribed by the Charter but it was an important step into the future.[158]

5. The Future

It was never foreseen or intended by the Charter that the Security Council could "save succeeding generations from the scourge of war" by simply handing a blank check to some UN members to go after the law-breaker without any UN controls to limit the combat and protect the innocent. The combined air, naval and ground forces of the many nations engaged in Persian Gulf war operations were not accountable to the Security Council - or to the Secretary-General or the General Assembly - but only to their own Unified Command led by an American General. That was never envisioned by the UN Charter or its members when they joined the club.

Despite the success in repelling aggression by driving Iraqi troops from Kuwait, and despite the fact that there was general UN authorization for military action by coalition partners, many thousands of innocent civilians were killed and many more died as a result of disease caused by damage to Iraq's water supplies and infrastructure. Whether the assaults exceeded the permissible limits of military necessity or proportionality will be debated, but - in the absence of an impartial tribunal - will never be legally resolved. Whether economic sanctions alone might eventually have accomplished the same result without the same deadly toll will never be known. International

---

158   *See* UN DPI Publication, United Nations Peace-keeping, (Aug. 1993).

military force was the only quick way to repel illegal aggression and annexation. The United Nations simply was not ready and did not have the tools in 1990 to do the job in a more humane or peaceful way.

Applications of unilateral or multilateral military force uncontrolled by the impartial guidance of the world body runs the risk of being abused for the political or self-serving purposes of powerful states rather than for the enforcement of international law. The UN was able to adopt a pragmatic approach to cope with a problem that could not otherwise be resolved. To avoid dangerous interventions in the future, new institutions or structures under international controls are necessary - imaginative improvisation is not good enough to cope with life and death on a regular basis.

At the end of January 1992, for the first time in its history, a special Summit Meeting of the Security Council, brought together the Heads of State from 13 member countries, as well as 2 Foreign Ministers, to consider the responsibility of the Council in the maintenance of international peace and security. Its Concluding Statement recognized that times had changed. They agreed:

> the world now has the best chance of achieving international peace and security since the foundation of the United Nations.[159]

The Council heads did not propose major Charter revisions or specific steps to be taken. Instead, they asked the Secretary-General to make recommendations.

In his impressive *Agenda for Peace*, Boutros Boutros-Ghali concluded:

> The United Nations was created with a great and courageous vision. Now is the time, for its nations and peoples, and the men and women who serve it, to seize the moment for the sake of the future.[160]

E- Social Justice

The final component in our projected view of what is what is right and what is wrong with international law enforcement is, in many respects, the most contentious. Laws are usually obeyed and treaties are usually honored. But unless those who are expected to accept and comply with new interna-

---

159 Press Release SC/5361, 31 Jan. 1992 at 4; S/PV.3046, 31 Jan. 1992 at 146-147.
160 B. Boutros-Ghali, *An Agenda for Peace*, UN Doc. A/47/277, S-24111, 17 June 1992.

tional rules understand clearly what is expected of them and are convinced that the requirements are fair and not merely designed to perpetuate an unjust status quo, compliance will be absent and enforcement will be difficult if not impossible.

In our modern society of instantaneous world-wide communications, a new framework of international and human relations is slowly being built. Set-backs are to be expected. Despair is never an acceptable substitute for hope. The future of human rights and social justice as a matter of law can be viewed optimistically if one considers the progress that has been made in a relatively short period of time.[161]

Despite significant advances made in recent years, we can not shut our eyes to the tragedies and perils that still surround us. In the world in which we live, many are affluent and overfed, yet millions of children die each year of starvation and malnutrition. Billions of people lack clean drinking water and go to bed hungry every night. Tens of millions of persons abandon their homelands in a desperate search for food to keep themselves and their families alive. We need not recite the detailed list of sufferings of the dispossessed, the sick, illiterate, homeless, helpless and hopeless human beings who inhabit this planet in degradation, fear and misery.[162]

Remember: revolting conditions inspire revolt; social justice and peace go hand in hand. If massive discontent - which ignites conflict - is to be diminished, the earth's resources must not be squandered on weapons of destruction and superfluous consumption but must be shared in a just way to improve the human condition. There can be no peace without justice and no justice without peace.

If we review the historical record we can see that much progress has been made in recent times. Yet much more remains to be done before social injustice is removed as a threat to peace. How can we fashion a rule of international law and create the legal institutions required to eliminate or ameliorate some of the miseries and discontents that inevitably give rise to violence among peoples and nations?

---

161   B.B. Ferencz, *The Future of Human Rights in International Jurisprudence*, 10 Hofstra L. Rev. 379 (1982); R. Bernhardt, *Schutz der Menschenrechte durch internationale Organe*, Lecture at University of Salzberg, 6 July 1990.

162   *See Report of the World Food Council*, GAOR, 47th Sess. Supp. No. 19 (A/47/19) 1992; *See* World Health Organization Report, *Nutrition and Development - a Global Assessment* (1992); L.R. BROWN et al., STATE OF THE WORLD, an annual publication of the Worldwatch Institute, (1984 - 1993).

1. The Search for Human Dignity

It was only after World War I that Western nations became officially concerned about human dignity and the welfare of people in other parts of the world. "Human dignity" has never been precisely defined but, as Professor David Forsythe of the University of Nebraska has noted:

> It accords roughly with justice or the good society...Concern for human rights is intertwined with concern for state security, economic health, and a sound environment. Human rights has arrived as one of the major subjects of world affairs.[163]

The focus on human rights is part of an evolving process of respect for the dignity of every human being.

The Constitution of the International Labor Organization, which was established in 1919, stated that universal peace could be established only if it was based on social justice. Improved working conditions at the national level required international cooperation. The ILO sought to eliminate degrading employment practices by securing fair and humane conditions of labor for men, women and children everywhere. Its studies and recommendations led to very many conventions that became legal obligations of signatory states. It provided impartial supervision of agreements voluntarily arrived at for the mutual benefit of all parties concerned.[164]

Art. 23 of the Covenant of the League referred to "just treatment of the native inhabitants of territories," preventing "traffic in women and children and... dangerous drugs," and "the prevention and control of disease." Red Cross Organizations were to help improve health and mitigate suffering throughout the world (Art. 25). Unfortunately, these goals were not binding rules but merely "endeavors" to be encouraged. They were not legal obligations and there was no international institution charged with overall responsibility for such programs.

After World War II, in a significant step forward, the UN Charter Preamble expressed the determination of the new organization not merely to maintain justice and respect for international law, but also

---

163 D.P. FORSYTHE, THE INTERNATIONALIZATION OF HUMAN RIGHTS (1991) at 1, 191. See D.V.JONES, CODE OF PEACE, ETHICS AND SECURITY IN THE WORLD OF THE WARLORD STATES (1992).

164 See A.ALCOCK, HISTORY OF THE INTERNATIONAL LABOUR ORGANIZATION (1971); W, GALENSON, THE INTERNATIONAL LABOUR ORGANIZATION: AN AMERICAN VIEW (1981).

> to promote social progress and better standards of life in larger
> freedom... and to employ international machinery for the pro-
> motion of the economic and social advancement of all peoples.

For the first time, the promotion of human rights, fundamental freedoms
for all and the collective solution of social and economic problems became
a principle goal of international society. A special agency, the Economic and
Social Council (ECOSOC) was created to *recommend* (but not enforce)
needed economic, cultural, educational, health and other social improvements.[165]

Individuals everywhere had new expectations and new demands.
People still continued to cherish parochial identifications and values but
there was a growing awareness of interdependence with larger and expanding groups, gradually extending to the whole of humankind. Recall
the conclusion reached by Professor Myres McDougal and his colleagues at
Yale: "No people can be fully secure unless all peoples are secure." [166]

Among the many inalienable and inviolable human rights proclaimed
by the 1949 Universal Declaration of Human Rights were the right to:

"[L]ife, liberty and security" (Art.3);

"Asylum from persecution" (Art.14);

"A standard of living adequate for the health and well-being... including food, clothing, housing and medical care" (Art.25);

"[T]he right to education" (Art. 26).

Furthermore, it declared:

> Everyone is entitled to a social and international order in which
> the rights and freedoms set forth in this Declaration can be fully
> realized. (Art. 28).

Being "entitled" implies that it will be made available. Many nations incorporated human rights into their national constitutions or legislation. An
international system providing social justice was promised - but it was only
a declaration with no means of enforcement beyond its own moral authority.

---

165 UN Charter, Chap.IX, X.
166 M.S. MCDOUGAL, H.D.LASSWELL AND L.CHEN, HUMAN RIGHTS AND WORLD
     PUBLIC ORDER (1980) at 49, 139.

By 1966 it was possible to draw up human rights Covenants in the form of treaties legally binding those states that elected to ratify them. Both the International Covenant on Civil and Political Rights and the Covenant on Economic, Social and Cultural Rights spoke of "the inherent dignity of the human person" and recognized that "the inalienable rights of all members of the human family is the foundation of freedom, justice and peace in the world" (Preambles). The inevitable and indivisible link between social justice and peace was again recognized.

One should not minimize the significant progress that is being made to move toward enhanced social justice for all. As we have pointed out, human rights *are* being protected to an ever-increasing degree through international legal action.[167] International concern for human betterment continues to grow and regional institutions created to protect such rights are gaining in respect and influence. The individual citizen is no longer at the unrestrained mercy of his government. As Professor Louis Henkin of Columbia has concluded, we have entered "the age of rights" where "every man and woman between birth and death counts, and has a claim to an irreducible core of integrity and dignity."[168] There has been an awakening of the international social conscience.

Many courageous journalists and non-governmental organizations keep a sharp vigil around the globe. News of human rights abuses is flashed across radios and television screens almost as soon they occur. The United Nations has its own worldwide network to disseminate human rights information. Diplomatic protests and the threat of sanctions amplify the voices assembled to protect the victims. No nation likes to appear as a villain or abuser of its own citizens. The power of shame, if conveyed by a united international community, can be, and often is, a powerful force for change.

The World Health Organization labors mightily to reduce health hazards and improve health conditions around the world - particularly in underdeveloped areas. Another specialized agency of the UN, the Food and Agriculture Organization, has, through its scientific research, helped to increase food production and raised the level of nutrition in many areas of poverty. Other UN agencies work to alleviate the plight of disadvantaged women, children, handicapped persons, prisoners, refugees and persons seeking asylum. The UN High Commissioner for Refugees seeks to ease the

---

167 Chapter Two, Section C-2, C-3.
168 L. HENKIN, THE AGE OF RIGHTS (1990) at 193.

plight of more than 18 million desperate refugees. In almost all areas where human suffering exists, the UN is trying - often under very difficult circumstances - to provide or organize humanitarian relief and create more favorable social conditions.[169]

Underdeveloped nations are not simply allowed to rot in their poverty - as they did in the not-too-distant past. In the vital area of economic aid, many new organizations have been created to enhance the well being of nations and peoples. The United Nations Conference on Trade and Development (UNCTAD), established in 1964, coordinates global economic policies to improve the industrial capacity of developing countries. The General Agreement on Tariffs and Trade (GATT) seeks to guarantee fair trade. The International Monetary Fund (IMF), the International Bank for Reconstruction and Development (IBRD), the UN Development Programs, the UN Industrial Development Organization, and the UN Commission on International Trade Law (UNCITRAL) are some of the leading multi-national agencies trying to alleviate economic disparities in an equitable way.

On the other hand, many states did *not* adopt national laws to protect human rights while some of those that did accept such obligations in legal theory ignored them in actual practice. The international community, restrained by a perceived duty not to interfere in the internal affairs of sovereign states, could do precious little to enforce obligations on states that chose to ignore them.

It was not merely a matter of greed - the rich refusing to share with the poor. Differences of culture, disparate social interests and entrenched perceptions inhibited acceptance of changes that would offer minimal living conditions for all members of the human family. Slavery and racial discrimination continued - despite the fact that they violated the UN Charter and internationally accepted human rights norms. It was reliably reported in 1970, for example, that slavery, debt bondage, the sale of children and marriage practices akin to slavery still existed in seventeen African countries, fifteen Asian countries and six Latin American countries.[170]

---

169 *See Report of the Economic and Social Council*, GA Doc. A/47/3, 21 Sept. 1992. According to Mrs. Sadako Ogata, UN High Commissioner for Refugees, there were almost 20 million refugees by the end of 1993 and an additional 24 million people had been forced into exile within their own countries. See P. Lewis, Stoked by Ethnic Conflict, Refugee Numbers Swell, N.Y. Times, Nov. 10, 1993 p. A6. See H. HANNUM, ed., DOCUMENTS ON AUTONOMY AND MINORITY RIGHTS (1993); L.B. SOHN & T. BUERGENTHAL Eds., THE MOVEMENT OF PERSONS ACROSS BORDERS (1993).

170 *Questions of Slavery and the Slave Trade*, UN Doc. E/CN.4/Sub.2/312 (1970). J. Brooke, *Slavery on Rise in Brazil, as Debt Chains Workers*, N.Y.Times report, International Section, May 23, 1993.

Comprehensive global economic laws and institutions, as some may have hoped for as part of a New International Economic Order, have not yet materialized. As we have noted, the draft of a Charter of Economic Rights and Duties of States contained provisions too abrasive and demanding to find broad acceptance by states expected to make sacrifices.[171]

Nations, through countless voluntary treaties and trade agreements, continue to balance the economic concerns of their own constituents against the recognized need to cooperate with others on a regional or global basis in the common interest. Trade confrontations, with the help of such new institutions as the Court of the European Communities, are normally settled by peaceful means. The peaceful regional precedents help create patterns which may offer useful lessons for coping with problems of economic and social cooperation on a global level. [172]

The time may be at hand when it is prudent to create new agencies to clarify legal obligations, resolve disputes and coordinate the many institutions now engaged in protecting basic human rights and interests. We shall examine such options when we deal with new law, courts and structures for peace enforcement.[173]

Models already in existence provide useful guides to the types of legal instruments and institutions required for a more equitable distribution of economic resources to benefit everyone. To discover what should be done on earth, it may be necessary to look back at ancient principles and look forward to see what is planned for the moon and the stars and the terrain beneath the seas as we reach for planetary solutions to our common global problems.

2. Our Common Heritage

Going back to ancient times, certain public areas were known as *res communis* - they were part of "the commons" or "common patrimony" which belonged to the community as a whole and were not the private property of any individual or nation. The concept that certain portions of this planet are "global commons" and therefore the "common heritage of mankind" has appeared in different contemporary contexts and has made remarkable

---

171 Chapter One, Section C-5. See M. BEDJAOUI, Ed., INTERNATIONAL LAW, ACHIEVEMENTS AND PROSPECTS (UNESCO 1991).

172 See Chapter Five.

173 Chapters Seven and Eight.

progress since it was first championed at the United Nations by Ambassador Arvid Pardo of Malta many years ago.[174]

In 1963, the United Nations unanimously adopted the Declaration of Legal Principles Governing the Activities of States in the Exploration and Use of Outer Space.[175]Through the efforts of a special UN Committee, a draft treaty was concluded in 1967 which provided:

> The exploration and use of outer space, including the moon and other celestial bodies, shall be carried out for the benefit and in the interests of all countries, irrespective of their degree of economic or scientific development, and shall be the province of all mankind (Art.1).[176]

By 1979, it was possible to draft a supplementary agreement defining and developing the accepted principles. In addition to assuring peaceful uses of the distant terrains, the Agreement stipulated:

> The moon and its natural resources are the common heritage of mankind...not subject to national appropriation... Neither the surface nor the subsurface...shall become property of any State...or of any natural person.

Perhaps even more important - the parties undertook to establish a new international legal regime to govern the exploitation and rational management of the resources of the moon. The regime would arrange for an equitable sharing of the benefits, taking into account the interests and needs of developing countries as well as those that had contributed to the moon's exploration (Art. 11).[177]

Professor Carl Q. Christol, a noted legal authority from the University of Southern California, hailed the new legal regime for outer space (which also included agreements to rescue astronauts, exchange information and assess liability for damages) as a "magnificent achievement." The Moon Treaty called for equitable sharing while also allowing risk-takers to benefit from their initiatives. According to Professor Christol,
"all of mankind will be the ultimate beneficiaries." [178]

---

174 *See* A.PARDO, THE COMMON HERITAGE (1975).

175 GA Res. 1962 (XVIII) 13 Dec. 1963.

176 The 1967 *"Principles Treaty"* is based on GA Res. 2222 (XXI), 25 Jan. 1967; UST 2410; 610 UNTS 205, TIAS 6347; By 1982 the treaty was in force for 80 states.

177 The 1979 *"Moon Treaty"* was adopted by consensus of the General Assembly, UN Doc. A/RES/34/68, 14 Dec. 1979, 18 ILM 1434 (1979).

178 C.Q. CHRISTOL, THE MODERN INTERNATIONAL LAW OF OUTER SPACE (1982) at xi, 328.

Looking into his crystal ball in 1991, Professor Christol saw a revitalization of international law mandated by the increasing interdependence of all nations and of peoples as humankind advances into the space age to share its common heritage and destiny.[179]

The principles for the rational and fair management of outer-space, the territory of the moon and other celestial bodies may serve as a useful model for parts of planet earth. The use of outer-space for vital telecommunications and placing satellites in geostationary orbit will be of increasing importance in the years to come. Nations which lack the funds or knowledge to exploit extra-terrestrial regions of our planet are still disadvantaged but there is an evolutionary process which now recognizes the common obligation to use such common resources for the common good.[180]

The Antarctic Treaty of 1980 gave assurance that Antarctica would be used only for peaceful purposes "in the interest of all mankind" (Preamble). Establishing an operational regime for the rational use of the vast natural resources that lie on and beneath the enormous areas of Antarctic ice is a matter for the future.[181] In an impressive study of the social, political and legal process already taking place in Antarctica, Emilio J. Sahurie shows how the values of human dignity are being furthered in a cooperative and peaceful way. He sees the emerging Antarctic order as a blueprint and a precedent of major importance:

> In the near future, human survival will depend on the coordi-
> nation of human activities on a global basis - roughly like the
> interaction achieved for a quarter of a century in Antarctica.[182]

In 1970, the General Assembly declared that resources located in the area of the sea-bed and the ocean floor, "are the common heritage of mankind."[183] The Law of the Sea Convention repeated the common heritage

---

179 C.Q. CHRISTOL, SPACE LAW, Past, Present and Future (1991).

180 A.D.ROTH, *LA PROHIBITION DE L'APPROPRIATION ET LES REGIMES D'ACCESS AUX ESPACES EXTRA-TERRESTRES* (1992).

181 F.M. AUBURN, ANTARCTIC LAW AND POLITICS (1982); K. SUTER, ANTARCTICA, Private Property or Public Heritage? (1991); *See* S.K.N. Blay, *New Trends in the Protection of the Antarctic Environment: The 1991 Madrid Protocol*, 86 AJIL (1992) 377; W.E. WESTERMEYER, THE POLITICS OF MINERAL RESOURCE DEVELOPMENT IN ANTARCTICA: Alternative Regimes for the Future (1984). R. WOLFRUM, THE CONVENTION ON THE REGULATION OF ANTARCTIC MINERAL   RESOURCE ACTIVITIES (1991).

182 E.J. SAHURIE, THE INTERNATIONAL LAW OF ANTARCTICA (1992) at 575. *See* M.N. ANDEM, INTERNATIONAL LEGAL PROBLEMS IN THE PEACEFUL EXPLORATION OF OUTER SPACE (1992).

183 UNGA Res. 2749 (XXV) 14 Dec. 1970.

commitment (Preamble and Art. 136). It was made explicit that all rights to such resources were "vested in mankind as a whole (Art. 137)... for the benefit of mankind as a whole ... and taking into particular consideration the interests and needs of developing States and of peoples..."(Art.140). The common heritage principle was paramount and could not be amended (Art. 311). The 119 delegates who signed the Convention were demonstrating their determination to achieve a "just and equitable economic order" governing ocean space.[184]

The Law of the Sea will go into effect only after it has been ratified by sixty nations; that number has not yet been reached. Several industrial nations, led by the United States, are still holding out for more favorable terms regarding sea-bed mining rights. The stated objections are largely ideological: opposition to bureaucratic interference with free enterprise. Markus G. Schmidt's careful study based on official records and interviews with the participants led him to conclude that "the mining industry lobby and conservative forces" are largely responsible for the impasse.[185] Many private citizens, companies and governments regard short-term gain for themselves as more important than long-range hopes for humanity based on a strengthened system of global cooperation. It is a sobering reminder that national political support is a vital pre-condition for the advancement of international law.

The law of the sea is a model still being formed. Like the emerging regime in Antarctica, it can be a blueprint and an inspiration. Its principles and practices can guide nations toward a rational use of the earth's plenty. The international legal body created to manage the common heritage that lies in the oceans is the Sea-Bed Authority - a forerunner in the expanding role of new international organizations. Parties to the Convention are *ipso facto* members of the Authority and its Assembly. A smaller Council will exercise authority over sea-bed mining, aided by specialized commissions and its own commercial arm, the Enterprise.

A revolutionary change in thinking about ownership of certain vital resources is occurring. A new regime to manage sea resources which are acknowledged to belong only to the community of humankind has been created. A way is being found to balance competing equities by giving special incentives to those whose private initiative produces increased

---

184 See *U.N. Convention on Law of the Sea* (UN Publ. 1983) Introduction.

185 M.G. SCHMIDT, COMMON HERITAGE OR COMMON BURDEN? (1989) at 310-311. As of March 31, 1993, the Law of the Sea Convention had received 55 of the required 60 ratifications. UN Doc. A/48/100, 15 June 1993.

benefits for all. National interests are taking international needs into account just as international interests must also take national needs into account. As Soviet leader Gorbachev pointed out:

> The necessity of effective, fair, international procedures and mechanisms which would ensure rational utilization of our planet's resources as the property of all mankind becomes ever more pressing.[186]

3. Our Common Environment

The tiny speck hurtling through the vast cosmos of space - which its human inhabitants call the Earth - is the only home we all know and share. Around its central core of iron is a crust of stone covered by a thin layer of soil which offers nutrients to plants and animals alike. A watery blanket of seas, rivers and lakes makes up the hydrosphere upon which other living creatures and all life depends. Everything is enveloped in a gaseous atmosphere without which all would perish. The entire living world - the biosphere - moves in an unfathomed rhythm of time that is known as evolution. Only in recent years has humankind discovered that it is completely dependent upon the ecology of its planetary home. It is only beginning to learn that this is a common environment that must be rationally shared for human survival.

One can not speak of social justice and the common entitlement to vast unexplored or unclaimed resources of water, food and minerals of the earth without considering the most important common heritage of all - the air we breathe. All nations and all living things are affected by climate change, deforestation, ozone depletion and other planetary changes which can not be altered by the actions of one nation alone - no matter how powerful. The earth will fall silent if humans fail to ration and preserve the ecological foundations on which all life depends.[187]

The first international conference to consider problems of the human environment took place in Stockholm in 1972.[188]Nations were alerted to the worldwide need for laws to measure and assess the environmental impact of various pollution-generating activities. A UN Environmental Program (UNEP) was created, with headquarters in Nairobi, Kenya, and several international agreements (dealing with such topics as atmospheric and

---

186 M.GORBACHEV, PERESTROIKA (1987) at 137.

187 See R.L. CARSON, SILENT SPRING (1962).

188 Report of the UN Conference on the Human Environment, 5-16 June 1972 (UN Publ.)

marine pollution, endangered species, conservation and waste disposal) went into effect. A World Charter for Nature was adopted by the General Assembly in 1982. It contained a number of general principles urging states and individuals to respect nature and the environment.[189] It should be recalled that war itself and the preparation for war is a major polluter of the environment.[190]

In 1983, The U.N. created The World Commission on Environment and Development headed by Norway's former Prime Minister Gro Harlan Brundtland.[191] The "*Brundtland Commission*" report of 1987 focused on the environment and stressed the need to relate available resources to the health, food, energy, housing and other physical needs of an exploding world population. It called for more rational management of the global commons upon which all of humanity was dependent. It outlined a program for "sustainable development" - economic progress that meets current needs without compromising the ability of future generations to meet its needs as well.

Success of the Brundtland Commission plan required a political system with effective citizen participation, an economic system capable of generating surpluses on a sustained basis, a social system to reconcile tensions, a production system (backed by trade and finance) that does not destroy its own ecological base.[192] Seventeen heads of state, meeting in the Hague in 1989, proposed (and more than 30 nations eventually agreed) that the solution to global environmental problems required a strengthened UN institution capable of taking decisions - "even if, on occasion, unanimous agreement has not been achieved." Said Gro Harlem Brundtland: "The principles we endorsed were radical, but any approach which is less ambitious would not serve us."[193]

Professor Edith Brown Weiss, of Georgetown University, pointed out that what we do with nuclear waste and planetary resources in one part of

---

189 UN General Assembly Res. 37/7, 28 Oct. 1982.

190 *See* articles by P. Szasz, M. Bothe, and A.W. Dahl in XV No. 2 *Disarmament* (1992).

191 GA Res/38/161 (1983); Brundtland had been a member of the Independent Commission on Disarmament and Security Issues ("Palme Commission") whose central conclusion was that, in the nuclear age, security *means* common security. COMMON SECURITY, A BLUEPRINT FOR SURVIVAL (1982).

192 OUR COMMON FUTURE (1987) at 65.

193 "*Hague Declaration*" from conference held Mar. 10-11,1989 and Brundtland speech at National Academy of Sciences, Washington DC. May 2, 1989, cited in H.F.French, Worldwatch paper 107, *After the Earth Summit: The Future of Environmental Governance* (1992) at 35; also Brundtland speech at the University of Cambridge, England on 14 Feb. 1991.

the world will affect natural and cultural systems elsewhere and impact the welfare of future generations. She argued that we need to change the way we think about the global commons, and must develop a planetary ethos which recognizes that we are trustees who "share the planet with all communities throughout time."[194]

There have been notable accomplishments in international environmental governance over a fairly short period of time. But there are many remaining challenges.[195] When he addressed the Security Council Summit Meeting of Heads of State in 1992, Mr. Rao of India deplored the fact that

> the world's natural resources - land, water and air, which are really humanity's common heritage are getting fast depleted by thoughtless acts of overexploitation and environmental degradation.[196]

Jyrki Kakonen, of the Tampere Peace Research Institute of Finland, wrote:

> Environmental problems have taken the place of nuclear weapons as a source of anxiety. People have begun to understand that environmental problems can also totally destroy human civilization.[197]

Mustafa K. Tolba, Executive Director of the United Nations Environmental Program pointed out that environmental problems are not restricted to national boundaries. What happens to the environment - atmospheric pollution, ozone depletion, climate change, marine and fresh water pollution, land degradation - has a global impact on development activities, human well being and world peace and security. He called for a "global partnership" to translate the good intentions and high-sounding declarations into action.[198]

Twenty years after the pioneer Stockholm Conference on Environment, the UN convened the Conference on Environment and Development (UNCED) - an "Earth Summit" where Heads of State were invited to assess world environmental problems and seek common solutions in the common

---

194 E.B.WEISS, FAIRNESS TO FUTURE GENERATIONS: INTERNATIONAL LAW, COMMON PATRIMONY AND INTERGENERATIONAL EQUITY (1989) at 291.

195 *See* E.B. WEISS, D.B.MAGRAW, P.C.SZASZ, INTERNATIONAL ENVIRONMENTAL LAW: Basic Instruments and References (1992).

196 S/PV. 3046, 31 Jan. 1992 at 96-97.

197 J. KAKONEN, Ed., PERSPECTIVES ON ENVIRONMENTAL CONFLICT AND INTERNATIONAL RELATIONS (1992) at 1.

198 MOSTAFA K. TOLBA, SAVING OUR PLANET, Challenges and Hopes (1992) Preface.

interest. A basic theme throughout the conference, that took place in Rio de Janeiro, was the need to build an environmentally clean planetary system which would allow sustainable development with priority given to the health, housing, food and other vital needs of poor countries. Recognizing that: "the struggle against poverty is the shared responsibility of all countries," a comprehensive "Agenda 21" set forth detailed plans for enabling the poor to achieve sustainable livelihoods in the twenty-first century.[199]

One hundred fifty- three governments signed a convention on climate change which recognized the climatic threat posed by gas emissions generated to largest extent by developed countries. They also signed a convention to conserve the biological diversity of the planet by protecting its flora and fauna. These conventions were less than what some of the planners such as its able Secretary-General Maurice Strong, had hoped for, but he saw it as a step forward in a time of transition. He put his finger on the problem:

> The carrying capacity of our Earth can only sustain present and future generations if it is matched by the *caring* capacity of its people and its leaders.[200]

Shridath Ramphal, former Prime Minister of Guyana and a leading champion of a more humane world, referred to "the enlightened global community of people" as he praised the new awareness of humanity's crisis that emerged from Rio.[201]

Another tangible result of the 10-day meeting was the *Rio Declaration on Environment and Development*. It sought to build upon the Stockholm initiative of 1972 by listing 27 principles on which there was general agreement:

> States had a responsibility to insure that activities within their control did not cause damage to the environment of other states (Principle 2);

> Eradicating poverty was an indispensible requirement for sustainable development (Principle 5);

---

199 A/CONF. 151/26 (Vol.I) 12 Aug. 1992, at 31; N. ROBINSON, Ed., AGENDA 21 AND THE UNCED PROCEEDINGS, 3 vols. (1992).

200 Address at the closing session of the Earth Summit. *See* World Goodwill *Newsletter* No. 4 (1992).

201 *See* I.S. RAMPHAL, OUR COUNTRY, THE PLANET: Forging a Partnership for Survival (1992).

Special priority had to be given to the least developed countries (Principle 6);

There had to be a "global partnership" to protect the earth's ecosystem (Principle 7);

"Peace, development and environmental protection are interdependent and indivisible." (Principle 25).

The World Bank embarked on a major effort to incorporate environmental concerns into all aspects of its work. Its strategy is to implement the provisions of Agenda 21 by supporting environmental projects, particularly those related to clean water, sanitation and energy efficiency.[202]

The main point here is not to what extent the ambitious goals have ben achieved or how soon they can be implemented. Everyone has now become aware that the biosphere affects us all and that it can only be managed on a global - and not a national - basis. The important fact is that the scope of environmental problems was not generally recognized even a few decades ago and now plans for global management finally *exist* and are receiving very broad public and international support. 29,000 participants and some 450,000 visitors came to Rio from about 171 countries to show their active support for environmental reform. That is the type of force which every political leader must reckon with in the days ahead - people power.[203]

How to cope with international environmental disputes, that will certainly arise, presents another organizational problem. If such disputes can not be resolved through the ordinary methods of peaceful settlement, adjudication may be necessary. But the World Court has serious drawbacks: only states may be official parties, it may lack technical competence - even with the help of assessors or small Chambers - and states are not eager to risk its unpredictable outcomes or to engage in its long, drawn out, and relatively expensive procedures.[204] The creation of new legal institutions competent to enforce binding environmental obligations is the necessary final act of implementation.[205]

---

202 *See* The World Bank, *The World Bank and the Environment* (1992). A series of annual reports (since 1987) records progress in helping developing nations cope with poverty reduction, population growth and environmental management on a global basis.

203 *See* '92 Global Forum journal, *Network*, No. 18, July 1992. The subject of people power will be further explored in Chapter Nine.

204 *See* J.SCHNEIDER, WORLD PUBLIC ORDER OF THE ENVIRONMENT: TOWARDS AN INTERNATIONAL ECOLOGICAL LAW AND ORGANIZATION (1979) pp. 187-192.

205 *See* ENVIRONMENTAL PROTECTION AND SUSTAINABLE DEVELOPMENT, Legal Principles and Recommendations, Adopted by the Experts Group on Environmental Law of the World Commission on Environment and Development, R.D. Munro, Chair (1986).

The General Assembly is already moving in the direction of creating a new environmental agency to scrutinize and report on the environmental record of all nations. A new 53-member group, including industrialized nations and others from all geographic regions, will form the Sustainable Development Commission to monitor how nations carry out Agenda 21. It is an embryo which, in its maturity, can help guide (but not compel) developing nations to build industries without endangering the environment. [206]

To be sure, the draining effect of debt and interest repayments from poor to rich nations, the continuing growth of world populations, and the hesitancy of some states to accept the burdens of sharing, will slow progress. But public awareness and demand for the elimination of prevailing social injustices has increased to such an extent that forward movement is inevitable. The declaration of accepted principles is a first step; to be followed by later acceptance of binding obligations. As we weigh what's right and what's wrong, there is reason for optimism that Agenda 21 and common environmental concerns have finally been placed high on the human agenda for the 21st century and appropriate enforcement mechanisms will soon be created.

The failure of the U.S. Government to sign some of the environmental protection accords accepted by most of the rest of the world at Rio in the summer of 1992 resulted in a storm of public protest. The Bush administration was voted out of office to be replaced by the Clinton-Gore team dedicated to U.S. leadership in preserving our environmental heritage. A few weeks before his election as Vice-President of the United States, Al Gore wrote:

> Understanding that the world does not belong to any one nation, and sharing a spirit of utmost urgency, we dedicate ourselves to undertake bold action to cherish and protect the environment of our planetary home.[207]

F - Evaluation

As we review what is right and what is wrong with the current system of international law enforcement, what emerges is a picture of a gradual awakening and slow progress toward a new order of international coopera-

---

206 GA Res. 47/191, 22 Dec. 1992; *See* article by Paul Lewis, *U.N.Implementing the Earth Summit*, NY Times Dec. 1, 1992 p. A16.

207 A. GORE, EARTH IN THE BALANCE: ECOLOGY AND THE HUMAN SPIRIT (1993) p. xx.

tion that holds greater promise than ever before. The blueprint for sound global structures can be seen - that is the first step toward building the new peaceful planet for the human family.

The historical record that we have briefly sketched shows that humankind, in its search for world peace, is - of necessity - experiencing a gradual evolutionary movement toward a new universal legal and social order. No doubt, different value systems will lead to different solutions to different problems.[208] But we all share a common planet and its rational management is essential for the common benefit of all. It is beyond dispute that in almost all important matters - global management, disarmament, sanctions, peacekeeping, economic development and environment - nations are dependent on each other and must work together for their mutual advantage.

Political leaders of the past were unable or unwilling to accept changes that were necessary. The need for new laws and new structures to enforce peace was frequently recognized but only during the past few years have significant advances become politically feasible. Recent events show that change is not only possible but is inevitable.

With more imagination, determination and education, it should be possible to reduce the size of existing UN bureaucracies and still cope with global problems in a more effective and peaceful way. A functional - rather than a political - approach may be the key. In this increasingly vulnerable world, we must turn away from destructive and dangerous rivalry and disorder to find more efficient techniques and more effective structures for maintaining peace. There are a few problems of such importance to world security that they demand highly expert handling to avert catastrophe.

No one in his right mind would resort to today's devastating warfare if important disputes could be resolved in any other way. The choices for peaceful resolution of conflict are so many and varied that it is almost inconceivable that sane people would not find at least one of them preferable to the use of massive force. Yet it must be anticipated that the legal prohibitions against the use of armed might will be ignored by some well-armed or terroristic fanatics who are not prepared to be bound by the rules and who refuse to recognize the enormous perils of the nuclear age.

---

208 See R.D. MCKINLAY AND R. LITTLE, GLOBAL PROBLEMS AND WORLD ORDER (1987).

The danger has been recognized by all responsible world leaders. Nuclear weapons are actually being destroyed under effective international controls. Other weapons of mass destruction are also being curbed or eliminated. The arms race which exhausted the resources of the superpowers seems to be waning. Plans for complete and comprehensive disarmament have been on the drawing board for decades. Now it may be possible to generate the political will to gradually put such plans into effect - if the other necessary preconditions can also be put in place. The problem is important enough to justify an early commitment to a new world peace program and the establishment of a special enforcement agency to bring about world disarmament.

Economic sanctions can be a potent weapon for peace but only if used in an effective way. The objective must always be to halt illegal activity by making its continuation physically impossible. Sanctions cannot be used as a weapon to injure the innocent in the hope that the guilty will repent or be replaced. The burdens caused by imposing sanctions must be equitably shared and supported by the world community which benefits from its peaceful coercive power. Legal systems to make sanctions effective have been outlined but never tried or tested. Where determination and patience are lacking, economic sanctions can not achieve their goal. A "UN Sanctions Agency" could be created to do the job with greater efficiency and impact.

As a last resort, enforcement by police action may be required. The UN Charter envisaged the use of international military forces but nations have never honored those Charter obligations. Necessity for intervention has been the mother of invention. New ways have been devised for the UN to help restore peace in various regions. UN peacekeeping is an expanding occupation and the Security Council is gradually moving closer to carrying out its mandate as prescribed in the Charter. As disarmament becomes a reality, and the need for arms for self-defence diminishes, there should be a greater willingness to rely on new international institutions and mechanisms to enforce international law for the benefit of all.

In his "Agenda for Peace," Secretary-General Boutros Boutros-Ghali called upon states to bring

> into being, through negotiations, the special agreements foreseen in Article 43 of the Charter, whereby Member States undertake to make armed forces, assistance and facilities available to the Security Council on a permanent basis.[209]

What he looked forward to was a new system - as outlined in the UN Charter and never tried - whereby states would provide units to be on call by the

Security Council. These peace-enforcement units could, as authorized by the Charter (Art.40), be sent into action as provisional measures to prevent the aggravation of dangerous situations. A "UN Police Force" could cope with enforcement problems. Its time is approaching.[210]

The emergence of human rights as a necessary goal and norm of international society is a fairly recent but compelling phenomenon. Improved enforcement of certain political, economic and social rights through new institutions and monitoring agencies are major achievements of the past few decades. Existing regional human rights agencies may serve as a model or inspiration for an expanded global structure to protect human dignity everywhere. But some fundamental human rights, such as the right to food, shelter, health and education, are universal rights deserving greater implementation. A new UN Social Justice Agency might incorporate the protection of the environment as a fundamental human right of humankind.[211]

There is still very much that needs to be done to replace international war by international law. The fact that "new thinking" is emerging can be a source of encouragement and inspiration. Professor W.E. Butler of London put it well:

> Underpinning these reformulations is the conviction that mankind shares a common fate and confronts common threats; that the hostilities of old, the risks of nuclear accident, the certainties of irreparable environmental harm, the horrors of war, whether local or otherwise, bear too high a price for the former pattern of inter-state relations to continue.[212]

The time has come for the UN to rely less on diplomats whose primary concern is their own national interest and to give greater authority to impartial experts for guidance in resolving those few world problems that threaten us all. It is also time for the voice of the people to be heard. The general public, relying on policymakers, never fully understood what was required of them to make the world system work. The advent of instantaneous global television stimulated rising expectations everywhere - followed by increasing demands for improved conditions. More than ever before, people now clamor for basic security and human dignity. As a

---

209   B. Boutros-Ghali, *An Agenda for Peace*, UN Publ. (1992) at 25.

210   *See* B. Boutros-Ghali, *Empowering the United Nations*, 71 Foreign Affairs 89 (Winter 1992-1993).

211   See Chapter Eight, Section A-5, Section B-3 and Section C-4.

212   W.E. BUTLER, PERESTROIKA AND INTERNATIONAL LAW (1990) at 4.

consequence, new institutions are slowly being created to meet new needs and new demands that proclaimed human rights be enforced.

We return again to our theme that everything is linked and interdependent. There can be no effective social engineering on vital issues without effective global management. Global security requires international control of national weapons that threaten global peace. Without universal disarmament, militarily powerful states can commit aggression, defy economic or penal sanctions and defeat an inadequate UN military force. Even universal arms controls and effective economic and military sanctions will not maintain peace if conditions of vast social inequality continue to mar the human landscape. Strong legal institutions may prove more powerful than strong armies in maintaining peace and security but only if they create a coherent organizational structure for peace.

When an improved UN is properly reorganized and all the new component structures are in place, the time will finally have arrived for relative world peace to become a reality. Caring and sharing is the best way to avoid grabbing and stabbing but that requires a change of heart as well as mind. How this can be done is the subject of our next chapters.

PART II

GLOBAL MANAGEMENT RECONSIDERED

The most fateful challenge to lawyers and scholars in our time may, accordingly, be seen to embrace the dual tasks of inventing the structures of authority and sanctioning procedures designed most economically to move the peoples of the world from our immediate, precarious balance of terror toward minimum security and a more complete world public order of human dignity, and after investigating controlling conditions, of recommending the measures in communication and other action most effectively calculated to affect the predisposition of leaders and peoples to accept these structures and procedures and to put them into practice.

Professors Myres S. McDougal and
Florentine P. Feliciano

Professor McDougal, whose name has long been associated with a renowned school of thinking at the Yale Law School, has posed a crucial challenge to international lawyers and all citizens concerned with a peaceful world order of human dignity. Can we invent the new structures of authority and new sanctioning procedures that will move us from our precarious balance of terror and can we make them acceptable to leaders and peoples so that they are put into practice? We believe it can be done and that it must be done. But not without changing our ways of thinking about a few entrenched conceptions and altering our present system of global management.

CHAPTER FOUR
NEW THINKING ABOUT OLD PROBLEMS

Today we are on the threshold of a new world system, but it will take a courageous leap on the part of world leaders to seize the opportunity offered. It is a leap which sooner or later must be taken.

Blaine Sloan, Professor Emeritus of Pace Law School, former Director of the UN's General Legal Division.[1]

In considering what's right and wrong with the present world legal order, we noted legal and structural shortcomings as well as evolutionary developments and significant advances being made in recent years. Now we shall propose new international *laws* for peace to eliminate ambiguities and thereby strengthen legal principles appearing in the Charter. We shall also propose changes to strengthen the *judicial* arm of the world community. In dealing with the problems of *enforcement*, we must reconsider the United Nations as a management organization and the possibility of making modifications likely to lead to desired objectives in the foreseeable future. But first let us review where we stand before we go on to consider new ways of thinking about some very old and vital questions.

A - Where Do We Stand?

The overburdened and underfinanced United Nations, now nearing fifty years of age, is desperately in need of revitalization and reorganization. Economic and political antagonisms combined with religious and ethnic diversities still find expression in armed conflicts. The search for consensus has hobbled the World Organization. Too much talk among too many people has too often become a substitute for effective action to maintain peace.

Our fundamental premise has been that every orderly society, including world society, depends for its tranquility upon clear *laws*, efficient *courts* and effective *enforcement* of the agreed norms. We have focused on those three essential elements of the international legal order - without which there can be no world peace. Our attention has hovered around the

---

1   B.SLOAN, UN GENERAL ASSEMBLY RESOLUTIONS IN OUR CHANGING WORLD (1991) at 143.

United Nations because it's the only world organization we've got and there is no other functioning global model available anywhere.

We began with a brief survey of the international *laws* of peace - the general legal agreements renouncing war, widely accepted international declarations concerning peace and some of the main codifications which, if violated, threaten the security of humankind. The historical record shows an evolutionary process in which international law develops to meet changing societal needs. But its progress is slow and lags behind social requirements. The tug of traditional thinking and practices produces norms with such a level of abstraction that ambiguous new legal rules are unable to play their proper role in maintaining peace.

Our scan of international *courts* shows a similar pattern. Various methods for settling disputes by peaceful means have been expanded and refined over the years. There is an increasing willingness to settle commercial differences with the help of third-parties, but, in matters perceived as affecting vital interests, states often prefer to rely on war rather than law.

The International Court of Justice is severely handicapped by the absence of compulsory jurisdiction that would require states to bring their dangerous disputes to the Court. But new ways are gradually being invented to expand the Court's utility. Chambers, with judges approved by litigants, are being used to encourage acceptance of the Court's authority. Poor nations are offered UN financial aid to encourage them to turn to the Court rather than combat to resolve differences. The emergence of specialized regional courts to deal with commercial and human rights violations and the proposed Law of the Sea Tribunal stimulates the hope that the international judicial arm will gradually be strengthened and that, in a more rational world, disputes of all kinds will be settled only by peaceful means.

The absence of any international criminal jurisdiction, to bring to justice those individuals responsible for violating international law, remains a major gap in the world legal order. As long as decisionmakers know that there is no personal price to pay for flagrant violations of the laws of peace, they are less likely to respect or be deterred by toothless legal prohibitions.

Effective *enforcement* of international law poses difficult problems of legal organization and management among sovereign states. The United Nations, charged with responsibility for maintaining international peace and security in conformity with justice and law, is the only agency of global scope that is competent to deal with world peace issues. But the structure of both the General Assembly and the Security Council, and some of its procedures - as well as ideological conflicts and social diversity - have made it difficult for the UN to function efficiently or to carry out some of its most vital purposes.

The Security Council has clearly failed to discharge its primary Charter obligation to maintain international peace and security (Art.24) or even to formulate plans for the regulation of armaments (Art.26). The consequence has been that - despite Charter prohibitions against the use of force - there have been countless wars of varying intensity all over the globe and there was precious little that anyone could do to prevent them. The world remains a tinderbox ready to explode.

Without effective disarmament, the peril of human annihilation hangs like a sword of Damocles over humankind. The cost of the arms race among fearful or hostile nations drains resources needed to sustain the burgeoning human population. Countless General Assembly resolutions calling for universal disarmament under effective international controls remain paper recommendations that have never been implemented. Until all nations are disarmed to a point that they cannot threaten their neighbors, there is no way to prevent or repel aggression by militarily powerful states. National sovereignty is the ancient shield still used to justify unlimited arms proliferation and to immunize those most responsible for aggression and crimes against humanity.

Non-military sanctions, to be able to curb unlawful state behavior, must be directed in a coordinated and equitable way; that has never been given a fair chance. Should economic and other sanctions fail, military force - as a last resort - will be needed to halt persistent lawbreakers. Self-help in the form of military intervention is a dangerous game - too subject to abuse for selfish national purposes. We see the beginnings of military force authorized by the Security Council, but sovereign states remain reluctant to accept or pay for a new UN policeman of the world.

Planet earth must be appreciated as one entity, shared by human beings who are all equally entitled to live in peace and dignity in a wholesome social, cultural and physical environment. Even though these aspirations are not yet defined with exact precision, the craving for minimum living standards has been growing everywhere. Much progress is being made, but a great deal more must still be done. Peace and order can not be bought for nothing.

If the improved effectiveness of the Security Council is to be more than a sporadic interlude prompted by parochial political or economic considerations, or stimulated by temporary public outrage at shocking inhumanities, it will be necessary to build a new structural firmament to assure that improvised "rescue missions" become solid institutional policies for general application in the future. New supervisory or coordinating organs are desperately needed to cope with the exploding hazards of the contemporary world.

We come thus to the crucial question: How can we bring about the necessary changes in international *law, courts* and *enforcement* to move us closer to our stated goal of a world of peace and dignity for all? All countries have a common interest in peace - that was the main reason they joined hands in the United Nations. Despite sporadic nationalism and intolerance that erupts in violence and hatred, the fundamental movement of nations is unmistakenly in the direction of democratic freedom and international cooperation for the simple and persuasive reason that it serves the common good. The public must become convinced that war is no longer a viable means of settling disputes and it is in their personal self-interest and to the common advantage of all nations and peoples to live by the rule of law.

The certainties of yesterday and today are not adequate to meet the needs of tomorrow. Closer examination will disclose that many principles generally considered to be immutably self-evident, or firmly established international law, actually contradict other principles which stand on equally firm foundations. Such stultifying paradoxes paralyze the power of law. Political leaders often seize interpretations which best serve their own political purposes - even if they are distorted and detrimental to the general human interest.

Albert Einstein warned that we must adopt a new way of thinking if we are to avoid the drift toward endless catastrophe. In a message to members of the bar, he wrote:

> The release of atomic energy has created a new world in which old ways of thinking, that includes old diplomatic conventions and balance-of-power politics, have become utterly meaning-less. Mankind must give up war in the atomic era. What is at stake is the life or death of humanity. [2]

Professor Richard B. Bilder called for "creative lawyering... constitutional engineering of the most innovative sort" to develop more specialized international organizations, structures and procedures to manage the emerging global problems.[3]

---

2   O.NATHAN & H.NORDEN, Eds., EINSTEIN ON PEACE (1960) at 407.
3   R.B. Bilder, *International Law in the "New World order": Some Preliminary Reflections*, Jour. of Transn'l Law and Policy 1 (1992) at 9, 15.

Even with new thinking, we must always bear in mind that, realistically, there are short-term and long-term goals. Some objectives are within reach now. Others may require several years. Still others, whether we like it or not, may take decades or more. International law is an evolutionary process that is still emerging and constantly developing. Some solutions may be less than perfect; others will cause turmoil and suffering. There is no instant evolution and no painless revolution.

Despite such hazards and shortcomings, the goal of a more peaceful and humane world *can* be reached. Only if optimistic faith is sustained can humankind muster the energy and imagination needed to overcome the reversals that are, from time to time, inevitable. The best we can do is to try, under difficult circumstances, to reach desired objectives as quickly as possible. We must strive to make inevitable what now appears impossible. Our collective fate depends upon our courage and ability to make matters better by challenging what seems unchallengeable and changing what seems unchangeable.

B - The Meaning of Sovereignty

The current international legal order was designed to regulate relations among independent and sovereign nation states. One of the reasons it is so difficult to enforce a system of world-wide law and social justice is that many independent nations, although they respect most international rules as a matter of habit or necessity, are prepared - as a sovereign right - to deviate from the norms in order to protect their own perceived vital interests.

(1) Traditional View:

The very word "sovereign" suggests that the power of the state is absolute and supreme and not subject to any higher authority. The traditional notion that the state or monarch is above the law is neither accurate nor useful. In fact, it is as misleading as it is detrimental.[4] Professor Paul Guggenheim of Geneva, writing over forty years ago, saw "the dogma of sovereignty" as the principle instrument of nationalism and imperialism that was blocking the evolution of international law and the development of an inter-state system adequate to the needs of the times.[5]

---

4   *See* C.SCHLOMING, POWER AND PRINCIPLE IN INTERNATIONAL AFFAIRS (1991);
      W. LEVI, CONTEMPORARY INTERNATIONAL LAW (1991).

5   P. GUGGENHEIM, *L'ORGANISATION DE LA SOCIETÉ INTERNATIONALE* (1949) at
      168.

Even in ancient times, the ruling "sovereign" was bound to behave justly in peace and in war. It was in the year 1215 that King John of England, confronted by his Lords and Bishops on the fields of Runnymede, pledged that the English Church would be free and that men in his kingdom would be guaranteed certain rights and liberties. His *Magna Carta* became a historical symbol showing that even the King was not above the law.[6]

It has taken a very long time to move away from the feudal and medieval notion that, by Divine Right, the Sovereign rules supreme and those who inhabit his realm are his subjects and they are duty bound to serve him loyally and obey his every command. With the increase of trade and travel, the traditional notion of sovereignty was gradually eroded. Nations recognized the need to accept binding treaties to govern their relations. To end the Thirty-Year War, the Treaties of Westphalia (1644-1648) created a European regime of secular national states that obliged sovereigns to respect territorial boundaries.

Sovereign states generally do not consider themselves bound by any rules other than those they have chosen to accept by custom, treaty or other binding legal obligation. Fledgling new nations argue that they should not be bound by old international standards and duties that were formulated without their participation or consent.[7]

(2) *Changing Conceptions:*

With the rise of democracy - stimulated by abuses of the Crown - the conception of sovereignty was crystallized. It was asserted that the sovereign is really the servant of the people and it is his duty to serve *them*. The U.S.Declaration of Independence of July 4, 1776 proclaimed as self-evident that all men are endowed with unalienable rights, and Governments are instituted to secure those rights, "deriving their just powers from the consent of the governed." The great German philosopher, Immanuel Kant, wrote that permanent peace required the sovereign state to be subordinate to international *laws* that would guarantee human freedom for everyone (*menschlichen Freiheit nach Gesetzen*).[8]

---

6   F. THOMPSON, MAGNA CARTA (1948).
7   *See* F.SNYDER AND S. SATHIRATHAI Eds., THIRD WORLD ATTITUDES TOWARD INTERNATIONAL LAW (1987).
8   I. KANT, *ZUM EWIGEN FRIEDEN*, (1795), Valentiner Edition, Stuttgart,(1953) at 5; *See* F.R. Teson, *Kantian Theory of International Law*, 92 Columbia L. Rev. 53 (1992).

The League of Nations recognized that independent states had to accept certain international controls if they wanted to maintain peace, but what they recognized in principle they failed to carry out in practice. In 1932, Albert Einstein wrote to his friend Siegmund Freud:

> The quest of international security involves the unconditional surrender by every nation, in a certain measure, of its liberty of action - its sovereignty that is to say - and it is clear beyond all doubt that no other road can lead to such security.[9]

But states remained unwilling to cede their prerogatives. Although nations seemed ready to accept certain mutually beneficial rules for the conduct of warfare, even such regulations were undercut in the name of state sovereignty.[10]

After World War II, it was universally acknowledged that fundamental human rights of every individual deserved protection everywhere. The Universal Declaration of Human Rights proclaims: "The will of the people (expressed by universal suffrage and secret vote) shall be the basis of the authority of government" (Art.21). The war-weary world was reconfirming the conception that sovereignty resides in every human being.

C. Wilfred Jenks, after surveying a number of legal systems and international decisions concluded that the sovereignty of the State consists of its competence as defined and limited by international law, the treaties it has signed and customary international law . Sovereignty is not a discretionary power which overrides the law." [11] Jenks called for the rule of law within nations while allowing certain sovereign obligations to be taken over by a global organization that could guarantee human rights and civil liberties on an international basis. His thesis of "sovereignty within the law" was shared by other outstanding legal scholars from different regions, religions and cultures.[12]

---

9   O.NATHAN & H.NORDEN, EINSTEIN ON PEACE (1960) at 189; *See also* H. NEWCOMB, HOPES AND FEARS (1992) at 106-7.

10   The concept that sovereign states can disregard binding norms of international behavior in times of *emergency* appears in the rules of warfare and in many human rights instruments. It was a price exacted by sovereign states for acceptance of the accords. It has often been abused. See K. RADKE, *DER STAATSNOTSTAND IM MODERNEN FRIEDENVöLKERRECHT (1988)*.

11   C.W. JENKS, THE PROSPECTS OF INTERNATIONAL ADJUDICATION (1964) pp. 255-258. See JENKS, THE COMMON LAW OF MANKIND (1958).

12   A.LARSON, C.W.JENKS, SOVEREIGNTY WITHIN THE LAW (1965) at 470-471.

The Nuremberg and Tokyo trials established that all of humanity would be guarded by an international legal shield and that even a Head of State could be held criminally responsible and punished for aggression and crimes against humanity. When West Germany - which had been led to disaster by glorifying state sovereignty - was admitted to the United Nations in 1973, its Chancellor Willy Brandt, winner of the 1971 Nobel Peace Prize, said:

> The Federal Republic of Germany has declared in its Constitution its willingness to transfer sovereign rights to supra-national organizations and it has placed international law above national law and made it directly applicable. This expresses the realization that the sovereignty of the individual and of nations can be secured only in larger communities, that the meaning and fulfillment of history can no longer be attributed to the nation-state...[13]

(3) *The Modern View:*

The needs of a changing society have forced the evolutionary decline of the old concept of absolute sovereignty. In their own common interests, States are obliged to cooperate, to form larger unions and to accept the tenets of an expanded international law. As World Court Judge Manfred Lachs put it in one of his last writings: "...new institutions come into being while others like national autonomy erode."[14]

Professor Ronald St. John Mcdonald, Judge at the European Court of Human Rights, has correctly concluded:

> Since the nineteenth century there has been a progressive retreat whereby the right to wage war has ceased to be within the sovereign prerogatives of States and has come to be regulated by international law.[15]

Recently, Strobe Talbott summarized the shift in notions of state sovereignty:

> Through the ages, there has been an overall trend toward larger units claiming sovereignty and, paradoxically, a gradual dimi-

---

13 Cited in D. KEYES, EARTH AT OMEGA (1985) at 61.

14 M. Lachs, *Thoughts on Science, Technology and World Law*, 86 AJIL 673 (1992) at 697. *See* O. Schachter, *International Law in Theory and Practice*, 178 Recueil des Cours at 109 (1982 V).

15 R.St.J. Macdonald, *The Use of Force by States in International Law*, Chap. 33 in M. BEDJAOUI, INTERNATIONAL LAW, ACHIEVEMENTS AND PROSPECTS (1991) at 735.

nution of how much true sovereignty any one country actually has.[16]

The gradual growth of human rights protection in Europe and the growing acceptance of the right of individuals to file complaints - even against their own governments - has strengthened the position of the private citizen against the sovereign.[17]

Two-dozen independent experts meeting in 1992 concluded:

Under pressure from internal and global economic, social and political forces, the sovereign power of nation-states is declining... This dilemma challenges the United Nations to consider serious adjustments to reflect the changing world.[18]

The international legal community is slowly waking up to the realities and needs of modern civilization. Prof. Thomas M. Franck, of the New York University School of Law, recently echoed the U.S. Declaration of Independence by pointing out that a state earns its place in the community of nations by demonstrating "a decent respect for the opinions of mankind." He suggests that states which ignore that obligation lose their legitimacy or are unworthy of international support.[19] States that ignore the requirements of social justice, including proclaimed human and economic rights, are equally undeserving. It is no longer acceptable for a state to hide behind the cloak of sovereignty to do as it pleases - or to refuse to do what is legitimately expected by international *law*.

It has been conclusively demonstrated by T.R. Surramanya of India that the individual is increasingly being recognized as the bearer of certain rights - and duties - which the sovereign state must respect and which international law enforces.[20] Professor Michael Reisman of Yale has persuasively pointed out that the notion of sovereignty in the traditional sense is now an anachronism. International law will protect sovereignty, but "it is the people's sovereignty rather than the sovereign's sovereignty."[21]

---

16 S.Talbott, *The Birth of the Global Nation*," Time, July 20 1992 at 70. *See* H. CLEVELAND, BIRTH OF A NEW WORLD (1993).

17 J.A. Frowein, *The European Convention on Human Rights as the Public Order of Europe*, Collected Courses of the Academy of European Law, Vol. 1 Bk. 2 at 267 (1992).

18 *Changing Concepts of Sovereignty: Can the United Nations Keep Pace?* Report of a Stanley Foundation conference (July, 1992).

19 T.M. Franck, *The Emerging Right to Democratic Governance*, 86 AJIL (1992) 46 at 91.

20 T.R. SUBRAMANYA. RIGHTS AND STATUS OF THE INDIVIDUAL IN INTERNATIONAL LAW (1984).

21 M. Reisman, *Sovereignty and Human Rights in Contemporary International Law*, Editorial Comments, 84 AJIL (1990) at 875; Reisman, *Statehood and Int'l Legal Personality*, 4 Pace Yrbk of Int. L 9 (1992) at 48.

Former Soviet Foreign Minister Shevardnadze, having experienced the overthrow of a tyrannical state, noted that the force of vital necessity would move nation states toward integration in supernational structures. "No one country in the world today is capable of taking upon itself the defense of global law and order." His book was entitled: "The future belongs to freedom."[22] People's groups of all kinds - religious, ethnic, social and political - have a power that has yet to be fully asserted. It is a force that can be used for good or evil. Unless necessary changes are made, the voice of the sovereign people - heard clearly during the American and French revolutions and in recent topplings of dictatorial governments in Eastern Europe and the Soviet Union - may become the roar of the lion.

The needs of the modern world have brought about such an erosion of the traditional role of absolute state sovereignty that it is more than an anachronism - it is obsolete. Thousands of treaties between states impose upon their people - including their leaders - duties they are legally bound to honor. Nations are voluntarily ceding sovereignty to many international institutions dealing with problems that are simply unmanageable on a national basis. International obligations, voluntarily accepted, do not diminish a nation's sovereignty but enhances its capacity to better serve the real sovereigns - its own citizens.

The modern world could not function for a single day were it not for the fact that states have recognized the necessity to surrender a portion of their so-called sovereignty for the common good. No letter could be mailed, no plane could fly or land, no radio or television set could operate, outerspace could not be explored or exploited, were it not for binding international rules accepted and honored by all states in the interest of everyone.[23] Efficient management of trade, finance, health, environment and a host of other problems that can only be dealt with globally, compel nations to work together - regionally and universally - in accordance with agreed and mandatory international regulation. Absolute sovereignty today would produce absolute chaos.

Authorizing municipal or federal authorities to lay down rules of the road enhances the individual's ability to drive safely. Authorizing global agencies to enforce global obligations enhances the individual's right to live

---

22   E. SHEVARDNADZE, THE FUTURE BELONGS TO FREEDOM (1991) at 107, 197-188.
23   *See* H. FREDERICK, GLOBAL COMMUNICATIONS AND INTERNATIONAL RELATIONS (1993).

in peace. No state is big enough, rich enough or powerful enough to cope with such global problems as world security, disarmament, meeting basic human needs or preserving the environment. The sovereign individual is not diminished but enriched by clear rules of international law which bind everyone - even his own national government.[24]

The same idea was expressed by several Presidents, including Borja of Ecuador, Perez of Venezuela and Bush of the United States. President Borja said:

> The liberty of states, which is called sovereignty, is not under-mined but rather is strengthened by the establishment of inter-national organizations.[25]

President Bush argued that no nation had to surrender "one iota of its sovereignty" by accepting a *pax universalis* - a universal peace characterized by shared responsibilities and the rule of law rather than resort to force.[26]

The Charter,"based on the principle of the sovereign equality of *all* its Members" (Art.2(1)), is committed to defending the territorial integrity and political independence of the nation-state. But we must never forget that its *primary* purpose is to maintain international peace and security and justice. What is fundamental must not become incidental. As new global needs become more apparent, drastic changes in the notion of sovereignty are being made and will have to be made in the future - or there may be no future at all.

In 1991, Secretary General Perez de Cuellar - a former Law Professor - moved by public outrage against the persecution of Kurds in Iraq, pointed to the Universal Declaration of Human Rights to challenge the "inviolable notion of sovereignty":

---

24   Alan Cranston, a distinguished U.S. Senator from California from 1969 to 1992, correctly pointed out that by agreeing to be bound by international law the state does not *give up* sovereignty but can *acquire* sovereignty it would otherwise not have. Sovereignty belongs to the individual but there are many things he cannot do alone and therefore he cedes certain rights to the city, state and nation to regulate matters that can only be handled effectively on a municipal, state or national basis. Remarks at a Wingspread Conference on "*Rethinking Basic Assumptions About the UN*," sponsored by the World Federalist Association and the Johnson Foundation, Dec. 4-6, 1992. Comments taken from notes by B. Ferencz. Conference Summary published by World Federalist Association (1993).

25   S/PV.3046, 31 Jan. 1992 at 27. *See* similar statement by President Perez of Venezuela at 57.

26   President Bush's address to the UN General Assembly, 23 Sept,. 1991, A/46/PV.4 at 82-83.

We are clearly witnessing what is probably an irresistible shift in public attitudes towards the belief that the defense of the oppressed in the name of morality should prevail over frontiers and legal documents.[27]

A leading Catholic theologian, Professor J. Bryan Hehir, addressing alumni at Harvard, described four different forces that had arisen during the past four decades to challenge the traditional notion of sovereignty: the moral challenge posed by the need for UN intervention to protect human rights against sovereign abuse; the strategic challenge arising from the inability of sovereigns to protect their own citizens from attack; the economic challenge by the inability of any sovereign to cope with economic and environmental interdependence, and finally, the political challenge as evidenced by the European Community's recognition that the nation state is no longer a viable political entity. "As a result of these four forces," said Father Hehir, "sovereignty is much more permeable than it used to be." [28]

Prof. Louis Henkin of Columbia University, President of the American Society of International Law, summed it up best:

> Governments raise iron curtains of 'sovereignty' to resist international cooperation and frustrate international norms and institutions, to conceal atrocities behind state boundaries, to prevent their investigation and discovery, to preclude judgment and condemnation under international law, and reaction by international institutions...It is time to bring sovereignty down to earth...[29]

C - Non-Interference in Domestic Affairs

Closely related to the idea of absolute state sovereignty is the concept that nations may, within their borders, do as they please without fear of interference in their internal affairs. The Charter makes plain that it does not authorize the United Nations "to intervene in matters which are essentially within the domestic jurisdiction of any state" (Art. 2(7)). The memory of colonialism, imperialism, and exploitation made these Charter prohibitions particularly appealing to many smaller states. "Non-interference" was justifiably coveted as a valid principle to protect weak states from abuses by

---

27 *See* Secretary-General's Address at University of Bordeaux, 22 April 1991, Press Release SG/SM/4560, 24 April 1991 at 6.
28 Harvard Divinity Bulletin, No. 4 (1993) at 7.
29 From an address by L. Henkin, reported in ASIL *Newsletter*, March-May 1993 at 1, 6.

the strong. Like the idea of national sovereignty, the concept of non-interference in domestic affairs is frequently misunderstood.

(1) *Traditional View:*

Nations have traditionally intervened to defend their own citizens from being abused by a foreign power. But, in the past, nations did not consider it their right or obligation to intervene - either individually or collectively - when an independent sovereign state committed atrocious acts against its own citizens. Diplomatic protests were not uncommon, as in the case of the 1915 massacre of Armenians in Turkey or the mass killings by Bolsheviks in Russia in 1918, or against the persecutions by Hitler Gernmany beginning in 1933. But verbal or written expressions of concern by foreign governments could be, and often were, rejected or ignored.

To be sure, nations may - in general - do within their own borders whatever they see fit. But that right, like the right to wage war, is not unlimited. Enlightened classical legal scholars had laid the foundations for protecting the common rights of humankind. [30] Gradually, the unlimited right of sovereigns to do as they pleased within their own territory was restrained by law.

There are situations where what happens *within* a state can be as perilous to peace as what happens between states. Internal conflicts among different ethnic groups and civil wars among political rivals may spill over national borders and embroil neighboring states and other members of the international community. The traditional view of non-interference did not preserve peace but only imperilled it.

(2) *Changing Conceptions:*

The Charter prohibition against interference in another country's domestic affairs was never intended as a license for governments to abuse its own people. Human rights conventions and accords accepted after the UN Charter was adopted should not be emasculated into insignificance by an unintended and illogical interpretation of the non-interference clause. All nations are now under a binding obligation not to violate the fundamental right to human dignity enjoyed by every human being.[31]

UN Charter Article 55 speaks of:

---

30   *See T. Meron, Common Rights of Mankind in Gentili, Grotius and Suarez*, Editorial Comment 88 AJIL 110 (1991).

31   *See* Chapter 1, Section B-1.

> the creation of conditions of stability and well being which are
> necessary for peaceful and friendly relations.... higher stand-
> ards of living...solutions of international economic, social,
> health and related problems... and human rights and funda-
> mental freedoms for all without distinction as to race, sex,
> language or religion.

All members of the UN have agreed that these goals are to be promoted.
Repeated declarations supporting fundamental rights have endowed them
with new strength.

It should be recalled that the Nuremberg Principles, including the
Charter and Judgment of the International Military Tribunal, which declared crimes against humanity to be punishable offenses, were affirmed
unanimously by the General Assembly of the United Nations in 1945. They
have become part of *jus cogens* and binding customary international law.
Humanitarian intervention - under UN control - to prevent or halt crimes
against humanity or major human rights violations is not only consistent
with both law and morality but may well be the only justifiable use of force.[32]

When a sovereign regime itself is illegitimate, having seized power in
disregard of the will of its citizens, or if the state uses its power to grossly
abuse those under its control, it violates international law. If the magnitude
of the violations is so great as to shock the conscience of mankind it becomes
a crime against humanity for which those responsible, regardless of their
rank or station, can and should be held to personal criminal account. Massive
violations of legal prohibitions that have acquired the status of binding law
justifies "interference" to halt outrageous illegal activity wherever and
whenever it occurs.[33]

"Non-interference" was never intended as an absolute prohibition. A
persuasive study by M.S. Rajan of India shows that the intervention prohibition has never been strictly interpreted by nations or the UN. Although
powerful states have abused their power by intervening illegally to impose

---

32   *See* F.R.TESON, HUMANITARIAN INTERVENTION: AN INQUIRY INTO LAW AND
MORALITY (1988) at 249; W.M.Reisman, Editorial Comment, *Coercion and
Self-Determination: Construing Charter Article 2(4)*, 78 AJIL 642 (1984).

33   *See* Chapter 1, Section D; M.T. KAMMINGA, INTER-STATE ACCOUNTABILITY FOR
VIOLATIONS OF HUMAN RIGHTS (1992).

their own views or systems, they have also intervened at times for the laudable and lawful purpose of upholding international humanitarian law. Any other view, says Mr. Rajan, "would have been truly appalling" and would have made it impossible to honor the Charter principles.[34] The Charter speaks of non-interference but it also speaks of human rights. If both goals are to be reconciled in the human interest, human rights must prevail over human wrongs. That's what international law is all about.[35]

(3) The Modern View:

In 1991, the UN Secretary-General reported:

> The protection of human rights has now become one of the keystones in the arch of peace...it now involves more a concerted exertion of international influence and pressure through timely appeal, admonition, remonstrance or condemnation and, in the last resort, an appropriate United Nations presence, than what was regarded as permissible under traditional international law...

> The principle of non-interference with the essential domestic jurisdiction of States cannot be regarded as a protective barrier behind which human rights could be massively or systematically violated with impunity.[36]

The conclusion reached by Professor Henry G. Schermers was that the protection of human rights was no longer a matter solely within the jurisdiction of each individual state. In extreme cases of human rights violations, the international community had not merely a right to intervene, but a duty to do so and it was time for the academic community to develop the rules needed to curtail such abuses by sovereign states. [37] At the Security Council Summit meeting in 1992, Belgium's Mr. Martens pointed out that the principle of non-intervention was intended to allow states to foster in freedom the well-being of their peoples. It could not be used as an excuse to condone abuses of human rights: "States rights are subservient to human rights."[38]

---

34   M.S.RAJAN, UNITED NATIONS AND DOMESTIC JURISDICTION (2d ed. 1961) at 354.

35   See B.B. Ferencz, The Nuremberg Principles and the Gulf War, 66 St. John's Law Rev 711 (1992); B.B. Ferencz, Crimes Against Humanity, Max Planck Inst., 8 Ency. of Public Int,. Law (1985) at 107. Dr. Abdelkader Abbadi, of the UN Dept. of Political Affairs, speaks of "the humanization of international relations." See Vol. 14 No. 12, U.N. Observer and International Report, Dec. 1992 at 5.

36   Report on the Work of the Organization (1991) A/46/1 at 12.

37   H.G. Schermers, The Obligation to Intervene in the Domestic Affairs of States, in A.J.M.DELISSEN & G.T. TANJA Eds., HUMANITARIAN LAW OF ARMED CONFLICT, CHALLENGES AHEAD (1991) at 592-593.

38   S/PV.3046, 31 Jan. 1992 at 73. See similar statement by Mr. Shamuyarira of Zimbabwe at 130.

Pope John-Paul II declared:

> The conscience of humanity ... demands that humanitarian intervention be made compulsory in situations which seriously endanger the survival of entire peoples and ethnic groups: this is a duty for nations and the international community.[39]

It is not merely a matter of conscience but also a matter of law. Non-interference in domestic affairs is subordinate to a superior legal right of peoples to be protected. International law does not require the world community to tolerate the intolerable.

Who decides when national conduct is tolerable and under what circumstances outside interference is both justified and necessary? The rules have yet to be clearly defined; new thinking is needed and clearer rules are needed.[40]

Major powers have seldom felt inhibited by the legal obligation of non-intervention when it served their political interests to ignore it. The invention of the "Brezhnev Doctrine," that socialist states could lawfully intervene to protect socialist solidarity, was used to "legitimize" Soviet invasions of Czechoslovakia, Hungary and Afghanistan. It had no basis in international law. The United States relied on the Monroe Doctrine, the Truman Doctrine and similar self-proclaimed rationales to justify *its* invasions and interventions in many Latin American, Caribbean and other countries. *Realpolitik* or political expediency frequently determined interventionist policies - even where they lacked legal justification and the end-product was added human suffering.[41]

The Charter does not authorize interference in domestic affairs for the purpose of achieving any political or economic advantage for the interfering state. On the other hand, Charter principles impose an obligation to respect "human rights and fundamental freedoms" (Art.55) and all states are pledged "to take joint and separate action in cooperation with the Organization" to achieve those purposes (Art.56). The door is open, therefore, for nations to act separately or jointly to achieve the human rights and funda-

---

39   Address to the International Conference on Nutrition, *cited in* Press Release FAO/3857, 7 Dec. 1992.

40   *See* Sir R. JENNINGS, Ed., OPPENHEIM'S INTERNATIONAL LAW (9TH Ed.) Sec. 131 pp. 439-447 (1992); *See* Stanley Foundation Report, *The UN Role in Intervention*, June 1993.

41   *See* R.A.JONES, THE SOVIET CONCEPT OF 'LIMITED SOVEREIGNTY' FROM LENIN TO GORBACHEV - The Brezhnev Doctrine (1990).

mental freedom goals prescribed by the Charter - providing they do it, as the Charter says, *in cooperation with* the UN!

As Professor Lillich of the University of Virginia School of Law has pointed out, if the UN fails to act, via the Security Council as the Charter intended, individual states may find the need to intervene irresistible.[42] It is very dangerous to allow a powerful nation to decide on its own when it may intervene against a presumed violator. No one should be entitled to take the law into his own hands. Extreme caution must be exercised to avoid unjustified interference by a heavily-armed state on the pretext that it is being done only to uphold the rule of law or principles of universal morality when in fact the intervenor is seeking some special advantage for itself. Intervention, to be lawful, must be an expression of the collective will of the community of states expressed through its lawfully designated channels.[43] Unilateral intervention not sanctioned by the international community must always be suspect. Aggression can not be disguised as humanitarianism.

The 1991 General Assembly, considering Iraq's crimes against the Kurds during the Gulf War, heard many world leaders, including those from the U.S., U.S.S.R., Italy, Germany, Canada, Hungary and Luxembourg, speak out forcefully for the "*duty* of democratic intervention" and the necessary limitation of state sovereignty. There was widespread agreement that something had to be done but no agreement about how to do it.[44] Italy's Foreign Minister Mr. de Michelis, was quite outspoken:

> Intervention that is primarily aimed at securing protection of human rights and respect for the basic principles of peaceful coexistence, is a prerogative of the international community, which must have the power to suspend sovereignty whenever it is exercised in a criminal manner.[45]

Professor Lori Fisler Damrosch of Columbia University has argued that even collective military intervention to enforce human rights should be eschewed. She noted that forcible intervention, either through the UN or regional organizations, runs the risk of escalating rather than confining the violence.[46] Forcible means should always be the last resort, but - unfortu-

---

42   *See* R. LILLICH, Ed., HUMANITARIAN INTERVENTION AND THE UNITED NATIONS (1973) at xii.

43   *See* H.BULL, Ed., INTERVENTION IN WORLD POLITICS (1984) at 195.

44   *See* General Assembly plenary debate, 1991.

45   Address to the General Assembly, 27 Sept. 1991, A/46/PV.12 at 32.

46   *See* L. Damrosch, *Commentary on Collective Military Intervention to Enforce Human Rights*, in DAMROSCH & SCHEFFER, LAW AND FORCE IN THE NEW INTERNATIONAL ORDER 215 (1991).

nately - peaceful means may not always be capable of achieving peaceful ends. Even her distinguished and cautious colleague, Professor Oscar Schachter, concluded:

> [T]he United Nations and regional organizations can be useful instruments for combatting aggression and preventing wars through judicious use of collective military force.[47]

Professor Frowein has gone so far as to suggest that if, despite persistent and gross human rights violations, the Security Council fails, or is unable, to discharge its duty to serve as the collective peace-enforcement arm of the world community, collective enforcement measures *without* Security Council authorization might be envisaged.[48]

If the Security Council can be by-passed, what happens to the global management plan envisaged by the Charter and what other peace enforcement process takes its place? These questions evoked no clear answers when the issues were considered at a meeting of distinguished experts in June 1993. The Conference Convenor, Richard H. Stanley, called for more radical UN reform and for new "global institutions that focus less on the inviolability of nations than the indivisibility of human life.[49]

To assure objectivity and facilitate speed in rescuing those being oppressed, Michael Bazyler has suggested the following criteria to determine whether intervention is lawful and permissible:

(a) Large scale atrocities being committed in the offending state;

(b) the predominance of humanitarian concern by the intervening parties;

(c) no unilateral intervention;

(d) other remedies must first be exhausted.[50]

---

47   *Id.* at 89. O.SCHACHTER, INTERNATIONAL LAW IN THEORY AND PRACTICE (1991) at 413.

48   J.A. Frowein, *Legal Consequences for International Law Enforcement in Case of Security Council Inaction*, in J.DELBRUCK, THE FUTURE OF INTERNATIONAL LAW ENFORCEMENT: New Scenarios - New Law; Proceedings of a Symposium of the Kiel Institute, Mar. 1992, at 124.

49   Report of the Stanley Foundation, *The UN Role in Intervention: Where Do We Go From Here?* at 31.

50   M. Bazyler, *Re-examining the Doctrine of Humanitarian Intervention in the Light of Atrocities in Kampuchea and Ethiopia"*, 23 Stanford J. of Int. L., 548 (1987). He was quite right in predicting: "Inaction now sows the seeds of future massacres."

To avoid abuse, and comply with the Charter, intervention must always be under strict Security Council control. As was demonstrated during the Gulf War, the Council has the capacity - when it has the will of its powerful members - to act with utmost speed. UN Charter Article 2(7) specifically provides that Security Council "enforcement measures under Chapter VII" can be carried out - despite the non-intervention clause. It does not authorize any nation, or combination of nations, to decide when it should intervene in another state's affairs. Nor can any regional enforcement measures lawfully be taken without prior Security Council authorization.[51]

The Security Council - and it alone - has the right and the obligation to extinguish peace-threatening fires before they become a raging inferno. The Security Council must have the will and the capacity to intervene to halt gross violations of human rights that threaten world peace. Appropriate means must be found to ensure that it does not fail in that duty.

D - The Right to Self-Determination

The principle of "equal rights and self-determination of peoples" is "enshrined" in the UN Charter (Art.1(2)). That "all peoples have the right to self-determination" appears as the first article in the International Covenant on Economic, Social and Cultural Rights as well as the Covenant on Civil and Political Rights and the African Charter of Human and People's Rights (Art.20). It is lauded in countless UN Resolutions and Declarations. Exactly what it means, however, is nowhere made clear. In the interest of maintaining peace, it is important to clarify who are the "peoples" who have such a right and what precisely is their entitlement?

(1) Traditional View:

Since biblical times, oppressed peoples have fought against foreign domination. Scholars like Las Casas and de Victoria, argued for the right of indigenous populations to be protected from annihilation and exploitation by imperialist powers. The American and French revolutions espoused the principle of government by consent of the governed. Despite such declarations, the seizure of enemy territory as an act of conquest or the reshuffling of national borders for political or economic reasons was fairly common throughout history. It was prohibited in principle but tolerated in practice. It should not be surprising that discord and violence would be fomented among different ethnic groups by such involuntary dislocations.

---

51   UN Charter Art. 53, Sec.1. See P. MALANCZUK, HUMANITARIAN INTERVENTION AND THE LEGITIMATE USE OF FORCE (1993).

With the collapse of the Ottoman and Austro-Hungarian Empires after World War I, dozens of ethnic minorities clamored for protection of their rights and recognition of their independence. Woodrow Wilson argued that self-determination would provide stability. His Secretary of State, Robert Lansing, perceptively feared that it would be a calamity by raising hopes that could never be realized.[52]

(2) Changing Conceptions:

Treaties signed by European states with large minority populations sought to protect the ethnic and cultural diversity of local groups whose linguistic, religious, racial or ethnic characteristics distinguished them from the dominant majority of the population.[53] The League of Nations took steps to ease future tensions by trying to protect native populations from oppressive rule by imperialist powers. Colonies - "inhabited by peoples not yet able to stand by themselves under the strenuous conditions of the modern world" - were placed under tutelage of "advanced nations" as a "sacred trust of civilization." These "Mandates" were to "guarantee freedom of conscience and religion, subject only to the maintenance of public order and morals" (Covenant Art.22). The Covenant made no reference to "self-determination", which remained largely a political rather than a legal concept.[54]

The UN Charter contained a "Declaration Regarding Non-Self-Governing Territories" (Chap. XI), and a new "International Trusteeship System" (Chap. XII). Political, economic, social and educational advancement of the inhabitants of the trust territories was to be progressively developed by an "Administering Authority" - usually the former colonial power. The objective: "self-governance or independence as may be appropriate", taking into account "the freely expressed wishes of the peoples concerned" (Art.76). A UN Trusteeship Council, including each of the Permanent Members, was to see that the obligations were carried out. Both Chapter XI and XII made specific reference to the need "to further international peace and security" (Art. 73(c), Art.76(a), Art. 84). Thus self-determination was always perceived as a means to assure peace - never as a mean to destroy it.

---

52   *See* D. Binder and B. Crosette, *As Ethnic Wars Multiply, U.S. Strives for a Policy*, N.Y. Times, Feb.7, 1993 at 1.

53   *See* L. Sohn, *The Rights of Minorities*, in L.HENKIN, Ed., THE INTERNATIONAL BILL OF RIGHTS (1981) 270; J. Robinson, *International Protection of Minorities, A Global View*, Israel Yearbook on Human Rights (1971) 61.

54   *See* D. Thürer, *Self-Determination*, 8 Encycl. of Pub. Int'l L. 470 (1985); F. Capotorti, *Minorities, id.* 385.

In 1960, the General Assembly unanimously adopted the Declaration on the Granting of Independence to Colonial Peoples. Its aim was to hasten the end of colonialism. It declared: "All peoples have the right to self-determination" (Art.2). Their right to independence, however, was to be exercised "peacefully" (Art.4). The Declaration was careful to point out:

> An attempt aimed at the partial or total disruption of the national unity and the territorial integrity of a country is incompatible with the purposes and principles of the Charter of the United Nations (Art.6).

The maintenance of peace and security remained paramount. Stimulated by the UN Declaration on Granting Independence, the colonial system gradually approached its end.[55]

The process of preserving peace by granting independence was not always peaceful. One need only recall Korea, Vietnam, Cambodia and the mass killings of Ibos in Nigeria, the massacre between Tutsis and Hutus in Burundi, periodic slaughters between Hindus and Moslems in India, the killing of Shiites, Sunni and Baha'i in Iraq, civil wars in Pakistan, Bangladesh and elsewhere. Millions died and countless millions more were driven from their homes to swell the ranks of terrified refugees. It was all done - and is still being done in former Yugoslavia, the former Soviet Union and other areas - in the name of the humanitarian right to self-determination!

(3) *The Modern View:*

Almost all countries have cultural, religious or ethnic minorities. Consider the Welsh and the Irish in the United Kingdom, the Palestinians in Israel, the Quebecois in Canada, the Hispanics, native Indians and Afro-Americans in the United States, and literally hundreds of other groups in the former Soviet Union, former Yugoslavia and other lands who have an ethnic affiliation or loyalty different from the dominant national authority. There are thousands of groups throughout the world bound together by common tribal, cultural, ethnic, religious, linguistic, territorial or historical bonds.[56] If, as various Covenants and Declarations imply, they *all* have a right to self-determination - and they may use every means to attain it - no boundary would ever be secure, nations would be in constant agitation and

---

55 *See* G.THULLEN, PROBLEMS OF THE TRUSTEESHIP SYSTEM; A STUDY OF POLITICAL BEHAVIOR IN THE UN (1964); N.MURRAY, THE UN TRUSTEESHIP SYSTEM (1957).

56 *See* H.O. Schoenberg, *Self-Determination: A right that's been wronged*, ADL Bulletin, Jan. 1978.

transformation, international anarchy would flourish and world peace would be in permanent peril.

As usual, international lawyers have divergent views about self-determination as a legal right, the circumstances under which it may lawfully be asserted and whether "peoples" as a group are endowed with legal personality that entitles them to seek protection in international law.[57] The General Assembly has no vested authority to either make or interpret law and its many declarations regarding self-determination are recommendations or affirmations of general principles but they are not automatically or necessarily binding legal obligations.[58] The absence of legal clarity regarding the limits of self-determination, and the absence of any judicial forum to which "peoples" can turn to interpret the law or any effective law-enforcement mechanism, deprives the international community of tools needed to suppress the type of ethnic slaughter that continues to devastate many lands.[59]

In 1970, a UN Special Committee - after eight years of effort involving hundreds of international lawyers and diplomats - reached a consensus Declaration on the *Principles of International Law concerning Friendly Relations and Cooperation Among States*.[60] According to knowledgeable U.S. representative Robert Rosenstock, the agreed formulation of the principle of self-determination was one of the most difficult tasks the Committee faced. African and Asian states in particular argued that immediate independence was a declared legal right that entitled people who considered themselves to be deprived of that right to use force as a form of self-defense against colonialism. Furthermore, there was a duty on the part of other states to provide all possible assistance to the self-liberators. The debates were tainted by antagonistic political considerations. Western states took quite a different view.[61]

What emerged, after skillful papering over by legal draftsmen, was a typical UN consensus compromise. The Declaration confirmed the legal right of a state freely to choose its own political system. It did not include

---

57   *See* J. CRAWFORD, Ed., THE RIGHTS OF PEOPLES (1988); P. THORNBERRY, INTERNATIONAL LAW AND THE RIGHTS OF MINORITIES (1993).

58   L.GROSS, ESSAYS IN INTERNATIONAL LAW AND ORGANIZATION, The Right of Self-Determination in International Law (1984).

59   *See* M.Weller, *The International Response to the ssolution of the Socialist Federal Republic of Yugoslavia*, 86 AJIL 569 (1992); *See* H.A.WILSON, INTERNATIONAL LAW AND THE USE OF FORCE BY NATIONAL LIBERATION MOVEMENTS (Doctoral thesis completed at Oxford, 1988).

60   *See* Chapter One, Section B-2.

61   *See* R. Rosenstock, *The Declaration of Principles of International Law Concerning Friendly Relations: A Survey*, 65 AJIL 713 (1971).

a general right of groups to secede from states of which they were a part or any right to take action that would dismember independent states which respected human rights. The right to self-determination was subordinate to other Charter principles upholding the sovereignty, territorial integrity and political independence of states. All disputes had to be settled by peaceful means.

Although some of the rather tortured wording was sufficiently vague to enable both sides to put their own interpretation on some of its clauses, what stands out throughout the Friendly Relations Declaration are repeated statements prohibiting the use of force, either to prevent self-determination or to exercise it. Which "peoples" had such rights, and what they were, was not defined. It was quite clear, however that whatever freedoms were to be assured to whichever groups that were seeking self-determination, it could only be done lawfully if it did not endanger world peace.[62]

When, in 1992, the General Assembly adopted the *Declaration on the Rights of Persons Belonging to National or Ethnic, Religious and Linguistic Minorities*, and called upon persons and states to uphold and support such rights, its concluding article was careful to state:

> Nothing in this Declaration may be construed as permitting any activity contrary to the purposes and principles of the United Nations, including sovereign equality, territorial integrity and political independence of states (Art.8(4)).[63]

The goal of self-determination is approved, but the use of force to attain it is prohibited. Peaceful means are paramount.

Instead of ambiguous verbiage in new Declarations, what is urgently required is a new way of thinking. Tolerance is the lubricant that leads to needed compromises. Professor Amitai Etzioni of George Washington University, noting the undemocratic and murderous activities of various movements for self-determination in former Yugoslavia, the Baltic states and other regions, pointed out:

> Self-determination should not be treated as an absolute value, trumping all others. Self-determination is meant to enhance justice in the world through self-government. However, in

---

62   GA Res. 2625 (XXV), Oct.24, 1970; *reprinted in* 65 AJIL 243 (1971).

63   Res.47/135, 18 Dec. 1992, adopted without a vote, Report A/47/678/Add.2, GAOR 47th Sess. Supp. No. 49 (S/47/49) at 212. *See* H.A. WILSON, INTERNATIONAL LAW AND THE USE OF FORCE BY NATIONAL LIBERATION MOVEMENTS (1988).

spite of its positive role in previous periods, the violence and destruction - even war - it now incites greatly undercut its legitimacy.[64]

What is required of the majority, the minority, as well as every sovereign state, is a degree of flexibility that allows diverse cultures to flourish together in peaceful harmony. What is called for is compassionate consideration for ethnic, religious, linguistic or cultural traditions within a framework of relative group autonomy that does not tear asunder the prevailing international order.

The heart of self-determination is respect for the human heart - the awareness that all people need a *feeling* of independence and self-fulfillment as well as a minimum basis for human dignity, free of outside exploitation. Lawful goals can not be sought by unlawful means. All forms of peaceful settlement are acceptable methods for achieving self-determination. Democratic voting procedures to ascertain and protect the rights and interests of minorities, an appropriate route toward self-determination, is receiving increasing support from the UN. During the past few years, UN Peacekeeping Forces have been used to encourage self-determination by the peaceful methods of free elections in Namibia, Angola, Cambodia, Mozambique and El Salvador, while those who used violent means to attain their self-determination goals were suppressed by the international community wherever possible.[65] But no search for self-determination can be considered lawful if it requires massive death and destruction of innocent people.

The cry of "Self-Determination" can not be an acceptable subterfuge for political power-seeking, racial or religious intolerance or war-mongering nationalism. Finding the proper balance between competing interests and creating institutions to resolve differences in a non-violent way are challenges the international community must face. As Hurst Hannum has pointed out:

> Law can be used to give a framework to that diversity which is a fact of modern society, promoting mutual respect rather than coercing obedience.[66]

---

64   A.Etzioni, *The Evils of Self-Determination, 89 Foreign Policy* (Winter 1992-93) at 25.

65   *See* SC Res.745, 28 Feb 1992 and Res. 792, 30 Nov. 1992 re Cambodia; SC Res. 693, 20 May 1991 and Res. 791 30 Nov. 1992, re El Salvador; SC Res. 690, 29 Apr. 1991 and Res. 809 (1993) re Western Sahara.

66   H.HANNUM, AUTONOMY, SOVEREIGNTY, AND SELF-DETERMINATION (1990) at 477.See H. HALPERIN & D. SCHEFFER, SELF-DETERMINATION IN THE NEW WORLD ORDER (1992).

Unfortunately self-determination is among those problems that can not be solved simply by redrawing a boundary or redrafting a law. Memories of ancient hatreds do not die quickly. Recent movements towards reconciliation betwen Palestinians and the state of Israel gives rise to the hope that changes are possible. Those whose freedoms have been suppressed and who have cast off the shackles of "coerced obedience" often seize new liberties as an opportunity to obtain vengeance or restore old powers - even if it wreaks havoc in the process. It is usually a brutal procedure with no thought of the human rights of its victims. That was not what any rational person had in mind when the right to self-determination was proclaimed.

In this interdependent world, no people can unilaterally determine its own destiny. The right to self-determination must be seen as a human right that can only be exercised lawfully if done in a cooperative and non-violent way. Self-determination means *peaceful* self-determination that shows consideration for the human rights and feelings of others. Dr. Harris O. Shoenberg has suggested the possibility of having the Security Council create a new organ under Article 29 of the Charter to cope with self-determination disputes that might threaten peace.[67] That is the only way that is consistent with the declared Charter goal:

> to encourage respect for human rights and for fundamental freedoms for all without distinction as to race, sex, language, or religion, and to encourage recognition of the interdependence of the peoples of the world.[68]

Over twenty years ago, Professor Emerson of Harvard suggested that new norms were needed to evaluate the legitimacy of claims to self-determination. He expressed the thought that perhaps the Security Council or the Assembly "or some newly created international agency" should be empowered to decide such complicated questions. He asked whether states and peoples had evolved sufficiently to accept the substitution of international decisions instead of the old fashioned trial by battle.[69] If there is to be peace in the world, the answer had better be yes.

---

67 *See* H.O. Schoenberg, *We're Not Bananas!:The Concept of 'People' in the Principle of Self-Determination and Its Implications for the United Nations,* Monograph 11, Center for UN Reform Education (1993) at 66-67.

68 UN Charter Art.76 (c).

69 R. Emerson, *Self-Determination,* 65 AJIL 459 (1971).

E - The Right of Self-Defence

The defence of the fatherland or motherland has been an inspiring rallying-cry for which millions have willingly sacrificed their lives. Nationalism and militarism are stirring sentiments that have been glorified for centuries. But, the old way of thinking has now become so dangerous that it threatens to destroy what it was intended to preserve. Even the hallowed notion of self-defence must be reconsidered to see if a safer and better way can be found to protect the national and common interest.

(1) Traditional View:

Self-defence is usually perceived as a method of lawful self-help against the unlawful act of another. As long as wars were a lawful method for sovereigns to attain their particular goals, the idea of self-defense of nations was given little thought. Since sovereigns were allowed to use force, it was obvious that other sovereigns could also use force to preserve their kingdoms or protect the interests of their subjects. Since war for many legitimate purposes was permissible - an inherent right - the right to wage war for self-defense was, of course, also permissible - an inherent right. The right of self-defence was considered "inherent" only because the right to wage war was inherent in the notion of absolute sovereignty and the right to wage war for defensive purposes was an obvious and logical corollary of the broader entitlement.

The moral philosophy of the Greeks, as evidenced by the writings of Socrates, Plato and Aristotle, led to Roman Codes based on theories of "natural law." Cicero spoke of "just" wars in defense of honor or safety - which presumably includes territorial integrity. After the collapse of the Roman Empire and the "Dark Ages," Roman concepts of natural and just wars were revived by Catholic Churchmen, such as St. Augustine, to protect the interests of the Papacy. International law, as we know it, did not yet exist.[70]

---

70   *See* FERENCZ, ENFORCING INT. L. vol. 1 Chapter One, *The Origins of International Law Enforcement.*

Morality was regulated by the Church. "Self-defence" was one of the moral justifications for permitting the use of force under the theologically approved concept of a "just war." But, to be just, no more force could be used in self-defence than was necessary to repel or halt the harm. Thus the principle of proportionality became another requirement before wars could be morally or theologically sanctioned.[71] There was yet another pre-requisite before self-defence could be justified: self-help was considered permissible *only* if there was no centralized authority with power to maintain the peace. As long as there was a competent authority available to maintain peace, self-help was *not* permissible and could only be relied upon *after* resort to that authority has been exhausted to no avail.[72] The notion that self-defense is an "inherent right", ordained by some divine authority or natural law is not substantiated by the historical record. When war ceased to be legally an "inherent right," self-defense ceased to be an "inherent right."

(2) Changing Conceptions:

As international law developed and the absolute power of the sovereign state was gradually eroded, new institutions were created to enforce international law through collective security measures. In the security plan of the League and the UN, the old notion of self-defense lost much of its rational justification as a needed means for the protection of states. It retained its vitality only as long as the proposed new international institutions or organs, designed to replace self-help, were unable to discharge their peace-keeping responsibility.

The UN Charter describes self-defence as an "inherent right" but what that means must be understood in the historical context as well as the overriding Charter provisions prohibiting the use of force in order to maintain peace. Any law that is interpreted in ways that defeat its own fundamental goals can not be validly sustained.

According to the UN Charter, States must:

---

71   *See* J.G. Gardam, *Proportionality and Force in International Law*, 87 AJIL 391 (1993).

72   The Catholic doctrine of "Just War", requires: (a) a Just Cause, such as to secure basic human rights, (b) a Competent Authority - war must be declared by those responsible for public order, (c) Comparative Justice - using only limited means as long as there is no common moral or political authority, (d) Right Intention - the pursuit of peace, (e) Last Resort - Pope Paul VI called the UN the last hope for peace, (f) Probability of Success, and (g) Proportionality - unnecessary or excessive devastation could not be justified. *See* U.S. Catholic Conference, *Pastoral Letter on War and Peace: God's Promise and Our Response*, 13 *Origins*, May 19, 1983.

refrain from the threat or use of force against the territorial integrity or political independence of any state or in any other manner inconsistent with the Purposes of the United Nations (Art.2 (4)).

On the other hand, the Charter allows

the inherent right of individual or collective self-defence if an armed attack occurs against a Member of the United Nations, until the Security Council has taken measures necessary to maintain international peace and security (Art. 51).

International lawyers have had a field day analyzing the interplay between the prohibition of force in Art. 2(4) - which seems to be fundamental - and the right of self-defence in Art. 51 - which seems to be strictly limited.[73]

(a) Conflicting Interpretations:

Because of Charter ambiguity, it can be argued:

(i) States need only *refrain* from the use of force; that is not an absolute prohibition.

(ii) Force not directed against the territorial integrity or independence of states may be permissible, providing it is consistent with Charter purposes - whatever that is interpreted to mean.

(iii) Self-defence is an *inherent* or natural right that exists quite apart from the Charter and hence can not be restricted by the Charter to be exercised only until the Security Council has taken "measures" - whatever that means.

(iv) What constitutes an "armed attack" is debatable; besides the Charter doesn't say that self-defense is permissible *only if* an armed attack occurs, hence it may be permissible under other circumstances.

---

73   *See,* for example, J.L. Kunz, *Individual and Collective Self-Defense in Article 51 of the Charter of the United Nations,* 41 AJIL 872 (1947); M.S.MCDOUGAL AND F.P. FELICIANO, LAW AND MINIMUM WORLD PUBLIC ORDER (1961); J.ZOUREK, *L'INTERDICTION DE L'EMPLOI DE LA FORCE EN DROIT INTERNATIONAL* (1974); O.SCHACHTER, INTERNATIONAL LAW IN THEORY AND PRACTICE (1991); also Schachter,*The Right of States to Use Armed Force,* 82 Mich. L. Rev. 1620 (1984); L.DAMROSCH AND J. SCHEFFER, Eds., LAW AND FORCE IN THE NEW INTERNATIONAL ORDER (1991); *The Nicaragua Case (Merits)* ICJ Reports (1986).

(v) Security Council "measures necessary to maintain international peace" may come too late to protect the victim and therefore cannot be relied on for security.

(vi) "Collective self-defense" is not defined and therefore, it is argued, assistance of any kind can come from any source - without limitation.

(vii) Nothing is said in the Charter about "preventive self-defense" or "anticipatory self-defence" or "putative self-defense" (e.g. against an anticipated or *feared* nuclear attack,) hence such actions, not being specifically excluded, may also be permissible.[74]

Because of the legal ambiguities, all wars of aggression - according to the aggressors - are now fought only in "self-defence." In short, the prevailing notions of self-defence have left the door to international violence conveniently unlocked.[75] How do we lock the door?

(b) *Innovative Thinking:*

It is unlikely that international lawyers will ever agree completely on how best to reconcile the dichotomy between Article 2(4) and the self-defence provisions of Article 51. International legal interpretations are anchored in inapplicable ancient traditions and tend to get ensnarled in parochial political considerations that ignore the purpose and intent of the law. Courageous thinking is required that will take account of the basic objectives of the UN Charter, new perils of modern warfare that impact the possibility for proportionality and basic needs of contemporary world society.

Let us consider some innovative views on self-defence as expressed by very distinguished military leaders who were thoroughly dedicated to the objective of world peace:

After World War I, Lt. General Jan Christian Smuts, who had won highest honors in law at Cambridge, submitted a thoughtful plan for the organization of the League of Nations. He warned that without advances in

---

74 *See* L.GROSS, ESSAYS ON INTERNATIONAL LAW AND ORGANIZATION, Vol. 1, Chapter IV, *Problems of Interpretation* (1984).

75 *See* T.M. Franck, *Who Killed Article 2(4)?*, 64 AJIL 809 (1970); L. Henkin, *The Reports of the Death of Article 2(4) Are Greatly Exaggerated*", 65 AJIL 544 (1971).

world organization, the war would have been fought in vain and greater calamities would follow. Smuts advocated that if a state breached the peace, it would be brought down by economic boycotts backed by collective military force. The defeated nation would then be subject to perpetual disarmament. What that meant was that it would, in future, be unable to defend itself but would be dependent for its security upon the peacekeeping regime established by the League.[76]

Had Germany been subjected to restraints after 1918 and not allowed to rebuild its military might for purported purposes of "self-defence", World War II would have been avoided. Had the Kellogg Pact of 1928 outlawing war not been circumvented by its secret protocols permitting self-defence - as defined by each sovereign state - the Second World War could not have happened.[77]

After World War II, U.S. General Douglas MacArthur as Supreme Commander of the Allied Powers in the Far East, approved a plan for Japan similar to the 1918 aborted proposal made by General Smuts after World War I. Under MacArthur's guidance, a provision was written into the new Japanese Constitution saying:

> Aspiring sincerely to an international peace based on justice and order, the Japanese people forever renounce war as a sovereign right of the nation, and the use of force as a means to settle international disputes.

> In order to fulfill the purpose of the preceding paragraph, no army, navy, air force or other war potential will be maintained.[78]

In his *Reminiscences*, MacArthur made clear that he intended to divest Japan of any capacity for self-defence. He wrote of his meeting with Japanese Prime Minister Baron Kijuro Shidehara who - to MacArthur's surprise - also felt that Japan should be completely disarmed and have no military establishment whatsoever. The Prime Minister reasoned that whatever resources the country had should be devoted to bolstering its destroyed economy.

Both General MacArthur and Japan's Foreign Minister recognized the need for innovative thinking. MacArthur explained:

---

76   J.C.SMUTS, THE LEAGUE OF NATIONS - A Practical Suggestion (1918), extracts *reproduced in* FERENCZ, ENFORCING INT.L. vol. I Doc. 21 (d), p. 283; J.C.Smuts, PLANS FOR A BETTER WORLD (1942). *See* Chapter One, Section A-2.

77   *See* Chapter One, Section A-2, A-3.

78   I am indebted to Klaus Schlichtmann, who is writing a dissertation on the subject at Sophia University in Tokyo, for this translation of Article 9 of the Japanese Constitution.

For years I have believed that war should be abolished as an outmoded means of resolving disputes between nations...my abhorrence reached its height with the perfection of the atom bomb.

Shidehara is reported to have replied:

The world will laugh and mock us as impractical visionaries, but a hundred years from now we will be called prophets.[79]

It was a reminder of Schopenhauer's oft-quoted wisdom:

All truth passes through three stages. First it is ridiculed. Second it is violently opposed. Third it is accepted as being self-evident.

There is considerable dispute among scholars whether the ideas for a demilitarized Japan originated with MacArthur or the pacifistic Japanese Prime Minister. There is no doubt, however that by surrendering its ability to defend itself Japan immeasurably enhanced its economic well being and the security of its citizens and the world. By giving up its capacity to exercise an "inherent" right to self-defence, Japan's security was not diminished but increased.[80]

For many years after World War II, occupied Germany was allowed no military means whatsoever to defend itself against any potential aggressor. During that time it prospered and enjoyed an "economic miracle" of rebirth. By not insisting upon an "inherent right" of self defence, Germany's safety was not diminished but enhanced; its power was not weakened but strengthened. Relying on collective security for its protection enabled Germany to use its resources to rebuild its nation for the benefit of its citizens and the world.

Nobel-Prize-winner Oscar Arias pointed out that Costa Rica, one of the outstanding democracies in Latin America, prides itself on the fact that it has no army. It's citizens have been safer and freer from conflict than all of its neighbors. It can point to its Court of Human Rights and its University

---

79   D. MacARTHUR, REMINISCENCES (1964) at 74.

80   *See* C.A. Kades, *The American Role in Revising Japan's Imperial Constitution*, 104 Political Science Quarterly, 215 (1989); O. Nishi, THE CONSTITUTION AND THE NATIONAL DEFENSE SYSTEM IN JAPAN (1987). A special law was required to allow Japan to contribute troops for U.N. Peace-keeping operations. *See Law Concerning Cooperation for United Nations Peace- keeping Operations and Other Operations*, June 15, 1992, *reproduced in* 32 ILM 215 (1993).

for Peace which have enriched the liberties of its citizens without the need for military defense.

Prohibiting war but allowing nations to prepare for self-defense with unlimited national arms has never led to peace. On the contrary, the old Roman maxim: "If you want peace, prepare for war" only proved that those who prepared for war usually got what they prepared for. If you want peace, you must prepare for *peace*.

(3) *The Modern View:*

War is not a safe road to peace. In modern warfare there are no real winners, only losers. Those who are killed include not only military personnel but increasingly large numbers of innocent bystanders who become victims of what is camouflaged under the cruel euphemism "collateral damage." Even the accidental killing of one's own comrades-in-arms by modern weapons of uncontrollable power is belittled as "friendly fire." We owe it to all citizens - civilian and military - to try to protect them from destruction. Should there be an all-out nuclear war, everybody will lose and lose everything. Even a non-nuclear war has now become devastatingly intolerable. There is need for new thinking about how to defend oneself, one's country and humankind from such tragedies.

This is not to suggest that any nation should be forced to stand helpless while awaiting an assault from its enemies. In today's world, that would be suicidal. The dilemma is that an escalating arms race and the absence of any centralized controls to maintain peace is equally suicidal. Self-defense is a necessity until such time as a more effective defensive system is in place. The obvious answer to the dilemma is to put such a system in place as quickly as possible. To have an effective system of defense it is necessary to end the arms race, arrange for effective sanctions and a police force under international control to maintain peace. In the next chapters, we shall consider how those goals can be attained. Our purpose here is to alert the reader to the need for new thinking about self-defense as part of a revised world order under law.

It may diminish the shock if it is recognized that we are already moving in the direction of a world where traditional ideas of self-defence are no longer applicable. We have pointed out that large portions of planet earth may - according to most nations - only be used for peaceful purposes. What that means is that no military weapons can be made, brought, or even tested in the peaceful zone and no military bases may be set up there. All measures of a military nature are strictly prohibited in all of Antarctica; the high seas (the traditional war arenas of yesteryear); the exclusive economic zone protruding 200 miles beyond all national coastlines; the Moon and Other Celestial Bodies; the Indian Ocean and some other areas of the earth are shielded from nuclear weapons being used there. In effect, no measures of prohibited self-defence can take place anywhere within that enormous mass of protected terrain.[81]

> The Latin American, South Pacific and Antarctic Treaties form a nuclear free zone stretching from the western borders of Australia to the eastern shores of Latin America and extending south from the United States to Antarctica.[82]

Ian Browlie's important study, INTERNATIONAL LAW AND THE USE OF FORCE BY STATES, has shown that - in contrast with the practice before the first World War - legal instruments to prohibit the use of force have become more emphatic and more widely accepted. He has correctly recognized that "in the era of nuclear and thermonuclear armament, self-help involves intolerable risks."[83] Despite vague clauses authorizing force in "self-defense," the unauthorized threat or use of force by states is an illegal violation of the UN Charter. The very few exceptions to the general prohibition must be strictly construed and limited.

Tel Aviv University Professor Yorim Dinstein, in a recent comprehensive study of war and self-defence, states:

> If every State were the final arbiter of the legality of its own acts, if every State could cloak an armed attack with the disguise of self-defence, the international legal endeavor to hold force in check would have been an exercise in futility.[84]

According to Dinstein, the decision about the legality of self-defence can only rest with the Security Council or the International Court of Justice. Certain objective criteria can be used to ascertain whether self-defence is legitimate. Following a rule proposed in 1841 by U.S. Secretary of State Webster, the state using force would have to show :

> a necessity of self-defence, instant, overwhelming, leaving no choice of means, and no moment for deliberation.[85]

---

81 *See* Chapter Three, Section B-3; *See* Center for Innovative Diplomacy, Irvine, California, *Bulletin of Municipal Foreign Policy* (1987-1990).

82 Arms Control Association, Washington D.C. *Arms Control and National Security* (1989) at 124.

83 I. BROWNLIE, INTERNATIONAL LAW AND THE USE OF FORCE BY STATES, (1963) at 436. *Compare* D.W. BOWETT, SELF-DEFENCE IN INTERNATIONAL LAW (1958).

84 Y. DINSTEIN, WAR, AGGRESSION AND SELF-DEFENCE (1988) at 192.

85 *Id.* at 227.

What may have been feasible in the "horse-and-buggy" days of over a century ago would be exceedingly dangerous in our modern era of high-technology. "Mutual Assured Destruction" may be possible, but many modern methods of annihilation leave no time for a response that will protect lives; retaliation is not defence. If "anticipatory self-defence" (as is sometimes proposed) is ever accepted as an inherent right, the peril facing humankind will only be increased.[86] Modern armed conflict among states inevitably employs weapons of such massive and uncontrollable destructive capacity that one can not speak of "proportionality" in wars of the future. A reasonable case can be made that any use of nuclear weapons would be unlawful and a similar case can be made against all weapons of indiscriminate mass destruction.[87]

Professor Dinstein, who is quite realistic in his appraisals, has recognized that, as a practical matter, self-help can only be eliminated when there is an international police force to maintain peace. He has sensed the need for change - as well as the possibility:

> It is not beyond the realm of the plausible that a day may come when States will agree to dispense completely with the use of force in self-defence, exclusively relying thenceforth on some central authority wielding an effective international police force...what is - and was -is not always what will be.[88]

In order to rule out the necessity for self-defense as well as the legal justification for it, what is required - as Dinstein says - is a central authority wielding an effective international police force. The central authority already exists: it is the Security Council. There is no other legitimate authority. The UN Charter specifically imposes restraints on the authority of regional organizations to apply measures of collective self-defense - as many of them wished to do. Their sovereignty and their right to use force in self-defence was curtailed by Art. 53:

> No enforcement action shall be taken under regional arrangements, or by regional agencies without the authorization of the Security Council.

---

86   *See* L.R. Beres, *Preserving the Third Temple: Israel's Right of Anticipatory Self-Defense Under International Law*, 26 Vanderbilt Jour. of Transnational Law 111 (1993).

87   A Joint Project of the International Association of Lawyers Against Nuclear Arms, the International Peace Bureau and the International Physicians for the Prevention of Nuclear War (headed by Nobel Laureate Dr. Bernard Lown) have prepared a legal memorandum By Nicholas Grief calling for a decision of the International Court on the legality of such weapons. *The World Court Project on Nuclear Weapons and International Law* (1992).

88   Id. 171.

It was the Security Council that alone was vested with ultimate authority to decide when collective force would be used. But that presupposed that the Council would have not only the authority but also the ability to wield its authority through an effective international police force. No such force yet exists.

The obvious answer is to create a UN police force as quickly as possible so that individual states will not be obliged or justified - or burdened - by having to rely upon self-help to protect themselves.[89] But what are nations to do in the meanwhile - until a more effective international security system is firmly in place - to protect their interest without resorting to military force?

(4) Defensive Defense:

Non-violent peace strategies have been developed by many outstanding scholars. U.S. sociologist Gene Sharp of the Center for International Affairs at Harvard University, has been in the forefront of plans for civilian based defence by non-violent means.[90] Professor Johan Galtung has persuasively argued that the road to peace can be found through conflict resolution, transarmament to maintain a balance of reduced military power, non-alignment, inner strength and useful cooperation among nations working together in peaceful collaboration.[91] Randall Forsberg, of the Institute for Disarmament Studies, in Cambridge Massachusetts, argues for "non-offensive defense" in which long-range attack weapons are replaced by less-threatening means for repulsing attack.[92]

Professor Burns Weston of Iowa calls for new legal norms, procedures and institutions for peace. Professor Lloyd Dumas, of the University of Texas, calls for a stabilizing and expanded global political economy as a means to peace. Dean Russet of Yale calls for more representative institutions; Yale's former Chaplain, Reverend Sloan Coffin, appeals for new moral perceptions as a means to peace. Robert Johansen of Notre Dame in arguing against the use of force concludes that "by transcending the current bounda-

---

89   See Chapter Eight, Section C-3.
90   See G.SHARP, THE POLITICS OF NON-VIOLENT ACTION, 3 vols (1980). Harvard University has a Program on Non-Violent Sanctions in Conflict and Defense.
91   GALTUNG, THERE ARE ALTERNATIVES (1984).
92   R. Forsberg, The Freeze and Beyond: Confining the Military to Defense as a Route to Disarmament, World Policy Journal, Winter 1984 p.285. See R.C.KARP, Ed., SECURITY WITHOUT NUCLEAR WEAPONS? (1992).

ries of thought and behavior, people can envisage more powerful and effective security policies for the future."[93]

While in the process of disarming - and until a UN police force is created - nations can still be safe. If long-range attack weapons, such as strategic bombers, could be eliminated, a nation could defend itself by less threatening types of force. Defensive forces such as tanks, could be repositioned to allow non-offensive defense, enabling an invaded nation to prevail against the attacker. Such is the type of new thinking required to replace the old confrontation by a new spirit of cooperation for mutual advantage and security.[94]

The reasons that justified self-defense as an "inherent right" no longer exist today. War is no longer a legal prerogative of sovereign states or anyone else. Self-help is, at most, a very limited exception for a very limited time. The UN Charter reference to self-defense (Art.51) must be strictly construed in favor of peace. Since there is now a central authority - the UN Security Council - not only legally authorized to cope with the defense of world peace, but now politically able to do so with the greatest speed when necessary, the legal justification for the traditional conception of self-defense disappears.

What it adds up to is the conclusion that self-defense in today's world is not a policy that is justifiable or one that can lead to a more peaceful world. The traditional justification of self-defence as an inherent right lost its *raison d'être* when the UN Charter designated the Security Council to be the central authority to maintain peace. It lost its moral and legal basis when the Council began to fulfill its enforcement function and when proportionality became impossible by virtue of the technology of modern warfare. It will lose its utility when alternative means of self-defense through non-military means - or UN police action - becomes an assured alternative.

Saying that defensive security seemed implicit in the UN Charter, Nazir Kamal has argued:

> Generally speaking, the prospects of defensive security as a
> distinct arms control concept would depend, in large part, on

---

93   B.H. WESTON, Ed., ALTERNATIVE SECURITY- LIVING WITHOUT NUCLEAR DETERRENCE (1990) at 225.

94   *See* D.FISCHER, W. NOLTE, & J. OBERG, WINNING PEACE, STRATEGIES AND ETHICS FOR A NUCLEAR-FREE WORLD (1989); Report of the UN Secretary-General, *General and Complete Disarmament: Defensive Security Concepts and Policies*, A/47/394, 22 Sept. 1992.

macro-level developments in the international system, such as progress towards 'collective security,' 'comprehensive security' or 'common security'. The imperatives for making efforts in these directions are clear - not only effectively to contain military threats in a fatefully interdependent world...but also to direct greater energy and resources towards tackling the various non-military threats to security which have assumed awesome proportions.[95]

Until a credible and effective alternative to military self-defense is created, the sad reality is that many innocent people will die because of the failure of the international system to erect legal safeguards to protect them. We must press forward as quickly as possible to remedy this very deplorable situation. How that can be done is the principle theme of this book and will be dealt with in the following chapters.

Military establishments all over the world have been trained to fight wars in the hope that they will win them. If the public and the armed forces are to be safeguarded, national defence departments must begin to think less about *winning* wars and more about *avoiding* them. Military budgets must move away from the creation and use of new instruments of mass destruction and use their resources instead for the development of new institutions to maintain peace. We need smart leaders more than we need "smart bombs." Unrestrained self-help is no help. Preserving peace is now the only means for effective self-defence.

F - The Illusion of Consensus

The UN charter says absolutely nothing about voting by consensus. Since that has become the most popular method for passing UN resolutions, let us briefly consider how that unauthorized procedure came about and just how useful it is in helping to achieve Charter goals.

(1) Origins of Voting by Consensus:

Consensus voting at the UN was an innovative response to a crisis of UN management. It should be recalled that when the United Nations was founded it had 51 members and was essentially a coalition of victorious Allied Powers primarily concerned with preserving the status quo. The admittance of many new states, following the sweeping decolonization after 1960, drastically altered the power structure of the UN organization. New coalitions were able to muster a majority and pass Assembly resolutions

---

95   N.Kamal, Senior Research Fellow at the Institute for Strategic Studies, Islambad, Pakistan, *Defensive Security in Regions Other Than Europe,* XV *Disarmament* No.4,(1992) at 149, 151.

overriding objections of a powerful minority. America's Permanent Representative Patrick D. Moynihan called the UN "a dangerous place."[96]

Passing a resolution is one thing; *enforcement* is another. The confrontation between theory and reality came to a head in the early 1960's when
some permanent members simply refused to pay their allocation for certain
UN expenses approved by the General Assembly, despite an ICJ advisory
opinion that payments were legitimately due.[97] According to the Charter,
members in arrears "shall have no vote in the General Assembly" (Art.19).
But to enforce that Charter mandate would mean that principle players
would be out of the game. To avoid dismembering the organization, some
new theory was needed to save the United Nations from being undermined
by having to admit that binding legal obligations could be ignored and
nothing could be done about it. It was a challenge that tested the imagination
of delegates and the flexibility of the Charter.[98]

The creative solution that was found was simply to disregard the
Charter requirement that said:

> Decisions of the General Assembly on important questions will
> be made by a two-thirds majority of the members present and
> voting.[99]

Instead, a new technique was invented to by-pass the Charter restraints -
resolutions could be passed *without* a vote! If no nation raised formal
objection, resolutions could be adopted by declaring there was a *consensus*
in favor of it - and no vote was necessary. *Voilà*!

Delegates were allowed to take the floor to explain their own view of
the legal instrument - even if their interpretation was quite contrary to the
letter or spirit of what had just been "accepted," "passed by consensus" or
"adopted without a vote." Consensus created the illusion of concurrence.
By taking a pragmatic approach, a way had been found to circumvent the
Charter and save the UN - even though the Charter never envisaged such a
possibility!

---

96   D.P. MOYNIHAN, A DANGEROUS PLACE (1978).
97   ICJ Advisory Opinion, *Certain Expenses of the UN*, 20 July 1962; *See* Annual Report of the
     Secretary-General, GAOR 20th Sess., Supp.No.1 (A/6001) 1965.
98   *See* E. Suy, *Consensus*, 7 Encycl. Public. Int. Law (1992) at 49.
99   UN Charter Article 18 (2).

(2) *The Pros and Cons of Consensus:*

There was much to be said in favor and against the imaginative solution to the voting problem generated by deadbeats that didn't pay their UN bills. Stipulating in advance that future decisions would be reached only by consensus offered reassurance that no one would be outvoted and thereby encouraged fearful nations to come to the negotiating table. To be sure, the search for consensus forced nations to try harder to reach agreement than might otherwise have been the case. That was a good thing and sometimes produced real compromises and substantive accords - even if it took many years. It also prevented negotiations being broken off in failure. A consensus, even if not completely satisfactory, was something that could be built on and clarified in the future - without having to start all over again.

Even the *process* of trying to reach agreement had an educational value in enabling states better to understand their divergent points of view. If repeated often enough, or officially interpreted in a consistent and useful way, a consensus agreement could, as we noted in our discussion of *jus cogens,* gradually acquire the power of a binding norm.[100] The practice of passing resolutions by consensus was thus not without its redeeming features.

But there's another side to the coin of consensus. As the League of Nations discovered to its sorrow, requiring unanimity as a condition for action is a recipe for disaster. What consensus means - in effect - is that every participant has a right of veto. To get unanimous agreement of some 180 nations on *any* subject is practically impossible. It forces nations to take the lowest common denominator if there is to be any progress at all. It is an invitation for tyranny by the minority.[101] Worse - it is a convenient mask for hypocrisy. Nations hide their real opposition by creating the false impression that they agree with the majority. They seek to avoid criticism by marching along with the crowd, hoping no one will notice that they are out of step. Symbolism replaces substance - what appears as a unanimous agreement is, in fact, no agreement at all.

---

100 Chapter One, Section D.

101 *See* C. Tomuschat, *Tyrannei der Minderheit,* 19 Germ Yrb'k Int. L. 278 (1976); E. Suy, *Role et signification du consensus dans l'élaboration du droit international,* in *Etudes en l'honneur de Roberto Ago,* vol.1, 521, (1987).

As we have seen from our description of the vague and contradictory consensus texts dealing with the international laws of peace, the apparent agreement was only a mirage.[102] Professor Julius Stone, in a rather bitter dissection of the consensus definition of aggression, referred to the UN method of reaching agreement as "Conflict through Consensus."[103] Conflicting parties remained free to interpret consensus texts for their own advantage. It was - *faut de mieux* - a form of diplomatic game-playing that manipulated the Charter and created the illusion of progress to cloak the reality of stalemate.

The so-called "consensus", which meant agreement only on ambiguous language, may have seemed a clever way to respond to the conditions of yesterday but it is not good enough to meet the needs of tomorrow. Matters affecting war and peace are too important to be dependent upon the tedious and failed practices of the past. Progress is destroyed by deadlock. We must find a quicker and more effective way to make international law clear and binding on the vital issues that concern all of humankind.

In order to prevent total paralysis through consensus, the Law of the Sea negotiators reached a sensible "Gentleman's Agreement" not to *vote* on substantive matters *until* all efforts at consensus had been exhausted. Real consensus was a goal, but if it was unattainable, binding decisions would be reached by vote. Without such an agreement, the Law of the Sea Treaty might have been devoid of substance or might never have materialized.[104]

We can learn the following from the practice of consensus voting at the UN:

(a) Nations are quite willing and able to interpret the Charter in ways never anticipated by the founding fathers.

(b) The justification for innovative interpretations lies in the pragmatic need to preserve the UN and better serve the Charter purposes.

---

102 See Chapter One.

103 J.STONE, CONFLICT THROUGH CONSENSUS (1977); J. Stone, *Hopes and Loopholes in the 1974 Definition of Aggression*, 71 AJIL 224 (1977).

104 *See* B. Buzan, *Negotiating by Consensus: Developments in Technique at the UN Conference on the Law of the Sea*, 75 AJIL 324 (1981) at 348; L.Sohn, *Voting Procedures in UN Conferences for the Codification of International Law*, 69 AJIL 310 (1975).

(c) The search for widespread agreement is a highly desireable procedure but it becomes counter-productive if it is allowed to continue beyond a reasonable time.

(d) Democracy and progress can be imperiled by the tyranny of a small minority.

G - Evaluation

One of the hardest things to change is a firmly held opinion. In considering new thinking about old problems the first thing to ask oneself is whether the present world order is a satisfactory one. If the answer is yes, there is no hope that stubborn minds can be changed - nor (from their point of view) is there any reason to do so. But, if (as one surveys the international scene with its carnage, devastation, poverty, killing of innocents, human degradation, universal insecurity etc.) one is convinced that improvements are necessary or even desirable, then the rational mind should come to the conclusion that changes are required in the way this globe is managed and that some solidly entrenched points of view will have to be altered.

Some of the proposed changes in the way of thinking about old problems may, at first, appear unrealistic or shocking because they seem to run counter to firmly ingrained traditions, immutable dogmas or seemingly well established principles of law. But, on further reflection and examination, it will be seen that what may have been a rational basis for old principles is no longer persuasive or justifiable. The old way of thinking stands in the way of building a new world order in which all people can live in peace and dignity.

It must be recognized that sovereignty no longer lies in medieval monarchs but now rests with the people they were supposed to serve. The right of every nation to conduct its own affairs as it sees fit no longer includes the right to commit genocide or other crimes against humanity against anyone. The right to self-determination does not include the right to determine that large numbers of innocent people must die to provide nationhood to every self-proclaimed ethnic entity. The right of self-defence does not include the right to render millions of people defenseless against poverty because they are condemned to an endless arms race that threatens all of humankind. Refusing to advance towards peace until there is a universal consensus on every step of the way, is to condemn the world to stand still.

If the old problems inherent in trying to create a more peaceful world are to be overcome, it will be necessary to remember the flexibility of the UN Charter and to adopt more flexible ways of thinking about old perceptions that have been stumbling-blocks on the road to world peace. The world is in fact - of necessity - already moving away from outmoded concepts, but the pace of change is too slow to cope adequately with the advanced speed of modern social and political interactions.

Since the experience of regional associations may also offer valuable lessons in how to deal effectively with common international problems, a brief survey of such associations may also be an instructive guide to finding improved methods of global management for peace.

CHAPTER FIVE
ROLE OF REGIONALISM

The feasibility of realizing this idea of Federalism, that should eventually cover all states and so lead toward perpetual peace, can be described. When luck ordains that a powerful and enlightened people can build themselves into a republic (which according to its nature must be inclined to perpetual peace) that would offer other states a central point around which to link their own associations with the federal union and more and more linkages of this kind can be further broadened and thereby secure the condition of freedom for all states in accordance with the principles of international law.

Immanuel Kant, 1795[1]

There are those who are still inclined to seek the road to peace via the path of expanding regional organizations. The joinder of diverse nations working in unity for their mutual benefit gives rise to the hope that competitive states may eventually be consolidated into one cooperative human family living in pluralistic harmony in a democratic republic or confederation of the world.[2] How far have we come along that road which Immanuel Kant projected two centuries ago as a path to permanent peace and how long might it still take to reach its inspiring destination?

A - Regionalism as a Road to Globalism

(1) Historical Origins:

As paradoxical as it may sound, world society has been in a constant process of integrating and disintegrating at the same time. History is replete with examples of regional unity followed by disunity that ended in tragic war. A classic illustration can be found in the ancient writings of Thucydides.

Four centuries before the birth of Christ, sovereign Greek city states joined together to lead Greece to victory against the Persian Empire. But the

---

1   I. KANT, *ZUM EWIGEN FRIEDEN*, T. Valentiner paperback edition, 1953 at 33-34. (Translation of the citation by B. Ferencz).

2   *See* W.B. LLOYD, WAGING PEACE, THE SWISS EXPERIENCE (1958).

allied cities of Sparta and Athens - differentiated by race, political constitutions and divisions between rich and poor - ended by fighting against
themselves. Thucydides tells us that no one wanted war but, driven by fear,
politics and self-interest, the voices of justice and mercy were unheard and
only power ruled as former allies killed each other on land and sea for over
a quarter of a century until almost all of the young male population of
Athens was dead.[3]

Biblical tribes, bound by geographic, family and religious ties, formed
small nations to protect their interests and their terrain. The chronicles of
their dispersions and defeats fills the sacred books of all peoples. The *Pax
Romana*, that kept the peace in a mighty Roman empire of conquered states,
ended with the fall of the great Roman civilization. Alliances of medieval
monarchs were unable to halt the ravages of violent strife based on religion
or opportunistic conquest. Catholics and Protestants killed each other for
thirty years until their mutual annihilation was halted by the Treaties of
Westphalia in 1648 that created the modern system of secular and independent nation states - relying on balanced power to maintain peace. It
didn't work.

Out of the myriads of conflicting sovereignties came new formations
of modern nation states. In Switzerland, Germany, Italy, France and elsewhere, including the great expanses of China, Russia and India, many
diverse peoples were consolidated - whether they liked it or not - under the
centralized control of a single government. In the new world, thirteen
colonies declared their independence. When their system of weak confederation proved unworkable without a common legislature, courts or system
of law enforcement, they formed a "more perfect union" - the United States
of America. Nationalism became a dominant force in world affairs. Too
often, adoration of the nation state became associated with despotism,
militarism and ethnocentrism - to the detriment of universal humanity and
individual freedom.[4]

(2) Nationalism, Regionalism, Universalism:

The enormous losses arising out of the first world war among leading
nation-states was a rude awakening to the realization that a new structure
of international society was needed if future wars were to be avoided. The

---

3   THUCYDIDES, THE HISTORY OF THE PEOLOPONNESIAN WAR, Edited by R.W.
Livingstone, Oxford, (1943) at 387-8.
4   *See* J.KIANG, ONE WORLD, Chapter III.

League of Nations - an expanded association of states - gave rise to the universal hope that militant nationalism might be subordinated to a new international union to maintain peace. But war was never outlawed by the League and without unanimous consent of every member there could be no peace enforcement - there was a gap in the Covenant. World War II was the price humanity paid for its shortsightedness.

When a new world charter was being considered in the summer of 1944, Nationalism again came face to face with its competitors Regionalism and Universalism. It was recognized that an improved system of collective security would be necessary to deter or defeat aggressive national ambitions that might again imperil the common welfare. But the planners of the new United Nations Organization had mixed objectives: Churchill felt that a regional association of European states was necessary to maintain peace in Europe - thereby enhancing the security of Britain; the Soviets wanted a regional association of Eastern European states - dominated by the Soviet Union - that could serve as a buffer against future invasions from the west; the United States objected to the attempted Soviet power-grab but wanted the same predominance for itself in the Western Hemisphere. In short: those that had power were not ready to relinquish it to any regional combinations that might not be under their control.[5]

By the time the San Francisco Conference was called to discuss and sign the UN Charter, the die was cast:

> One thing was certain: the central organization had to be master, not the servant of any regional bodies.[6]

Small states, fearful that powerful nations would continue to exploit them as they had in the past, favored the creation of their own regional associations able to defend the interests of their local communities. American states had formed a regional association as early as 1899 and several of them spoke up at San Francisco when the draft Charter was being debated.[7] But the founders insisted upon retaining sole responsibility for peace enforcement in the Security Council (which they controlled) and no small nation could stand up to the mighty allies that had saved the world from barbarism. The outcome in 1945 was a reminder of Thucydides:

---

5   See Chapter Three, Section A.

6   C.HILDEBRAND. DUMBARTON OAKS (1990) at 164.

7   *See* Documents of the UN Conference on International Organization (UNCIO) Vol. 12 pp. 661-866, Minutes of Meetings, Commission III, Committee 4, May 5, 1945 - June 8, 1945.

8   Thucydides at 267.

You know and we know, as practical men, that the question of justice arises only between parties equal in strength, and that the strong do what they can, and the weak submit.[8]

The "compromise" that appeared in the final UN Charter was that the Security Council (with its veto intact) remained the only body authorized to use force to maintain peace. "Regional arrangements or agencies" were encouraged to seek *peaceful* settlements and could deal with such matters relating to peace "as are *appropriate* for regional action", but they could take no enforcement action "without the *authorization of the Security Council*." The Charter required regional organizations to keep the Council fully informed at all times of activities "undertaken *or in contemplation*" under regional arrangements.[9]

In matters of peace *enforcement*, all regional arrangements or agencies - whatever their constellation - were clearly and deliberately subordinated to the centralized power of the Security Council. But it was not - as seemed to be the case - a triumph of universalism over regionalism or nationalism. Retaining power in the hands of a few members of the Security Council, was motivated more by national political considerations and self-interest than concern for the future welfare of humankind - despite the contrary impression that was given to the public.[10]

It was not long after the Charter was signed that it became obvious that its peace-keeping mechanism could not succeed. The Covenant of the League was based on the flawed assumption that all nations would act unanimously against aggression. The Charter peace plan was based on the flawed assumption that all of the five permanent members would be in agreement; sadly, that was not the case. Just as there had been a fatal gap in the Covenant of the League, there existed a papered-over gap in the Charter - the regional agencies had no authority to enforce peace and the Security Council had neither the political ability or the military capability to do so. Until these shortcomings could be overcome and the gap closed, there would be no way to maintain peace in the world.

Since the major powers had insisted upon retaining their privileged position and their rights regarding peace enforcement, they should have

---

8   Thucydides at 267.
9   UN Charter, Articles 52, 53, 54, emphasis added.
10   R. Dolzer, *Universalism and Regionalism*, in A.GRAHL-MADSEN AND J.TOMAN, THE SPIRIT OF UPPSALA (1984) 513; *See* B. ANDEMICAEL, Ed., REGIONALISM AND THE UNITED NATIONS (1979).

been ready to assume the obligations and duties that (according to the Charter) went with the privileges. But that would have entailed risks and burdens they were not always ready to take. The inability of the new world organization to retain the solidarity on which peace and social justice depended made it essential that new ways be found to manage global problems that could no longer be dealt with on a national basis.

B - Regionalism as Pragmatism

Regionalism evolved not as a preferred transitional stage away from the nation state toward a universal order but as a pragmatic necessity that arose from the political inability of major powers to create a universal solidarity within the UN system capable of maintaining peace and human dignity.[11]

In 1947, Latin American states - with U.S. support - signed a mutual defense treaty.[12] The following year, twenty American Republics and the United States accepted a common Charter for the Organization of American States. The regional association promised joint action to repel aggression, and enhanced economic cooperation as well as peaceful settlement of disputes among its members.[13] Despite the promise, the region was soon torn by civil wars and internal and external subversion. The OAS system, dominated by the United States, proved too rigid, bureaucratic and inattentive to deal effectively with such local problems as the debt burden, poverty, and oppression. A genuine inter-American community working together to enhance the welfare of all of its inhabitants did not exist.[14]

Eastern European states, dominated by the Soviet Union, formed military and economic alliances to confront similar alliances of western European states led by the United states.[15] In the Middle East, the Arab League sought to unite Arab states to protect their special interests. In Asia and the Far East, nations formed regional associations for security and economic reasons.[16] In Africa, the Organization of African Unity sought to speak for

---

11 R.J.YALEM, REGIONALISM AND WORLD ORDER (1965) p. 142.

12 *Inter-American Treaty of Reciprocal Assistance*, the Rio Treaty, signed in Brazil in 1947.

13 *Charter of the Organization of American States*, April 30, 1948, 119 UNTS 3; Amended by Protocol of Buenos Aires, Feb., 27, 1967, 721 UNTS 266; *See* F.V. GARCIA-AMADOR, THE ANDEAN LEGAL ORDER (1978).

14 *See* L.R.SCHEMAN, THE INTER-AMERICAN DILEMMA (1988) at 194-196; A.V.W. THOMAS & A.J.THOMAS, THE ORGANIZATION OF AMERICAN STATES (1963).

15 *See North Atlantic Treaty* (NATO), 34 UNTS 243(1949); *Warsaw Treaty*, 219 UNTS 24 (1955).

16 *Southeast Asia Collective Defense Treaty*, 219 UNTS 28 (1955).

a wide array of disparate African nations with a large variety of problems.[17] With few exceptions, post-war regional organizations emphasized one function - either military, economic, social or political - without challenging national sovereignty.[18] Professor Ruth Lawson wrote:

> It should not escape attention that, whereas the principal multi-lateral regional-security arrangements of this era have originated as traditional alliances, under the pressure of necessity they have evolved into organizations whose institutions and procedures, and in some cases powers, have been pragmatically, if often reluctantly, devised.[19]

Just as multi-national industrial corporations and financial institutions discovered that efficiency and cost-effectiveness required global planning and control, a multi-national process evolved among many other groups to find pragmatic solutions and help meet a variety of universal human needs that were not dealt with under the global authority of the United Nations. Of necessity, the traditional integrated state system moved away from its rigid Westphalian national characteristics toward a broader area of international functional interaction.[20]

The most important and most advanced regional association that has been developed anywhere in the world is the European Community that arose out of the ashes of World War II. It was stimulated by a combination of idealism and pragmatism and found fertile ground in the blood-soaked soil of nations that had borne the heaviest brunt of two world wars. It is still evolving, but it may serve as a model from which new insights may be gained and many lessons learned.

C - European Community as Model

We have already briefly described the origins and workings of the Court of Justice of the European Communities as well as the European Court of Human Rights and the significant impact those institutions had in stimu-

---

17 *See* D.W. BOWETT, THE LAW OF INTERNATIONAL INSTITUTIONS, 4th Ed. (1982) Part Two; W.J.FELD, G.BOYD, COMPARATIVE REGIONAL SYSTEMS (1980); J. CHARPENTIER, *INSTITUTIONS INTERNATIONALES* (1989).

18 *See* G.BOYD, Ed., REGIONALISM AND GLOBAL SECURITY (1984).

19 R.C. LAWSON, INTERNATIONAL REGIONAL ORGANIZATIONS (1962) at viii.

20 L.H.MILLER, ORGANIZING MANKIND (1973) pp. 346-347. Trans-sovereign contacts among subnational governments, such a Quebec's attachments to the United States and France, are described in I.D. DUCHACEK, D.LATOUCE & G. STEVENSON, Eds.,PERFORATED SOVEREIGNTIES AND INTERNATIONAL RELATIONS (1988).

lating the establishment of similar courts in other regions of the world.[21] Here we are concerned with Europe as a regional association formed originally to end the destructive rivalry between France and Germany and evolving over the last four decades from a Common Market toward an enlarged economic and political union that should be considered as a possible blueprint for other regions as well as a catalyst for an expanded regime for global peace.[22]

Building on the dream of Jean Monnet and other great founders of the idea of an integrated Europe, a dozen sovereign states, eager to enhance the peaceful management of international cooperation, freely formed a supranational organization for the benefit of their respective citizens. The European Community was seen as a movement away from nationalism. According to S.F. Goodman:

> Europe is passing out of the phase of the dominance of the nation state and entering the era of cooperative decision making.[23]

As Europe moved toward greater integration and political cohesion its security was increased; the threat of warfare among its members disappeared and its need for military preparation diminished.[24]

The European Community (EC) that now encompasses twelve nation states has made its greatest advance in the field of economic integration - a component of social justice vital to world peace. As Ernest Wistrich has noted:

> Interdependence generated by integration has made war between its members not only unthinkable but no longer practicable. Europe's living standards, as the world's largest trader, largely depends on the preservation of peace in the rest of the world...Growth in its own prosperity depends on the living standards and purchasing power of its trading partners rising too. That is why the European Community, more than most, has

---

21 Chapter Two, Section C.

22 The European Community was created in Rome on 25 March 1957 by France, West Germany, Italy, Belgium, Netherlands and Luxembourg, and was later joined by Denmark, Ireland and the U.K in 1973, by Greece in 1981 and by Spain and Portugal in 1986. The early plans for the development of European integration and the treaties by which the various institutions have been created are found in A.H. ROBERTSON, EUROPEAN INSTITUTIONS, 2d Ed. (1966).

23 S.F. GOODMAN, THE EUROPEAN COMMUNITY (1991) at 182.

24 See B. BUZAN et al. THE EUROPEAN SECURITY ORDER RECAST (1990).

a direct interest in helping developing countries to grow out of their poverty.[25]

Even if motivated primarily by self-interest - and perhaps because of it - a working system of economic regional cooperation that enhances security and prosperity for its members can be an important motivating force for others to join together in similar unions for similar purposes. Any system that moves toward the desired goal of global peace deserves support and serious consideration as a model for global order.

Although the Community has become the worlds largest trading block, it is still only half formed. In the political field it still has a long way to go. National political considerations rather than regional or global aspirations still dominate many of its important decisions. Short-term domestic benefits - rather than long-term international or regional solidarity - determine the speed and parameters of more comprehensive European integration.[26] The European Parliament, elected by over 100 million voters, was the first supranational parliament in history. But it was more a symbolic milestone than a substantive one - power remained in the hands of the Council of Ministers representing the national interest of each member state. The nation-state remained the pivotal axis around which the European Community revolved. The European Parliament started as an over-bloated bureaucracy that was ridiculed as:

> an opera buffo, with over 500 characters (the MEPs) [Members of the European Parliament]), 12 acts (the member-states), seven plots (the transnational party groupings), playing in two theaters (Brussels and Strasbourg). Nine Languages are spoken, but none are listened to, and the EP is engaged in the symbolism of politics without its essence.[27]

The Single European Act (SEA) that came into force in 1987 was a rather belated commitment to negotiate a full Economic, Monetary and Political Union of Europe by 31 December 1992.[28] It was intended to move the Community from a system of "political cooperation" to one of "closer cooperation" that would enable the Community to speak with one voice at

---

25   E. WISTRICH, AFTER 1992 - THE UNITED STATES OF EUROPE (1991) at 126-127.

26   See A.CLESSE & R. VERNON, Eds., THE EUROPEAN COMMUNITY AFTER 1992; A NEW ROLE IN WORLD POLITICS? (1991); A.M. WILLIAMS, THE EUROPEAN COMMUNITY - THE CONTRADICTIONS OF INTEGRATION (1991).

27   L.HURWITZ, THE EUROPEAN COMMUNITY AND THE MANAGEMENT OF INTERNATIONAL COOPERATION (1989) at 241.

28   25 ILM 503 (1986); See G.A. Bermann, The Single European Act: A New Constitution for the Community? , 27 Colum. J. Transnat'l Law 529 (1989).

the United Nations and to act jointly on matters of common defense. But, local parliaments, when called upon to ratify the implementing Treaty on European Union signed in the Dutch town of Maastricht in 1991, balked at provisions regarded as detrimental to their local interests.[29] Efforts to create a unified European currency and monetary system were also faced by stormy opposition on the national level. Even among a dozen neighboring states of similar cultural and economic background, obtaining the necessary unanimous consensus on important questions proved to be a very slow and difficult process.

Creating an expanded "United States of Europe" or a politically stable European community to include the region from the Urals to the Atlantic - the "common European home" called for by Mr. Gorbachev - may be next to impossible in the near future. Amalgamating the western region with eastern European or North African regions - of different religions, ethnic identities, languages, cultural, economic and social affiliations - may present intractable problems.[30]

Regional associations of developing countries face even greater difficulties than those encountered by the European Community: they must penetrate new world markets, compete with highly industrialized countries, acquire new technologies, obtain additional resources and overcome a host of natural, political and economic barriers. The Third World itself is highly stratified. Despite immense oil wealth of many rulers, their populations remain backward, and different states in adjacent regions may be in fierce political or economic competition.[31] If one contrasts the degree and tempo of integration of the advanced European Community with the current level of existing regional associations in Latin America, Sub-Saharan Africa, Asia and the Middle East, it becomes readily apparent that a global amalgamation of such diversity can not realistically be seen as a feasible possibility in the near future.[32]

The prospects for integrating the Chinese "region," with its billion people bound by ancient tradition and totalitarianism, into an expanding

---

29   See Treaty on European Union and Final Act, Done at Maastricht, Feb.7, 1992, reproduced in 31 ILM 247 (1992).

30   *See* I. SEIDL-HOHENVELDERN, *AUF DEM WEGE NACH EUROPA - FRAGEN ZUR EUROPAISCHEN INTEGRATION* (1991) pp.1-7.

31   *See* R.KOTHARI, FOOTSTEPS INTO THE FUTURE (1977) pp.135-138.

32   *See* R.J. LANGENHAMMER, U. HIEMENZ, REGIONAL INTEGRATION AMONG DEVELOPING COUNTRIES (1990). The emerging international region of the Arctic is just beginning to come alive. *See* K. MOTTOLA, THE ARCTIC CHALLENGE (1988).

and merging world-wide regionalism appears even less promising in the foreseeable future.[33]   A mixed regional association of global reach is not likely to find much acceptance in fundamentalist Islamic nations - even if Islam could be interpreted (as Professor Majid Khadduri and others insist is the correct interpretation) to require the faithful to coexist in peace with the non-Islamic world community.[34]

In short, when one considers the enormous diversity of cultures and economic levels of different countries within Europe and of different regions outside of Europe, it appears most unlikely that a common law of humanity can soon be found through the role of an expanded European Community leading to a universal peace. The great peoples of China, India, Africa, the Middle-East and Latin-America will, for many years, be absorbed with raising the living standards of their own diverse populations and it will be a very long time before they will be able to focus on the longer-range goals of global integration.

This is not to suggest that the European Community itself will not gradually move closer together as a larger and more integrated federation of states. Professor Joseph H. Weiler of Harvard has persuasively demonstrated that an evolutionary movement is already under way whereby EC nations are developing a new structure and process in which the interpretation of law and the application of politics interact to produce pragmatic solutions to common problems. The resulting legal-political equilibrium - strengthening both the Community and its Members - is obtained by giving states the assurance that their interests will be protected and by giving the members a principle role in the decision-making process:

> ...by virtue of the near total control of the Member States over the Community processes, the community appeared more as an instrument in the hands of the governments than as a usurping power..The key to success of the 1992 strategy occurred when the Member states themselves agreed to majority voting.[35]

Professor Weiler can not predict when complete political integration of Europe will be a reality but he has pointed to the process of mutual confidence-building as a stimulus to movement in the right direction.[36]

33   *See* G. KAMINSKI, *CHINESISCHE POSITIONEN ZUM VöLKERRECHT (1973).*

34   M. KHADDURI, WAR AND PEACE IN THE LAW OF ISLAM (1941); See S. SIYAR, THE ISLAMIC LAW OF NATIONS, Translated, with notes by Majid Khadduri (1965); I.K. SALEM, ISLAM UND VOLKERRECHT (1984); M.T. AL GHUNAIMI, THE MUSLIM CONCEPTION OF INTERNATIONAL LAW AND THE WESTERN APPROACH (1968).

35   J.H.H. Weiler, *The Transformation of Europe,* 100 Yale L.J. (1991) 2405 at 2449, 2458.

36   Weiler, mindful of the dangers that a new European nationalism or European regionalism might turn into a super-state, feels that politically (but not legally) the EC is already a

Confidence building through a sense of shared participation may be a slow and arduous process but if it produces visible movement toward the integration of a world community, it is a process worth encouraging and emulating. The same lesson can be drawn from another European experience in multi-national cooperation and peace-building.

D - The "Helsinki Process" of the CSCE

Some regional combinations developed in ways that neither the UN Charter nor the parties themselves ever anticipated.[37] The Helsinki Accords signed in 1975 by 35 states participating in a Conference on Security and Cooperation in Europe (CSCE) were designed primarily to assure Eastern Soviet-bloc states that their borders would not be challenged by NATO forces of the west. In exchange for that "concession," the west extracted promises that human rights in eastern European states would be enhanced. Perhaps most important, it was agreed that follow-up conferences would be held regularly to monitor and report on progress. The Helsinki Final Act of 1975 was just a beginning.[38]

From its unofficial and non-binding origins, the CSCE nations developed a process of confidence-building that held the potential for playing an important role in the future development of Europe - all without a heavy bureaucratic superstructure or any military force.[39] Expert meetings were convened regularly and frequently to ease East-West tensions by proposing disarmament, human rights liberalization and specific confidence-building measures. Following the disintegration of the Soviet empire starting around 1987, Europe was engulfed in a flood of new problems that threatened peace.[40]

---

*con*federation and that it may take a period of adjustment before it can become a federation acceptable to all its members. *Id.* at 2481.

37 *See* P. Porstila, *The Helsinki Process: A Success Story and New Challenges,* 4 *DISARMAMENT - A Periodic Review by the UN* (1992) p. 26. V. MASTNY, THE HELSINKI PROCESS AND THE REINTEGRATION OF EUROPE 1986 -1991: ANALYSIS AND DOCUMENTATION (1992).

38 Follow-up meetings took place in Belgrade in 1977-78, in Madrid in 1980-1983, in Helsinki in 1985, in Vienna in 1986 and 1989, in New York and Paris in 1990, in Berlin in 1991 and in Prague in Jan. 1992 to be followed by a Summit meeting in Helsinki in July 1992 and frequent meetings thereafter.

39 *See* B. KOHLER-KOCH, *REGIME IN DEN INTERNATIONALEN BEZIEHUNGEN* (1989); W.KOREY, THE PROMISES WE KEEP (1993).

40 To what extent the liberalizing influence of the CSCE, and its well-publicized reviews contributed to the collapse of the Soviet Union, and whether an over-emphasis on self-determination rather than tolerance contributed to keeping the spirit of *revanchism* alive, are both speculative.

Ethno-national conflicts, economic and environmental crises, mass migration of populations, disputes about ownership of military and other resources are among the many problems that plunged the Balkans and other areas into armed conflicts. NATO, which had been created to repulse any possible Soviet invasion of the west, had lost its mission and purpose and seemed paralyzed by its own legal restraints. What mechanism would prevail to protect human rights, promote economic integration and maintain peace in a disintegrating Europe was quite uncertain.

UN resolutions - restrained by the Charter prohibition against interference in internal affairs, did little to halt the genocidal bloodshed that emerged in several regions and seemed to be spreading. New strategies were needed to cope with the new regional problems. While the UN dithered, the CSCE, with all of its organizational limitations, tried to jump into the breach. A 1990 "Charter of Paris" proclaimed a new role for the CSCE.[41]

CSCE membership was increased to 52 by admitting the states of Eastern Europe. Decisions of less than vital importance could be reached by less than consensus voting - an important step forward. At its Helsinki summit meeting of Heads of State in July 1992, its expanded institutional structure was approved and CSCE considered itself authorized as a "regional arrangement" under Chapter VIII of the UN Charter to seek to settle European disputes by peaceful means.[42] In implementation of the Paris Charter, it was agreed:

> 1 - A review conference would be held every two years with the Heads of State or Government of each member;
>
> 2 - A Council, consisting of the foreign ministers of the member states, would meet at least once a year;
>
> 3 - A Committee of Senior Officials (CSO) - a management control mechanism to prepare the work for the Ministers - and a central forum for political consultations would meet at least every three months. In the interim,

---

41   On 21 Nov, 1990, at a Paris meeting of Heads of State, the *Charter of Paris for a new Europe* was signed (A/45/859), primarily to plan the creation of a new CSCE institutional structure to cope with the new European problems.

42   The Final Document was adopted on 10 July 1992 (A/47/361 - S/24370); *reproduced in* 4 *DISARMAMENT* (1992) p. 172.

they would consider reports from experts and a new High Commissioner on National Minorities who would serve as part of an early-warning system for "preventive diplomacy."

4 - New permanent institutions would be created:

A - A Secretariat, to be located in Prague;

B - A Conflict prevention center in Vienna;

C - An Office for free elections (later expanded to cover democratic institutions and human rights) in Warsaw;

D - A Parliamentary Assembly, representing the national parliaments of the members, was to meet annually to assess the workings of the CSCE and the implementation of its decisions.[43]

CSCE thus set up a mini-mechanism to deal with crises of various kinds, political, military and human. It was hoped that by using experts rather than national delegates and relying on democratic principles and voting procedures, disputes could be settled peacefully by a streamlined system that would be more efficient than the prevailing bureaucracies. An optimistic analysis prepared in Germany - one of the main moving partners - concluded:

> If the CSCE is not used as a 'blueprint' but is primarily considered to be a 'process', then the knowledge about its structure and mechanism can contribute to the development of peace strategies which would also be suitable for other regions of the world.[44]

American analysts saw the CSCE in a far less optimistic light. They noted that efforts by CSCE fact-finders and negotiators to resolve the conflicts in Nagorno Karabakh, Moldavia, Abkhazia and elsewhere were singularly ineffective. CSCE negotiators were able to bring some of the parties together for talks but - in the absence of any enforcement authority - the impact was minimal.[45] CSCE Efforts to reach agreement on a new treaty mandating dispute settlement by peaceful means was opposed by the

---

43   The Parliamentary Assembly held its first meeting, in Budapest, in July 1992. For an overview of the CSCE *See* N.ROPERS & P. SCHLOTTER, THE CSCE, MULTILATERAL CONFLICT MANAGEMENT IN A TRANSFORMING WORLD ORDER (1993).

44   Id. at 39.

45   See Report of *"Roundtable on the Conference on Security and Cooperation in Europe (CSCE): Mechanisms for the Peaceful Settlement of Disputes,* Oct. 6, 1992, USIP Journal pp.9-10; R. Bonner, *War in Caucasus Shows Ethnic Hate's Front Line,* N.Y. Times, International, Aug.2, 1993 p.A6.

United States as superfluous.[46] A report, prepared by American staff members of a U.S. Congressional Committee appointed to monitor the implementation of the Helsinki accords, concluded that CSCE weaknesses showed that participating states were concerned with parochial national interests first and foremost:

> ...[T]he record of CSCE's institutions and structures is far from impressive. Two years after their creation, not only have they failed to solve any of the deepening conflicts in the former Yugoslavia, the Caucasus and across the former Soviet Union but they have also remained peripheral to efforts to address those crises, as well as other conflicts plaguing participating states... understaffing, duplication and lack of expertise threaten to undermine their functioning further....Procedures will have to be streamlined, areas of action prioritized, and the institutions granted some degree of independence in order to ensure smooth support for CSCE initiatives...[47]

Acting on behalf of 52 nations, well-intentioned diplomats sent monitor missions to Yugoslavia and other Eastern states to plead for moderation and peaceful settlement. They competed with similar missions acting in the name of the European Community, the Secretary-General and UN organs such as the UN High Commissioner for Refugees. Non-Governmental Organizations like Amnesty International, the Red Cross and others also did their best to halt atrocities and bring peace to troubled areas. They held meetings, carried on discussions, negotiations, convened conferences and issued reports. But none of them had any power to enforce anything. They were political symbols more than problem solvers.[48]

The principal lesson to be drawn from the ambitious CSCE restructuring seems to be that despite efficiencies in rational organization on a minimal and non-bureaucratic basis, without the support of the United Nations - and the military backing of the Security Council in particular - all that the CSCE negotiators could do was to *talk* - and that may have been marginally helpful but it wasn't good enough to maintain or restore peace to the region.

---

46   *See* Report prepared by the Staff of CSCE, submitted to 103d Congress 1st Sess., Mar. 1933. For the CSCE draft *Convention on Conciliation and Arbitration within the CSCE, see* 32 ILM 551 (1993).

47   Report prepared by CSCE Staff, Washington D.C.(Senator Dennis DeConcini, Chairman), *Beyond Process - The CSCE's Institutional Development 1990-1992* (Dec. 1992) at 37-39. *See* "The Helsinki Commission" DIGEST Jan. 1993.

48   See S.C. Res. 874, 14 Oct. 1993.

E - Evaluation:

Regional associations have their advantages and their hazards. They allow functional integration to exist with regard to specific common problems without the need for territorial expansion or conquest.[49] They demonstrate a movement away from the parochialism of nationalism and a more rational approach to dealing with world-wide problems. Regionalism may be seen as a partner rather than a competitor of universalism since it moves in the direction of rational global management.[50]

But the world is not formed of separate and neat regional compartments. There is an overlapping and interaction of regions and their problems. There must be global solutions to global problems. Professor Dieter Ruloff of the University of Zurich argues optimistically that the nation state will not disappear in the foreseeable future but since no state can solve global problems without international cooperation they will learn to work together for their own political, social, cultural, financial, security and ecological reasons.[51] Professor R.P. Anand of New Delhi is not that optimistic. He concludes:

> In spite of the absolute interdependence of states, we are living in a divided world...Based on historical, political, ideological, economic and cultural factors, there are seemingly irreconcilable conflicts. Divided by ideology and aspirations, the world reposes uneasily in fragile peace...International peace has become everyone's responsibility.[52]

Regional associations run the risk of developing their own autonomies that might engender competition and conflict against rival regional groupings. Regional groups organized for political pressure purposes can be a means of exacerbating rather than diminishing frictions.[53] Regionalism is only a pragmatic compromise between nationalism and the presently unattainable universalism - an interim step forward in a world that lacks global

---

49   *See* E.SENGHAAS-KNOBLOCH, *FRIEDEN DURCH INTEGRATION UND ASSOZIATION* (1969).

50   See O. Kimminich, Peace Keeping on a Universal or Regional Level, in R. WOLFRUM, Ed., STRENGTHENING THE WORLD ORDER, UNIVERSALISM V. REGIONALISM (1989).

51   D. RULOFF, *WELTSTAAT ODER STAATENWELT?* (1988).

52   R.P.ANAND, CONFRONTATION OR COOPERATION? INTERNATIONAL LAW AND THE DEVELOPING COUNTRIES (1987), Preface.

53   *See* R.A.FALK & S.H. MENDLOVITZ Eds., REGIONAL POLITICS AND WORLD ORDER (1973).

controls. It is a necessary advance - but inadequate and incomplete. Regionalism can not solve problems that extend far beyond the region. The risk that regionalism may become an expanded form of competitive and violent nationalism can best be diminished by enforcing global order globally through global authority. No regional association has legitimation or power to do that - the UN Charter assigned that function primarily to the United Nations Security Council.

Immanuel Kant's vision of an evolving world order flowing naturally from expanded regionalism still seems like quite a distant dream. As we approach the end of the 20th century, the only accepted plan for peaceful world relations is based on a United Nations Charter that is almost half-a-century old and has many obvious organizational deficiencies.[54] Despite its shortcomings, it is to the United Nations that we must look for the ultimate protection of peace and human dignity.

---

54   *See* Chapter One, Section A-4; Chapter Three, Section A-3.

CHAPTER SIX
REVIEWING THE UN CHARTER

The UN is underfunded, poorly organized, and yet - by nearly universal agreement - indispensable.

Ambassador Samuel Lewis, on retiring as President of the independent U.S. Institute of Peace.[1]

In addition to new ways of thinking, we must find new ways of organizing international society so that its inhabitants may live in greater peace and dignity. Let us take a closer look at some of the UN structural shortcomings and see what has been and can be suggested to improve the world organization.

A - Structural Defects

Those criticizing the United Nations frequently maintain that the organization as a managing agency for the world is conceptually and structurally defective:

(1) It is undemocratic and unfair. It is not democratic because the Assembly's one-nation-one-vote principle disregards enormous population differences among its members. The "peoples" are not represented at all. The Security Council was designed to give preferential treatment and control to those large powers that set up the organization.

(2) It lacks the necessary authority of a legislature. Contrary to popular misconception, the General Assembly has no authority to legislate. Without world laws there can not be world peace.

(3) It lacks courts with compulsory jurisdiction. The International Court of Justice is only competent to cope with legal issues voluntarily submitted by sovereign *states*; it never has jurisdiction over individuals or groups. The World Court has no independent enforcement powers; it must depend on the Security Council. There

---

1   USIP *Journal*, 3 Feb. 1993 at 4.

is no international criminal court to penalize individuals who violate laws of peace.

(4) The UN enforcement arm is completely lame; the Security Council is a political body that can be immobilized by a veto of any one of its few privileged members. The Charter plan to regulate armaments has never been implemented; UN sanctions are ineffective; the UN army envisaged by the Charter has never been assembled.

(5) The UN has no source of independent funding; it is unable to meet its financial obligations. It must depend upon remittances from states that protest or refuse to pay the costs of the bloated bureaucracy and some of its peace-enforcement expenditures; it has no way to collect its unpaid assessments.

Without seeking to minimize any of its shortcomings, it should be recalled that the UN Charter, drafted almost fifty years ago, was only a beginning with many of its defects recognized by governments and scholars.[2] It seemed to be, and probably was, the best that could be done under the circumstances then prevailing. By the time of its 20th anniversary, - during the Vietnam war - Secretary-General U Thant candidly admitted that the Charter was already obsolete.[3] We have indicated that a General Conference to review the Charter, which the Charter itself indicated would take place within ten years - at the latest - was never convened.[4]

Some would argue that nothing less than a complete structural change of the UN is now required; the old worn-out prototype should be discarded and a new organization created that is more capable of coping with contemporary needs. Advocates of total reform often point to the experience of the new American states in 1787, when the Founding Fathers set out to revise the Articles of Confederation only to discover that a completely new Constitution of the United States was essential to make the country viable.[5] With

---

2   *See* FERENCZ, ENFORCING INT.L. vol. 2 Chap. Ten.

3   *See* Center for the Study of Democratic Institutions, *A Constitution for the World* (1965) at 4.

4   UN Charter Art.109 (3) requires that "If such a conference has not been held before the tenth annual session...the proposal to call such a conference shall be placed on the agenda... and the conference shall be held if so decided by a majority vote of the members of the General Assembly and by a vote of any seven members of the Security Council." *See* J.P.BARATTA, GRENVILLE CLARK, WORLD FEDERALIST (1985).

5   *See* B. BAILEY, Ed., THE DEBATE ON THE CONSTITUTION (1993); C.D. BOWEN, MIRACLE AT PHILADELPHIA (1966); C.V. DOREN, THE GREAT REHEARSAL (1986). The domestic analogy in various world order proposals is appraised in H. SUGANAMI, THE DOMESTIC ANALOGY AND WORLD ORDER PROPOSALS (1989).

so many defects - the argument goes - the best thing to do is to chuck the old Charter and start all over again.

Instead of drawing up a completely *new Constitution* for the World, others - fearful that any comprehensive overhaul might be rejected as utopian - would settle for *amendments* to the existing Charter to meet only those needs that are vital for global survival. Cautious "realists" would favor an even more modest endeavor and rely on broader *interpretations* of the existing Charter. Bearing in mind that entrenched bureaucracies are prepared to defend their prerogatives and seldom willing to surrender power gracefully, let us appraise each of the three alternatives.

B - Replacing the Charter

For hundreds of years, great scholars have drafted plans for a peaceful world order. None of the plans was ever given a fair chance.[6] Stimulated by public protests against the staggering losses of World War I, the League of Nations was formed as a hesitant first step toward a more tranquil international regime. The League, inadequate in its conception, stumbled along for less than two decades before it collapsed into World War II.

The United Nations was the next small step forward. With its Charter shortcomings rather obvious, countless new drafts were prepared by professors, concerned citizens and non-governmental organizations seeking an improved legal structure that might finally preserve world peace.[7] A few of the more recent proposals, for either a new Charter or drastic revision of the present one, can be outlined:

(1) *The Hutchins Constitution For the World*:

Toward the end of 1945, Robert M. Hutchins, respected Chancellor of the University of Chicago, assembled ten distinguished professors to draft a new Constitution for the World. For over two years, legal scholars, social

---

THE DOMESTIC ANALOGY AND WORLD ORDER PROPOSALS (1989).

6   *See* FERENCZ, ENFORCING INT. L. vol.1; H. NEWCOMB, DESIGN FOR A BETTER WORLD (1983); G. LLYOD AND E.WYNNER, SEARCHLIGHT ON PEACE PLANS (1944): J. KIANG, THE EARLY ONE WORLD MOVEMENT (1992); *See also* Reports of the World Federalist Association, Washington D.C.

7   *See* J.P. BARATTA, STRENGTHENING THE UN, A BIBLIOGRAPHY ON UN REFORM AND WORLD FEDERALISM (1987).

scientists, political philosophers and their assistants labored to produce a Preliminary Draft of a World Constitution.

Its Preamble proclaimed that "the age of nations must end, and the era of humanity begin." Its opening Declaration of Rights and Duties imposed an obligation on everyone everywhere to "abstain from violence, except for the repulse of violence as commanded or granted under law." It spoke of "release from the bondage of poverty," "the dignity of the human person," and proclaimed the four elements of life - earth, water, air and energy - "the common property of the human race."

The World Constitution was to be binding on all of the communities in the Federal World Republic. Peace was to be maintained by the promulgation of laws binding all communities and individuals. The World Government's jurisdiction would include: "the limitation and control of weapons," the "organization and disposal of federal armed forces" and the "collecting of federal taxes." Powers not delegated to the World Government and not prohibited to its members were reserved to the several states. Sovereignty, it said, "resides in the people of the world." Bravo!

Under the Hutchins Plan, world management was to be vested in 5 bodies:

(a) The *Federal Convention*, consisting of 99 delegates, was to be elected (by secret ballot) directly by the people of all nations, subdivided into nine geographic regions of the world. The Convention could debate issues but was given no legislative power.

(b) The *President* was to be elected by an Electoral College from the Regions. The President would be the chief executive with the right to initiate legislation.

(c) The *Council* was to be the legislative branch.

(d) The *Grand Tribunal* (composed of 60 justices divided into 12 Benches to deal with different types of conflicts) would be governed by a Supreme Court drawn primarily from the Benches. A Tribune of the People was authorized to appear on behalf of the rights of individuals and groups.

(e) The *Chamber of Guardians* was assigned the role of enforcing the peace through the use of armed forces under the Chairmanship of the President as Protector of the Peace. Guardians were to be elected by secret ballot and proportional voting.[8]

The Hutchins draft Constitution of the World - providing for a system of laws, courts and enforcement - was a serious document worked out by serious people. There is no indication that it was ever given serious consideration by serious decisionmakers.

(2) *The Clark and Sohn Plan*:

One of the foremost plans for comprehensive Charter revision appeared in Clark and Sohn's classic book WORLD PEACE THROUGH WORLD LAW.[9] Grenville Clark and Louis B. Sohn proposed an article-by-article overhaul of the UN Charter - with detailed commentary and annexes. Recommended structural changes included:

(a) A radical revision in the powers, composition and method of voting in the General Assembly. In place of one-nation-one-vote, there would be a system of weighted voting according to population, with no nation having more than 30 representatives and none less than 1. Representatives would be chosen by a system of popular election. The Assembly would be aided by two standing committees: one for Peace Enforcement Agencies and one for Budget and Finance. The Assembly would be given authority to enact legislation regarding threats to the peace and such laws would be binding upon "member Nations and all the peoples thereof" (Art.10).

(b) The Security Council would be replaced by an Executive Council composed of 17 representatives elected by the General Assembly, with certain priorities given to the largest nations. The veto would be abolished. "Important matters" would require the vote of 12 of the 17, including majorities from the larger countries entitled to more than 15 representatives in the Assembly. The Council would serve as the Executive arm, but always subordinate to the Assembly.

---

8   Center for the Study of Democratic Institutions, *A Constitution for the World* (1965); A preliminary draft, with background information, appears in G.A.BORGESE, FOUNDATIONS OF THE WORLD REPUBLIC (1953).

9   G.CLARK AND L.B. SOHN, WORLD PEACE THROUGH WORLD LAW (1st ed.1958, 2d Ed. revised 1962, 1966; Introduction revised 1984, 1960).

(c) An annex to the Charter provides a detailed plan for the gradual but comprehensive elimination of all national armaments, including a system for verification. The plan is over a hundred pages long.

(d) A World Police Force - created as a subsidiary organ - would be responsible for guaranteeing that the disarmament plan is carried out and that any attempted international violence is suppressed and deterred. A professional army of between 200,000 and 600,000 persons is envisaged.

(e) The judicial and conciliation system is to be strengthened by authorizing the Assembly to direct that all legal disputes likely to endanger peace must be submitted to the International Court of Justice. The Court would have compulsory jurisdiction in such cases - in addition to its general authority to interpret the Charter. Enforcement of Court decisions would be by the General Assembly applying sanctions or, if necessary, military force. A World Equity Tribunal would be created as an organ of the Assembly to resolve non-legal disputes. A World Conciliation Board would also be made available to settle disputes that might threaten peace.

(f) Individual violators of disarmament provisions would be subject to prosecution in UN or Regional Courts.

(g) A World Development Authority - also an organ of the Assembly - would assist in economic and social development.

(h) Reliable financial support would be assured by a new United Nations Revenue System based on a sharing of national tax revenues.

(i) Later drafts included provisions for an Environmental Protection Agency and a UN Outer-Space Authority and Ocean Authority, as guardians of "the common heritage".

Clark and Sohn wished to make it crystal clear that their proposals were not dogmatic and that if some other method proved more feasible they "would be very ready to adopt it in order to reach the end in view."[10] If either

10   1960 edition at xliii.

a new organization or a major Charter overhaul would not prove acceptable, consideration could be given to separate treaties to be negotiated among states consenting to such things as a World Disarmament or a World Development Organization. Said Professor Sohn, in 1982:

> Many variations are, of course possible. Details are not crucial: the important point is to find a plan for peace that would be both effective and generally acceptable. If a sufficient effort is made, the collective wisdom of mankind can find the right combination.[11]

Unfortunately, the world community has, thus far, failed to make sufficient effort or to mobilize sufficient collective wisdom to find the right combination. The Clark and Sohn draft was a serious document worked out by serious people. There is no indication that it was ever given serious consideration by serious decisionmakers.

(3) *World Federalist Proposals*:

The World Federalist Association, now headquartered in Washington D.C., has long been in the forefront of the movement for major Charter reform. Its former President Norman Cousins, Editor of *The Saturday Review*, was a prolific writer on the subject. World Federalists argue that the federal principle, similar to the U.S. model, is the best basis for free and democratic societies. They point to at least seventeen other federations around the world (including Switzerland, Germany, Canada and Mexico) that have existed for a long time in relative peace.[12]

The Federalists and their affiliates throughout the world have supported a 14-point program to reform and restructure the UN system. These are some of the changes called for:

> (a) An improved General Assembly, with weighted voting (taking population and UN contributions into account,) a second legislative chamber composed of delegates selected on a modified population basis; an

---

11   CLARK AND SOHN, WORLD PEACE THROUGH WORLD LAW, (Revised 1984 edition) at 6.

12   *See* J.P. Baratta, *The Spirit of Federalism: From Philadelphia in 1787 to the World in 1987*, in B.M. WALKER, Ed., WORLD FEDERALIST BICENTENNIAL READER (1987) 131; E. McWHINNEY, FEDERAL CONSTITUTION-MAKING FOR A MULTI-NATIONAL WORLD (1986); I.BERNIER, INTERNATIONAL LEGAL ASPECTS OF FEDERALISM (1973); E.L.MILLARD, FREEDOM IN A FEDERAL WORLD (1961).

advisory body composed of former parliamentarians and non-governmental organizations.

(b) Eliminating the veto-power in the Security Council when considering enforcement of World Court decisions or cases where a Permanent Member is a party to the dispute.

(c) An International Disarmament Organization to work for disarmament and to verify implementation.

(d) A UN Conciliation and Mediation Service and a Charter amendment to compel parties to arbitrate or take their dispute to the World Court.

(e) A Permanent UN Peacekeeping Force, with independent training and financing and authority to intervene without consent of the states involved.

(f) Adequate and stable UN revenues financed by such means as a tax on international mail, shipping, communications, or national military expenditures.

(g) Increased use of the International Court of Justice by granting the Court compulsory jurisdiction in all matters referred to it by the Security Council as issues posing a threat to peace. The Advisory capacity of the Court would also be expanded.

(h) An International Criminal Court to try international terrorists.

(i) A UN High Commissioner for Human Rights, as well as stronger environmental protection and economic development programs.

Despite many publications and large convocations of non-governmental organizations supporting their objectives, the efforts of World Federalists have, thus far, made some progress but not achieved any of their goals.[13] The comprehensive World Federalist proposals were serious documents worked out by serious people. There is no indication that their proposals for

---

13   World Federalist Association, *Structures for Peace Convocation, Summary of Proceedings* (1989); *See* T.A. HUDGENS, WE NEED L.A.W. - Let's Abolish War (1986); L. GREEN, JOURNEY TO A GOVERNED WORLD (1992); World Federalist News Magazine; World Federalist News; *World Peace News*, a weekly publication of the American Movement for World Government, Thomas Liggett, Publisher and Editor.

drastic Charter reform were ever given serious consideration by serious decisionmakers.

(4) The Stassen Plan:

Harold Stassen (one of the signers of the original UN Charter, disarmament negotiator for President Eisenhower and frequent unsuccessful candidate for U.S. President) proposed a new Charter in 1985. On the 40th anniversary of the original signing, he said:

> I do not consider the difficulties [of Charter change] to be as great as were those we confronted in making the original start 40 years ago...I emphasize that a new United Nations is imperative.[14]

The Stassen plan consisted of 162 articles divided into 27 Chapters. It was similar in most respects to the existing UN Charter. Among new additions to augment the General Assembly and Security Council he proposed:

(a) An expanded Security Council to include Germany, Japan, India and Brazil as Permanent Members (Art.23).

(b) A UN Peace Force of no more than 250,000 volunteers to maintain peace and combat terrorism (Art. 39-47).

(c) An Inspection Corps to serve as a verification agency (Art. 48-51).

(d) A Central Cabinet of 22 Administrators elected by weighted voting (based on population, gross national product and per capita production) to exercise primary jurisdiction over "common heritage" areas (Art.64-75).

(e) A one-percent tax on import and exports of all nations to guarantee independent UN funding (Art.76).

(f) World Panels of Mediators, Arbitrators and a Court of Equity to settle controversies peacefully (Art. 123-148).[15]

---

14 *The Stassen Draft for a New United Nations*, Glenview Foundation, Phil. Pa., (1985) at 5-6.

15 *Id.* Several of Stassen's proposals - such as authorizing nuclear weapons to be used against members "engaged in massive military aggression" (Art.2) - were bound to be controversial.

The Stassen plan was a serious document worked out by a serious person. There is no indication that it was ever given serious consideration by serious decisionmakers.

(5) *Other World Order Plans*:

A number of other plans calling for a total revision or replacement of the UN Charter have also appeared over the years. Only a few can be sketched here.

(a) *The World Constitution and Parliament Association Plan:*

After consultation with many dedicated persons, a new world constitution was recently drafted by The World Constitution and Parliament Association, headed by *Philip Isely* of Lakewood, Colorado. It is over 70 pages long and provides for a World Parliament composed of three houses: Peoples, Nations and Counsellors. A World Executive and Cabinet, a Judiciary and Enforcement System as well as an ombudsman to protect the Bill of Rights for citizens of the earth. Its nineteen articles and forty-five sections spell out details about how the World Constitution would work.[16]

A worldwide network of non-governmental organizations is being established to ratify and elect delegates to Isely's proposed new World Parliament. Endorsements from organizations, purporting to represent millions of people in Pakistan, Bangladesh, India and elsewhere, attest to the yearning of peoples everywhere for an improved system of international relations.[17]

(b) *The John Logue Plan:*

Professor John Logue, of Villanova University and Director of the Common Heritage Institute in Swarthmore, Pennsylvania, has argued that comprehensive UN reform, backed by public support, is the only way to attain peace for the human family. He feels that narrow perceptions of national interest will defeat any minimalist or piecemeal approach. He urges American statesmen to follow in the footsteps of such U.S. Presidents as Washington, Jefferson, Madison, Lincoln, Wilson, Franklin Roosevelt, Truman and Kennedy, by supporting

---

16 World Constitution and Parliament Association, *A Constitution for the Federation of Earth* (1991); *Reproduced in* E.E. HARRIS, ONE WORLD OR NONE (1993), Appendix.

17 *See Bulletin of the World Constitution & Parliament Association*, March 1993.

a movement to reform, restructure and strengthen the United Nations ...with the power, authority and money to keep the peace and to promote economic and social progress.[18]

(c) *Variations on the Same Theme:*

Variations on the theme of a new world legal structure can be found in such works as that of *Clarence Streit* who argued for a new Federal Union starting with free and democratic states, and *Garry Davis* who gained prominence by echoing Thomas Paine's cry: "My country is the world."[19] A similar thought appears in the work of Professor *Dieter Senghaas* who, using the European Community model, argues for a Federation of European states from the Atlantic to the Urals.[20] A comprehensive and scholarly study by *John Kiang*, a retired librarian from Notre Dame, Indiana, contains a blueprint culminating in an evolutionary world government offering "Permanent Peace on Earth and the General Happiness of Mankind."[21] Professors *Richard Falk* of Princeton and *Saul Mendlovitz* of Rutgers have devoted years of their lives seeking a model world order that could ensure peace and justice.[22]

No doubt, the noble aspiration for a united world society living in peace has inspired, and still inspires, many individuals and organizations. But, if past action is any guide, pointing to new highways leading to the promised land of peace is not likely to attract many voyagers from the UN diplomatic corps. It is not enough for a plan to be desirable and feasible - it must also be *acceptable* to nations that now control world organization. And there's the rub!

A 1993 report of an independent bi-partisan U.S. Commission reflects the divisiveness that inhibits Charter reform. As a result of lobbying by various peace groups, the U.S. Congress was persuaded in 1987 to create a commission to study the workings of the UN and to make suggestions for

---

18   *See* J.Logue, *A More Effective United Nations*, N.J. L. Jour. Nov. 26, 1985, *reprinted in* World Federalist Bicentennial Reader 123 at 127 (1987); *Testimony of Dr. John Logue to U.S. Commission on Improving Effectiveness of UN*, Oct.22, 1992.

19   C.K. STREIT, UNION NOW (1940). *See* G. DAVIS, MY COUNTRY IS THE WORLD (1961).

20   D. SENGHAAS, *EUROPA 2000, EIN FRIEDENSPLAN* (1990).

21   J. KIANG, ONE WORLD (1984).

22   R.FALK and S. MENDLOVITZ, Eds. THE STRATEGY OF WORLD ORDER 4 vols. (1966); *See* R. FALK, KIM and MENDLOVITS, THE UNITED NATIONS AND A JUST WORLD ORDER (1991). *See also:* H. HOLLINS, A.POWERS, & M. SOMMER, THE CONQUEST OF WAR - Alternative Strategies for Global Security (1989); D.KRIEGER, F.KELLY, Eds., WAGING PEACE (1988). *See also* Parlementarians for Global Action, 15th Parliamentary Forum, UN, N.Y. 28 Oct. 1993. Reference should be made to the original publications for a more comprehensive presentation than the brief outline herein.

improvements. The idea was opposed by the Republican administration and no public funds were allocated for the study. By the time they were appointed, the 16 Commissioners represented a broad spectrum of political opinion. Congressman James Leach, who had sponsored the legislation, was joined as Co-Chairman by former U.S. Ambassador Charles Lichtenstein who had gained notoriety when he publicly invited the UN to take its business elsewhere by sailing off into the sunset. After conducting hearings in half a dozen cities throughout the land, the Commission issued its Final report. Not surprisingly, the Commission was unable to reach consensus on any of its principle findings or recommendations.[23]

Congressman Leach wrote of the "the corrosive cynicism of the 'realist' clique", by which was meant the six Commissioners who had filed dissenting views (p.14). The only points on which there seemed to be general agreement related to: the creation of a UN Rapid Reaction Force guided by the Military Staff Committee; creating a High Commissioner for Human Rights and a Human Rights Court to uphold the rule of law, establishing an International Criminal Court by treaty under UN auspices, creating cost efficient cabinet-type structures within the Secretariat, and eliminating the practice of using nationality as a basis for assignments to various posts. A key point - adopted without debate - was: "Reforms should be made within the confines of the Charter" (P. 91).

We must face the sad reality that most nations are most unlikely to consent to any revolutionary transformation of the world's legal structure at this time - no matter how cogent any new blueprint may be. That does not mean that such plans should be abandoned; efforts to enlighten and improve the world should never cease. But, as a fall-back position, it might be prudent and more productive to consider less drastic alterations that may have a more promising prospect for acceptance in the foreseeable future.

C - Amending the Charter

Proposals for a few basic changes have come from many distinguished persons who argue not for a completely new Charter or drastic alteration but simply for Charter renovation.[24] Finn Seyersted, Professor of International Law and International organizations at the University of Oslo and an

---

23   *Final Report of the United States Commission on Improving the Effectiveness of the United Nations* (US Gov't Printing Office 1993).

24   *See* H. Morganthau, *The New United Nations and the Revision of the Charter*, The Review of Politics 16 (1954).

experienced UN diplomat, wrote: "The first condition for a strong international organization is a more realistic voting system."[25]

(1) Voting Procedures in the General Assembly:

The General Assembly operates on the principle of "one state, one vote."[26] Small states, fearing to be overrun by large ones, are inclined to stick with that system. China, with a billion people, probably would like a louder voice than San Marino with its population of 24,000. The Canadian Peace Research Institute considered various forms of weighted voting that might be suitable for international organizations by taking into account such factors as population, geographic location, financial contributions, level of development, education, culture, religious ties, political affiliations or a combination of these and other factors.[27] The possibilities are almost unlimited - if there exists the political will for change. But no proposals to alter the basic voting rules in the General Assembly have ever been seriously debated at the UN.[28]

The Center for War/Peace Studies, headed by *Richard Hudson*, has long advocated a charter amendment to put a new voting system into practice that would, in effect, convert the General Assembly into a legislative body. The idea behind what he calls *"The Binding Triad"* is that important issues before the General Assembly would be subjected to three parallel, simultaneous votes: one based on the existing practice whereby each member state gets one vote; the second vote would be weighted according to population and the third vote on the same issue would be weighted based on contribution to the UN regular budget. If all three votes produced a two-thirds majority in favor of the particular resolution it would be passed and would thereby become not merely a *recommendation* but *binding law* for all countries.

The reasoning behind the Hudson plan is that if the overwhelming majority of states, and the world's population, as well as nations having the most economic strength, are overwhelmingly in favor of the resolution, the minority should not be able to defeat it and it should automatically become

25   Nordic Journal of Int. Law, Vol. 56, No.3, *reprinted in* H.NEWCOMB, HOPES AND FEARS (1992) at 82.

26   UN Charter, Article 18 (1).

27   C. Barrett and H. Newcombe, *Weighted Voting in International Organizations*, Peace Research Reviews, April 1986.

28   *See* A. CASSESE, INTERNATIONAL LAW IN A DIVIDED WORLD (1986).

vested as international law binding on all. The Binding Triad idea could be grafted on to the present Charter by a simple amendment.[29] But no nation has ever put a Binding-Triad amendment on the UN agenda. Never.

(2) *Voting Procedures in the Security Council:*

Many people have criticized - not without cause - the preferential veto right enjoyed only by the five permanent members of the Security Council.[30] There are those who acknowledge that the veto power is undemocratic but insist that any attempt to change the system would be counter-productive since it would disrupt the delicate balance that now exists. They argue that the subject is highly political and once changes are on the table, there is no way of knowing what demands or bargains will be made and which states might refuse to ratify the new system.[31]

Some even argue that the unfair veto right is really a good thing and should be retained in the common interest. They say it is to be credited with solving many of the world's problems peacefully since - like requiring consensus - it forces powerful nations to negotiate and compromise in order to get results. According to Anjali V. Patil:

> It doesn't really matter who enjoys the veto power in the Security Council, international peace and security cannot be maintained until all states accept the need to identify with the whole of humanity.[32]

Eliminating, restricting or modifying the veto power is theoretically possible in a number of ways:

> (a) It could be restricted so that it could only be authorized under certain grave circumstances; for example, if a permanent member was being required to send its troops into battle.

---

29 Paul Szasz, formerly of the UN Office of Legal Affairs, has suggested the wording for possible amendments that would achieve the Binding-Triad goals. See 34 Global Report (1991); Publications of the Center for War/Peace Studies are available from its office at 218 E. 18th St., New York NY 10003.

30 UN Charter Article 27(3). *See* J. Baratta, *The Veto: Abolition, Modification or Preservation?* in W.HOFFMAN,Ed., A NEW WORLD ORDER: CAN IT BRING SECURITY TO THE WORLD'S PEOPLE?, World Federalist Association (1991).

31 *See* Comments of Paul Szasz in B. FERENCZ, Ed., WORLD SECURITY FOR THE 21ST CENTURY (1991) 23-32.

32 A.V. PATIL, THE UN VETO IN WORLD AFFAIRS, 1946-1990 (1992) at 464.

(b) It could be modified by requiring at least two, or more, of the permanent members to join in the veto before it could be counted.

(c) As was suggested by the Austrian Government in 1972 and by President Carter in 1978, Security Council members could agree in advance that certain subjects would be regarded as "procedural" and hence, under Article 27(2), not subject to veto.

(d) The veto might be ruled out if it would negate a decision of the World Court, or a finding that aggression or a threat to peace existed.

(e) There could be a written agreement to institutionalize what now appears to be a tacit "gentlemen's agreement" among the Permanent Members not to exercise the veto.[33]

None of these five alternatives - that may not require Charter amendment - to modify the veto power has ever been put on the UN agenda. Never.

(3) *Expanding the Council:*

Another way to water-down the veto power and to alter voting procedures is to formally expand the Security Council. Rich states, like Germany and Japan today, (that Charter Art. 107 still describes as enemies) can be expected to argue - as the founding Members did in 1945 - that those who are asked to pay the piper should have a greater say in calling the tune. It has been proposed that the number of Permanent Members be increased to include the new economic powers, Germany and Japan, as well as India, Brazil and Nigeria as representatives of the three populous continents of Asia, South America and Africa - but not necessarily extending the right of veto.[34] Foreign Minister Andreatta of Italy, in his address to the General Assembly on 30 Sept. 1993 suggested a third-category of "semi-permanent members" - those capable of making a special contribution to achieving UN objectives. The general question of equitable representation on the Security Council has been on the UN agenda many times. It was considered in 1979, was raised again in 1992 and was mentioned by many states during the General Asembly plenary debates in September and October 1993.[35]

---

33 *See* SG/SM/4932, Feb. 19, 1993; World Peace News, May 1993, p.1.

34 *See* S.D.BAILEY, THE PROCEDURE OF THE UN SECURITY COUNCIL (1988) at 159. Proposal by Mr. de Michelis of Italy, A/46/PV.12, 27 Sept. 1991 at 34.

35 *See* A/34/246; GA Res. 47/62, 11 Dec. 1992; Forty-Eight General Assembly Plenary, Sept.-Oct. 1993.

In submitting their views to the Secretary-General, most states pointed to the unfairness of the present procedures and advocated changes in the composition of the Security Council to reflect the increase in UN membership and the shift in economic and political power structures since the UN was founded.[36] What was most striking however was that no *Permanent Member* - not one - stated clearly that it was really prepared to accept such changes at this time.[37] It has been reported in the press that the United States was in favor of granting seats on the Security Council to Germany and Japan.[38] But there is a difference between political rhetoric and reality. In addressing the General Assembly in September 1993, neither Germany nor Japan pressed for inclusion in the Council - although they would be prepared to do their duty.[39]

If any one of the Permanent Members really wanted to extend the veto right, or expanded participation in Security Council power, to either Japan, Germany or any other state, that could be arranged - in substance - without Charter alteration. All it would really take would be a brief written commitment from France or the U.K., for example, that it would not vote in the Council without prior (formal or informal) clearance with its European partner, Germany. China could offer the same privileges to its Asian neighbor, Japan. Any member of the Security Council could offer to share its voting authority with any of its allies who would in effect become silent partners as far as public appearance was concerned but actual partners and participants in the functioning of the Council.

To be sure, being a partner is not as prestigious as being an independent sovereign - but form should not be allowed to triumph over substance. The principle of cooperative consultation or voting is not new; many regional associations already vote only as a bloc. Inviting other states to consult would strengthen solidarity between nations. Of course, no official has suggested such a simple and sensible pragmatic solution to solve the unfair veto problem.

The truth is that, despite all of the flowery rhetoric suggesting the contrary, the powerful nations that now control the Security Council are not

---

36 *See* UN Doc. A/48/264, 20 July 1993 and Add.1, 26 July 1993 and Add.2, 27 Aug. 1993.
37 Views of China, France, Russia, U.K. and U.S. are all in A/48/264, 20 July 1993.
38 *See* Paul Lewis, *U.S. Backs Council Seats for Bonn and Tokyo,* N.Y. Times Jan. 30, 1993 at 5.
39 Statement by the Prime Minister of Japan, Mr. Hosokawa, 27 Sept. 1993 and Statement by Dr. Kinkel, the Foreign Minister of Germany, 29 Sept. 1993.

prepared to weaken their present position. A slight ray of hope can be glimpsed from the statement by the United States:

> The creation of one or more subsidiary bodies of the Security Council pursuant to Article 29 of the Charter is a possibility worthy of consideration.[40]

(We shall consider this possibility in the next chapter.) The subject of Charter amendment is being dealt with by the Sixth Committee and the *Special Committee on the Charter of the United Nations and on Strengthening of the Role of the Organization* that was formed in 1975 and which has accomplished practically nothing in nearly two decades.[41] What the UN will actually *do* about amending the Charter, remains to be seen. The only agreement reached by consensus in 1993 was to continue talking in 1994.[42]

(4) Difficulties of the Amendment Process:

Perhaps the most serious objection to attempts to amend the Charter is the amendment process itself. Amendments require approval by *two-thirds* of the member states, *and* later ratification by the constitutional processes of two-thirds of all governments including *all five* of the Permanent Members (Art. 108). It took the U.S. Senate 40 years, and numerous reservations and special understandings, before it was willing to consent to ratification of even the Genocide Convention.[43] How long would it take for the U.S., or China, or Russia, to ratify a Charter amendment abolishing its right to veto enforcement measures?

Significant opposition and long drawn-out debates can surely be anticipated for major Charter changes altering the structure of the Assembly, the Security Council, the ICJ or other principal organs of the world organization. Judging by attitudes reflected during many years of fruitless debate by the UN Special Committee on the Charter, and the suspicions, fears and

---

40   A/48/264,*supra* at 92.

41   See V.Morris & M.Bourloyannis, The Work of the Sixth Committee at the Forty-Seventh Session of the UN General Assembly, Current Developments, 87 AJIL 306 (1993).

42   Summary Records of the Sixth Committee, 6 Oct. - 14 Oct. 1993; Report of the Special Committee on the Charter, GAOR 48th Sess. Supp. No. 33 (A/48/33) 27 May 1993; A/C.6/48/L.18, 26 Nov. 1993.

43   In a recent article, Prof. David D. Caron of the University of California at Berkeley, noted difficulties of amending the Charter in any significant way. He recognized the need for some process to institutionalize world governance without risking abuse of power that might be inherent in an uncontrolled Security Council. D.H. Caron, *The Legitimacy of the Collective Authority of the Security Council*, 87 AJIL 552 (1993). Professor Thomas Franck addressed the problem in his book THE POWER OF LEGITIMACY AMONG NATIONS (1990). No solution has yet been found.

traditional thinking that still exist among governments, the prospects for major Charter amendments to correct existing inequities or alter voting procedures are - regrettably - not very promising.[44] It must always be recalled that if changes are actually to come about, proposals must be not merely desirable and workable but also *acceptable*.

This is not to suggest that efforts should not be made to persuade nations to think globally and move toward a more democratic and peaceful international structure. Such efforts should certainly continue in the hope that there may be a break-through. But hope without progress loses some of its vitality and it is therefore necessary to keep searching for other alternatives that may prove more acceptable as a means of enhancing the UN's effectiveness as an agency for peace in the foreseeable future.[45]

D - Carrying Out the Charter

As every Foreign Minister knows, today's crisis can not wait for tomorrow's Utopian dream to come true. The plans that we have outlined for replacing, revising or amending the Charter are replete with ideas that would certainly improve the functioning of the existing international order, but - in the light of the historical record - the prospects for early acceptance of such ideas must be seen as practically non-existent. Is there a better or a faster way to move toward a more rational world order?

There are several lawful ways - without discarding or amending the Charter - to enhance the ability of the UN to manage global problems more effectively in the interests of world security. Let us re-examine some of the possibilities and options:

---

44   *See Report of the Special Committee on the Charter*, GAOR Forty-Seventh Sess. Supp. No. 33 (A/47/33) (1992).*See* B. Broms, *The Special Committee on the Charter of the United Nations and the Strengthening of the Role of the Organization*, 20 German Yrbk of Int. L. 77 (1977).

45   In a recent article, Prof. David D. Caron of the University of California at Berkeley, noted difficulties of amending the Charter in any significant way. He recognized the need for some process to institutionalize world governance without risking abuse of power that might be inherent in an uncontrolled Security Council. D.H. Caron, *The Legitimacy of the Collective Authority of the Security Council*, 87 AJIL 552 (1993). Professor Thomas Franck addressed the problem in his book THE POWER OF LEGITIMACY AMONG NATIONS (1990). No solution has yet been found.>

(1) *The Traditional Route:*

The traditional method for bringing about changes in international law has always been the drafting of a treaty or legal convention setting forth new commitments and obligations that would bind those parties that finally ratified the accord. Nations willing to be bound by a particular UN resolution can always sign a treaty making it binding among themselves - without involving the Charter - and leaving out those states that prefer to go their own way. This could by-pass hesitant or obstructionist states and avoid the "tyranny by the minority" that often blocks effective action.[46]

The "separate treaty" technique could be most effective where the overwhelming majority of nations are ready and willing to be bound by the terms of a convention but a small minority is holding out for some perceived advantage. Once hold-out countries are convinced that they cannot have their way by obstructionist tactics, they may eventually be persuaded that it is in their own interest not to stand aloof and apart from the rest of the world.[47] The traditional treaty route remains a possibility - but it may be a slow and difficult terrain.

We have pointed out that arriving at a widely acceptable text of such an agreement - particularly in the peace field - usually takes years of tedious and patient negotiation. As we have seen, it's end-product is frequently an ambiguous compromise that binds no one. Ratifications - when and if they materialize - often subject the text to crippling reservations and understandings. Many states never ratify at all. Ratification by only a small number of states confirms that the treaty or convention has little international legal significance.

Professor Karl Zemanek of Austria, in appraising the utility of traditional international conventions to codify international law, correctly concluded that it was an exercise in futility. The hope that a real compromise might be reached was naive and the process "too brutal a method for success." He cited many cases where conventions were not ratified and simply ignored and nothing could be done about it. He suggested, as an interim step, that instruments less stringent than treaties, such as joint

---

46   *See* B. SLOAN, UN GENERAL ASSEMBLY RESOLUTIONS IN OUR CHANGING WORLD, (1991) p. 125.

47   *See*, for example, the Treaty on European Union, done at Maastricht, Feb. 7, 1992, 31 ILM 247 (1992). This may also apply to the United States regarding its refusal to accept the Law of the Sea Treaty. *See* D. Pitt, *U.S. Seeks to 'Fix' Mining Provisions of Sea Treaty*, N.Y. Times Aug. 28, 1993 at L-3.

declarations, might gradually edge states into accepting its provisions. Such procedure seemed to him to be "more promising than the adoption of still-born codification conventions for the archives of chancelleries." He recognized that it would take considerable time.[48] It must be made possible to move toward a peaceful regime more quickly than via the tortuous path of traditional international law.

(2) *Interpreting the Charter Pragmatically:*

Professor Sloan has also pointed out that the Charter is both a treaty and a world constitution. Its broad principles require interpretation. The framers certainly intended that the Charter would be interpreted to meet changing conditions which they could not have foreseen.[49] There are many precedents showing that this has, in fact, been the practice - even if it required a stretch of the legal imagination. For example:

(a) When the Soviet Union walked out of the Security Council in 1950, the remaining Council members, including a Chinese representative whose seat was being challenged, did not hesitate to adopt peace-enforcement resolutions designed to halt the war in Korea.[50] In its "uniting for peace" resolution (actually voting for war), the General Assembly asserted its authority to pass peace enforcement resolutions whenever it decided that the Council was enable to discharge its primary responsibility.[51] The Charter contained no such authorizations.

(b) The Charter provision that specifically requires Security Council decisions to be made by "the concurring votes of the permanent members" has been interpreted to mean that *abstention* will be regarded as an *affirmative* vote![52]

(c) The Charter says:

---

48 K. Zemanek, *Codification of International Law: Salvation or Dead End?* in *Études en l'honneur de Roberto Ago*, vol.1, at 600-601 (1987).

49 *See* B.SLOAN, *The UN Charter as a Constitution* 1 Pace Yrb'k Int. L. 118 (1989).

50 SC Res.S/82, 25 June 1950, S/83, 27 June 1950.

51 GA Res. 377 (V), 3 Nov. 1950; *See* H. KELSEN, RECENT TRENDS IN THE LAW OF THE UN (1951).

52 UN Charter Art. 27. *See* C. Stavropoulos, *The Practice of Voluntary Abstentions by Permanent Members of the Security Council under Article 27, Paragraph 3, of the Charter of the United Nations*, 61 AJIL 737 (1967); ICJ Decision in *The Namibia Case*, ICJ Reports (1971) at 22.

> The expenses of the organization shall be borne by the Members as apportioned by the General Assembly (Art. 17).

But some members refused to pay the Assembly allocation. If the organization was to continue to function, new sources of funding had to be found outside the regular budget - even if the Charter made no provision for it. In addition to making special peacekeeping assessments, the UN is forced to appeal to nations for *voluntary* contributions to enable it to carry on much of its humanitarian and social activities.[53] That certainly is not what the framers of the Charter had in mind.

We have referred to the fact that the Charter stipulated that members in arrears "shall have no vote" in the Assembly, but honoring that provision was not considered useful. Obviously, the Charter can be a very flexible instrument - when there is a political will to interpret it pragmatically.[54]

(3) Activate Dormant Charter Provisions:

The United Nations Association of America, which is conservative in its approach, has listed many steps that could be taken to make the UN more effective without amending the Charter. They suggest that certain provisions of the Charter which have been allowed to lie idle be put into practice:

(a) Encourage the Secretary General (as authorized by Article 99) to exercise "preventive diplomacy" by alerting the Security Council when danger is brewing anywhere in the world. Greater use of Article 99 has recently been advocated by many others and seems to have good prospects for acceptance.[55]

(b) The Military Staff Committee called for in the Charter could finally be activated to do what it was required to

---

53 *See*, for example, *UN Appeals for $840 Million for Former Yugoslavia*, UN Press Release IHA/480, REF/10129, 17 Mar. 1993; *Member States and Public Invited to Contribute to UN Assistance Programmes for Southern Africa*, UN Press Release, SAF/154, 16 March 1993. *Financing an Effective United Nations*, A Report of an Independent Advisory group, Ford Foundation (1993).

54 *See* Y. BLUM, ERODING THE UNITED NATIONS CHARTER (1993).

55 *See* B. RAMCHARAN, THE INTERNATIONAL LAW AND PRACTICE OF EARLY WARNING AND PREVENTIVE DIPLOMACY (1992); AN AGENDA FOR PEACE Report of the Secretary-General pursuant to the statement adopted by the Summit Meeting of the Security Council on 31 Jan. 1992, A/47/277, S/24111, 17 June 1992. *See* P. Szasz, *The Role of the UN Secretary General: Some Legal Aspects*, 24 NYU J. of Int. L and Politics 161 (1991).

do. The Chiefs of Staff of the permanent members were mandated to form a committtee to:

> advise and assist the Security Council on all questions relating to the Security Council's military require- ments for the maintenance of international peace and security, the employment and command of forces placed at its disposal, the regulation of armaments and possible disarmament (Art. 47).

For over forty years, members of the Military Staff Committee, often re- splendent in full dress uniforms, have met 26 times each year - to do nothing. The very high-ranking officers greet each other, spend a few minutes in noting that they have nothing to do and then adjourn to continue the silly game two weeks later.[56]

To be sure, the Charter anticipated that the Security Council would have military forces at its disposal and that the Council would regulate armaments and possible disarmament. The time has come for these vital obligations to be fulfilled.

(c) Regional Arrangements (under Charter Chap. VIII) could be strengthened and given greater enforcement authority. The NATO forces were given hundreds of billions of dollars on the assumption that they would be strong enough to repel a massive Soviet invasion. Yet they played no role in squelching relatively minor European insurrections. Something seems to be very wrong.

(d) UN peace-keeping activities - as recent experience shows - can be expanded without Charter alteration.

(e) Intervention to stop crimes against humanity might be permissible if called for by an advisory opinion from the World Court.

(f) New verification regimes could be created to supervise global disarmament programs.

(g) Members who violate the rules may be suspended or expelled as provided in Articles 5 and 6. Those who

---

56   *See annual Reports of the Security Council*, GAOR Supp. No. 2.

deliberately fail to pay their dues may lose their vote, as provided in Article 19.

All of these measures or interpretations could, without requiring Charter amendment, enhance the effectiveness of the United Nations as a peace-management agency. Professor Louis Sohn, in recent writings, seems to have come around to this type of pragmatic thinking.[57]

Ralph Zacklin, Director of the UN Office of the Legal Counsel, noting that the veto power of the Permanent Members makes it very difficult to obtain Charter *amendment*, has suggested that it may be more expedient to bring about change by other means. He suggests that new interpretations can bring about change. Failure to enforce certain Charter provisions is another means to alter the Charter. It is also possible to bring about change by supplementary agreements that are not contrary to Charter purposes. These devices may not be as open and effective as normal amendment procedures (that now work well in some of the Specialized Agencies of the UN that do not demand consensus) but they will provide the Charter with the needed flexibility to do what needs to be done until such time as formal Charter amendments may become politically acceptable. [58] If we wish to make progress, it may therefore be prudent to look to new devices, rather than Charter amendment, to bring about needed changes in the near future.

(4) *Create New Organs for Peace:*

A promising possibility to establish new structures for peace is to *create new organs* to perform special functions - as already authorized by the Charter.[59] The General Assembly is specifically empowered to "establish such subsidiary organs as *it* (emphasis added) deems necessary for the performance of its functions (Art.22). The Assembly's right to do so is practically absolute.

The Security Council is specifically authorized to do the same (Art.29). No reference is made to any preferential treatment of permanent members. It should be noted that Security Council resolutions creating new organs to help it carry out its responsibilities are properly regarded as procedural matters. [60] All that is required for procedural decisons, according to the

---

57 *See* L. Sohn, Ed., *The Common Defense: Peace and Security in a Changing World*, United Nations Association, Washington DC (1992).

58 R. ZACKLIN, THE AMENDMENT OF THE CONSTITUTIVE INSTRUMENTS OF THE UNITED AGENCIES AND SPECIALIZED AGENCIES (1968).

59 UN Charter Art.7, 22, 27, 68.

Charter, is an affirmative vote by any nine of the fifteen members. **No veto applies.**[61]

It is a well established fact that many new UN organs were never mentioned in the Charter and have been created to play important roles without any Charter amendment or interpretation. The Charter, for example, makes no reference to Human Rights Commissions or Human Rights Tribunals, any environmental organizations, UN peace-keeping forces, and many other very important UN agencies that exist today. With some courageous and imaginative innovations, it may be possible - now that the Cold-War is over - to create new agencies to make the Charter more democratic and effective in the search for peace.[62]

In fact, the United Nations, driven by necessity, is already moving in the direction of discovering new legal interpretations, inventing new procedures and creating new organs to help discharge peacekeeping responsibilities. For example:

(a) The Security Council - in addition to exercising its Chapter VII enforcement powers in response to Iraq's aggression against Kuwait - broadened its own authority under the Charter by setting territorial boundaries, mandating disarmament, imposing environmental controls and applying economic sanctions. Furthermore, it directed the Secretary-General, in consultation with existing agencies, to plan the formation of a Special Commission for on-site inspection and destruction of prohibited weapons. The Council directed the Secretary-General to present plans for the setting up of a Fund to pay claims against Iraq and to establish a Commission to see that it was done.[63] New agencies were quickly formed, approved by the Council and put

---

60 See Repertory of Practice of UN Organs, Vol.II p. 104 (1955). Compare p. 65, 72-73.

61 UN Charter, Article 27, Sec.2.

62 The Conferences on a More Democratic United Nations, a non- governmental organization headed by Harry Lerner of New York and Jeffrey Siegel of London, has led a campaign to have a special "Peoples Assembly " added as a subsidiary organ of the General Assembly to give greater voice to individuals and non-governmental organizations. *See* F. BARNABY, Ed., BUILDING A MORE DEMOCRATIC UNITED NATIONS (1992); Report of the Second Conference on a More Democratic UN (1991) at 19. The idea is also supported by Professors Falk, Kim and Mendlovitz in THE UNITED NATIONS AND A JUST WORLD ORDER (1991). *See also* L. Sohn, *Consultative Assembly of the United Nations*, 35 Amer. Bar Assn J. 860 (1949) and Sohn, *The Need for the Democratization of the UN*, The Federalist, Jan-Feb. 1966.

63 The Council went even further when it exercised its enforcement powers by requiring all states to transfer the proceeds of Iraqi petroleum sales to a compensation fund for the victims. SC Res. 778 (1992).

into action to carry out the new mandates.[64] And all of this by simple resolution - without Charter amendment or alteration!

(b) Similar action was taken by the Security Council to expand the judicial function when it requested the Secretary-General to designate a panel of experts to collect evidence of war crimes in former Yugoslavia and to establish a criminal tribunal to try those responsible for crimes against humanity.[65] More shall be said about this later.[66]

(c) Another illustration of the extended reach of Security Council resolutions under the broad peace-enforcement authority granted by Charter Chapters VI and VII can be found in the economic sanctions imposed against Libya for refusal to cooperate in investigating two Libyan nationals accused of terrorism.[67] The World Court rejected Libya's request for a protective injunction.[68]

(d) On 3 December 1992, the Security Council authorized the use of

all necessary means to establish as soon as possible a secure environment for humanitarian operations in Somalia.

It requested the Secretary-General and participating states to establish a unified control and command of military forces that would be involved. It appointed an ad hoc Council commission to report on implementation.[69]   It

---

64   SC Res. 687 3 April 1991, SC Res. 699, 17 June 1991, SC Res.706, 15 Aug. 1991, SC Res. 715, 11 Oct. 1991.

65   SC Res.780, 6 Oct. 1992, SC Res. 827, 25 May 1992.

66   *See* Chapter Eight, Section B.

67   SC Res. 731 (1992), SC Res. 748 (1992). UN sanctions were tightened on Nov. 11, 1993, effective Dec. 1, 1993. See P. Lewis, *UN Tightens Sanctions Against Libya*, N.Y. Times, Nov. 12, 1993 p. A 10; SC Res. 883, Nov. 11, 1993.

68   *Libya v. United States*, 1992 I.C.J. 219, April 14, 1992, 31 ILM 662 (1992).

69   SC Res. 794, 3 Dec. 1992. Press Release SC/5516, 3 Dec. 1992. On 13 Oct. 1993, the Security Council imposed sanctions on Haiti for its failure to allow a UN Mission to discharge its Security Council mandates; S/RES/873; see also S/RES 867 (1993). Following the assassination of Haiti's Justice Minister, the Council tightened its sanctions (Res. 873, 16 Oct. 1993) and threatened stronger action. SC/5729, 30 Oct. 1993.

was yet another illustration of the authority the Security Council has recently unfurled under the prevailing Charter.

E - *Evaluation*

As we review the UN Charter its structural defects seem overwhelming. The temptation to cast the document aside and begin again is very great. But realism dictates that such an effort would now be almost in vain. Sovereign states are not ready to yield their power gracefully. Nothing is more obstinate than an entrenched bureaucracy controlled by persons unwilling to diminish their significant privileges or prerogatives. Those that have power are not ready to give it up and those that do not have power are unable to do much about it. Alas!

The only realistic alternative left is to try to make the present Charter work. And - with a little imagination and a lot of determination - it can be done. All that is really required is a willingness (on the part of 15 nations rather than the current 184) to carry out the original intent and fundamental purposes of the binding legal obligations that all states accepted when they became members of the United Nations. They have all vested the Security Council with the authority and duty to maintain peace. The Council has demonstrated that it has the power and political ability - when it chooses to do so - to reinforce the three components of *law, courts* and *enforcement* on which peace depends.

Cooperation by the Secretary General, other UN agencies and powerful member states was certainly necessary to implement the resolutions referred to above. But in all of these recent actions to enhance peace and security, no new Charter was required and no new Charter amendments were required. Where did the impetus come from to make the UN more responsive to current needs for peace? When an outraged public demanded action, all that was needed to make the UN effective was the stimulus of a few resolute Security Council resolutions!

PART III
MAKING THE SYSTEM WORK

No more than any other form of organization do federal structures have value in themselves: like the others they may become the instrument of political or economic antagonisms that divide peoples. The redistribution of power can be efficacious only when based on solid realities; it can be beneficent only if it guarantees order and peace.

Professor Charles de Visscher, 1960[1]

Something must be done to redistribute power in a realistic way so that the system of world management can guarantee order and peace for everyone. Scholarly theories that only gather dust on library shelves will not halt the slaughter and universal misery that continues to plague large segments of humankind. There must be a new approach that offers the prospect of a more humane world in the foreseeable future.

---

1   C.D. VISSCHER, THEORY AND REALITY IN PUBLIC INTERNATIONAL LAW, revised ed. translated from the French by P.E Corbett (1968) at 406.

CHAPTER SEVEN
SECURITY COUNCIL AS SECURITY GUARDIAN

A growing number of member states are concluding that some problems can be addressed most effectively by U.N. efforts. Thus, collective security is finally beginning to work as it was conceived.

UN Secretary-General Boutros Boutros-Ghali,
Aug. 20, 1993.[1]

Everyone agrees that it would be highly desirable if the UN Charter could achieve its primary goal of protecting peoples from the scourge of war. No one doubts that the UN organization *should* function more efficiently and effectively. But there is considerable disagreement about how to achieve these shared objectives. A better way must be found. It seems to be staring us in the face. The Security Council has a key role to play as the world's peace-keeper - and is finally beginning to play it.[2]

A - A New Approach

We have seen that it takes many generations to create binding "customary law" and even then its parameters are usually uncertain. It usually takes many years to negotiate treaties or international conventions related to peace and many more years must pass before they receive the necessary number of ratifications - often subject to debilitating interpretations or "understandings." Even when treaties are solemnly accepted and finally ratified and supposedly binding, they are subject to repudiation whenever states believe that their own vital interests are at stake.[3] Traditional methods of treaty negotiation, drafting and ratification - that failed to achieve the goals of peace in the past - are not good enough for the maintenance of peace in the future.

Traditional diplomacy required fifty years to reach a consensus definition of aggression - which was largely ignored and surely did not deter or diminish aggression. Terrorism and crimes that threaten the peace are yet

---

1   B.Boutros-Ghali, *Don't Make the U.N.'s Hard Job Harder*, Op-Ed. N.Y. Times, Aug. 20, 1993 at A29.

2   On 26 September 1985, the Security Council held a special meeting on the level of Foreign Ministers to commemorate the fortieth anniversary of the United Nations. All agreed that there was an urgent need to enhance the effectiveness of the Council in discharging its principal role of maintaining peace and security in the world. Compare Security Council meeting at the level of Heads of State, dealing with its responnsibility for the maintenance of peace and security; S/PV.3046, 31 Jan. 1992.

3   *See* S/PV. 3212, 11 May 1993; *North Korea, Fighting Inspection, Renounces Nuclear Arms Treaty*, N.Y. Times article by David E. Sanger, March 12, 1993, at 1; SC Res. 825, 11 May 1993; SC Res.841, 16 June 1993.

to be defined by the international legal community.[4] Surely, the worn-out, plodding, confusing, inefficient and ineffective methods of protecting international security - which has been the rule - must be changed if peace is to be preserved. New procedures for clarifying and enforcing binding legal obligations for peace must be quicker, clearer and more effective than present practices. Contemporary international law does not offer any sense of real security to anyone.

In light of the failure of the United Nations to achieve its most fundamental purpose, the temptation is great to discard the entire present system and replace it with an improved new UN Charter or Constitution for the World. But, as we have seen from our brief review of such proposals and the more modest plans for Charter amendments, the prospects for achieving drastic overhaul in the foreseeable future seem to range somewhere between hopeless and impossible.[5] We are challenged therefore to use our creative imagination to find a new approach, one that utilizes many of the fine suggestions for Charter reform, suggested by many serious thinkers, that have been outlined in the previous chapter and one that may prove more acceptable to those who hold the reins of power in their hands.

One of my esteemed college professors, Morris Raphael Cohen, taught that the legal order can prevail only to the extent that it promotes a maximum attainable satisfaction to all groups.[6] Law must be judged by the extent to which it meets the moral standards and practical needs of society. If the moral standards and practical needs of international society are to be met, the following action now seems called for:

(1) International law must be interpreted so that it becomes possible to *achieve*, rather than to *defeat*, the most fundamental Charter goals.

(2) New procedures must be adopted and new organs of management created that make it possible to meet the practical needs for world peace and security.

(3) The new proposals must be so structured that the present members of the international community rec-

---

4   *See* Chapter One, Section C. "Measures to eliminate international terrorism" was still being discussed by the UN's Legal Committee in October, 1993; A/C.6/48/L.1, 1 October 1993.

5   Recent efforts by the UN, the Council of Europe and the 52 nations forming the Conference on Security and Cooperation in Europe (CSCE) to agree on a binding treaty that would mandate such obvious advantages as peaceful settlement of international disputes have not yet succeeded. *See* Commission on Security and Cooperation in Europe, 101st Congress, 1st Sess., *Update on Peaceful Settlements of Disputes in the CSCE Process* (1993).

6   M.R. COHEN, REASON AND LAW (1950) at 8.

ognize that their own vital interests are best protected
by the new system.

B - The Best Choice Now

Fortunately, there is no real need to be dependent upon new international treaties or conventions which require long negotiations, ambiguous compromises and uncertain ratifications in the distant future. A better way is at hand.

We have seen that by new thinking about old problems some changes can come about by correct *interpretations* of the present Charter to make it more effective in maintaining peace.[7] Most important of all, we have seen in several recent events, that - given the political will - there is a legal and quick method that is already being used to enhance the effectiveness of the United Nations as an enforcement arm of the world community. The Security Council has - by resolution - articulated the law and then mandated the Secretary-General to create a number of new organs to help secure the peace in Iraq, Yugoslavia, Somalia and elsewhere.

Action by the Security Council now offers the best hope for effective implementation of established international norms and the creation of new agencies needed for a more peaceful world. In order to encourage the Council to act quickly and decisively, only those minimum changes that are vital for peace are suggested. Stability of the international order is important but stability does not mean rigidity - stability requires flexibility.

To reinforce the *laws, courts* and *enforcement* mechanisms on which world security depends, we propose that the Security Council adopt twelve new resolutions - which we shall draft hereafter - to strengthen its capacity to maintain peace and security. For clarity of comprehension, we divide these twelve resolutions into the three categories that we have postulated as essential structures for world peace:

(1) *Laws:*

The Council, in order to discharge its security obligations, must reinforce our inadequate legal system by new clarifying resolutions having the force of law. Five such resolutions are proposed: 1- to mandate peaceful settlement and non-use of force; 2- to redefine aggression - without loopholes; 3- to define and prohibit crimes against humanity; 4- to end the arms race while enhancing national security; 5- to draft a Charter for Enhancing

---

7   See Chapter Four.

Social Justice so that human beings everywhere may live in peace and dignity.

(2) Courts:

The Council must reinforce the present, inadequate, international judicial system. Three new Security Council resolutions are proposed to achieve that goal: 1- The International Court of Justice must be strengthened; 2- an International Criminal Court must be created; 3- a World Tribunal for Social Justice must be started.

(3) Enforcement:

The Council must create new structures or procedures for peace that will see to it that the new resolutions for peace are in fact carried out. The creation of four new organs of enforcement are proposed at this time: 1- A UN Disarmament Enforcement Agency; 2- a UN Sanctions Agency; 3- a UN Police Agency; 4- a UN Social Justice Agency.

By combining the five Security Council resolutions clearly articulating the international law of peace, adding three resolutions strengthening the judicial system, and then supplementing the package by four additional resolutions creating structures for peace enforcement, a comprehensive new regime can be created to curtail the current international anarchy. All twelve resolutions can be combined into one omnibus and comprehensive resolution in which the Council asserts its lawful authority to maintain peace. A proposed omnibus resolution is drafted as a single consolidated text to offer a comprehensive overview of the preceding twelve new resolutions. If this new and relatively simple approach can become a reality, a new path to peace may have been found.

Will it be possible to gain acceptance for even these relatively few changes in current UN practice and procedures? Only time will tell. But it should be much easier to persuade a group of fifteen sophisticated diplomats on the Security Council to take action needed to save the world than to convince representatives of over 180 competing nations in diverse stages of social development. It should be much easier to focus public attention, understanding and support for clear and limited peace objectives on which their future depends than on the myriad toothless declarations and exhortations that now flow from an incomprehensible assortment of international bodies. How nations that have the power to implement (or defeat) the resolutions may be persuaded to embrace such a new peace regime will be dealt with hereafter.[8]

---

8   See Chapter Nine.

It is appropriate to ask at the outset: Is the Security Council legally authorized and legitimately empowered to take the type of comprehensive security action here suggested?

C - The Council's Legal Jurisdiction

The United Nations Charter is an international treaty that legally binds all member states and which, all have agreed, takes precedence over any other international agreement (Art.103). Even states that are not members are expected to act in accordance with Charter principles regarding peace (Art.2 (6)). The United Nations Charter itself defines and sets the legal parameters for action by any of its organs.

To make it possible for the United Nations to carry out its mission of enforcing peace, all members have specifically conferred on the Security Council :

> primary responsibility for the maintenance of international peace and security and agree that in carrying out its duties under this responsibility the Security Council acts on their behalf.[9]

The only restraint on Security Council peace-keeping authority is the requirement that it discharge its duties "in accordance with the Purposes and Principles of the United Nations" (Art. 24 (2)). The very first article of the Charter lists among its purposes: "to maintain international peace and security" and "to take other appropriate measures to strengthen universal peace" (Art. 1). The Preamble proclaims the determination of "We the Peoples"..."to save succeeding generations from the scourge of war" and reaffirms "faith in fundamental human rights, in the dignity and worth of the human person..." As long as these principles are respected, the Security Council is vested with a broad power of attorney that it has already received from all states that have accepted membership in the United Nations.

The Council is charged with the duty of determining "the existence of any threat to the peace" and to "decide what measures shall be taken...to maintain or restore international peace and security" (Art. 39). All members have already agreed "to accept and carry out the decisions of the Security Council" (Art. 25). No Charter revisions or new amendments or new ratifications are required to authorize the Security Council to do what it is supposed to do. Even though political considerations in the past made it difficult or impossible for the Council to discharge its obligations, these

---

9   UN Charter, Article 24 (1). How it may proceed to carry out its responsibility is spelled out in the Charter Chapters VI, VII, VIII and XII.

barriers seem to be significantly diminished and the Council should now be able to assert its legitimate and vested general authority to maintain peace.

(1) Council Jurisdiction to Clarify Binding Norms:

It is only logical and reasonable to recognize that a Council that has authority to impose sanctions and use military force to maintain peace (as it may clearly do under Articles 41 and 42,) also has authority to take more moderate steps such as to articulate, interpret and expound the binding norms on which peace depends.

Recognizing that such authority to articulate and expound the law is, by implication, already vested in the Security Council (with regard to security issues *only*) makes it possible to see more clearly that binding international legal obligations concerning peace *can* be clarified and authoritatively reconfirmed in a short period of time. Whether they realize it or not, the Security Council - driven by necessity - is already moving in that direction and no nation has seriously challenged its authority to do so.[10]

Christiane Bourloyannis, of the UN Codification Division, has persuasively confirmed the authority of the Security Council to enforce widely accepted obligations to respect the laws of war as laid down in various Hague Conventions.[11] If the Council can enforce humanitarian laws in war (despite the fact that the applicable conventions envisage an enforcement regime by national states) the Council may surely exercise its vested authority by interpreting and enforcing laws of peace to prevent war.

Acting within its constitutional authority under Chapter VII of the UN Charter, the Council has authorized unlimited military force to repel aggression, it has imposed economic sanctions against many nations, controlled production, monitored free elections, supervised cease-fires, mandated humanitarian relief, helped reestablish civil governments and taken, authorized or directed a wide variety of similar actions aimed at maintaining peace all around the world.[12] Clarifying binding international norms or interpreting the Charter in a manner that enables its fundamental purposes to be realized, and in such a way that it becomes possible - rather than impossible - to maintain peace is clearly within the authority validly asserted by the Security Council. The old order is changing and a new order knocks at the gates.

---

10 *See* ASIL *Proceedings* 1993, Comments by Bruce Rashkow of the U.S. State Dept. and others on a panel discussing *"The Security Council, It's Authority and Legitimacy,* April 1, 1993.

11 *The Security Council of the United Nations and the Implementation of International Humanitarian Law,* 20 Denver Jour. of Int. Law and Policy 335 (1992).

12 *See An Agenda For Peace,* A/47/277 (1992) and *Report on the Work of the Organization* (Sept. 1992).

(2) *Jurisdiction to Create New Organs:*

The world community has not only delegated to the Security Council the authority to articulate existing legal obligations where necessary to preserve peace but it has also given the Council the authority to create new agencies to help carry out its mandates. The UN Charter specifically authorizes the Security Council to create "such subsidiary organs as it deems necessary for the performance of its functions" (Art.29). All states, by accepting the Charter, have already consented to such arrangements and it has frequently been exercised without protest.[13]

Nearly 25 years ago, Secretary-General Dag Hammarskjold pointed out that new UN organs would be needed to cope with problems that exceeded the capacity of the Secretariat.[14] Literally dozens of new organs not envisaged by the Charter have been created as part of the UN system to perform a variety of activities. UN regional associations of states have also found it necessary to create specialized organizations to discharge specialized responsibilities.[15]

There is no need to rely on diplomatic conferences or conventions that require long and complicated negotiations, ambiguous compromises and uncertain or conditional ratifications of treaties or conventions in the distant future. We have pointed out that many new agencies to deal with many issues have been based on simple resolutions of the General Assembly or other UN bodies. It would be unthinkable to argue that the Security Council lacks the authority to do the same regarding vital issues of war and peace. We have noted many recent instances where the Council - with the help of new organs - has begun to exercise its powers in a broad and rather effective manner.[16] Such innovative and relatively swift Security Council decisions and interventions manifested a dramatic shift when compared to the Cold-War paralysis that frequently stymied Security Council action in the past. The Council was finally starting to do what is was supposed to do under the Charter!

---

13   The power to create subsidiary organs has been delegated under the Charter to each of the five principal organs; UN Charter Art.7, 22, 29.

14   *See* B. URQUHART, HAMMARSKJOLD (1972) at 325.

15   *See* KAPTEYN et. al. Eds.,INTERNATIONAL ORGANIZATION AND INTEGRATION, Annotated Basic Documents and Descriptive Directory of International Organizations and Arrangements, 4-vols.,(1984); I. SEIDL-HOHENVELDERN, *DAS RECHT DER INTERNATIONALEN ORGANISATIONEN EINSCHLIESSLICH DER SUPRANATIONALEN GEMEINSCHAFTEN* (3rd ed. 1979); H. SCHERMERS, INTERNATIONAL INSTITUTIONAL LAW, 2 vols. (2d ed. 1980); D.W.BOWETT, THE LAW OF INTERNATIONAL INSTITUTIONS 3rd Ed. (1975).

16   See Chapter Four, Section C.

We see, therefore, that the Charter provides complete legal authority for the Security Council to pass resolutions reasserting binding legal obligations to maintain peace and to create new organs to help it in that task. What is required now is for the Council to do its job.

D - Guiding Principles for Council Action

If the Security Council is to fulfill its assigned role in maintaining international peace and security, it will have to be guided by principles that will make its decisions and actions acceptable to the international community as a whole. The Security Council can not become a dictatorial agency that exists primarily to protect the interests of the privileged against the cries of the needy. It must take into account the legitimate concerns of all members of the human family. Tyranny by the majority or tyranny by the minority is still tyranny and must be avoided.

It is important that other agencies of the United Nations participate, and have a sense of participation, in whatever decisions are taken by the Security Council on behalf of peace - whether it be by new legal formulations or new organs of peace enforcement. All of its actions must in fact, as well as perception, be motivated solely by the sincere desire to build a peaceful world of human dignity and justice for all - while protecting the right of all nations and peoples to govern themselves in all other matters as they may see fit.

Maintaining a sense of shared community and dedication among those who are expected to be bound by new rules is a vital prerequisite for compliance with new mandates. If the power that is vested in such a small group as the Security Council is to be accepted by other members of the world community, it will be necessary for the Council to adopt guidelines that will minimize the dangers of oppression or exploitation by major powers and assure smaller nations - as well as powerful non-permanent members - that their voices are being heard and seriously considered.

(1) Guiding Principles for Clarifying Legal Norms:

There is a fine line between *expounding* the law and *expanding* the law - one must tread the boundary with caution. The Council can not act arbitrarily or inconsiderately in clarifying or articulating binding rules for future legal behavior of nations and peoples. Legal interpretations by the Security Council - which is a political and not a judicial body - must grow out of legal seeds that have already been planted.

Although we have stipulated that a new way of thinking is required, that does not mean that one should disregard or discard hallowed customs or practices. We must honor traditions of the past when considering needs of the present. International stability requires respect for existing laws, institutions and procedures. Proposed changes which depart too-radically from established traditions run the risk of generating such opposition, turmoil and uncertainty that the goals being sought may be rendered unacceptable and unattainable; consequences may be counter-productive or unpredictable.

This is not to suggest that the future must be a slave to the past. Respect for tradition does not demand blind obedience. Progress depends on change that builds on what has gone before. Law must be allowed to grow in order that the promise held out to the people of the world may be fulfilled. The best way to respect the Charter is to interpret it, and its apparent inconsistencies and vagaries, in ways that allow the fundamental principles and objectives of the Charter to be achieved - even if it requires a new way of thinking about old problems.[17]

In elucidating binding legal norms, the Council - above all else - must be sure to honor the basic peace-keeping purposes of the UN Charter. Those who accept interpretations which allow the goals of the United Nations to be frustrated show their contempt for the organization and for international law. Interpretations that defeat the primary Charter determination "to save succeeding generations from the scourge of war" should be rejected as erroneous and detrimental. Before articulating legal interpretations, the Council should not hesitate to seek guidance from legal bodies or recognized experts who are free of political taint or national bias.

Obviously, the International Court of Justice - "the principle judicial organ" of the UN - has a significant role to play in clarifying international law. The Charter specifically authorizes the Security Council to "request the International Court of Justice to give an advisory opinion on any legal question.[18] The Council should, as a matter of prudent practice and the exercise of wise discretion, in all cases of reasonable doubt, seek an advisory opinion regarding any significant Security Council interpretation of prevailing international law. The interplay between Court and Council is a desireable method to disperse power and provide a check against mis-interpretations or arbitrary action. By turning for guidance to recognized legal authorities, the Council will demonstrate that it is not a dictatorial regime but one that is prepared to cooperate with others in maintaining peace through law as part of an invigorated global management process.

The Council must be careful not to exceed its authority under the Charter. Any nation, acting through the General Assembly, should be authorized to request the International Court of Justice to render an advisory opinion regarding the validity of a Council decision that a threat to the peace

---

17   See Chapter Four.
18   UN Charter, Article 96 (2).

exists and that the proposed Council action is reasonably likely to diminish or eliminate that threat.[19] An opinion by the Court that the Council has exceeded its constitutional authority should be respected. By shining the light of transparency on Council deliberations and requiring more frequent Council reports to the General Assembly on issues that affect war and peace, the power of legal and public opinion can be mobilized as an additional bulwark against the dangers of arbitrary or unjustified Council action.

(2) *Guiding Principles for Creating New Peace Structures:*

The last thing this world needs is to add more bureaucracy to the already overcrowded UN bureaucracies. But members of the Security Council lack the time and usually lack the qualification to deal personally with details of the complicated and specialized problems that must be mastered to manage global peace. Not all new problems can be loaded on the over-burdened shoulders of the UN Secretary-General. It was well put by Mr. Rao of India:

> The Secretary-General cannot, I submit, be expected to be inspecting basements and searching for bombs. This can hardly succeed as anyone can see. There must be some other way.[20]

Transfering responsibility to qualified experts is essential. To attain the desired goals of peace and human dignity in the most efficient way and in the shortest period of time, a pragmatic approach is necessary. Delegates must be able to delegate.

Existing UN structures - or parts of them - that are effective and essential should, if needed, be preserved. It is not necessary to demolish or disregard everything that has gone before or that is already being done to make this a more peaceful and better world. To assure efficiency, as well as maximum acceptance by existing agencies and the worldwide public, the purposes and operational mechanisms of proposed new organizational structures should be defined in the authorizing instrument. A small group of experts in the Secretariat - or recruited for that purpose by the Secretary-General - can be charged with responsibility for drawing up recommended guidelines to be followed by any new organs created by the Security Council.[21]

---

19 Whether the ICJ has authority to review and overrule a decision of the Security Council is a more difficult question. *See* M. Higgins, *The United Nations and Lawmaking: The Political Organs*, 64 AJIL 37 (1970) at 46.

20 S/PV.3046, 21 Jan. 1992 at 99.

21 The Codification Division of the Office of Legal Affairs, which has drawn up an excellent Handbook on the Peaceful Settlement of Disputes between States as well as Statutes for a new International Criminal Court to deal with crimes in former Yugoslavia, would be very competent and suited for such an assignment.

The prescribed guidelines for all new Security Council organs should include the following:

(a) Mission and Rules of Procedure:

Not every detail of the mission of any new Security Council organ need be set forth in the basic statute creating the agency. It would be desirable if "Guiding Principles" were incorporated and agreed to in advance by the principal UN bodies; but the rules should not become a bureaucratic straight-jacket. Each such organization can establish its own operational regulations consistent with the effective discharge of its basic responsibilities to carry out and further the proposed new Security Council resolutions.

(b) Staffing:

Any proposed new organs should be strictly limited to the size needed to do the job efficiently. It should *not* have representatives from each of the more than 180 nations - as now exists in major UN Committees. The work of those large or universal committees can be reduced or eliminated and their time (and cost) saved by having problems delegated to a small number of more competent specialists who will perform the duties normally expected of corporate executives or of efficiency-experts. The quality of the staff and its leadership will determine the quality of the organization and its effectiveness.

For example: The Sixth (Legal) Committee is now composed of representatives from all UN member states. Hundreds of participants sit for weeks on end discussing issues previously discussed - often for years - without any significant progress. It is all done and reproduced in several languages - with expensive interpreters and transcribers. On many of the issues, the Sixth Committee receives reports and recommendations from the 35-member International Law Commission. The ILC has no power other than to make recommendations. Many ILC members also sit on the Sixth Committee, so they are, in effect reporting to themselves. If a smaller group had greater executive authority - backed by the Security Council - it could eliminate much of the waste of time, energy and expense of the present bureaucracy.

To assure objectivity and efficiency, the organs must be staffed by independent professional experts of known competence in their assigned field of activity.[22] Such persons may be drawn from dedicated Secretariat staff with demonstrated skill in that particular subject or area. To assure that they are democratically selected, they should - if reasonably possible - come

---

22   *See* F. MORGENSTERN, LEGAL PROBLEMS OF INTERNATIONAL ORGANIZATION (1986).

from various regions of the world so that different cultural backgrounds and legal systems are taken into account. To enhance acceptance of their actions, they must respect the pluralistic nature of the international community and the need to preserve peaceful diversity wherever possible. They should be career international civil servants under the general supervision of the Secretary-General.[23] They should not hesitate to recommend *reduction* of existing bureaucracies that do more harm than good because they are unable, or unwilling, to move expeditiously toward the attainment of the declared goals.

(c) Management:

The management must be able to command respect of the world community for its fairness and determination to serve the general interests of all of humankind.Each new agency for peace should be run by a Director (or similar title) who will be directly responsible for its operations. Nominees for the position can be submitted by member states, interested organizations or individuals or recruited by independent employment specialists. The appointment of the heads of the new organs here proposed should be made by the UN Secretary-General after taking into consideration the requirements of competence and impartiality prescribed by the authorizing statute.

The appointment should be for a term sufficient to assure independence of the Director; four years with right of re-election would seem to be a minimum. To assure widespread confidence and support, the nominee for the position of Director should require approval by two-thirds vote of both the General Assembly and the Security Council.

(d) Funding:

Funding for new organs must come from the UN's regular budget. The Charter provides that the General Assembly shall consider and approve the budget of the Organization and apportion the expenses among the Members. The International Court of Justice has given an Advisory Opinion confirming that where an organ is created by the Security Council to help discharge its responsibility for maintenance of peace and security, the expenses incurred by the Secretary General in carrying out those functions must be honored by the Assembly and allocated as part of the regular budget.[24]

---

23 Art. 101(3) of the UN Charter requires the Secretary-General to appoint staff as necessary for "securing the highest standards of efficiency, competence and integrity. Due regard shall be paid to the importance of recruiting staff on as wide a geographical basis as possible."

24 UN Charter Article 17 (2);. ICJ Decision, *The Expenses Case*, ICJ Reports 1962 p.164. *See Proposed Programme Budget for the Biennium 1994-1995*, A/48/6, 20 Aug. 1993.

Money spent on the maintenance of peace is an investment in security. Its costs can reduce national defense budgets while providing more real national security than spending countless billions on murderous weaponry. High-level independent experts recently pointed out:

> The United Nations remains the only existing framework for building the institutions of a global society. While practicing all the requisite managerial rigor and financial economy, it must have the resources - a pittance by comparison with our society's expenditures on arms and illicit drugs - to serve the great objectives that are set forth in the Charter.[25]

But - if past experience is any guide - it may be anticipated that some of the major contributors to the UN's general budget may balk at payments for purposes they have not approved. To accommodate such concerns, a rule can be adopted, if necessary, to require that all large contributors (to be defined) must be included in the two-thirds majority now needed for General Assembly budgetary decisions.[26]

If the Assembly should refuse to allocate funds needed for the operations of new security organs created by the Council, the Secretary-General can always seek voluntary contributions, as he now does to cover other unfunded responsibilities. It is not a desirable alternative. If the contributions should prove inadequate, the Security Council has authority to employ such other means of enforcing its mandates as will prove effective - including "all necessary means" for that purpose. A UN tax on trade, defense expenditures, gross national product or other indicators of wealth, are possible sources of regular UN revenue which the Security Council might command as a price for peace. It is more hypocritical than reasonable for the world community to direct the Security Council to maintain peace and then refuse to give it the tools - and the money - to do the job.

(e) Possible Models:

There are many existing UN organs that can be used as a model or guide in creating effective new executive structures for peace. Of course, no mold can be rigidly applied. Some enforcement assignments can be carried out by a team of a few experts; others may require an army. Modifications to adapt to different needs will be necessary. It may be wise to give added voice to those countries that have a greater involvement or interest in the particular problem. New concepts of human needs and entitlement are

---

25 *A Report of the Independent Advisory Group on U.N. Financing*, Co-Chairmen: Shijuro Ogato of Japan and Paul Volcker of the U.S., Ford Foundation (1993) at 24.

26 UN Charter Art. 18 (2). *See* Report of the Committee on Contributions, GAOR Forty-eighth Sess., Supp. No. 11 (A/48/11) 26 July 1993.

constantly emerging and new legal structures must always be created to cope with them effectively. Requiring complete consensus or unanimity would paralyze action. The UN Charter prescribes that decisions of ECOSOC and the Trusteeship Council shall be made by majority vote.[27] By following those patterns that have been widely accepted and have functioned well in the past, apprehensions about untried innovations may be reduced and valuable lessons learned.

For example: The UN High Commissioner for Refugees is an organ of the General Assembly and has twice won a Nobel prize for its work.[28] The United Nations Administrative Tribunal functions as a small and independent judicial body which resolves disputes regarding UN employment.[29] It is appointed by the General Assembly and has functioned efficiently and well.[30] The UN's fifteen "Specialized Agencies," such as the World Health Organization, the Food and Agriculture Organization, d the International Monetary Fund, follow organizational patterns common to the cumbersome UN system, but may provide some guidance as to what should - or should not - be done by new Security Council organs.[31]

Another useful model can be found in the International Atomic Energy Agency, where effective decision making is entrusted to a small Board of Governors composed of ten experts on atomic energy. A problem that sparked the Iraq-Kuwait war has been handled by a small Demarcation Commission, aided by two independent experts, acting in cooperation with other UN agencies. They completed a new demarcation of a very contentious border after only 11 sessions. The Council expressed its appreciation to the Commission and the Secretary General hailed it as a noteworthy international success where law, technology diplomacy and security came together in a unique UN endeavor.[32]

In a very thoughtful article, Sir Geoffrey Palmer, Professor of Law at the University of Wellington in New Zealand, has suggested ways to make international environmental law effective and binding on sovereign states. He calls for an innovative and conceptual leap forward in institutional terms. He recognizes that some vital decisions must be made even if unanimous consent is lacking. He suggests a series of secretariats for separate

---

27   UN Charter Art. 68, 87.

28   *See Reports of the UN High Commissioner for Refugees*, UN GAOR 1951, Supp. 1951 to date.

29   *See* ICJ Advisory Opinion, 13 July 1954, ICJ Reports p.47.

30   See B.KOH, THE UNITED NATIONS ADMINISTRATIVE TRIBUNAL (1966).

31   *See* D. MITRANY, A WORKING PEACE SYSTEM, AN ARGUMENT FOR THE FUNCTIONAL DEVELOPMENT OF INTERNATIONAL ORGANIZATION (1943); E. LUARD, INTERNATIONAL AGENCIES: THE EMERGING FRAMEWORK OF INTERDEPENDENCE (1977).

32   *See* SC Res. 687 (1991); SC Res. 773 (1992) UN Press Release SG/SM/499, 20 May 1993.

environmental issues or the creation of a new organ so that "the law can cope effectively with a new problem." [33] That is exactly what is needed now to cope with the major problems that threaten global security and world peace.

(f) Checks and Balances:

A system of checks and balances regarding the creation of new organs to help with peace enforcement is essential to help overcome opposition from governments or bureaucrats that might otherwise consider their interests jeopardized. The Charter already requires the Secretary-General to keep all members informed of deliberations by the Security Council (Art. 12 (2)). But current practice is rather diffuse and Professor Reisman has correctly argued for the creation of a "Chapter VII Consultation Committee" composed of a cross section of only 21 Assembly members to share views with the Council *before* enforcement decisions are reached.[34]

Involving the Assembly in funding Security Council organs and in approving appointment of Directors enhances checks and balances. Similarly, turf or jurisdictional disputes with other UN agencies, or challenges that the new organ has unlawfully exceeded its mandate, can be resolved by advisory opinions from the International Court of Justice or by referral, where appropriate, to the UN Administrative Tribunal.

Before the Security Council decides to use force it should invite the nation that is expected to contribute toward enforcement to participate in the Council's decision. That is essentially what is required by the Charter itself.[35] Consultation and, if feasible, coordination with other UN organs, committees, commissions and similar agencies dealing with related problems must be made mandatory. Representatives of such institutions should be invited to meetings and consulted informally on issues that might affect the workings of their agencies. Maximum consultation and consideration before binding decisions are reached should be the rule. Such cooperation further diminishes the risk that the Council will act in a high-handed and unacceptable manner. The executive head of each new agency must be regarded as a Coordinator, Facilitator or Expeditor - and not as an Executioner.

Without impeding the discretion that is often essential to successful negotiation of sensitive problems, there must be greater openness so that the public understands fully and clearly the motivation and justification for

---

33   G. Palmer, *New Ways to Make International Environmental Law* 86 AJIL 259 (1992) at 283.

34   M.A. Reisman, *The Constitutional Crisis in the United Nations,* Notes and Comments, 87 AJIL 83 (1993) at 99.

35   UN Charter Art. 44).This point was made by Italy's Foreign Minister Mr. Beniamino Andreatta when he addressed the General Assembly on 30 Sept. 1993.

Council action. Where public disclosure may jeopardize the success of a negotiation or mission, disclosure of details may, of course, be temporarily delayed but public support must remain paramount for without it no enforcement measures by the Council can prevail. The role of non-governmental organizations and other interested groups must not be underestimated and should be reinforced.

Fortunately, the changes here suggested do not stretch far beyond what has already been recognized to be essential. A Group of High-level Intergovernmental Experts, appointed by the General Assembly, has for years been dealing with the problem of making the UN more effective. The UN agenda calls for *Review of the efficiency of the administration and financial functioning of the United Nations.*[36] The experts recognize the relationship between peace and security, economic and social development, transparency in recruitment practices and the need to divide major Secretariat activities along functional lines in a limited number of consolidated departments to enhance coordination and streamlining.[37] The Secretary-General is struggling to try to put some of the expert proposals into effect.[38] To expect the Secretary-General to accomplish so much is expecting too much. Maintaining peace and security is - according to the Charter - primarily the responsibility of the Security Council.

Involvement of the Secretary-General, the Assembly, the World Court, coordination with other UN agencies and openness to the public produces an important network of checks and balances to protect both nations and peoples from dictatorial abuse by the Security Council. Vesting operational responsibility in new organs of the Security Council to enforce specific Council resolutions for peace is a small transitional step in the inevitable direction of delegating authority to specialists in an increasingly specialized and integrating world. Nations and individuals, if they are determined to stop war, must be ready to take a chance for peace.

(g) Security Council as Ultimate Authority

The new organs will, in effect, be acting under the Secretary-General's administrative control but actually as agents of the Security Council to see that their assigned specialized peace tasks are effectively discharged - either by the new organs directly or in collaboration with existing agencies. These are Security Council responsibilities which members of the Council cannot possibly carry out directly and which they must therefore delegate to a limited number of impartial and qualified professionals serving the common interest.

---

36   A/48/100, 15 June 1993, Agenda Item 123.
37   id. at 391.
38   *id.* at 392.

It is hoped that the excellence and specialization of the new organs, the reputation of its Director and the wisdom of its recommendations and enforcement actions, will carry such weight that neither the Assembly nor the Council will want to override the conclusions of its own recognized and approved experts. Unless there is clear and overwhelming justification, it is difficult and politically risky to overrule the considered recommendations of outstanding authorities assigned to carry out their peace-maintenance assignment for the benefit of all. Public awareness of decisions taken by the new structures for enforcing peace will enhance greater public support and help to overcome diplomatic or bureaucratic hesitation or intransigence. It is assumed that members of the Security Council are persons of intelligence and integrity who will recognize that the public interest in security is also their own personal interest and the interest of every country.

D- *Evaluation*

The framers of the Charter intended the Security Council to be the world's guardian for peace. It has never been given the chance or the means to carry out its assignment. If nations and peoples are to break out of the straightjacket that binds them to be helpless victims of the war system, they must allow the Council to do its job. It is the only authorized agent and the only available alterative that holds forth the possibility of creating a new universal regime of peace within a reasonable period of time.

What has been here proposed is a balanced new technique for expounding, clarifying, supporting and carrying out the law of peace and building new structures to enforce it under Security Council control. The new institutions that will be created by Security Council resolutions (details of which will be spelled out in the next chapter) will - if properly constituted - relieve the principal organs of the UN of burdens and detailed responsibilities they were never able to fulfill.

Such quasi-independent institutions with direct operational responsibilities to be carried out under Security Council control and Secretary-General observation or administration can address urgent problems quickly and efficiently - in contrast with the endless and indecisive *talk* that now plagues so many diplomatically organized large UN Commissions and Committees struggling hopelessly - and often endlessly - for consensus. Coordination and cooperation, rather than dominance or confrontation, should be the goal and the rule. It must remain clear, however, that - after adequate consultation and fair consideration - the final decision to enforce peace must remain in the hands of the Security Council - where the Charter put it.

If one studies the September 1993 *Report of the Secretary-General on the Work of the Organization*, what emerges is a picture of an overworked Secretary-General who has no independent authority to enforce anything, who lacks funds to carry out his peace-keeping assignments and no special skills or experience for the many military command functions that now absorb most of his time. It depicts an impossible task being inadequately done because its basic assumption is that all states (who are his employers) must agree on all vital issues - an assumption that makes it quite impossible to do what needs to be done to secure peace in the world.[39]

In addressing the General Assembly on September 27, 1993, President William J. Clinton of the United States referred to the way governments were now re-inventing how they operate. "Now the time has come," he said, "to reinvent the way the United Nations operates as well."[40]It is our contention that global peace problems can most expeditiously be resolved by a new three-pronged approach - led by the Security Council:

(a) Five Security Council resolutions clearly defining the *legal obligations* essential for peace.[41]

(b) Three resolutions empowering international *judicial* organs to interpret the laws of peace, adjudicate disputes and punish violators.[42]

(c) Four resolutions setting up special *enforcement* agencies to see that every peace mandate is fully implemented and carried out in the shortest possible time.[43]

The attainment of the three objectives for world order (effective laws, courts and enforcement) will be possible by the adoption of a small number of new Security Council resolutions mandating the minimal requirements to safeguard the future.

We will reiterate the reasons why each new resolution is required, how it is expected to work to improve world security and we shall also propose a draft text of each resolution designed to achieve the stated goal. Like a "baker's dozen," we will then add one omnibus resolution consolidating all twelve in the hope that what then emerges is a picture of an improved and attainable world order based on peace, justice and human dignity for all.

---

39   A/48/1, 10 Sept. 1993.
40   Release USUN 140-(93) Rev. 1, Sept. 27, 1993 at 10.
41   See Chapter One.
42   See Chapter Two.
43   See Chapter Three.

CHAPTER EIGHT

TWELVE SECURITY COUNCIL RESOLUTIONS FOR PEACE
Their Justification and Substance

> Logic, and history, and custom. and utility, and the accepted
> standards of right conduct, are the forces which singly or in
> combination shape the progress of the law...Uniformity ceases
> to be a good when it becomes uniformity of oppression. The
> social interest served by symmetry or certainty must then be
> balanced against the social interest served by equity and fair-
> ness or other elements of social welfare.

Judge Benjamin N. Cardozo[1]

We have shown that a new way of *thinking* is necessary if we are to
move toward a more rational world order in which the basic purposes of
the UN Charter can be achieved.[2] Now, as an essential part of our revised
world structure, we propose a new way of *acting*. The principle actor is the
Security Council doing its duty in the common interest as the duly-desig-
nated guardian of the world community. Its tool is the adoption of binding
and enforceable resolutions articulating legal obligations relating to world
security.

To respect the past, the proposed peace-enforcement resolutions are
limited to norms, edicts or institutions that have already been generally
approved in principle. For foundation-stones and guidance, the Council
should select only the clearest and most widely accepted legal instruments.
As Belatchew Asrat of Ethiopia has noted:

> As the constitution of a near-universal world body, the Charter
> is a unique international instrument. Its provisions need to be
> given the interpretation which makes them relevant for the
> period to which they pertain.[3]

Clauses and phrases or interpretations that served to undermine the purported peace objectives in the past must be eliminated to safeguard the
future. The authority of the International Court of Justice must be strengthened and violations of the laws of peace must be made a criminal offense

---

1 B. CARDOZO, THE NATURE OF THE JUDICIAL PROCESS (1921) p.112-113.
2 See Chapter Four.
3 B. ASRAT, PROHIBITION OF FORCE UNDER THE UN CHARTER (1991) at 243.

for which individual perpetrators will be held personally accountable. New enforcement agencies are essential.

We shall deal only with the substance of a few generally accepted legal concepts and the strengthening or creation of a few institutions that are already in existence, in formation or on the near horizon. In the proposed new Security Council resolutions, non-binding preambles are omitted. What is offered is a bare-bones skeleton to be fleshed out as required - without diminishing the firmness of the basic legal obligation. Inspired by Justice Cardozo and guided by logic, custom, utility and "the accepted standards of right conduct," we hope to shape the progress of the law.[4]

A - Five Resolutions to Strengthen *Laws* of Peace

In order not to get too far ahead of reality, we limit our proposal to only five legal doctrines that have already been universally or widely accepted in principle: peaceful dispute settlement, prohibiting aggression and crimes against humanity, ending the arms race and enhancing social justice. If laws are to fulfill their proper role in governing human society, they must be unambiguous and equally binding on everyone. To be meaningful, laws must be clear, mandatory and unequivocal.

(1) *Mandating Peaceful Settlement*

The reasons why such a resolution is needed should be fairly obvious - the present mandates don't work. In Chapter One, we sketched the progress of what, for lack of a better description, we termed International Laws of Peace. We saw that, for at least a hundred years, sovereign states professed a desire to stop war by the rule of law. The Treaties, Agreements, Covenants, Pacts and Charters signed by leading nations of the world all stipulated that the use of armed might to settle disputes would be outlawed. After World War II - if not before - there was no doubt that aggressive war was an international crime. The binding legal texts were reinforced by countless official Declarations that confirmed fundamental juridical principles designed to invalidate resort to war.

All of the cited treaties and proclamations for peace received overwhelming public support. The authors of the documents were hailed as national and international heros by a grateful public that had grown weary of the barbarism and madness of man's brutality to his fellow human beings.And yet, wars raged on. All of the professed legal measures to assure peace turned out to be chimerical.

---

4   Of course, none of these suggestions purports to be the last word on the subject. If anyone has a better way to achieve the desired goal of a peaceful world, let them come forward; all improvements would be most gratefully received.

We have suggested some of the reasons for the failure to prevent wars: sovereign states were not really ready to live up to their professed declarations; hallowed traditions extolling the "glories" of war and nationalism anchored diplomatic thinking to the past; the uncertainty about the outcome of peaceful settlements and the absence of international courts capable of guaranteeing peace with justice served to undermine sincere acceptance of heralded legal obligations. We noted ambiguities and loopholes deliberately written into all of the international laws of peace in order to free the hands of signatories. Despite such self-serving "safeguards," many treaties were never ratified or were later repudiated to protect "honor" or "vital interests."

War has been the traditional way of settling disputes between sovereign states - and it was legal in the sense that it was not prohibited by international law. The 1899 Hague Convention for the Pacific Settlement of International Disputes was probably the most important legal instrument up to that time that purported to restrain man's capacity for slaying his fellow man in combat.[5] It outlined procedures for the use of "Good Offices and Mediation," "International Commissions of Inquiry," and "International Arbitration," and was somewhat improved at the second Hague Conference in 1907. But the parties only agreed "to use their best efforts," "as far as possible," or "as far as circumstances allow." With such debilitating reservations, the Convention turned out to be practically useless. It surely did not cause states to settle all their disputes by peaceful means.

After World War I, the League of Nations sought to limit warfare as a legitimate way to settle disputes between sovereign states. But it still permitted war as a lawful activity - providing there was a delay of three months after peaceful methods failed. The widely-accepted Kellogg-Briand Pact of 1928 appeared to renounce and condemn *all* recourse to war; it consisted of only two substantive Articles. The reasons the Pact failed - secret reservations regarding self-defence and vital interests - have already been described.[6]

After World War II, the UN Charter prohibited the use of force but also allowed exceptions for "self-defense" and imposed no effective penalties for violations. More recent legal instruments, such as the Friendly Relations Declaration and the 1982 Manila Declaration on the Peaceful Settlement of Disputes were also replete with such terms as *"should, "bear in mind," "consider," "whenever appropriate"* and similar non-binding qualifications which meant that the document expressed vague wishes but surely could not

---

5   *See* Chapter One, Section A-1. The Hague Convention of 1899 is *reproduced in* FERENCZ, INTERNATIONAL CRIM. CT Vol. 1 Doc. 1 at 111.

6   Chapter One, Section A-3.

compel anyone to be bound by its apparent restraints.[7] In the face of such vacillation and uncertainty, new wars were unavoidable. The general public, unable to perceive the legal machinations of diplomats who pretended to be statesmen, were misled into believing that their destinies would be controlled by law and not by war. But law never lived up to the promise to the people.

We now seek to correct these fatal shortcomings in the international legal documents - prohibiting recourse to force by making their provisions absolute and unambiguous. The succinct Kellogg Pact, as well as the UN Charter, serves as our model for a new resolution for peaceful settlement of disputes but the new resolution demands the unequivocal renunciation of the use of armed force and also penalizes those who violate its mandates.

DRAFT RESOLUTION MANDATING PEACEFUL SETTLEMENT

THE SECURITY COUNCIL, acting pursuant to its authority under the Charter of the United Nations, declares that all members of the organization are bound by the following resolution:

ARTICLE 1 - All states, groups or individuals are legally prohibited from using armed force for the settlement of controversies of any kind, or for any purpose not specifically authorized by the Security Council of the United Nations.

ARTICLE 2 - All states, groups or individuals are legally bound to settle all disputes or conflicts of whatever nature or origin by peaceful means in accordance with Chapter VI of the UN Charter.

ARTICLE 3 - There may be no exceptions whatsoever, under any circumstances, to the mandates of Articles 1 and 2.

ARTICLE 4 - Violators of these rules are subject to individual criminal punishment. Leaders, organizers, instigators, and accomplices participating in the formulation or execution of a common plan or conspiracy to violate this resolution shall be

---

7   *Reproduced in* FERENCZ, ENFORCING INT. L. vol.2 Doc. 75 (b) at 855.

held responsible. **Those who aid and abet persons accused of violating these rules, either before or after the commission of the crime, will share criminal responsibility.**

ARTICLE 5- **The interpretation of these rules and their implementation and enforcement shall be the responsibility of the Security Council or such organs as it may designate for that purpose.**

COMMENTARY:

The Preamble makes clear that the Security Council will only be involved where there is a threat to the peace, breach of the peace or act of aggression, as set forth in Chapter VII, Article 39 of the Charter.

Article 1 leaves open the possibility that armed force may be used for enforcement purposes, but only if it is done pursuant to Security Council decision and control - as now provided in the UN Charter.

Article 2 follows the Kellogg-Briand example and the principles in UN Charter Chapter VI. The reference to "groups or individuals" in both Articles 1 and 2 makes it more comprehensive than the Charter term "parties" which might be interpreted as being limited to state entities or members of the UN.

The Article eliminates the need for any new law, treaty or convention for the peaceful settlement of disputes. It contains none of the evasive clauses that appeared in the Hague Convention for the Pacific Settlement of Disputes, the Friendly Relations Declaration or the Manila Declaration and relies instead on the options clearly specified in the Charter.

Article 3 is intended to eliminate unauthorized national self-defence and collective self-defence as well as "national emergency," "honor," "vital interests" or any similar rationales that have been used to justify self-help by the use of force in the past. Defence of a peaceful world order is to be an obligation of the international community. Only the Security Council can authorize the use of force.

Article 4 criminalizes violations but leaves open the procedures for trial and the nature of the punishment. Whether aggression has occurred must be decided by the Council but the door is left open for the Council to seek an advisory opinion from the International Court of Justice or to use some other means for obtaining independent "outside" support for its conclusion.

Accused individuals may be tried by the International Criminal Court as proposed hereafter. As confirmed by the Nuremberg Principles, planners and accomplices can not escape responsibility. Those who aid and abet the accused will also have to face trial. This is intended to inhibit the granting of political asylum or sanctuary to the accused. Art. 4 reinforces Art. 2 since punishing violators may encourage states to settle disputes peacefully.

Article 5 envisages the creation of a new Security Council organ to deal with international crimes - as discussed hereafter under the proposed Resolution Creating An International Criminal Court. Implementing regulations may define the circumstances under which local police action is permissible to repress ordinary crimes within national jurisdictions. Security Council involvement is only permissible where the infractions pose a threat to peace.

Making it absolutely clear that the illegal use of force will be penalized is only a first step in reinforcing the law of peace. The argument most frequently raised to justify the use of international force is that it was not illegal because it was necessary to achieve a lawful objective. To discredit such evasions, it is important to re-define without ambiguity what constitutes the crime of aggression.

(2) *Clearly Defining Aggression*

Aggression is a crime against peace. The 1945 Charter of the International Military Tribunal at Nuremberg, the Court's judgment and the unanimous resolution of the UN General Assembly have confirmed that aggression is an international crime. Even though aggression was characterized as "the supreme international crime" it was not defined. When a definition was reached by consensus, 29 years later, it was, as we have noted, more sieve than substance.[8]

The definition of aggression adopted without a vote by the General Assembly in 1974, on consensus recommendation of the Legal Committee, purported to be a legal instrument designed to define the offence clearly so that it could deter unlawful behavior and help the Security Council decide whether aggression had occurred. But the inclusion of exculpating clauses, allowing conduct that would normally be condemned as aggression to be considered lawful if done in pursuit of certain legitimate goals, made the definition practically useless. Although the definition was mentioned from time to time, it had no significant legal impact.[9]

The loopholes deliberately written into the law became an added invitation for evasion by those who preferred to use military might rather than peaceful settlement. It should have come as no surprise that the

---

8   Chapter One, Section C.
9   The consensus definition was reaffirmed in several international declarations, such as the Declaration on International Detente, Res. 32/155 (1977), Declaration for Societies for Life in Peace, Res. 33/73 (1978), Declaration on the Non-Use of Force, Res. 42/22 (1988) and it was mentioned in the ICJ decision in Nicaragua v. U.S., ICJ Reports 1986 p. 103.

definition that was supposed to serve as the basis for triggering peace-keeping action by the Council has been all but ignored in practice. It certainly proved inadequate as a guide to peace enforcement.

When Security Council resolutions condemned Iraq's invasion and annexation of Kuwait, they made frequent reference to Charter Chapter VII, but the consensus definition of aggression was never mentioned.[10] The Council acted by simply passing a resolution authorizing member states to use "all necessary means" to evict Iraq and "to restore international peace and security in the area."[11] In submitting a revised definition of aggression, we have taken the prevailing consensus definition as our starting point. Exculpatory clauses, inserted by the parties in the consensus definition of 1974 - in order to satisfy the parochial political interests of competing groups - have been deleted.[12]

DRAFT RESOLUTION CLEARLY DEFINING AGGRESSION

THE SECURITY COUNCIL, acting pursuant to its authority under the Charter of the United Nations, declares that all members of the organization are bound by the following resolution:

ARTICLE 1 - The use of armed force in violation of the Security Council Resolution Mandating Peaceful Settlement is a breach of the peace. It shall also constitute an act of aggression if it includes:

(a) Invasion or attack by armed forces.

(b) Bombardment from land, sea or air, using nuclear, chemical, bacteriological or any other weapons capable of destroying human life directly or indirectly.

(c) Blockade of ports, coasts, cities or regions.

---

10   See SC Res. 660, 661, 662, 664, 665, 667, 670, 674, 677 (1990).

11   SC Res. 678 (1990).

12   The clauses which have been deleted appeared in Article 2, 4, 6, 7 and 8 of the consensus definition.

(d) Sending armed bands, groups or mercenaries to carry out acts of armed force in violation of Security Council prohibitions.

ARTICLE 2 - No consideration of whatever nature, whether political, economic, military or otherwise, may serve as a justification for aggression.

ARTICLE 3 - An act of aggression is a crime against international peace. No territorial acquisition or special advantage resulting from aggression shall be recognized as lawful. No nation, group or individual shall be allowed to benefit from any act of aggression.

ARTICLE 4 - Violators of these rules are subject to individual criminal punishment. Leaders, organizers, instigators, and accomplices participating in the formulation or execution of a common plan or conspiracy to violate this resolution shall be held responsible. Those who aid and abet persons accused of violating these rules, either before or after the commission of the crime, will share criminal responsibility.

ARTICLE 5 - The interpretation of these rules and their implementation and enforcement shall be the responsibility of the Security Council or such organs as it may designate for that purpose.

COMMENTARY:

Article 1 goes beyond the consensus definition, which is limited to action by States against States and designed primarily to protect "the sovereignty, territorial integrity or political independence of another State." The new article seeks to protect the peace of everyone. By making a distinction between "breach of the peace" and "aggression" - which Charter Article 39 does not make clear - it is implied that the former is a lesser violation that may not be criminally punishable. The International Law Commission, in dealing with State Responsibility, has made a similar distinction between "crimes" and "delicts".[13]

---

13   GAOR 44th Sess. Supp. No. 10 (A/44/10) (1989) pp.194-199.

Sections (a) to (d) of Article 1 are based on the listing in the 1974 definition but made somewhat more inclusive.

Article 2 is taken verbatim from the 1974 definition Art.5.

Article 3 is also taken verbatim from the 1974 definition, except that the term "war" has been replaced by "act".

Sec.(a) is based on, but goes beyond, the 1974 definition which said: "No territorial acquisition or special advantage resulting from aggression are (sic) or shall be recognized as lawful."

Article 4 is stronger than the 1974 text which said: "Aggression gives rise to international responsibility."

The resolution defining aggression builds on the currently prevailing ambiguous formulation of law by giving notice that aggression, as more clearly defined, is a punishable international crime. The two resolutions (1 and 2 above) serve as a double warning that the use of armed force and aggression are illegal and will not be tolerated. Since there are other crimes that may threaten peace, a new resolution spelling out how the Security Council will react to certain other crimes against humanity is also proposed.

(3) Prohibiting Crimes Against Humanity

We have been warned by Grotius to remember our humanity "lest by imitating wild beasts too much, we forget to be human."[14] The Charter and Judgment of the International Military Tribunal at Nuremberg listed three categories of punishable international crimes:

    (a) Crimes Against Peace - aggression, which has been
       dealt with above.

---

14   Grotius, LAWS OF WAR AND PEACE, Book III, Chap. XXV, Sec.II.

(b) War Crimes - the breaches of customary or conventional rules for the conduct of hostilities are defined in various Hague Conventions and Protocols, as well as military manuals, and judgments of war crimes trials.[15] Since we are concerned here with laws of peace rather than war, we shall not suggest any revisions of existing laws dealing with the conduct of warfare. The best way to avoid war crimes is to avoid war.[16]

(c) *Crimes Against Humanity:* The Nuremberg Charter defined Crimes Against Humanity as:

> murder, extermination, enslavement, deportation, and other inhumane acts committed against any civilian population, before or during the war; or persecutions on political, racial or religious grounds...whether or not in violation of the domestic law of the country where perpetrated.[17]

The difference between War Crimes, ordinary criminal acts and Crimes against Humanity was never made quite clear.[18]

What distinguishes Crimes against Humanity from ordinary crimes is that their magnitude reaches such proportions as to shock the conscience of

---

15 *See* A.DELISSEN AND G. TANJA, Eds. HUMANITARIAN LAW OF ARMED CONFLICT: CHALLENGES AHEAD, Essays in Honor of Frits Kalshoven (1991); M. BOTHE, Ed., NATIONAL IMPLEMENTATION OF INTERNATIONAL HUMANITARIAN LAW (1990); G.PLANT, ENVIRONMENTAL PROTECTION AND THE LAW OF WAR (1992).

16 Henry Dunant, founder of the International Red Cross after the first World War, became convinced that the only way to avoid the horrors of war was to abolish war itself. That opinion was shared by Prof. B.V. Roling, head of the Polemological Institute at Groningen and a Judge at the Tokyo war crimes trials. *See* B.V.A. Roling, *Aspects of the Criminal Responsibility for Violations of the Laws of War,* in A.CASSESE, Ed., THE NEW HUMANITARIAN LAW OF ARMED CONFLICT 199 (1979) at 231. Retired U.S.Admiral Noel Gaylord has aptly described the rules of war as "the attempts of civilization to put limits to barbarism." *See* D.A.WELLS, WAR CRIMES AND LAWS OF WAR (1991) at xi.

17 IMT Charter Art.6.

18 Listing Crimes Against Humanity as a distinct offense was stimulated by outrage against Hitler's genocidal persecution of Jews and political adversaries. The International Military Tribunal gave a restricted interpretation to the IMT Charter, holding that, to be punishable, persecutions had to be connected to the crime against peace and therefore had to be committed *during* the war. The restrictive view was later expanded by Allied Control Council Law No. 10 and later Nuremberg decisions confirmed that Crimes Against Humanity are punishable whenever and wherever committed. See FERENCZ, DEFINING INT. AGRESSION, Vol. 1 at 43. A meticulous analysis of the wording of the IMT Charter appears in M.C. BASSIOUNI, CRIMESS AGAINST HUMANITY IN INTERNATIONAL CRIMINAL LAW, Chapters 4 and 5 (1992).

humanity - which thereby becomes the offended party and the appropriate complainant. There is no clearly demarcated threshold which marks the point where violence reaches the level of barbarity and outrage to qualify as a cri me against humankind. Genocide, piracy, slave trade, apartheid, terrorism and torture are examples of generally recognized Crimes against Humanity.[19]

Reasonable arguments have been made that the use of nuclear weapons should be a crime against humanity because its devastating explosive and ecological impact would unavoidably destroy innocent civilian populations.[20] Although a clear-cut definition has yet to be formulated and accepted, there is no doubt, as Professor Bassiouni has concluded, that the concept of crimes against humanity and its legal viability has been constantly reinforced.[21]

We have noted that several international legal instruments have tried, after many years of negotiation, to deter such international crimes as hostage-taking, aerial hijacking, crimes against diplomatically protected persons and terrorism. None of them proved effective.[22] In almost identical language, the legal conventions contained exculpating clauses to exonerate killers who could argue that they were merely seeking "self-determination" or "freedom from alien domination." Political motives allowed the crime to be excused or permitted perpetrators to escape by finding asylum in a friendly country. The legal instruments supposedly condemning terrorism, made a mockery of international justice.

The truth is that some nations were unwilling to agree on clear-cut obligations to halt all murderous activities. State-sponsored terrorism became a clandestine political weapon to be used with impunity. Since there existed no international legal mechanism to prevent terrorism, unilateral counter-measures of vengeance or retribution were unavoidable even though they ran the risk of inciting even more retaliatory violence. Hostage-taking and aircraft bombing or hijacking so infuriated victim states or their nationals that vengeful unilateral retaliation was provoked. Assassination,

---

19 *See* B. Ferencz, *Crimes Against Humanity*, 1 Max Planck Institute, Encyclopedia of Public International Law 869 (1992); M.C. BASSIOUNI AND V. NANDA, A TREATISE ON INTERNATIONAL CRIMINAL LAW, Vol.1 (1973); C.L.BLAKESLEY, TERRORISM, DRUGS, INTERNATIONAL LAW AND THE PROTECTION OF HUMAN LIBERTY (1992).

20 See, for example, A. MIATELLO, L'ARME NUCLEAR EN DROIT INTERNATIONAL (1987), E.L. MEYROWITZ, PROHIBITION OF NUCLEAR WEAPONS (1992); H. Meyrowitz, Les Armes Nucleaires et le Droit de la Guerre, in A.DELISSEN and D.TANJA, HUMANITARIAN LAW OF ARMED CONFLICT (1991).

21 M.C.BASSIOUNI, CRIMES AGAINST HUMANITY IN INTERNATIONAL CRIMINAL LAW (1992) p. 527.

22 See Chapter One, Section C.

even if only attempted or planned, aroused strong emotions and brought nations to the brink of war.[23]

It can not be expected that over 180 nations that have vacillated for decades will suddenly reach agreement on clear conventions or treaties to eliminate terrorism or other crimes against humanity. If such crimes have become intolerable to the world community, it is up to the Security Council to act on its behalf and to make the rules of the game unmistakably clear in advance. It is the duty of the Security Council to recognize threats to peace and to take measures to prevent them. Failure of the Security Council to act increases insecurity.

In 1992, the Security Council intervened when - in its judgment - international crimes threatened peace. Acting in its authorized capacity as the world's agent to protect the peace, the Council passed resolutions demanding that Libya cooperate with a request by the United States and France that it hand over for trial two Libyan nationals suspected of bombing civilian aircraft with heavy loss of life.[24] When Libya failed to comply, the Council, acting under its enforcement powers bestowed by Chapter VII of the Charter, passed another resolution imposing aerial, arms and diplomatic sanctions against Libya.[25] Security Council intervention and enforcement measures were upheld as legal by the International Court of Justice.[26] Surely, action via the Security Council as the authorized representative of the world community and confirmation of legality by the World Court is a much safer (and more lawful) way of dealing with terrorism - or any problem - than allowing nations to decide for themselves when to use force in retaliation or vengeance against a perceived wrong

On October 13, 1993, the twelve former Soviet Republics condemned "any act of terrorism, whatever its motive and called for punishment by an international tribunal[27] When Haiti's Minister of Justice was assassinated, Haiti's representative on the Security Council declared:

---

23   For example, the United States bombed Libya in 1990 as a warning to Muammar el-Qaddafi, the head of state, to halt state-sponsored terrorism. See A.D'Amato, The Imposition of Attorney Sanctions for Claims Arising from the U.S. Air Raid on Libya, Editorial Comment, 84 AJIL. 705 (1990). The United States, which itself had been accused of complicity in the assassination of President Allende of Chile and planned assassination of Fidel Castro in Cuba, bombed Iraq in response to an alleged plot by Iraqi agents to assassinate former U.S. President Bush. *Transcript of President Clinton's address*, N.Y. Times, June 27, 1993 p. L 13.

24   S.C. Res. 731 (1992).

25   S.C. Res.748 (1992). See Chapter One, Section C, Chapter Two, Section D.

26   *Libya v. U.S.*, 1992 ICJ 219 (Apr.14); 31 ILM 662 (1992).

27   A/C.6/48.

A handful of criminals cannot be allowed to defy with impunity the international community and hold hostage an entire people that desires to recover its rights and freedoms.[28]

It is to clarify and uphold the rule of law that the following resolution is proposed. In keeping with our principle of limiting Security Council intervention as much as possible and not trying to expand its authority, it relates only to well-recognized crimes that threaten peace. Crimes against humanity that do not rise to a level that threatens peace are not subject to Security Council jurisdiction and will not be considered here.[29] The determination whether the illegal action threatens peace is, according to the Charter, for the Security Council to make. When such crimes do pose a threat to the peace, it is the *obligation* and not merely the *right* of the Security Council to intervene to put a stop to them.[30]

DRAFT RESOLUTION PROHIBITING CRIMES AGAINST HUMANITY

THE SECURITY COUNCIL, acting pursuant to its authority under the Charter of the United Nations, declares that all members of the organization are bound by the following resolution:

ARTICLE 1- The following acts, when determined by the Security Council to constitute a threat to the peace, are absolutely prohibited as Crimes Against Humanity:

(a) Genocide, by which is meant any act committed with intent to destroy, in whole or in substantial part, any racial, national, linguistic, religious or political group of human beings. Such acts shall include: killing or causing serious physical harm or inflicting conditions calculated to bring about the destruction of the group.

---

28   S/PV. 3293, 10 October 1993 at 3.

29   Nuclear contamination might reach a level to pose a threat to peace, but no conventions have yet beeen reached making that an international crime. See V. Morris, Protection of the Environment in Wartime: The UN General Assembly Considers the Need for a new Convention, 27 the International Lawyer (Fall, 1993) 775.

30   UN Charter Art.39.

(b) Terrorism, by which is meant any threat or illegal act of violence intended to coerce, intimidate or cause a state of panic, fear, insecurity or terror among a civilian population. Such acts shall include political assassinations, hostage taking, dangerous interference with civilian aircraft, destruction of public buildings, systematic kidnaping, massive physical abuse or torture and similar acts of illegal violence designed to terrorize the public.

(c) Apartheid, by which is meant the practice of racial discrimination and segregation on a scale to constitute a threat to international peace and security, including acts for the purpose of establishing and maintaining domination of one racial group of persons over any other racial group of persons and systematically oppressing them.

ARTICLE 2 - No consideration of whatever nature, whether political, economic, military or otherwise, may serve as a justification for crimes against humanity.

ARTICLE 3 - Violators of these rules are subject to individual criminal punishment. Leaders, organizers, instigators, and accomplices participating in the formulation or execution of a common plan or conspiracy to violate this resolution shall be held responsible. Those who aid and abet persons accused of violating these rules, either before or after the commission of the crime, will share criminal responsibility.

ARTICLE 4- The interpretation of these rules and their implementation and enforcement shall be the responsibility of the Security Council or such organs as it may designate for that purpose.

COMMENTARY:

Article 1 (a) is drawn from a combination of the Genocide Convention and an earlier draft prepared by the Economic and Social Council.[31] The text has been abbreviated and simplified. The word "substantial" has been added for clarity and to avoid the inclusion of minor atrocities that may not

---

31 Both documents are *reproduced in* FERENCZ, INT. CRIM. CT., vol. 2, Doc. 19, (UN Doc. A/362, 25 Aug. 1947) and Doc. 24, (*The Genocide Convention* adopted as GA Res. 260 (III) 9 Dec. 1948).

threaten peace and should be punished as ordinary crimes without Security Council intervention. "Political" groups have been included since they are a frequent target of genocidal acts that may threaten peace.

Article 1(b) is a composite based on existing laws and conventions. There is no agreed definition of terrorism.[32]

Article 1(c) is extracted - omitting the elaboration - from the International Convention on the Suppression and Punishment of the Crime of Apartheid.[33]

Article 3 is taken verbatim from the Charter of the International Military Tribunal, Art.6.[34]

It could be argued that war itself should be outlawed as the greatest Crime against Humanity. It might also be argued that even the costs of *arming* the world - about $2.5 billion *each day* - should also be a crime against humanity since, as General Eisenhower said, it robs the poor of the resources they need to live in human dignity. But the international legal community has - unfortunately - not yet reached the stage of civilization where war and armaments are legally prohibited. The next step on the way to a more humane world is putting a stop to the arms race that imperils everyone.

(4) *Ending the Arms Race*

Eliminating the arms race is absolutely vital. The use of national military force can not be effectively outlawed in a highly militarized world any more than local law-enforcement authorities can effectively eliminate crime in streets filled with well-armed criminals. Experience shows that nations with large arsenals are inclined to use them. Peace can never be enforced against lawless nations that are stronger and better armed than the peace-enforcers.

Repeated promises to eliminate the arms race have never been honored.[35] After the horrors of World War I, 45 leading nations covenanted that

---

32   See Chapter One, Section C-3; Hague Academy of International Law, *The Legal Aspects of International Terrorism* (1988) Introduction by Prof. J.A. Frowein; Colloquium, University of Bruxelles, *Reflexions sur la definition et la repression du terrorism* (1974); Symposium, *Terrorism and the Law*, 19 Connecticut Law Rev. (1987). Prof. C. Blakesley argues for universal jurisdiction - similar to piracy - over all forms of terrorism. *Id.* 895.

33   UNGA Res. 3068 (XXVIII) 30 Nov. 1973. *See* M.C. Bassiouni and D.H. Derby, *Final Report on the Establishment of an International Criminal Court for the Implementation of the Apartheid Convention and Other Relevant International Instruments*, 9 Hofstra Law Rev. 523 (1981).

34   *Reproduced in* FERENCZ, INT. CRIM. CT. vol.2 p. 457.

35   See Chapter Three, Section B.

armaments would be limited to only those weapons needed to maintain domestic tranquility and enforcement "by common action of international obligations." Nations were required to disclose the size of their arsenals and arms industries. The private manufacture of weaponry was recognized as undesirable. The Council of the League was authorized to control the level of all arms.[36] None of these solemn promises was ever kept.

After even greater horrors and losses in World War II, the promises of disarmament were repeated. The very first General Assembly of the new United Nations resolved to eliminate all weapons of mass destruction. The Security Council was obligated by the Charter to prepare a disarmament plan and to arrange for international military forces to maintain peace under Security Council control. These obligations have not yet been fulfilled. In 1992, the UN Secretary-General was still urging nations to eliminate all nuclear weapons.[37]

The willingness of nations to disarm and to rely for their defense upon measures of collective security was confirmed by men of intelligence and good faith, yet they never did what they promised to do. We have already described the reservations and loopholes in some of the arms-limitation treaties - as well as recent progress.[38] Hanspeter Neuhold has tried to explain the reasons for the roadblocks:

> By now, decision-makers can draw on a sizeable backlog of treaty practice which ought to facilitate arms control agreements. As in the past, the way toward arms control is not paved with technological and legal difficulties as the principle stumbling stones; the main roadblocks are rather political: the lack of mutual trust and political will.[39]

Nothing can be gained by recriminations about whose fault it was that promises were not kept or that progress was hesitant. Slowing the arms race is not good enough - the arms race must be *ended*. The world has been given another chance; it may be its last.

The dilemma: States are not likely to agree to eliminate their armaments unless a better security plan can replace military force as the ultimate means to protect national safety and interests. Before universal disarmament can become a reality there must be something more desirable and useful to take

---

36 Covenant of the League, Art. 8.
37 *New Dimensions of Arms Regulation and Disarmament in the Post-Cold War Era*, A/C.1/47/7-S/24111 (17 June 1992).
38 Chapter Three, Section B.
39 H. Neuhold, *Legal Aspects of Arms Control Agreements*, in BOCKSTIEGEL et. al., LAW OF NATIONS, LAW OF INTERNATIONAL ORGANIZATIONS, WORLD ECONOMIC LAW, *Festschrift fur Ignaz Seidl-Hohenveldern* (1988) at 448.

its place. No nation will, or should, disarm completely until there is some reasonable assurance that the world-wide elimination of weaponry will be enforced and a new security system of effective non-military sanctions and a UN peace-keeping capability will be firmly established. That is precisely why a comprehensive plan and action by the Security Council is needed now.

The contents of any comprehensive disarmament package - to be acceptable - must include the following:

(a) Verified and Gradual Arms Reductions:

Every nation must preserve the right to retain at its disposal sufficient force to maintain law and order within its own territory. That does not mean that its weaponry must be of such magnitude and power as to strike justifiable fear into the hearts of its neighbors or other nations of the world. The citizens right to bear arms, which may be included in constitutions of democratic states, was never intended as a license to commit international aggression.

It should be quite obvious that no nation should be required to strip itself of every defensive capacity and stand militarily naked and helpless before its enemies.[40] Arms reductions of all nations must go hand in hand so that the relative security of any state is not diminished in the process. Furthermore, there must be a fool-proof system of verification to make sure that no nation cheats or acquires an unfair, and dangerous, advantage.[41]

(b) Minimizing Hardships of Dislocation:

Consideration must also be given to the economic dislocation that is inevitable in any massive disarmament program. Members of armed forces and employees of defense industries who have dedicated themselves to the service of their country can not be discarded as useless surplus. Revolutionary social turmoil can best be avoided by making sure that soldiers, scientists and others who may be displaced in the process of eliminating the arms race are reintegrated into new fields of more productive social betterment.

A massive shift from military activity to peaceful activity has occurred after every war. Admittedly, there have been some hardships caused by unemployment and difficulties of retraining and absorbing displaced workers into a peace economy. That would hardly justify carrying the burdens of a useless, and very expensive, military establishment indefinitely. With

---

40 See Chapter Four, Section E.

41 Walter Dorn, of Parliamentarians for Global Action, a non-official body with headquarters in New York City, has written extensively and persuasively on establishing a UN agency capable of effective disarmament verification. *See* W.A. Dorn, *The Case for a United Nations Verification Agency: Arms Control by International Means*, May 5, 1990 (unpublished).

proper industrial planning and government help, such problems have been overcome in the past and can be overcome in the future. Conversion from military to peace economies has led to an industrial renaissance in such countries as Germany and Japan as well as the United States - before it was dragged deep into debt by the weight of its military budget. The public has much more to lose from a war economy than a peace economy.[42]

(c) Effective Sanctions as an Alternative:

Whatever disarmament plan is proposed must include a credible and less violent alternative system to maintain peace among nations. The collective security plans of both the League of Nations and the UN Charter have been outlined and we have indicated why economic sanctions failed to restore peace. What is required now are clearer legal obligations for more effective non-violent coercion, implemented and *enforced* by new organs under Security Council control - which we shall deal with hereafter.

(d) UN Military Force:

There will always be some lawbreakers - in national as well as international societies. A country without an effective police force would be a country in chaos. A world without a military force to maintain peace is a world in chaos.

No country has been designated to be the policeman of the world and no single nation should assume or be given that role. The world's security system is not based on unilateral military intervention or dominance by one or more super-powers. It is based on the theory that only the Security Council, as agent for all nations, can act to restore the peace. It can no longer be tolerated that some states - unilaterally or in concert with its allies - have sufficient power to pose a threat to world security. Remember McDougal's warning: "No nation can be secure until all nations are secure." We are all in the same boat.

It is our contention that, in fulfillment of its clearly stated Charter responsibility to limit armaments and to maintain peace, it is incumbent upon the Security Council to take decisive action to *end* the arms race and also to create an alternative peace enforcement agency. Recognizing that national arms can not be eliminated without creating a substitute security system, the proposed new Security Council resolution to end the arms race links universal disarmament with Security Council peace enforcement via

---

42 Columbia University Professor of Industrial Engineering, Seymour Melman, who heads a National Commission for Economic Conversion and Disarmament, has been in the forefront of those who have written extensively and convincingly on the subject. *See* S. MELMAN, THE PERMANENT WAR ECONOMY (1985), and writings of Professor Llyod Dumas of Texas, including L.J.DUMAS & M. THEE, Eds.,MAKING PEACE POSSIBLE, THE PROMISE OF ECONOMIC CONVERSION (1989).

economic and other sanctions as well as a UN military force (to be described hereafter) as the world's policeman. Ad hoc solutions may be the product of necessity but a system of international law and order should have a firmer legal foundation than expedient political improvisations.

In drafting new binding legal obligations for disarmament, we turn for our model to the McCloy/Zorin (M/Z) agreement for General and Complete Disarmament - primarily because it was universally hailed and unanimously endorsed by the United Nations General Assembly in 1961.[43]

DRAFT RESOLUTION ENDING THE ARMS RACE

THE SECURITY COUNCIL, acting pursuant to its authority under the Charter of the United Nations, declares that all members of the organization are bound by the following resolution:

ARTICLE 1: All states shall have at their disposal only those non-nuclear armaments, forces, facilities, and establishments as are agreed by the Council to be necessary to maintain internal order and protect the personal security of its citizens.

ARTICLE 2: States shall support and provide manpower for a United Nations Peace Force when called for by the Security Council.

ARTICLE 3: The Security Council, or such organ as it may designate, shall establish rules to implement the program for general and complete disarmament, including:

---

43   See Chapter Three, Section B. A/RES/1722 (XVI) 20 Dec. 1961. The McCloy/Zorin Agrement, UN Doc. A/4879, Sept. 20, 1961 is *reproduced in* FERENCZ, ENFORCING INT. L. vol. 2 Doc. 76 (a) p. 858. A comprehensive disarmament plan is also contained in CLARK AND SOHN, WORLD PEACE THROUGH WORLD LAW (1960 ed.) pp.206-313.Marcus Raskin, of the Institute for Policy Studies in Washington D.C., has outlined a thoughtful Draft *Treaty* for Disarmament and Common Security, consisting of eighty-two articles. The system would be controlled by a new International Disarmament Organization to end the arms race; M.G. RASKIN, ABOLISHING THE WAR SYSTEM (1992).

(a) Disbanding of armed forces, dismantling of military establishments, including bases, cessation of the production of armaments as well as their liquidation or conversion to peaceful uses;

(b) Elimination of all stockpiles of nuclear, chemical, bacteriological, and other weapons of mass destruction and cessation of the production of such weapons;

(c) Elimination of all means of delivery of weapons of mass destruction;

(d) Abolishment of the organization and institutions designed to organize the military effort of states or other entities, cessation of military training, and closing of all military training institutions;

(e) Discontinuance of military expenditures.

ARTICLE 4: The disarmament program mandated above shall be implemented in a sequence until it is completed, with each measure and stage carried out within specified time-limits after verification by the Security Council that there has been compliance, that no military advantage has been gained and that security is ensured equally for all.

ARTICLE 5: All disarmament measures will be implemented from beginning to end under such strict and effective international control as will provide firm assurance that all parties are honoring the obligations set forth herein. Any organ created by the Security Council to implement control over and inspection of disarmament shall be assured unrestricted access, without veto, to all places as necessary for the purpose of effective verification.

ARTICLE 6: During and after the implementation of general and complete disarmament, the Security Council shall take the necessary measures to maintain international peace and security, including the use of economic and other sanctions, UN peacekeeping forces, other forces placed at its disposal pursuant to Article 2 above, and all other means it may consider necessary to deter or suppress any threat or use of arms in violation of the purposes and principles of the United Nations.

ARTICLE 7: In carrying out the program of comprehensive and complete disarmament, the Security Council, and whatever organs may be created to implement the program of disarmament, sanctions or policing, shall consult with the General Assembly and with existing agencies dealing with similar problems with a view to making implementation effective in the widest possible area at the earliest possible date with the minimum possible economic hardship to persons and industries affected by the transformation.

ARTICLE 8: Violators of these rules are subject to individual criminal punishment. Leaders, organizers, instigators, and accomplices participating in the formulation or execution of a common plan or conspiracy to violate this resolution shall be held responsible. Those who aid and abet persons accused of violating these rules, either before or after the commission of the crime, will share criminal responsibility.

COMMENTARY:

Article 1 is taken verbatim from the McCloy/Zorin (M/Z) Agreement, except that the reference to the Security Council has been added after the word "agreed" in order to make clear that it is the decision of the Council which will be determinative and binding.

Article 2 is taken verbatim from the M/Z agreement except that the word "agreed" has been deleted before "manpower" and the phrase "as called for by the Security Council" has been added. Detailed plans for a U.N. Peace Force are contained in CLARK AND SOHN, *supra* at pp.314-334.

Article 3 is taken verbatim from M/Z except there has been added the reference to an "organ" in sentence 1. It is anticipated that the Council's responsibility will be delegated to a special organ or organs competent to deal with disarmament problems.[44]

---

44   Chapter Eight, Section C.

Article 3(d) adds the phrase "or other entities" to make the prohibition more inclusive and comprehensive.

Article 4 follows points 4 and 5 of M/Z closely but is abbreviated without altering substance.

Article 5 is taken, in substance, from Point 6 of M/Z but the word "will" replaces "should be" and "would" in order to make it mandatory.

Article 6 follows the substance of M/Z point 7. Drawing on the goal stated in principal 1 of M/Z to make "effective arrangements for the maintenance of peace in accordance with the principles of the UN Charter," it adds the authorization, already in the Charter, for the Council to employ economic and other sanctions as well as a UN military force or police agency - which will be a separate organ of the Council as proposed hereafter.

Article 7 is based on Point 8 of M/Z which aimed at *agreement* of states through uninterrupted negotiation. The reference to the General Assembly and to other agencies is intended to give some assurance that the Council will not act arbitrarily and that the views, and problems, of all nations and related organs or committees will be taken into account when implementing the program. It also specifically authorizes the creation of new organs such as the UN Sanctions Agency and the UN Police Agency which is proposed hereafter. Its last clause is intended to encourage comprehensive approaches to problems of economic dislocation and conversion to peaceful production.

Even in a disarmed world, where peaceful settlements have been mandated and aggression and crimes against humanity have been outlawed by clear laws, more changes will still be needed if peace is to be maintained. If the peace is to be secure, the United Nations will have to take action to improve the social conditions of those who, through no fault of their own, suffer the deprivations of being destitute. Revolting conditions inspire revolt.

(5) *Enhancing Social Justice*

World poverty is a threat to world peace. A world that is one-fifth rich and four-fifths poor can not be a secure world. A world that has a depleting supply of clean water and clean air to be shared by an increasing and ever more demanding population can not be a secure world. A world that is half slave and half free can not be a secure world. The need to create conditions of minimum social justice for all peoples has long been recognized as a humanitarian prerequisite for peace and security. Declaring shared goals is one thing, making them a legal duty is another.

Humanitarian principles, even if universally acclaimed, are not automatically binding obligations that can be characterized as enforceable international *law*.[45] Let us recall that the movement toward a world of enhanced social justice through law is still in its infancy.[46] The 1948 Universal Declaration of Human Rights heralded human entitlement to civil and political rights (Arts. 3-21) and to fundamental economic, social and cultural rights (Arts. 22-27,)[47] but these were only recommendations - not legally enforceable by any international body.

By 1953, the European Convention on Human Rights went into force and by 1959 the European Court of Human Rights was established. By 1965, a European Social Charter went into effect purporting to set forth a variety of economic rights. Since the Charter was not self-executing and national legislation was required to implement the declared rights, they remained little more than declarations of principle which might - one day - become binding law. Nations were required to report progress but there was no right of individual complaint nor any court or enforcement mechanism to redress violations of accepted norms.[48]

International Covenants elaborated the proclaimed civil and political rights as well as economic, social and cultural rights.[49] They again spoke of "human dignity," the "human family" and the rights of every human being. These ringing manifestations of increasing human aspirations never reached the level of legally enforceable human entitlement.

The clear delimitation and description of specific legal standards to improve human welfare and assure human dignity in a disparate multi-cultural society poses a very difficult challenge. Before laws or new institutions can resolve the problems of social justice in the world, more knowledge and more public commitment on a broad scale will be required. Without such knowledge and dedication it will be very difficult to articulate established norms to be protected or to obtain approval for new administrative organs to implement and enforce minimum standards of worldwide human decency.[50]

---

45   *See* S.P.SINHA, WHAT IS LAW? (1989).

46   *See* C.W. JENKS, SOCIAL JUSTICE IN THE LAW OF NATIONS -the ILO Impact After Fifty Years (1970).

47   GA Res. 217 A (III) 10 Dec. 1948.

48   European Social Charter, 529 UNTS 89-139 (1965);   D.J. HARRIS, THE EUROPEAN SOCIAL CHARTER (1984).

49   International Covenant on Civil and Political Rights, GA Res. 2200 A (XXI) 16 Dec. 1966; International Covenant on Economic, Social and Cultural Rights, GA Res. 2200 A (XXI) 16 Dec. 1966.

50   *See* M.S.MCDOUGAL et.al. HUMAN RIGHTS AND WORLD PUBLIC ORDER (1980).

Thirty-eight states participating in the Conference on Security and Cooperation in Europe (CSCE) met in Paris in 1990 and, in a Charter for a New Europe, agreed:

> Ours is a time for fulfilling the hopes and expectations our people have cherished for decades: steadfast commitment to democracy based on human rights and fundamental freedoms; prosperity thorough economic liberty and social justice; and equal security for all our countries.[51]

They promised to promote "economic activity which respects and upholds human dignity" and to "promote social justice and progress and further the welfare of our peoples"[52] They recognized the need for new structures and institutions to implement and enforce the shared objectives for the common welfare. But the implementation has been very slow in coming. As William Korey concluded in his enlightening survey of human rights, the Helsinki process and American foreign policy: "promises are only as good as their keeping."[53]

This is not to suggest that no effort has been made to fulfill some of the human rights promises. The United Nations Development Program, in cooperation with the World Bank and others, has been trying to improve opportunities and prospects for international economic growth and social development in Africa and other underdeveloped regions. Its detailed reports show progress is being made but they also depict areas of continuing desperate need.[54] A recent collaborative report of the United Nations Development Program, the UN Environment Program and the World Resources Institute shows that sustainable development requires economic growth, improvements in human health and the quality of life, environmental protection and the use of earth-friendly technologies by industrialized countries. They are all part of one process for human betterment - and it has hardly begun.[55]

A host of other UN Organs, Commissions, Committees and Sub-committees have sought to improve the human condition in an increasingly large number of ways.[56] These encouraging efforts reflect the growing trend

---

51   J. BOROWSKI, SECURITY FOR A NEW EUROPE (1992) at 208.

52   *Id.* at 210, 215.

53   W.KOREY, THE PROMISES WE KEEP (1993) at 438.

54   *See* UNDP and World Bank Reports: *African Economic and Financial Data* (1989) and *African Development Indicators* (1992):LESTER BROWN et. al., STATE OF THE WORLD (Annual). *See* Meeting of the Standing Ministerial Committee for European Cooperation of the Non-Aligned Movement, A/48/338, 23 Aug. 1993, Annex.

55   *See* WORLD RESOURCES, 1992-1993.

56   UN Headquarters in New York maintains liaison, for example, with the Geneva-based UN High Commissioner for Refugees; the UN Environmental Program and Center for

toward gradual fulfillment of the great political and social ideal that all humans are entitled to live in human dignity. Yet these important advances have been forced to rely to large extent upon voluntary support that has proved inadequate to emancipate whole populations from justified discontent.[57] Until nations recognize that it is in their own self-interest to respect fundamental rights of individuals everywhere, one must look to the Security Council to detect and diminish the human anguish that may rise to a level that threatens peace.

The 1991 *Stockholm Initiative on Global Security and Governance* - with its very distinguished panel of world leaders - recognized that:

> Member countries of the Security Council should give a lead in taking on to their agenda issues now so inescapably linked to the peace of the world and the security of its people as poverty and economic and ecological interdependence.[58]

The Security Council, that has been granted primary responsibility for maintaining peace and security in the world, can not remain indifferent to the hazards caused by prevailing social disparities which stimulate massive migrations that penetrate national boundaries, threaten economic disruption and generate massive violence born of desperate discontent.[59]

If prevailing social abuses of any kind pose a threat to peace, the Security Council has been vested with authority to intervene. In line with the recommended "Guiding Principles" for Security Council clarification of law, the Council's resolutions can not get too far ahead of what is generally accepted by the world community. Human rights declarations have flowered and new environmental standards have come into the human conscience, but the recognition of clear economic rights and the acceptance of concomitant duties remains an orphan in the family of nations.

Using as its basic model those few relevant articles that received almost unanimous endorsement when the General Assembly voted for the *Charter of Economic Rights and Duties of States* in 1975,[60] the following Resolution for

---

Human Settlements situated in Nairobi; the World Food Council in Rome; a Center for Social Development and Humanitarian Affairs, located in Vienna; and a very large network of sprawling agencies dealing with trade, human rights, population control, disaster relief, protection of women and children, population control and similar concerns.

57   *See* M. MOSKOWITZ, INTERNATIONAL CONCERN WITH HUMAN RIGHTS (1974).

58   COMMON RESPONSIBILITY IN THE 1990's, (1991) at 25.

59   *See* T.C. Schelling, *Rethinking the Dimensions of National Security*, in G.ALLISON and G. TREVERTON, Eds.,RETHINKING AMERICAN SECURITY:BEYOND COLD WAR TO NEW WORLD ORDER (1992) p. 200.

60   A/RES/3281 (XXIX) 15 Jan. 1975, *reproduced in* XIV ILM 251 (1975).

Enhancing Social Justice is proposed to make certain minimum human entitlement a mandatory right. Admittedly, because of the generality of some of its declarations, it is more a guiding light and a beacon of hope than a clear legal mandate for specific action. But if we don't see where we are trying to go, we will surely never get there.

DRAFT RESOLUTION FOR ENHANCING SOCIAL JUSTICE

THE SECURITY COUNCIL, acting pursuant to its authority under the Charter of the United Nations, declares that all members of the organization are bound by the following resolution:

ARTICLE 1 - Every state has the duty to cooperate in promoting a steady and increasing expansion and liberalization of world trade and improvement in the welfare and living standards of all peoples, in particular those of developing countries.

ARTICLE 2 - The protection, preservation and enhancement of the environment for the present and future generations is the responsibility of all states. All states have the responsibility to ensure that activities within their jurisdiction or control do not cause damage to the environment of other states or of areas beyond the limits of national jurisdiction.

ARTICLE 3- All human beings are entitled to a minimum standard of human dignity, including: clean air and water, food, shelter, medical care, education, gainful employment and religious and political freedom.

ARTICLE 4 - The Security Council will establish a separate organ, or organs to help carry out these mandates.

ARTICLE 5 - The Security Council will use all necessary means to protect the rights enumerated in this Charter when it determines that their violation poses a threat to the peace.

COMMENTARY:

Article 1 is taken verbatim from the first sentence of Art. 14 of the 1975 Economic Charter which was opposed by only 1 vote out of 115.

Article 2 is extracted verbatim from Art. 30 of the Economic Charter. It received 126 affirmative votes against 3 negative.

Article 3 is an extract of fundamental principles expressed in almost all human rights declarations.[61]

Article 4 recognizes that the Security Council shares responsibility for economic and environmental issues that threaten peace. The reference to additional "organ or organs" is authorization for the creation of a World Tribunal for Social Justice to interpret social justice laws and resolve disputes regarding them. It also contemplates the creation of a new UN Social Justice Agency to implement and enforce the Charter for Enhancing Social Justice.[62]

Article 5, by asserting the Security Council's authority, lends credence and support to the proclamation in the Universal Declaration of Human Rights: "Everyone is entitled to a social and international order in which the rights and freedoms set forth in this Declaration can be fully realized" (Art.28).

No article has been added to criminalize violations since the stated social justice obligations lack the specificity required by a criminal statute.

As we review the five proposed new Security Council resolutions designed to reinforce the international laws of peace, it should be apparent that they seek to build on norms that have been universally acclaimed and accepted by people of good will. But these declared legal norms have never been clearly articulated in detail or adequately implemented. Laws do not interpret themselves and laws without courts lose their power. Peace also requires that defects in the international judicial structure be repaired. Here too, the Security Council can play a vital role.

61　*See* R.MULLER, THE BIRTH OF A GLOBAL CIVILIZATION (1991).

62　See Chapter Eight, Section B and Section C.

B - Three Resolutions to Strengthen *Courts* for Peace

The public interest in world peace cannot properly be served without decisions of wise and dedicated judges in courts of international law. In our sketch of international courts, we described the gradual growth and use of different methods to settle disputes by peaceful means. We noted the emergence of new regional courts and human rights courts and plans for a new Law of the Sea Tribunal with compulsory jurisdiction and the stirring of an *ad hoc* criminal tribunal to hear charges of genocide and mass rapes in former Yugoslavia. These were significant advances.

We also pointed to shortcomings of the present system that does not compel parties to turn to the World Court - even with disputes that threaten peace. There exists no permanent international criminal tribunal competent to try those individuals who flout the international laws of peace, although progress in that direction is being made. An international court to decide whether minimum social justice norms are being met is not even in the planning stage.

We shall again look to the Security Council as the instrumentality for improving the international judicial system as a means of preserving peace. New Council resolutions can set the framework for enhancing the authority of the World Court and for creating new organs to implement and carry out new judicial approaches to peace enforcement.

(1) Enhancing the World Court

In our outline of the evolutionary development of the International Court of Justice, we pictured a court severely handicapped by the unwillingness of many states to turn to the Court or to be bound by its decisions. The fact that the World Court lacks compulsory jurisdiction undercuts its effectiveness as a tribunal for the settlement of legal disputes that might lead to war. If peace is to be more secure and the rule of law is to be strengthened, it is essential to strengthen the ICJ.

The authority of the World Court needs to be strengthened so that parties engaged in legal disputes that threaten peace are obliged to turn to the Court if other means of peaceful settlement fail. It must also be clear that where the failure to comply with an ICJ decision threatens peace, the Security Council will step in to see that the decision is enforced.

The UN Charter provides that "legal disputes should as a general rule be referred by the parties to the International Court of Justice." But it then adds: "in accordance with the provisions of the Statute of the Court".[63] The Court Statutes provide that the Court has jurisdiction only over cases "which the parties refer to it."[64] Thus, the UN Charter says that nations *should* accept the jurisdiction of the Court, but the ICJ Statute, which is annexed to the

---

63   UN Charter Art. 36 (3).
64   ICJ Statutes Art. 36 (1).

Charter, says they don't really *have* to. The time has come to move beyond that kind of paralyzing vacillation. The Charter must be interpreted to uphold the rule of peace through law.

To be sure, those who drafted the Charter of the UN and the Statute of the Court did not *want* to invest the tribunal with compulsory jurisdiction at that time. But they did express the hope that eventually, as the Court earned the confidence of nations, it would be more widely accepted. It is therefore consistent with the wishes expressed by the "founding fathers" to now seek ways to make the Court more accessible and productive.

The world has changed considerably since nations first thought of creating a court with binding authority to settle international disputes. In the intervening years, the World Court has earned the confidence needed for greater acceptability. Judges for the ICJ are democratically elected by both the General Assembly and the Security Council from a list of highly qualified legal experts representing the principal legal systems of the world.[65] Despite valid criticism of the political campaigning which takes place to fill a vacancy on the Court, and normal differences of view regarding certain judges or decisions, it would be fair to conclude that the ICJ has earned general respect and is usually held in high regard.

Professor Thomas M. Franck recently found it reassuring "to note that the Court has carefully, and quietly, marked its role as the ultimate arbiter of institutional legitimacy."[66] Professor Eli Lauterpacht, a distinguished scholar of the Court, has questioned the continuing validity of the requirement that jurisdiction may not be exercised without consent.[67] An increasing number of states have been accepting the compulsory jurisdiction of the Court or limiting their reservations. In 1990, even the Soviet Union - which had always opposed compulsory jurisdiction as a violation of national sovereignty - seemed ready, as was the United States, to accept compulsory ICJ jurisdiction for disputes involving a limited number of human rights declarations.[68] Indications that both superpowers were prepared to agree that human rights violations should be submitted to the binding jurisdiction of the World Court encourages the hope that they might consent to a further expansion of ICJ competence.

---

65   Statute of the ICJ, Art. 2, Art. 9.

66   Editorial Comment: *The "Powers of Appreciation": Who is the Ultimate Guardian of UN Legality?* 86 AJIL 519 (1992) at 523.

67   *See* E. Lauterpacht, *Aspects of the Administration of Criminal Justice*, Vol. IX in the Hersch Lauterpacht Memorial Lecture Series (1991).

68   Report of the ICJ, GAOR 44th Sess. Supp. No.4 (A/44/4) (1989) p.2; *See* FERENCZ, WORLD SECURITY pp. 57-58.

Past experience clearly indicates that there is no realistic expectation that all sovereign states will voluntarily accept the binding jurisdiction of the ICJ on all issues that affect war and peace. Nor is it at all likely that basic amendments to the ICJ Statute will be accepted and *ratified* by two-thirds of all nations including all the permanent members of the Security Council - which is the required procedure.[69] If the present stalemate is to be broken, some more "creative lawyering" will be required.

In light of the gradual evolution and growth of the ICJ and its record of increasing acceptance by many nations, it is not unreasonable for the Security Council to expand the Court's authority by making greater use of advisory opinions and by vesting the ICJ with compulsory jurisdiction on those legal issues where the Council considers it necessary to secure peace. Let us consider how that can be done without breaching any existing legal obligations.

There are several steps that can be taken by the Security Council to enhance the role and authority of the International Court of Justice:

(a) Greater Use of Advisory Opinions:

The UN Charter entitles the Security Council to request advisory opinions from the ICJ on any legal question.[70] We have suggested as a "guiding principle" that the Security Council turn to the World Court for advisory opinions whenever apparent breaches of international law pose a threat to peace. The very fact that an ICJ advisory opinion has been requested would serve as a warning to transgressors that the Council is contemplating enforcement action. It would also have a deterrent effect and a form of "preventive diplomacy" on behalf of peace. The ICJ could decline to render is opinion where there was no international legal issue involved or the Court felt that it could not reach a fair determination without hearing the parties.[71] Regular interaction between the Security Council and the Court - each acting within its Charter competence - would help avoid abuses of power by the Council and give public reassurance of its objectivity.

(b) Mandatory Submissions to the ICJ:

In addition to advisory opinions, the Court's competence can be enhanced by other means. It must become a binding obligation that all legal

---

69   U.N. Charter Art. 108 and ICJ Statute Art. 69.

70   UN Charter Art. 96.

71   ICJ President Sir Robert Jennings, informally addressing the UN's Legal Committee on October 7, 1993, was careful to point out that the World Court is a legal body that renders its important service best by sticking to international *legal* issues and - as far as possible - avoiding decisions influenced by political considerations.

disputes which the Security Council decides constitute a threat to peace *must* be submitted to the Court for final decisions if other means of peaceful settlement fail. That can be accomplished by an innovative, but accurate, interpretation of the UN Charter backed by a suitable Security Council resolution.

We must bear in mind that disputing parties always retain all of their negotiating options - except the right to start using force and killing those who disagree with them. The legal obligation not to resort to war, already articulated in the Charter and many other legal instruments, is reinforced by being unequivocally reiterated in the proposed new Security Council Resolution that mandates the peaceful settlement of all disputes.

The Charter provides that if the parties are unable to settle a dispute by any of the peaceful means of their choice and its continuation is likely to endanger peace and security, the parties are legally *obliged* to refer it to the *Security Council* for action.[72] The Council is authorized to "recommend appropriate procedures" and "as a general rule" the parties would be referred to the World Court.[73] But if the parties, taking advantage of the Court's optional Statute, decide NOT to submit the issue to the ICJ, what then? Must the Security Council be stymied in its search for peace? If the "general rule" does not produce the desired results because of the intransigence of one or more of the parties, the Security Council still has the right, under the Charter, to

> decide what measures shall be taken in accordance with Articles 41 and 42, to maintain or restore international peace and security.[74]

If peaceful settlement or judicial procedures fail, and Council recommendations are ignored, the Council remains empowered to remove threats to peace by enforcement action under Chapter VII. Articles 41 and 42 authorize economic sanctions or military force to give effect to Council decisions. If the Council is empowered to impose sanctions and to use unlimited military might to maintain peace, it should certainly have the authority to insist that the parties first submit the dispute to a court of law. Surely it is consistent with Charter purposes and language to allow the Security Council to require warring states to bring their legal disputes to a courtroom rather than a battlefield.

The Council's failure to use its enforcement powers in the past was caused by political, not legal, restraints.[75] As long as it is discharging Charter

---

72   UN Charter Art.37 (1).
73   UN Charter Art. 36.
74   UN Charter Art.39.
75   *See* C.W.JENKS, THE PROSPECTS OF INTERNATIONAL ADJUDICATION (1964) pp. 692-695.

purposes to maintain peace and it does not flagrantly abuse its discretion, there is practically no limitation on the Security Council's authority or power. The enforcement powers of the Council under Chapter VII includes the implied right to *order* the parties to take their argument to the ICJ - a very mild method of enforcement as compared with other actions the Council is authorized to take. Any other interpretation would be contrary to the objectives of Chapter VI mandating Pacific Settlement of Disputes. Denying the Security Council's right to compel the parties to turn to the World Court would impose unwarranted restrictions on the Council's broad enforcement powers granted under Chapter VII. To compel the Council to resort to harsher measures of enforcement because peaceful avenues are closed to it would be standing the normal sequence and procedures on its head.

What is being proposed here is much less violent than what the Security Council - as authorized by the Charter and the world community - is already doing to suppress threats to the peace in Iraq, Libya, former Yugoslavia and elsewhere. Non-military economic sanctions have been ordered by the Council to enforce its resolutions and Members have also been authorized to use "all necessary means" (including aerial assaults) to enforce Council decisions. Would it not have better served the cause of peace if Iraq had been directed by the Council to take its border dispute with Kuwait to the Court and rely on briefs rather than bombs?

Directing the parties to the World Court as an enforcement measure under Chapter VII is within the Security Council's overriding competence and responsibility for peace. It would be absurd to maintain that the Council is authorized to send the parties to war but not to law. Such a conclusion would justify the comment of Mr. Bumble in Dickens' Oliver Twist: "the law is a ass, a idiot." The time has come for the Security Council to deputize the World Court to help enforce peace by peaceful means.

If parties remain adamant and absolutely refuse to present their case to the Court, the ICJ, on application of an entitled party or request from the Security Council, can decide the issues "in absentia" and render its opinion without the obstructionist party taking advantage of the opportunity to argue its own cause; the defendant's appearance before the Court remains "optional."[76]

Most decisions of the World Court are honored for a variety of reasons: the parties have voluntarily submitted the case for decision, Article 94 of the UN Charter requires the parties to comply, they may fear public scorn or

---

76   For example: Iran did not appear in the case concerning *U.S. Diplomatic and Consular Staff in Teheran ("The Hostages Case")*, ICJ Judgment, 24 May 1980 ; the U.S. did not appear in the case of *Nicaragua v. United States*, ICJ Judgment 27 June 1986.

the boomerang effect of the precedent of non-compliance if they undermine international law, etc. But, in the last analysis, the effectiveness of the Court's decision depends upon its enforceability - and that depends on the Security Council. If any party fails to perform its obligations under a judgment rendered by the Court, the other party may have recourse to the Security Council which - under the Charter - may decide upon measures to be taken to give effect to the Court's judgment.[77] To buttress the Court's authority, it must be made clear that ICJ decisions *will* be *enforced* by the Council - without bias - whenever the Council determines that failure to do so jeopardizes peace.

DRAFT RESOLUTION ENHANCING THE WORLD COURT'S AUTHORITY

THE SECURITY COUNCIL, acting pursuant to its authority under the Charter of the United Nations, declares that all members of the organization are bound by the following resolution:

ARTICLE 1: Any legal dispute which the parties have not settled by peaceful means, and the continuation of which the Council determines is likely to endanger the maintenance of international peace and security, must be submitted to the International Court of Justice for binding decision.

ARTICLE 2: In all cases where the Security Council determines that failure of any of the parties to honor a decision of the International Court of Justice poses a threat to the peace, the Security Council will use all necessary means to see that the decision is enforced.

ARTICLE 3: No national of a party to a dispute which is the subject of an opinion or decision by the International Court of Justice may vote on such decision or on any Security Council measures in enforcement thereof.

---

77   UN Charter Art. 94(2).

COMMENTARY:

Article 1 draws its authority from interpretation of existing Charter principles. It borrows language from Charter Art.34. It makes clear that once the
Council has determined that (a) there is a legal dispute; (b) the parties have
been unable to settle it peacefully and (c) it threatens the peace, the Council
has, as a matter of principle, decreed as an enforcement measure that the
dispute *must* go to the ICJ for final decision. Should the ICJ decide that the
dispute is not legal in nature, the Court could decline to decide the issue.
This would contribute to the desired system of checks-and- balances.

Article 2 builds on the Council's Art. 39 authority to decide what measures
should be taken. It combines that authority with the Art. 41 and 42 authority
to apply sanctions and military force. It assures enforcement backing to the
ICJ decisions.

Article 3 excludes from the decision and its enforcement those who are
unlikely to be objective or who may block justice to protect their own
interests. A similar point was urged when both the Covenant of the League
and the UN Charter were being debated. It is a principle of basic fairness
which has already been recognized in Charter provisions which exclude
parties to a dispute from voting on matters regarding *pacific* settlements
under Chapter VI or certain regional actions for peace.[78] It also diminishes
the power of the veto which those who do not share that discriminatory
privilege find objectionable.

These interpretations and proposed resolutions are completely consistent with UN Charter language and its fundamental purpose and intent.[79]
Failure to proceed in the indicated direction undermines Charter purposes
and leads to the very dangerous world in which we find ourselves. The ICJ
Statute, appended to the UN Charter, can not be allowed to defeat basic
Charter objectives for peace. An interpretation which allows the Court more
effectively to serve the peace purposes of the UN is a positive and accurate
approach. No additional action is required to give the World Court the
binding authority and enforcement backing needed to transform it into a
more effective instrumentality for world peace through law.

Since the International Court of Justice would still lack jurisdiction to
try *individuals* for crimes of any kind, a new court for that purpose should
be created to cope with crimes that threaten peace.

---

78   UN Charter Art. 27 (3).
79   *See* T.O. ELIAS, THE UNITED NATIONS CHARTER AND THE WORLD COURT (1989).

(2) Creating An International Criminal Court

We have already described in some detail the origins and slow emergence of international criminal courts to deal with international crimes.[80] We saw that nations - particularly powerful ones - were most reluctant to have the legality of their actions judged by any impartial tribunal. States were ready to try enemies defeated in war but not really ready to risk having their own nationals or leaders put on trial for similar deeds. Failure to create a court to try those responsible for atrocious crimes of aggression, terrorism and other crimes against humanity did not deter but only encouraged more criminality.

The international legal community can no longer stand helpless in the face of blatant aggression and massive criminal violations of human rights that threaten peace. The time has come for a permanent International Criminal Court to be created to deter or punish international criminals - regardless of their motivation, rank, station or nationality. The security of humankind depends upon it.[81]

The Statute of the International Court of Justice does not provide the ICJ with jurisdiction to try individuals on criminal or any other charges. Criminal proceedings - with presumptions of innocence, testimony of witnesses and questions of guilt and extenuating circumstances - are quite different from the ponderous deliberations of international law that usually occupy the World Court. ICJ procedures are cumbersome and time-consuming and may be inappropriate for a criminal proceeding where speedy trial is a human right. Criminal jurisdiction is usually separated from civil jurisdiction - for good reason.

Amendment of the ICJ Statute to create a new Criminal Chamber is conceivable but mustering the needed two-thirds majority of both the General Assembly and the Security Council appears to be politically difficult or impossible.[82]

Our proposed new Security Council resolutions clarifying the international laws of peace made clear that individual violators would have to face trial and punishment. Needless to say, no one should be convicted without a fair trial and sentence should only be imposed after a duly-constituted and

---

80   Chapter Two, Section D.

81   In an independent survey commissioned by the World Federalist Association of Washington in 1993, it was found that almost 80% of the American public favored the creation of an International Criminal Court by the UN, even if it had authority to try American Presidents for alleged war crimes or serious human rights violations. Americans Talk Issues Foundation, *Survey* #23, May 10, 1993 at 7.

82   *See* Statute of the ICJ Article 69; FERENCZ,INTERNATIONAL CRIM. CT, vol.2 Part Two describes the historical background of UN views on international criminal jurisdiction.

impartial court has found the accused guilty beyond a reasonable doubt. The creation of a new International Criminal Tribunal should be consistent with the UN Charter and its principles. In addition to respecting human rights standards, it should also build on precedents already established and accepted by the world community.

It would be unreasonable to expect the Council, composed largely of trained diplomats and foreign service officers, to assume the responsibilities of participating in the operations of an international criminal tribunal. Council members certainly lack the time and usually lack the qualification for such an added assignment. A criminal court needs qualified jurists to carry out that obligation. A subsidiary organ - authorized by the Charter - is necessary to help the Council discharge its responsibility.

The Charter of the International Military Tribunal (which influenced our proposed Security Council resolutions prohibiting aggression and crimes against humanity) offers a blue-print for a criminal court by following a pattern that has already been unanimously approved by the United Nations. Rigid adherence to the model is not necessary; it can be modified and improved when required to meet changed circumstances.

The Nuremberg Tribunal was, for example, criticized as a court of victors trying the vanquished. To overcome any such objection, the Court should be created as a permanent institution, available to uphold the laws of peace whenever they are violated. There should be a widesprad search for suitable judicial candidates. The list of nominees can be reduced to a manageable level after screening by an impartial panel of qualified and impartial authorities from different regions or by the Secretary-General. Selection of judges can follow procedures prescribed for the International Court of Justice.[83]

The number and qualifications of judges needed for different types of criminal cases may vary. Whether there be eleven, nine or five judges is not decisive. Whether judges meet *en banc* or in smaller Chambers may depend upon the case load and practical efficiency. The impartiality and qualification of the judges and their democratic election is vital. The judges of the proposed new International Criminal Court should be authorized to draw up their own rules of procedure. The Rules for the International Military Tribunal, which took several legal systems into consideration, may be a helpful guide.[84]

---

83   The Statutes of the ICJ require that "in the body as a whole the representation of the main forms of civilization and of the principal legal systems of the world should be assured" (Art. 9). Judges must win approval by an absolute majority vote in both the General Assembly and the Security Council (ICJ Statute Art. 10).

84   The Rules of Procedure of the IMT are *reproduced in* FERENCZ, INT. CRIM. CT., vol.1, Doc. 13 at 464. *See also* 15 TRIALS OF WAR CRIMINALS, *Procedures, Practices and Administration* (1949).

After many years of effort by the International Law Commission, a small Working Group Chaired by Mr. Abdul Koroma of Sierra Leone recently drafted statutes for a new International Criminal Court.[85] It suggests that a treaty be drawn up and that states then have the choice of accepting such a court or not. There is no need to wait for the long-drawn out process that treaty procedures usually require. In addition to the Charter for the Nuremberg Tribunal or the ILC draft, there are a large number of more recent draft statutes for such a court that can quickly be adopted by the Security Council to meet contemporary needs.[86]

As an organ of the Security Council, the new court would have to be financed by the UN. Its budget would be subject to General Assembly approval, thereby involving the other branch of the United Nations and enhancing the principle of balance-of-powers.

Perhaps the best model is the most recent statute for an *ad hoc* war crimes tribunal to deal with crimes in former Yugoslavia after 1991. Although the jurisdiction of this *ad hoc* criminal court is circumscribed in scope and purpose, it is a big step forward. The proposed Statute for the court is based on the Charter for the Nuremberg Tribunal, modified to take the views of governments and more recent developments into account. As we noted, it met with unanimous Security Council acceptance on 25 May 1993.[87] It was drawn up by a small team of dedicated legal experts from the UN Secretariat and they accomplished more in ten weeks than was accomplished by the ILC in more than ten years.

The International Criminal Court was anchored by the ILC into the uncompleted draft code of crimes which would be subject to the Court's jurisdiction. That hurdle can also be overcome and eliminated as an obstacle if there is the will to do so. Professor Bassiouni's trenchant observation written on 16 July 1993, is an appropriate prod:

---

85   ILC Doc. A/CN.4/L.490, 19 July 1993 and Add.1. *Report of the ILC* on the Work of Its Forty-fifth Sess., GAOR Forty-Eight Sess. Supp. No. 10 (A/48/10) 30 July 1993. See *ante* Chapter Two, Section D-. UNGA Res.47/33, Nov. 25, 1992; *See* Eleventh Report on the Draft Code, ILC Doc. A/CN/4/449, 25 March 1993; V. Morris & M.C. Bourloyannis, *The Work of the Sixth Committee at the Forty-seventh Session of the UN General Assembly*, 87 AJIL 306 (1993). Mr. Koroma was elected as a member of the International Court of Justice for a term beginning on 6 February 1994. *See Journal of the UN*, 11 Nov. 1993

86   *See* Ferencz, *An International Criminal Code and Court*, 30 Col. Jour. of Transnational Law 375 (1992) at 389 n. 65; Professor M.Cherif Bassiouni of DePaul University, has, with the help of other experts and the International Association of Penal Law which he heads, recently prepared comprehensive statutes for a new International Criminal Tribunal, DRAFT STATUTE INTERNATIONAL TRIBUNAL, *Association Internationale de Droit Penal* (1993).

87   SC Res.827, 25 May 1993; S/PV.3217, 25 May 1993. *See* Chapter Two, Section D-4.

If the legal office of the United Nations can produce a draft statute for an International Tribunal for the former Yugoslavia in less than sixty days, which the Security Council adopted without change, then surely the distinguished members of the ILC can produce an acceptable Draft Code in less than half a century.[88]

As long as the fundamental requirements of fairness and clarity are met, the precise form of the Statute or rules of procedure for an International Criminal Court is not decisive. What is important is that the Security Council demonstrated that, in the exercise of its lawful authority, it had the ability to create an international criminal tribunal - at least on an *ad hoc* basis - in a short period of time.

The gradual and moderate approach manifested by the establishment of very limited criminal jurisdiction for crimes in Yugoslavia after 1991 is perhaps understandable and in some ways desirable if it reflects the political need for progress in slow stages. But enforcement of law is not a selective process; to avoid charges of hypocrisy, law must apply to everyone. Those who respect the rule of law have nothing to fear. It is time to take another small step forward.What is called for now is a new Security Council resolution mandating the creation of a *permanent* international criminal tribunal to deal with crimes that threaten peace.

DRAFT RESOLUTION CREATING AN INTERNATIONAL CRIMINAL COURT

THE SECURITY COUNCIL, acting pursuant to its authority under the Charter of the United Nations, declares that all members of the organization are bound by the following resolution:

ARTICLE 1- The Secretary-General of the United Nations is instructed to establish an International Criminal Court as an organ of the Security Council.

ARTICLE 2- The International Criminal Court shall be competent to deal with all crimes that the Security Council determines

---

88 M.C. BASSIOUNI, Ed., COMMENTARIES ON THE INTERNATIONAL LAW COMMISSION'S DRAFT CODE OF CRIMES AGAINST THE PEACE AND SECURITY OF MANKIND (1993) at ix. On 29 Nov. 1993, the Sixth Committee recommended that a draft statute be submitted in 1994 and that governments comment on the draft articles by 15 Februaary 1994. Press Release GA/L/2809, 29 Nov. 1993.

constitute a threat to the peace, breach of the peace or act of aggression. Such crimes shall include violations of the following Security Council resolutions or mandates:

(a) The Security Council **Resolution Mandating Peaceful   Settlement,**

(b) The Security Council **Definition of Aggression,**

(c) The Security Council **Resolution Prohibiting Crimes Against Humanity,**

(d) The Security Council **Resolution Ending the Arms Race,**

(e) The Security Council **Charter for Enhanced Social Justice,**

(f) A Security Council **mandate to submit legal disputes to the** International Court of Justice, **and**

(g) A Security Council **mandate to comply** with a decision of the International Court of Justice.

ARTICLE 3- Judges of the International Criminal Court shall be elected in accordance with the procedures laid down in the UN Charter for the election of judges for the International Court of Justice. Nominees may also be submitted by non-governmental organizations, universities or other qualified sources. The judges shall create their own rules of procedure consistent with the requirements of fair trial and the most efficient methods for carrying out the Court's assignment.

ARTICLE 4: The Security Council will use all necessary means to see that decisions of the International Criminal Court are enforced.

COMMENTARY:

Article 1 charges the Secretary-General to establish the court. The Secretariat is experienced in creating many UN organs. It was charged with a related responsibility when asked by the Council to submit "specific proposals" for the creation of an International Tribunal "to prosecute persons responsible for serious violations of international humanitarian law committed in the territory of the former Yugoslavia since 1991."[89]

Article 2 spells out the competence or jurisdiction of the Court. It is limited to crimes which have generally been recognized as posing a threat to peace. Whether the crime constitutes a threat to peace must be determined by the Security Council before the Court acquires jurisdiction. This rules out trials for minor lapses or infractions.

Article 3 assures that the judges of the International Criminal Court will be qualified and democratically elected in accordance with well established procedures. The rules for the court's operations would be established by the judges themselves.

Article 4 puts teeth into the Court's decisions and is similar to the support given by the proposed Resolution Strengthening the World Court.

The proposed International Criminal Court becomes the enforcement link to the five Security Council laws-of-peace resolutions previously proposed. By involving the Secretary-General and the Secretariat there is an increased division of authority. But what of a World Tribunal for Social Justice? How can a court be created to adjudicate norms that consist largely of inexact generalities? Can the World Court in the Hague perform such functions? Is the time really ripe for a new social tribunal on a global level?

(3) *Creating A World Tribunal for Social Justice*

The concept of "social justice" is as broad as it is vague. The Security Council Charter for Enhancing Social Justice, which we have outlined above to clarify the *law*, remains admittedly imprecise in many respects. To speak about human dignity, economic advancement and environmental protection without spelling out the specific details does not create very firm legal obligations. To give it more than symbolic significance, it will require more exact definition as *law*, and only then can it be interpreted by a *court* or implemented by effective *enforcement*.

The first thing that needs to be done is to clarify what rights are protected or assured by the general formulations of law contained in the proposed Security Council resolution for Enhancing Social Justice. Since the principles of the Social Justice Charter are not precise, they must be construed by independent and impartial judges who are mindful of the diversity of views and who will try to balance those views in a manner best suited to maintain peace. It will have to be similar to the Supreme Court of the

---

89   SC Res. 808, 22 Feb. 1993. *See* SC Res. 827, 25 May 1993.

United States defining what is meant by the U.S. Constitutional requirement of "due process of law " - terms that found their definition only in judicial decisions.

Social justice is a personal entitlement. It belongs primarily to individuals, groups or peoples. This is particularly true where a state itself may be the perpetrator of wrongs to its own citizens. In the past, states were the only recognized subjects of international law and it was only the state that was authorized to appear before an international court or to speak for or represent its nationals when asserting international claims for damages or wrongdoing. The idea that individuals or peoples are entitled to protection of international law in their own right is a fairly recent phenomenon.[90]

It has recently been reported that the World Court has appointed seven of its members to serve as a special Chamber for Environmental Matters in order to respond to environmental cases under its jurisdiction.[91] This is a positive recognition that environmental cases may involve special problems and that the Security Council itself cannot deal with such matters. But the International Court of Justice has jurisdiction to deal only with legal disputes between *states*. It is statutorily not competent to consider *individual* complaints of any kind. To interpret and protect the individual human rights, which the Council by its proposed new resolution has proclaimed, some new juridical body to represent the interest of individual complainants is required.

We can approach the problem pragmatically by focusing on only those rights which, if grossly violated, are most likely to pose a threat to peace. It is only in such cases that the Security Council has authority to intervene in any way. We can then consider what type of court or other institutional mechanism would be best suited to deal with those particular problems.

(a) Human Rights Generally:

We have postulated that human rights are universal and that human beings everywhere are entitled to live in peace and dignity. Some of these rights are already being protected by special regional or local tribunals enforcing national constitutional or statutory legislation. For those regions not much more needs to be done at this time.[92]

---

90   *See* L.B. Sohn, *The New International Law: Protection of the Rights of Individuals Rather than States*, 32 Amer. U. Law Rev. 1 (1982); *See* J. CRAWFORD, Ed.,THE RIGHTS OF PEOPLES (1988).

91   *International Observer* July 1993 at 6.

92   See Chapter Two, Section C.

The European Convention on Human Rights was the first to create a Commission and a Court to adjudicate rights that the European Community had recognized in a binding treaty.

Professor Frowein has pointed out:

> There is general agreement today that fundamental human rights must be protected as individual rights everywhere...[O]ne should certainly not forget the great importance of social and economic rights for the individual human being and his right to live in dignity.[93]

The existing Human Rights Courts in Strasbourg and Costa Rica can also serve as models of what needs to be done and what can be done in those many nations where there are no laws, treaties or tribunals to protect the public from human rights abuses.

The 18-member Human Rights Committee of the UN, established under the Optional Protocol to the International Covenant on Civil and Political Rights, is competent to receive complaints from individuals. But not all states have opted to accept the Protocol and hence are not bound by it. Furthermore, the Committee can do little more than issue reports and rely on public opprobrium to bring about a modification of prohibited behavior; it lacks the compelling force of a judicial body.[94]

T.O. Elias of Nigeria, who became a Judge on the World Court, proposed that the UN create an International Court of Human Rights to deal with human rights violations on a global basis; the proposal got nowhere.[95] René Cassin of France, who won the Nobel Prize for his Universal Declaration of Human Rights, called for an International Bureau of Human Rights. Others called for a High Commissioner of Human Rights; all to no avail.[96] On the hundredth anniversary of the French Declaration of Human Rights, a large group of young people met in Strasbourg, home of the European Court of Human Rights, to call for a World Court of Human Rights.[97] Attorney Luis Kutner of Chicago has long advocated a World Tribunal to enforce *habeas corpus* rights everywhere.[98]

---

93   J.Frowein, *The European Convention on Human Rights...* at 279.

94   *See* Report of the Human Rights Committee, GAOR, Forty-Seventh Sess., Supp. No. 40 (A/47/40) 1992; also (A/48140) 1993.

95   UN Doc. A/Conf.32/L.3, 15 Feb. 1968 pp.19-20.

96   W. Korey, *The Key to Human Rights - Implementation,* 570 International Conciliation (1968). At a World Conference on Human Rights that took place in Vienna in June 1993, the U.S. Secretary of State called for the appointment of a UN High Commissioner on Human Rights; *See* N.Y. Times article by Elaine Sciolino, June 15, 1993 p. A-18; Paul Lewis, *Differing Views on Human Rights Threaten Forum,* N.Y.Times International, June 6, 1993. Several states, including the U.S. supported the idea during the Plenary debates of the General Assembly in Sept, and Oct. 1993. See U.S. draft resolution, A/C.3/48/L59 29 Nov. 1993.

97   *See* R.MULLER, THE BIRTH OF A GLOBAL CIVILIZATION (1991) p.78.

98   L.KUTNER, WORLD HABEAS CORPUS (1962).

Since human beings everywhere are presumed to be entitled to the same fundamental rights, a World Tribunal empowered to interpret the human rights standards articulated by the proposed Security Council Charter for Enhancing Social Justice would be an improvement over the few regional human rights organizations that exist today - even if its jurisdiction were limited to only those gross violations that the Security Council decided posed a threat to peace.

Too frequently, the pleas of private individuals or organizations seeking to vindicate human rights fall on deaf national ears because there is no international court to which they can turn. A World Tribunal competent to deal with serious human rights complaints could assure uniform interpretations of the Universal Declaration and other human rights conventions that seem vague and illusory. It could reconcile discrepancies in decisions of regional human rights tribunals or agencies and serve as an appellate body from national or regional human rights bodies. These are powerful arguments for creating a new world tribunal to protect individuals everywhere from major human rights abuses.[99]

(b) Environmental Protection:

In 1986, experts called for environmental protection by: establishing a Special UN Commission, designating an International "Ombudsman", expanding participation of non-governmental organizations and by imposing criminal liability for environmental damage. Their thoughtful study showed the need for a new international legal structure or agency to deal more effectively with important problems of environment and development that may threaten world security.[100]

On March 11, 1989, a declaration was issued in the Hague by 24 heads of state who called for the development of a new environmental authority within the UN system that would be responsible for the preservation of the earth's atmosphere and could take effective action "*even if on occasion unanimous agreement has not been achieved.*"[101] The UN Conference on Environment and Development that took place in Rio in June 1992 dealt with the problem of providing an effective legal and regulatory framework to carry out the comprehensive environmental protection goals of Agenda 21. It was clear that law-making in many countries was piecemeal and inadequate and

---

99   *See* E. McWHINNEY et. al., FROM COOEXISTENCE TO COOPERATION (1991) at 283.

100 *See* R.D.MUNRO, J.LAMMERS et. al.,ENVIRONMENTAL PROTECTION AND SUSTAINABLE DEVELOPMENT (1986).

101 Cited in D. Heinrich, *The Case for a United Nations Parliamentary Assembly*, World Federalist Movement Booklet (1992) at 20.

"has not been endowed with the necessary institutional machinery and authority for enforcement and timely adjustment."[102] Desiring to make laws more effective and responsive to complaints by individuals, groups and organizations, the delegates called for

> judicial and administrative procedures for legal re-
> dress and remedy of actions affecting environment
> and development that may be unlawful or infringe on
> rights under the law...[103]

A Non-Governmental Organization, the Mandate for Life on Earth, is trying to get 100 million signatures on a document authorizing the creation of a World Court for the Environment.[104]

The United Nations has appointed various committees to consider a comprehensive strategy for the efficient utilization of water in order to avoid a global crisis in the foreseeable future.[105] Water is an essential element for life. The use of international waterways has been and will continue to be a source of conflict or potential conflict between states. "Water Law" is just beginning to be taught. An unofficial International Tribunal for Water Rights has been created by private individuals and organizations in the Netherlands.[106] The UN has hardly begun to move in the direction of a world tribunal to cope with potentially very dangerous disputes about water rights or other alleged international environmental law violations.[107]

The knowledgeable Bertran Schneider, Secretary-General of the Club of Rome, suggested that environmental problems, beyond the reach of national governments, are so important that they must be handled by an over-arching UN body - a new Security Council for the Environment.[108] The Independent Commission on the Future of the UN also suggested that a special Security Council for the Environment be created.[109]

---

102 A/CONF.151/26 (Vol.I) 12 Aug. 1992, p.104.

103 *Id.* p.105.

104 World Peace News May 1993 p.3, cites as source THE FEDERALIST - A Political Review XXIV #3 p. 240.

105 *See* UN Committee on Natural Resources, Report E/C.7/1991/8, 13 Feb. 1991.

106 An International Water Tribunal Foundation, headquartered in Amsterdam has established an unofficial International Water Tribunal to deal with disputes regarding the aquatic environment.

107 *See* Report of the UN Water Conference, Mar del Plata, UN Doc. E/CONF. 70/29 (1977); UN Conference on Desertification, Nairobi, UN Doc. A/CONF. 74/36 (1977); B.R. CHAUHAN, SETTLEMENT OF INTERNATIONAL WATER DISPUTES IN INTERNATIONAL DRAINAGE BASINS (1981); *Water Resource Management*, A World Bank Policy Paper (1993).

108 Address by Bertran Schneider at the Annual Conference of Non-Governmental Organizations at UN Headquarters 13-15 Sept. 1989.

109 Conference Report, *Toward Common Goals* (April 1993) p.6.

(c) Economic rights:

Acclaimed economist and social historian, Kenneth Boulding has pointed out that this politically fragmented and diverse world is rapidly becoming a single economic, cultural and communications system that is dependent upon mutual cooperation rather than threats and war.[110] Environment, economic development and peace are all closely linked. Poor people forced to burn wood to heat meager rations are not convinced by arguments that the rain forests which provide their fuel must be preserved - particularly when the admonitions come from rich industrialized nations primarily responsible for massive pollution of the planet. An impartial judicial agency to resolve such fundamental differences in point of view is needed to diffuse tensions that may explode.

Drastic disparities in standards of living stimulate mass migration, flooding affluent countries with massive numbers of economic refugees from underdeveloped areas. Countries of haven reach a saturation point when their own residents feel displaced and ugly violence often ensues.[111] According to the 1993 Report of the UN Development Program, ninety percent of people have no control of their lives and many of today's struggles are simply for access to land, water, work and basic social services.[112] Over one billion people subsist on less than one dollar per day.[113]

A team of 30 researchers from four continents recently concluded that land scarcity and population growth and the scarcity of renewable resources are contributing to dislocation and violent conflicts in various parts of the world. The brutal ethnic hatreds that are beginning to emerge raise the risk of social disintegration, mass migrations, civil war and insurgency, as scarcity sets the stage for greater conflagrations.[114] The earth's carrying capacity is not unlimited and a legal process must be developed to control the rate and direction of resource consumption. This will require judicial-type decisions of the highest legal and social character.[115] It has been sug-

---

110 K.E. BOULDING, THE WORLD AS A TOTAL SYSTEM (1985); K.E. BOULDING, THREE FACES OF POWER (1989).

111 *See* J. TINBERGEN, WORLD SECURITY AND EQUALITY (1990). Tightening of the laws of political asylum in Germany in 1993 was a direct consequence of public protest against the "foreigners." *See* L.B. SOHN & T. BUERGENTHAL Eds., THE MOVEMENT OF PERSONS ACROSS BORDERS (1993).

112 *Diplomatic World Bulletin*, May 24-31, 1993, at 5.

113 World Summit for Social Development. E/1993/77, 10 June 1993, p. 13.

114 *See* T. Homer-Dixon, *Destruction and Death*, N.Y. Times, OP-ED, Jan. 31, 1993. report on the Project on Environmental Change and Acute Conflict, by a research group sponsored by the American Academy of Arts and Sciences and the University of Toronto.

115 *See* M.A. SANTOS, MANAGING PLANET EARTH - Perspectives on Population, Ecology, and the Law (1992).

gested that a UN Economic Security Council, composed of 20 members from both developed and developing countries be created to deal with problems of global human security.[116]

The fact that distinguished and knowledgeable persons have called for a specialized World Court of Human Rights, a new Security Council for the Environment and a new Economic Security Council clearly indicates that existing institutions are not adequate to cope effectively with mounting human rights, environmental or economic problems. A new judicial structure, competent to cope with interrelated legal issues of social justice may be needed to satisfy justified concerns that may jeopardize peace.

The existing regional Courts of Human Rights could serve as a useful model in creating the structure for new World Tribunal for Social Justice. It is not necessary to carry over all of its institutions if they are not essential. For example, the European *Commission* of Human Rights, that screens and blocks access to the Court, may be eliminated. Since ECOSOC is responsible for dealing with many of the issues which such a court would have to face, it may be desireable to give ECOSOC a special role in nominating or electing the judges.[117]

Another model may be found in the recent judicial mechanism authorized by the Security Council to deal with personal claims arising from Iraq's aggression in the Gulf War.[118] Under the general guidance of a Governing Council representing all members of the Security Council, a small group of experts, nominated by the Secretary-General and aided by a small Secretariat, was created to adjudicate claims for compensation for injuries arising from such human rights violations as illegal detention, serious physical or mental harm, torture, and environmental damage.[119]

Rather than trying to create several specialized world tribunals to adjudicate or interpret human rights, environmental or economic disputes, it is suggested that one Social Justice Tribunal be created. The Tribunal should be competent to handle any social justice issue if the Security Council

---

116 *See* E. Adler, *Keynoters Survey "New Realities"*, Disarmament Times, May 1993, p. 1, citing Ambassador Douglas Roche of Canada and Mahbub ul Hag of the UN Development Program. DISAMAMENT - NEW REALITIES (1993) at 57, 61. A similar suggestion by Maurice Bertrand will be dealt with in Chapter Eight, Section C dealing with a UN Social Justice Agency.

117 ECOSOC has 54 members elected by the GA. See Art.61 UN Charter. The Rio Conference recommended that ECOSOC assist the General Assembly in implementing Agenda 21. Report of the UN Conference on Environment and Development, A/CONF.151/26 (Vol.III) 14 Aug.1992 Chap. 38 at p.89.

118 SC Res.687, April 3, 1991, *reprinted in* 30 ILM 846 (1991); Secretary-General Report UN Doc. S/22559 (1991) is in 30 ILM 1706 (1991).

119 *See* J.R. Crook, *The UN Compensation Commission - A New Structure to Enforce State Responsibility*, 87 AJIL 144 (1993).

decides that the dispute is not suitable for handling by the International Court of Justice and that it poses a threat to world peace and security.

DRAFT RESOLUTION CREATING A WORLD TRIBUNAL FOR SOCIAL JUSTICE

THE SECURITY COUNCIL, acting pursuant to its authority under the Charter of the United Nations, declares that all members of the organization are bound by the following resolution:

ARTICLE 1- The Secretary-General of the United Nations is instructed to establish a World Tribunal for Social Justice as an organ of the Security Council. It may sit on an *ad hoc* or permanent basis, as may be necessary to discharge its responsibilities.

ARTICLE 2- The World Tribunal for Social Justice shall be competent to decide all legal questions concerning the interpretation of the Security Council Charter for Enhancing Social Justice, if the Security Council determines that failure to resolve the issues constitutes a threat to peace.

ARTICLE 3- Judges of the World Tribunal for Social Justice shall be elected by the Economic and Social Council in accordance with procedures laid down for the election of judges for the International Court of Justice. Nominees may be submitted by non-governmental organizations, universities or other qualified sources. The judges shall create their own rules of procedure consistent with the requirements of fair trial and the most efficient methods for carrying out the Court's assignment.

ARTICLE 4: The Security Council will use all necessary means to see that decisions of the World Tribunal for Social Justice are enforced whenever the Council decides that such enforcement is necessary to maintain world peace or security.

COMMENTARY:

Article 1, by declaring the tribunal to be an organ of the Security Council, limits its jurisdiction to issues that pose a threat to peace. It charges the Secretary-General to establish the tribunal, thereby enhancing the desired checks-and-balances. The Secretary-General has already been directed to create such an *ad hoc* criminal tribunal to deal with gross human rights violations in former Yugoslavia.[120]

Article 2 spells out the competence or jurisdiction of the Court. It reinforces the limitation of jurisdiction to violations that pose a threat to peace. Whether a threat to peace exists must be determined by the Security Council before the Court acquires jurisdiction. This rules out trials for infractions that do not have a peace-threatening potential and assures the Security Council that the court will not be inundated with non-peace-threatening complaints.

Article 3, by involving ECOSOC, is intended to enhance the checks -and- balances of the system and to give a greater voice to the UN principal agency that has been responsible for similar social issues.

Article 4, by asserting the Security Council's authority, lends credence and support to the proclamation in the Universal Declaration of Human Rights: "Everyone is entitled to a social and international order in which the rights and freedoms set forth in this Declaration can be fully realized" (Art.28). No article has been added to criminalize violations since the stated social justice obligations lack the specificity required by a criminal statute and prosecutions might encounter *ex post facto* legal objections until that shortcoming is corrected.

Resolutions can be passed quickly, but implementation is difficult and time-consuming. Until all of the component parts of the interconnected and comprehensive plan are firmly in place, the world remains in jeopardy. In addition to new *laws* and *courts*, it will be necessary to reinforce the existing mechanisms and create new structures for *enforcing* peace as vital components of any comprehensive peace plan.

C - Four Resolutions to Strengthen Peace *Enforcement*

We propose the creation of four new executive agencies that can be put in place quickly to help enforce the laws of peace. The hope and expectation is that these new structures will enable the United Nations to do what it was legally obliged to do and has failed to do effectively since the organization was founded. The objective is to replace the present world order that tolerates the use of armed might by a new system that will enforce the new Security Council resolutions mandating universal disarmament, economic sanctions, UN police action and enhanced social justice.

---

120 SC Res. 808, 22 Feb. 1993. *See* SC Res. 827, 25 May 1993. See J.C. O'BRIEN, The International Tribunal for Violations of International Humanitarian Law in the Former Yugoslavia, 87 AJIL 639 (1993).

In the hope that changes may prove acceptable, we suggest only such new organs as are absolutely necessary to achieve the stated goals on which world security depends. We are very mindful of the advice of World Court Judge Manfred Lachs who cautioned that the edification of the future required "the placing of one brick upon another."[121]

(1) Creating A UN Disarmament Enforcement Agency

Experience has shown that maintaining peace by military power generates more insecurity than security. Disarmament has remained a fundamental objective of the world community since the first world war. The regulation of armaments has repeatedly been confirmed as a goal of the United Nations,[122] and some slow progress is being made in that direction.[123] But sovereign states normally accept voluntarily only what is perceived to be in their national interest. Because Foreign Ministers and politicians remain skeptical about untried new structures for world order, and because the old order still appeals to those who benefit from it, the arms race can only be ended if nations are convinced that it is part of a package that includes an effective substitute for war as the ultimate means for safeguarding their security and vital interests.

To respect the legitimate concerns of all nations that they will not be endangering themselves by radical changes, the twelve draft resolutions are all linked. Disarmament depends on the concomitant creation of a better and less-violent method for protecting legitimate interests. Enforcement of disarmament is absolutely vital if the war system is to be replaced by a peace system. At a 1991 symposium of experts on arms control, Ambassador Nabil Elaraby of Egypt, a highly-respected UN diplomat, bemoaned the difficulties of negotiating multilateral arms control treaties as he called for new and innovative approaches. He emphasized the guiding role that must be played by the Security Council.[124] Only the UN Security Council - or an organ that it may create - is legally authorized and competent to create a world disarmament agency with binding power.[125]

We have already proposed that the first prong of the disarmament pincer be a Security Council resolution, (based on the comprehensive

---

121   M. LACHS, THE TEACHER IN INTERNATIONAL LAW (1982) at 203.

122   UN Charter Art.11, 26, 41-48.

123   See Chapter Three, Section B.

124   J.DAHLITZ, D.DICKE, Eds., THE INTERNATIONAL LAW OF ARMS CONTROL AND DISARMAMENT, *Proceedings of the Symposium*, Geneva 28 Feb.-2 March 1991. *See* R.C.KARP, Ed., SECURITY WITHOUT NUCLEAR WEAPONS? (1992).

125   In their June, 1993 issue, Parliamentarians for Global Action called for the establishment by 1995 of an organ of the Security Council to plan for the regulation of arms, as called for by the Charter.

McCloy/Zorin Agreement) ending the arms race by mandating universal disarmament as a *legal obligation* of all states.[126] The second (judicial) prong consists of the proposed Council resolutions to strengthen the World Court and to create an International Criminal *Court* to penalize individuals who defied the law. As the third prong, we here propose that the Council create a new organ to help *enforce* the disarmament resolution - a UN Disarmament Enforcement Agency (UNDEA).

The primary function of UNDEA is to see that universal disarmament is carried out in a rational, non-political, impartial and decisive way as quickly as possible. The multitude of agencies now coping with disarmament problems would have to be coordinated and a number of clearly defined objectives would have to be attained. Let us spell out how the new UNDEA might go about achieving those specific objectives that are essential if the proposed new Security Council mandate to end the arms race is to be enforced.

It should be noted that all of the objectives have already been approved in principle and endorsed by prominent persons and important UN committees as well as experts from academia and non-governmental organizations.[127] Furthermore, all of the proposed enforcement measures have already been started on a limited scale.[128] There is no persuasive reason for states not to apply the same principles to broader areas of threat.

No rational disarmament plan can work until and unless at least the following five objectives can be met:

(i) Ascertaining existing military capabilities;

An arms census is the logical starting point for the control of arms. To begin with, UNDEA will have to know the size and nature of the problem being dealt with. One of the primary pre-conditions for any system of universal disarmament is a reliable accounting of the weapons and military units that now exist throughout the world. In addition to a clear picture of

---

126 See Chapter Eight, Section A.

127 *See* A/48/100/Add.1, 9 Oct. 1993; A/C.1/48/L.35, .L37, L39, .L47, 4 Nov. 1993; GA Res. 43/75, Dec. 1988, Report of a Group of 12 experts, chaired by Maj Britt Theorin of Sweden, that focused on nuclear weapons and which the Assembly commended without a vote on 4 Dec. 1990, Res. 45/58E. *See also* reports of conferences convened in 1989, 1991 and 1993 in Kyoto, Japan; Report of the UN Office of Disarmament Affairs, DC/2430, 2 April 1993. See GA/DIS/2977, 8 Nov. 1993.

128 The *Chemical Weapons Convention* (CWC), signed by 137 states, is a good illustration of recent actions that give effect to the necessary objectives. *See UN Convention on the Prohibition of the Development, Production, Stockpiling and Use of Chemical Weapons and on Their Destruction* (CWC), signed in Paris on Jan. 13, 1993 ; 32 I.L.M. 800 (1993). A.W. Dorn and A. Rolya, The Org. for the Prohibition of Chemical Weapons and the IAEA: A Comparative Overview, 35 IAEA Bull. 44 (1993).

the composition of military forces, there must be a comprehensive inventory of the many types of weapons, their location, fire-power and the speed and accuracy of their delivery systems.

The idea for an arms census is not new. As we have noted, it was repeatedly proposed by France, going back to the days after the First World War, and was, apparently, accepted in principle by the United States.[129] Although it makes good sense, it has yet to be accepted or implemented. States refused, and still refuse, to divulge the size of their military arsenals. Keeping details of their armed might a top secret is supposed to enhance security by not revealing weakness - which might tempt their adversaries - or not revealing strength - which might further stimulate the arms race. The reasoning is not convincing.

Much of the information about the military prowess of various nations is already in the public domain or at least is well known to most major intelligence services. The arms *trade* in weapons of all kinds is overwhelming and many of its details are common knowledge to everybody in the business.[130] The General Assembly resolution calling for a *voluntary* register of conventional arms *transfers* is a confidence-building measure and a very small step toward the objective of a comprehensive registry of all weapons. It is not good enough.[131] The hesitancy of some nations to list their arms trades indicates how difficult it is to get voluntary cooperation from sovereign states that want to be free to do business as usual - even if it jeopardizes peace.

As early as 1955, President Eisenhower put forth an "Open-Skies" proposal.[132] Today, remote sensing by military reconnaissance satellite as well as national means of observation and published reports of ships and planes built by various countries offer a rather complete picture of every nation's real military potential. If a few rifles are hidden in a haystack it doesn't usually threaten world peace. If the arms race is to be ended, transparency in armaments must replace secrecy. Keeping hidden the destructive capacity of a nation certainly threatens its neighbors as well as the rest of the world. The Security Council is fully justified and authorized to *demand* complete disclosure to the extent necessary to carry out its resolution

---

129 See Chapter Three, Section B.

130 The Stockholm International Peace Research Institute (SIPRI) publishes highly-regarded annual reports showing the approximate size of military expenditures of all nations. In 1991, according to the SIPRI Yearbook, the U.S. accounted for 51 per cent of global trade in major weapons.

131 *See* GA Res. 47/52 L. 15 Dec. 1992. Disarmament Times, 23 Nov. 1993. A proposed *Convention on the Monitoring, Reduction and Ultimate Elimination of the International Arms Trade* has been drafted by Professor Saul Mendlovitz and the Lawyer's Committee on Nuclear Policy headed by Peter Weiss of New York.

132 *See* W.W. ROSTOW, OPEN SKIES: EISENHOWER'S PROPOSAL OF JULY 21, 1955 (1982).

for universal and complete disarmament. The risk to peaceful national interests is minimal. Sovereignty should not be allowed to conceal a threat to human security.

(ii) Halting production of new military capabilities;

Three related arms-control measures have been on the international table for a long time - all aimed at ultimately stopping the production of arms that threaten peace:

A *Comprehensive Test Ban Treaty* (CTBT) is the first logical step toward halting production of nuclear weapons. It has been argued that:

> The history of the Nuclear Weapons Complex is a tale of strategic overkill, contamination, health hazards, and cost overruns...The United States cannot credibly ask other countries not to build nuclear arms if it continues to develop and test new weapons.[133]

The proposed CTBT is a pre-condition linked with non-proliferation. As long as states that already have nuclear missiles insist on building new ones or testing and improving the old ones, those that do not have such lethal weapons are not very reassured about the intentions of the others and are therefore not eager to bind themselves to remain without nuclear arms forever. On 10 August 1993, the Conference on Disarmament took an historic decision to begin negotiation of a comprehensive test ban treaty in January 1994.[134]

A Nuclear Non-Proliferation Treaty (NPT):

In 1970, 150 states that had no nuclear weapons agreed not to produce them. In exchange, those nations that already possessed nuclear weapons promised to eliminate their own nuclear arsenals as soon as possible. The International Atomic Energy Agency was designated to verify compliance. But, as we have noted, powerful nations did not live up their promises.[135]

States that had no nuclear weapons were ready to forego the doubtful and expensive privilege of joining the nuclear club on the express condition

---

133 FACING REALITY: A Citizen's Guide to the Future of the U.S. Nuclear Weapons Complex, The Tides Foundation, San Francisco, CA (1992) at p.1, 3. President Clinton agreed to extend a nuclear testing moratorium until September, 1994 as long as no other country tests nuclear weapons before then. Clinton Extends Ban on U.S. Nuclear Tests. N.Y. Times, July 3, 1993 p. A-4.

134 See Disarmament Times, 22 Sept. 1993 at 1.

135 See Chapter Three, Section B.

that nuclear nations divested themselves of their military advantage. The clear implication of the drawn-out NPT negotiations was that there would soon be a nuclear-free world. But what actually happened was that the five nuclear weapon states *increased* their nuclear fire-power and were even suspected of selling nuclear materials and technology to non-nuclear states trying to build nuclear arsenals of their own.[136] Not wishing to remain in a vulnerable position, some of the NPT signatories are secretly or openly disregarding the treaty, repudiating their obligation not to produce nuclear weapons or threatening not to renew the NPT when it expires in March 1995.[137]

Conventional Weapons Reductions still have a very long way to go before peace can be enforced. On November 19, 1990, 22 NATO and former Warsaw Treaty Organization states signed the Treaty on Conventional Forces in Europe (CFE), to mark the end of the Cold War.[138] Although it provided for reductions in the size of conventional arsenals in Europe, the destructive capacity of modernized air, sea and "conventional" land weapons in other areas remains undiminished. Existing "conventional weapons" can be quite annihilating - as the recent conflict in the Persian Gulf demonstrated.[139]

The proposed UNDEA, unfettered by the futile search for consensus agreement by recalcitrant states, could do whatever was necessary to see that the Security Council resolution to end the arms race is fully implemented. This would include regulations -backed by the Council - banning the testing of nuclear weapons, prohibiting their proliferation and halting further production of all conventional weapons that may threaten peace.

(iii) Destroying existing military capabilities;

According to many published reports there are at least 50,000 nuclear weapons spread around the world today. Their explosive power exceeds one million Hiroshima atomic bombs.[140] The former Soviet Union possessed enough nuclear weapons to destroy the world many times over. (The U.S. presumably had at least the same capacity.) Those devastating Soviet weapons are now in the hands of independent and ethnically diverse

---

136 *See,* The Stanley Foundation, *Preventing Weapons Proliferation: Should the Regimes be Combined,* a Report by Leonard Spector and Virginia Foran on a Conference of 73 foreign policy professionals held in Oct. 1992.

137 *See* Report by the Director of the International Atomic Energy Agency on Non-Compliance by the Democratic Peoples Republic of Korea; A/48/133, 12 April 1993.

138 See Chapter Three, Section B.

139 See Chapter Three, Section D.

140 UN Publication, Disarmament Facts No. 77, Comprehensive Study on Nuclear Weapons (1991) p. 5.

Republics of the new Commonwealth of Independent States that are reluctant to hand over control to Russia or to anyone else. The threat to world peace remains enormous.[141]

In 1985, President Reagan and President Gorbachev agreed: "A nuclear war cannot be won and must never be fought." The INF Treaty showed that, given the political will, nuclear arms can be safely destroyed under effective controls. But the treaty took many years to negotiate and will take many more years to be carried out. The elimination of intermediate-range nuclear weapons in Europe will decrease the world's nuclear arsenal by less than 5%. UNDEA would seek a more expeditious procedure to destroy the remaining 95%.

The 1991 Strategic Arms Reduction Treaty (START) is aimed at significantly reducing the number of tactical nuclear weapons held by the U.S. and the former U.S.S.R. Dismantling nuclear weapons is a dangerous process that requires great care, skill, and money. It is estimated that reducing the Soviet arsenal will take about 20 years, during which time the wapons will have to be stored, safeguarded and maintained adequately to avoid the risk of accidental explosion--"a difficult and expensive business."[142]

Any nuclear weapons held by any nation must be destroyed, and problems that arise from that process must be solved on a universal and not merely a bilateral basis.[143]

Douglas Roche, Former Ambassador for Disarmament of Canada, at a meeting on disarmament organized by many non-governmental organizations, stated that even the possession of nuclear weapons should be banned as a matter of law. Retention of such weapons by anyone leads not only to more proliferation of nuclear weapons but to an increased demand for more conventional arms.[144] "Conventional weapons," improved by modern technology, can be almost as dangerous as nuclear weapons. Only the Security Council, or an organ created and backed by the enforcement powers of the Council, can order and supervise the destruction of weapons of all kinds that now hang like an albatross around the neck of humankind.

(iv) Verifying that there are no evasions:.

Verification regimes have already been built into the existing agreements for arms reductions. The INF Treaty, the Chemical Weapons Treaty

---

141   See M.R. Gordon, *Ukrainian Official Backs U.S. Plan on Atom Arms*, N.Y. Times, June 6, 1993 p. A 7.

142   F. Barnaby, The Role And Control Of Weapons In The 1990's (1992) at 176.

143   See Chapter Three, Section D.

144   Disarmament Times, article by Enid Adler, May, 1993 p. 1 at 4. See E.L.MEYROWITZ, PROHIBITION OF NUCLEAR WEAPONS: The Relevance of International Law (1990).

and others provide for on-site inspection, challenge inspections and other safeguards. The proposed UNDEA would, of course, have to coordinate its actions with such existing control mechanisms as the International Atomic Energy Agency and special enforcement groups created to supervise the destruction of weapons under the treaties already in force.[145] Cooperation with other groups studying verification in all its aspects would also be necessary.[146]

(v) Conversion to peaceful production:

Coordinated plans for conversion of military plants to more-useful forms of production and retraining displaced scientists, engineers and other workers will have to go hand in hand with the program of arms reductions. In fact, new and more constructive employment may be provided by the program for arms destruction that will also be necessary to secure peace. Cleaning up the toxic legacy of discarded weapons and nuclear-testing may also provide new avenues for useful re-employment.

Eliminating the cost of weaponry would be a significant boost to the standard of living everywhere. A "peace dividend" may finally become available for social purposes and thereby serve not merely to create new jobs but as an additional enhancement of world security. Underdeveloped countries, which spend a disproportionate amount of their income on armaments, may be offered new economic incentives in exchange for agreements to disarm.[147]

A new and specialized Security Council organ can expedite the disarmament process. As Sergey Batsanov, Chairman of the Conference on Disarmament's *ad hoc* Committee, noted when commenting on the Chemical Weapons Convention:

> The world cannot afford waiting another 20 plus years in order to have another militarily significant global arms control treaty...This calls both for a review of global negotiating institutions and for a reassessment of approaches to a number of implementation mechanisms.[148]

---

145 See Chapter Three, Section B.

146 *See* GA Res.47/45, 9 Dec. 1992.

147 Tables showing military spending by countries and regions are contained in the Yearbooks of the Stockholm International Peace Research Institute (SIPRI).

148 S. Batsanov, *Some Observations on the Chemical Weapons Convention*, XVI Disarmament 31 (1993) at 39.

What is urgently needed is a comprehensive program for disarmament without requiring years of unproductive wrangling between adversaries whose real desire to sever their own military limbs may be questionable.

If one counts all the agencies working on the problem of disarmament - the First Committee representing every member of the UN, the Conference on Disarmament that operates by consensus, the UN Disarmament Commission, the UN Office for Disarmament Affairs, and many others - and compares that with the results they have achieved, it becomes quite obvious that organizational improvements are required.[149]

By way of contrast (and model) one may consider the work of the UN Special Committee (UNSCOM) established as a subsidiary organ of the Security Council to implement the terms of the cease-fire with Iraq.[150] It is headed by an Executive Chairman supported by a small full-time office at UN Headquarters in New York, and aided by a few experts abroad who are qualified to cope with disarmament inspection and other problems. Ambassador Rolf Ekeus, the respected Chairman of the Special Commission, expressed hope for greater Security Council involvement in preventing the proliferation of nuclear weapons everywhere.[151] The General Assembly has recognized the need for a unified, integrated structure and professional advisors to carry out the varied peacekeeping responsibilities. [152] It has also pointed to the competence of the Security Council in disarmament matters.[153]

Robert S. McNamara, Secretary of Defense under U.S.Presidents Kennedy and Johnson and Director of the World Bank, wrote:

> The United Nations Security Council could play a central role in stopping the further proliferation of all types of weapons of mass destruction...[T]here is no alternative to collective coercive Security Council action...[154]

The concluding statement when the Heads of State met at the Security Council Summit in 1992, indicated a readiness on the part of the Council to curb all weapons of mass destruction as a threat to peace and to use the Council's powers under Chapter VII to enforce such a rule.[155]

---

149 See Report of the Disarmament Commission, GAOR Forty-eighth Sess., Supp.No. 42 (A/48/42) 8 July 1993.

150 See SC Res. 687, 3 April 1991.

151 See S/26451, 16 Sept. 1993; Disarmament Times, May 1993 p.2.

152 See A/48/100, 15 June 1993 at 228-230.

153 Id. at 187.

154 R.S. Mcnamara, Nobody Needs Nukes, N.Y. Times Op-Ed, Feb. 23, 1993 at A21.

155 S/PV.3046, 31 Jan. 1992 at 145.

Since none of the five vital objectives (ascertaining stockpiles, halting production, destroying existing arsenals, verification and conversion) has yet been adequately achieved, the work of UNDEA in enforcing the Security Council disarmament objectives set down in its new resolution to end the arms race is a necessary and challenging assignment. A special staff of qualified and independent experts, empowered by the Security Council to get the job done as quickly and safely as possible, would be a much more efficient, faster and more effective procedure than what has been tried and failed in the past. A new approach is desperately needed. Now.[156]

DRAFT RESOLUTION CREATING A UN DISARMAMENT ENFORCEMENT AGENCY

THE SECURITY COUNCIL, acting pursuant to its authority under the Charter of the United Nations, declares that all members of the organization are bound by the following resolution:

ARTICLE 1- The Secretary-General of the United Nations is instructed to establish a UN Disarmament Enforcement Agency (UNDEA) as an organ of the Security Council to carry out the disarmament objectives of the Security Council Resolution Ending the Arms Race in as fair, efficient and speedy manner as possible.

ARTICLE 2- Pursuant to Article 3 of the Security Council Resolution Ending the Arms Race, UNDEA shall serve as the agent of the Security Council in supervising the implementation of the program of general and complete disarmament as set forth in that resolution and in drawing up such rules as shall be necessary for that purpose.[157]

ARTICLE 3- The Secretary-General shall invite nominations for the position of Director of the UN Disarmament Enforcement

---

156 See A.H. LAKHDHIR, Ed., DISARMAMENT, New Realities: Disarmament, Peace-Building and Global Security - Excerpts from the panel discussions organized by the NGO Committee on Disarmament (Vernon Nichols, Pres.) held at the UN in N.Y. from 20 to 23 April 1993. Over 500 participants, including many outstanding experts, seemed to agree that greater attention had to be paid to improving the well-being of all people in all countries and to take practical steps to eliminate all nuclear weapons as soon as possible (at p. ii).

157 See Chapter Eight, Section A.

Agency from members of the UN Disarmament Commission as well as other competent organizations or agencies. The list of nominees shall be screened by the UN Secretary-General and reduced to no more than 20 and no less than 10. The appointment shall be made by majority vote of the Security Council and require approval by a majority of the members of the General Assembly.

ARTICLE 4 - The Security Council will use all necessary means to enforce the provisions of the Resolution Ending the Arms Race and the decisions and rules of UNDEA whenever the Council decides that failure to do so would constitute a threat to the peace.

COMMENTARY:

Article 1 charges the Secretary-General to establish UNDEA. The reference to fairness and efficiency is intended to convey an obligation to employ only qualified and independent persons who will be considerate of the interests of all sides.

Article 2 is intended to make clear that UNDEA as an organ of the Security Council is backed by Security Council authority. It also seeks to limit the responsibility of UNDEA to disarmament problems rather than those related to non-military sanctions or the use of military force by the United Nations; these functions will be assumed by the proposed UN Sanctions Agency and UN Police Agency dealt with hereafter.

Article 3 is intended to provide a system of checks-and-balances in selecting the Director of UNDEA. It follows general principles approved by the Security Council for designating judges for the new *ad hoc* International Criminal Court to deal with crimes in former Yugoslavia.[158]

Article 4 reinforces the authority of UNDEA yet retains ultimate enforcement power in the hands of the Security Council - where the Charter put it.

What has been here proposed is not intended to be set in concrete; variations are possible. It is intended to indicate how the problem of world disarmament has to be approached if it is ever to become a reality and remove the heavy shackles of armaments that now burden humankind.

We have stipulated that universal disarmament can only become acceptable if it is coupled with other effective means for securing a more

---

158 See Chapter Two, Section D-4 and Chapter Eight, Section B (2).

rational world order. We turn, therefore to consideration of other UN agencies needed as part of a new regime to maintain the peace.

(2) *Creating A UN Sanctions Agency*

The idea of using economic and diplomatic sanctions to achieve political goals has been around since ancient days. The Covenant of the League of Nations held out high hopes that the "Economic Weapon" would replace war as the method for conflict resolution. But, as we pointed out, it didn't work.[159] Unilateral or even multilateral sanctions never succeeded in preserving or restoring peace.[160] Only in recent years, has the Security Council been in a position to reactivate sanctions as a tool for peace - but a great deal still remains to be done before sanctions can be enforced effectively as envisaged by the proposed new Security Council Resolution Ending the Arms race.[161]

The first thing that needs to be done is to understand more clearly how sanctions may be made to work. The next thing that must be done is to create an instrumentality whereby imposed sanctions can be organized, implemented and globally enforced.

(i) *Make initial sanctions comprehensive:*

There should be, as was prescribed in the Covenant, complete interruption of all economic relations, diplomatic relations and communication with the transgressor. Such a comprehensive approach would demonstrate the seriousness and determination of the entire international community to put a stop to the unlawful behavior. It would be very difficult, if not impossible, for any government to function for long without telephone, post, radio or other means of communication with the outside world. Blocking all road, train, ship and air travel as well as the cessation of all banking, trade and other contacts - even if imperfect - would be economically devastating. It would be a sharp blow and would get immediate attention. Its symbolic value as a measure of disapproval would be invaluable - even if it had to be subsequently ameliorated because of unbearable and unjustifiable hardships unavoidably imposed on innocent civilians.

(ii) Spare the innocent:

The goal is not to punish the populace but to make it physically impossible for the lawbreaking government to continue its illegal activity.

---

159   See Chapter Three, Section C.

160   *See* G.C.HUFBAUER, J.J.SCHOTT & K.A. ELLIOTT, ECONOMIC SANCTIONS RECONSIDERED, 2 Vols. 2d Ed. (1990); B.E. CARTER, INTERNATIONAL ECONOMIC SANCTIONS (1988).

161   See Chapter Eight, Section A.

Exceptions - under strict controls - may be made for humanitarian reasons to prevent undue suffering by those who are not supporting the prohibited activities. Goods which in no way affect the illegal behavior can also be excluded from embargo.[162]

(iii) Share the burdens equitably:

Peace should not be a privilege enjoyed only by rich and powerful states that can impose their will on the poor and the weak. All nations are entitled to world peace and to share its benefits equitably. But the burden and costs of peace-enforcement measures should also be borne equitably by everyone - bearing in mind their capacity to pay. A system of universal sharing of the costs of peace-maintenance must be planned on a global basis if it is to minimize the burdens on each and serves as a form of life insurance for all.

The UN Charter provides that any state that finds itself confronted with special economic problems arising from enforcement measures ordered by the Security Council,

> shall have the right to consult with the Security Council with regard to a solution of those problems.[163]

A right "to consult" does not put bread on the table. A nation's economy can be ruined and peace thereby threatened unless relief is available when needed.[164]

It would be prudent to create a Compensation Fund in advance so that financial relief can be provided quickly.[165] Relief must encompass more than merely prompt monetary compensation for lost trade. Boycotts may cut off vital lifelines (such as oil or grains) of countries cooperating in applying UN sanctions against lawbreakers. Imports as well as exports must be globally regulated and global resource sharing may be essential to make the sanctions system workable.

The principle that a wrongdoer should pay for injuries caused is a general principle of law and justice. The imposition of economic sanctions

---

162 The argument has been made that economic sanctions imposed by the United States alone, and involving only manufactured goods, would be adequate to bring down any aggressor. H. BREMBECK, THE CIVILIZED DEFENSE PLAN (1989).

163 UN Charter, Article 50.

164 Bulgaria's President complained that his country's economy was being ruined by the need to abide by the sanctions imposed against Serbia. See President Zhelev's address to the General Assembly on 5 Oct. 1993 and General Committee recommendation in GA/8558, 22 Oct. 1993.

165 See Reports of the Special Committee on the Charter of the UN, GAOR, 47th Sess., Supp. No. 33 (A/47/33) (1992) pp. 37-45, and subsequent Reports; Sixth Committee debate 12-20 Oct. 1992; UN Press Release, L/2661, 17 Mar. 1993.

against Iraq for its aggression against Kuwait involved the seizure of Iraqi accounts and assets abroad, as well as Iraqi oil stocks and proceeds from the sale of Iraq's petroleum to reimburse the UN for its costs in eliminating Iraq's weapons of mass destruction and providing humanitarian relief.[166] Any Sanctions Agency would have to keep in mind that reparations after peace has been restored may impose unbearable burdens on innocent populations and may, if excessive, prove to be counter-productive - as was the case with German reparations after World War I.

(iv) Target vital resources:

Economists would have to track the changing economic needs of nations and particulary the vital resources upon which aggressors would have to depend for military adventures. Much of this information should already be on hand in military intelligence establishments. It was the basis for strategic bombing of German defense industries during World War II. Similarly, there must be contingent planning for future resource targeting should it become necessary. Just as the military has honed its highly technical skills for destroying potential military targets, it will be necessary to develop skills for coercing lawbreakers by less violent - and less expensive - means aimed at the economic-military potential of belligerent states.

An efficient legal instrumentality to make sanctions work effectively has not yet been created. Many recent Security Council sanctions have been hastily improvised under great pressure by overburdened diplomats dependent upon distant home offices for instructions. Swamped by a constant flood of crises around the globe, many of them have neither the time nor the specialized qualification to do the job properly.[167] Monitoring the implementation of the most recent resolutions was assigned to different special committees, each with its own Chairman and each with a membership consisting of all 15 members of the Security Council.[168] Every member of the Security Council was expected to deal with all of the problems related to sanctions enforcement - in addition to their other problems.

The UN has not yet organized an effective system of burden-sharing to provide quick relief to those unintended targets that indirectly suffer hardships resulting from economic sanctions. The Committee designated by the Security Council to deal with sanctions against Iraq, including requests for burden-sharing under Charter Art. 50, is only an embryo that is not yet fully developed.[169] The problem of insulating or compensating

---

166 SC Res. 778 (1992), see SC 3117th Meeting PM, 2 Oct. 1992.

167 See SC Res.661 (1990) against Iraq; SC Res. 724 (1991) against former Yugoslavia; SC Res. 748 (1992) against Libya; SC Res. 751 (1992) against Somalia; SC Res. 841 (1993) against Haiti.

168 See UN Press Release SC/5535, 11 Jan. 1993.

169 *See* SC Res. 669 (1990).

innocent states from the financial burdens arising from economic sanctions were passed back from the Council to the Secretary-General for his recommendations.[170] A coordinated global sanctions-planning organization is badly needed.

The organizational structure and procedures for a new United Nations Sanctions Agency (UNSA) should be governed by the Guiding Principles suggested heretofore.[171] UNSA - acting in consultation or cooperation with existing mechanisms - would have to organize the international legal and factual basis for imposing import, export and other restrictions in case of need. Computerized information, already available regarding natural resource, industrial production, trade and finances of various lands now makes the type of sanctions planning possible that was impossible in the past. UNSA could draft model sanctions statutes to be offered for adoption by national legislatures.[172]

A new Sanctions Agency could keep track of the basic needs of different lands and determine how burdens can most equitably be distributed and controlled in case of emergency. It could detect violations or evasions and suggest appropriate corrective action. It would help to avoid the risks of unilateral sanctions imposed as counter-measures by an aggrieved state. Once an effective UN sanctions agency became operational, the dangers of uncontrollable national counter-measures could be diminished or eliminated.

In 1992, the International Law Commission, discussing counter-measures, expressed its fear that inequality among states would "unduly operate to the advantage of the strong and rich over the weak and needy." The ILC drew attention to:

> the absence in the international community, of any institutionalized remedies to be put into motion against a State which committed an internationally wrongful act...the imperfect structure of the international society which had not yet succeeded in establishing an effective centralized system of law enforcement.[173]

---

170 S/PV. 3154, 30 Dec. 1992.

171 See Chapter Seven, Section D.

172 See D.L.BETHLEHEM, Ed., THE KUWAIT CRISIS: SANCTIONS AND THEIR ECONOMIC CONSEQUENCES (1991).

173 Report of the ILC, A/47/10 (1992) at 40.

A new United Nations Sanctions Agency would be the type of organ needed to close the institutional gap noted by the ILC in the present imperfect structure of international society.

DRAFT RESOLUTION CREATING A UN SANCTIONS AGENCY

THE SECURITY COUNCIL, acting pursuant to its authority under the Charter of the United Nations, declares that all members of the organization are bound by the following resolution:

ARTICLE 1- The Secretary-General of the United Nations is instructed to establish a UN Sanctions Agency (UNSA) as an organ of the Security Council to carry out the sanctions objectives of the Security Council Resolution Ending the Arms Race in as fair, efficient and speedy manner as possible.

ARTICLE 2- Pursuant to Article 6 of the Security Council Resolution Ending the Arms Race, UNSA shall serve as the agent of the Security Council in supervising the implementation of the program of economic and other sanctions as set forth in that resolution and in drawing up such rules as shall be necessary for that purpose.[174]

ARTICLE 3- The Secretary-General shall invite nominations for the position of Director of the UN Sanctions Agency from members of the Special Security Council Committees dealing with sanctions, as well as from other competent organizations or agencies. The list of nominees shall be screened by the UN Secretary-General and reduced to no more than 20 and no less than 10. The appointment shall be made by majority vote of the Security Council and require approval by a majority of the members of the General Assembly.

ARTICLE 4 - The Security Council will use all necessary means to enforce the provisions of the Resolution on Ending the Arms

---

174 See Chapter Eight, Section A.

Race and the decisions and rules of UNSA whenever the Council decides that failure to do so would constitute a threat to the peace.

COMMENTARY:

The Resolution for a UN Sanctions Agency follows the lines of the Resolution Ending the Arms Race; the two are linked.

Article 1 charges the Secretary-General to establish UNSA. The reference to fairness and efficiency is intended to convey an obligation to employ only qualified and independent persons who will be considerate of the interests of all sides.

Article 2 is intended to make clear that UNSA is an organ of the Security Council and hence backed by Security Council authority. It also seeks to limit the responsibility of UNSA to non-military sanctions problems rather than those related to the military aspects, such as disarmament or the use of force by the United Nations; those function will be assumed by the special UN Disarmament Enforcement Agency and the UN Police Agency, to be proposed hereafter.

Article 3 is intended to provide a system of checks-and-balances in selecting the Director of UNSA. It follows general principles approved by the Security Council for designating judges for the new *ad hoc* International Criminal Court to deal with crimes in former Yugoslavia.[175]

Article 4 reinforces the authority of UNSA yet retains ultimate enforcement power in the hands of the Security Council - where the Charter put it.

As a last resort, if non-forcible measures prove inadequate, international military operations by land, sea and air forces can be employed to whatever extent required to restore and maintain peace. The application of unilateral military might (even within the vague restraints of self-defense and proportionality prescribed by the UN Charter) runs the risk of being abused for self-serving national purposes. Self-help is more likely to jeopardize world security than enhance it. To avoid dangerous improvisations, new institutions are needed to maintain the peace in a systematized and collective way. Let us consider what can be done to further enhance security measures under United Nations guidance or control.

---

175 See Chapter Two, Section D-4 and Chapter Eight, Section B (2).

(3) *Creating a UN Police Agency*

Law without force is farce. As long as the enforcement provisions of the Charter remained chilled and dormant during the decades of the cold-war, most people in the world did not take the UN very seriously. The organization created after two world wars for the purpose of preserving the peace failed in its basic responsibility. According to Worldwide Watch:

> Since 1945, some 135 wars, most of them in the developing world, have killed more than 22 million people - the equivalent of World War III.. There were 18 million officially recognized international refugees in 1992...and another 20 million displaced *inside* their own countries.[176]

The end of the cold-war made it possible for the Security Council to begin to discharge its basic responsibility. More peace-related operations were created in the past four years of the UN than in the first forty. The improvised expansion of peacekeeping activities during recent years - with over 80,000 military and civilian police personnel serving in thirteen missions throughout the world by June 1993 - reflects innovative responses to meet irresistible needs. But more than imaginative improvisation is now required.[177]

The challenge that the UN faces is to institutionalize the use of military might along lines originally foreseen in the Charter and to create a truly international peace force that by its availability and presence may deter or put a stop to massive violence wherever it occurs. The time has come for a more comprehensive and systematic approach to peace enforcement. A Comprehensive Review of the Whole Question of Peace-Keeping Operations in all Their Aspects is on the UN agenda. [178]

The first thing that must be done is to clarify the authority and competence of the Security Council and UN peace forces. Boutros-Ghali's *Agenda for Peace* outlined four ways to maintain peace:

Preventive diplomacy - early identification of tensions and efforts to remove the danger *before* violence erupts. He recommended preventive troop deployment but only "at the request of the Government or all parties concerned, or with their consent." Said the Secretary-General:

---

176 *See* M.Renner, *Critical Juncture, The Future of Peacekeeping*, Worldwide Watch Paper No. 114 (May 1993) at 8-9. Confirmed by the UN Secretary-General in his *Agenda for Peace* (1992) at 7.

177 Recommendations of Special Committee on Peace-keeping Operations GA/PK/119, 19 May 1993.

178 *Report of the Special Committee on Peace-keeping Operations*, A/48/173, 25 May 1993; Provisional Agenda, A/48/100, 15 June 1993 at 224.

In these situations of internal crisis the United Nations will need to respect the sovereignty of the State; to do otherwise would not be in accordance with the understanding of Member States in accepting the principles of the Charter.[179]

Peace-making - peaceful conflict resolution, but if peaceful means fail, the use of military force as prescribed by Chapter VII of the Charter - *even if not requested by the parties.*

Peace-keeping - deployment of a UN presence to preserve the peace once fighting has been halted, *providing it is with the consent of the parties.*

Peace-building - restoring institutions and eliminating the social injustice that might cause a relapse into conflict. This being a counterpart of preventive diplomacy would presumably also require the prior consent of the parties concerned.

The Secretary-General recognized that peace-*making* may require the use of military force *without* the consent of the parties. Any other view would render Chapter VII meaningless or nonsensical. In all other cases, however, sensitive to the concerns of sovereign states and past practice, he considered the use of UN forces permissible only *with* the consent of the parties affected. There seems to be something illogical and self-defeating about the Secretary-General's polite, and deferential, interpretation of the UN Charter. Let us analyze the Charter provisions a bit more closely.

The first article of Chapter VII requires the Security Council to determine the existence of "*any threat* to the peace" and the Council has authority to decide upon *any* necessary military action "to *maintain*" as well as to "restore international peace and security."[180] It does not limit the use of UN force only to those circumstances where there has already been "a breach of the peace or act of aggression." In requiring that states immediately report any military measures taken in self-defence, the Charter clearly reaffirms that such action

> shall not in any way affect the authority and responsibility of the Security Council under the present Charter to take *at any time* such action as it deems necessary in order to *maintain* or *restore* international peace and security.[181]

In both articles, the Charter makes explicitly clear that it is the Council that has the authority and responsibility to act and that it may *at any time* take

---

179 *An Agenda For Peace*, Paragraph 28-29.
180 UN Charter, Art. 39, emphasis added.
181 UN Charter, Art.51, emphasis added.

such action *as it deems necessary* in order to *maintain* or *restore* international peace. Neither article says a word about requiring the consent of the parties. A contrary view would be as if to say that a suspected criminal can only be arrested when and if he agrees to go along with the police officer. Kofi Annan, Under-Secretary-General for Peacekeeping Operations was quite right in his statement:

> There can be no doubt that the Security Council is the ultimate legal and political authority in deciding on a United Nations operation.[182]

Smoldering disputes, or failure to respect Security Council peace-keeping mandates, may pose a threat to peace that can best be averted by a show of UN military force. Keeping UN troops on the ground after a cease-fire may be just as important to maintain peace as interjecting them to halt an artillery barrage in progress. To say that the latter can be done without consent but the former needs permission from the parties is an illogical and unjustified limitation on the authority of the Security Council. A correct interpretation of the Charter - consistent with both its language and purposes - is to recognize that UN Forces have complete authority to do whatever the *Security Council* decides is necessary to remove a threat to the peace - whether the states concerned like it or not.[183]

Retired Major-General Rikhye, President of the International Peace Academy, put it well when he concluded:

> The members of the Security Council must show greater will to support their resolutions, for there will be little progress if there are no teeth for implementing the Council's decisions.[184]

The Secretary-General, in calling for NATO help in Bosnia, has recognized that he has neither the staff nor the expertise to take over daily command of large numbers of UN peacekeepers scattered over the world.[185] Pleading to nation states to offer help in creating stand-by forces is no way to run an army or a peace mission. The time has come for the Security Council to insist that nations honor the Charter security plan they all freely accepted. The Charter (Art.43-45) calls for members to make armed forces and air contingents available to the Security Council to maintain peace. Details were to be worked out by the Military Staff Committee representing the Chiefs of Staff

---

182 *See* Kofi A. Annan, *UN Peacekeeping Operations and Cooperation with NATO*, NATO Review (Oct. 1993).

183 See Chapter Seven, Section C.

184 I.J.RIKHYE, THE FUTURE OF PEACEKEEPING (1990) AT 197.

185 P. Lewis, *U.N.Leader Backs Takeover of Force in Bosnia by NATO*, N.Y. Times Sept. 20, 1993 at A10.

of the Permanent Members. The anticipated agreement was never concluded.[186] The fact that the agreement has not yet been reached casts serious doubt about the sincerity of the declared allied willingness or intention to reach such an understanding.

Dietrich Fischer, a former MacArthur Fellow in International Peace and Security at Princeton, has pointed out that for each country to maintain its own military forces is as wasteful as if every house in a community had its own fire-engine.[187] If the international community is to be safeguarded against conflagrations, an international fire-brigade is what is required. The proposed Security Council Resolution Ending the Arms Race links the process of step-by-step universal disarmament with the simultaneous build-up of UN forces capable of maintaining peace. National disarmament goes hand in hand with the enhancement of UN force as nation states hand their military baton over to the Security Council in the final lap ending the arms race. This difficult and dangerous process requires constant supervision and specialized coordination and cooperation of the highest political and military calibre.

We have seen that UN forces are engaged in a wide variety of functions: monitoring a cease-fire or truce, observing and patrolling a buffer-zone, guarding a border, supervising an election, enforcing a weapons embargo, protecting the delivery of humanitarian relief supplies, quelling local disorders or - as in the case of Iraq - delegating authority to a coalition of independent states to use all necessary means to repulse aggression and restore the sovereignty and boundaries of a member state, collect funds, pay claims and take undefined other measures to restore peace to the area.[188]

The size, nature and composition of UN forces will vary with different missions. A UN Police Agency must be so structured that it can call upon its resources at any time to meet emergencies of different urgency and gravity. "Preventive Diplomacy," for example, requires observers and negotiators more than tank commanders. Monitoring an election does not need supersonic aircraft. Suppressing aggression or a major military insurrection that threatens world peace may require intensive military counter-strikes. The Security Council must be able to cope effectively with whatever peace-threatening emergency may arise.

In addition to stand-by and reserve units to cope with missions of varying size and type, the UN must eventually have available its own rapid-deployment forces that can move quickly to put out a brush fire before

---

186 See Chapter Three, Section D.
187 D. FISCHER, NON-MILITARY ASPECTS OF SECURITY - A SYSTEMS APPROACH (1993).
188 See Chapter Three, Section D.

it becomes a major conflagration. An elite force of UN "Blue Beret" Police-men or Marshals for Peace can be recruited from the best of those forces being demobilized by nations as part of the mandated world disarmament process. How such contingents can be created, their size and command structures raise questions that require expert military judgments. To place ultimate operational responsibility for all of these missions on the shoulders of one Secretary-General - no matter how competent - is as unreasonable as it is unfair and unwise.

The Secretary-General has been forced to delegate many specialized functions to different groups, Commissions, and other special agencies created to cope with each particular crisis situation. But the missions are increasing in number, size and complexity and the need for coordination has become imperative.[189] Financing peacekeeping operations has been a growing problem. The costs in 1992-1993 are expected to exceed three billion dollars. Although this is less than the costs of two stealth bombers, or worldwide military expenditures for three *days*, many nations refuse to pay their allotted share and only 10% pay on time.

In line with our declared policy of not moving too far too fast, let us begin by looking to agreements that were reached in principle in 1947 when the Military Staff Committee was trying to carry out its Charter obligations. Those tentative agreements can now be completed to serve as a basic guide for the creation of the anticipated (but never realized) UN military force.

The UN Charter says that the Military Staff Committee, consisting of the Chiefs of Staff of the Permanent Members, or their representatives, shall

> advise and assist the Security Council on all questions relating to the Security Council's military requirements for the mainte-nance of international peace and security, the employment and command of forces placed at its disposal, the regulation of armaments, and possible disarmament.[190]

In 1947, the Military Staff Committee began to do what it was supposed to do under the Charter; it drafted a plan for a UN Military Force. It reached unanimous agreement on almost all major points:

> Armed forces made available to the Council would be com-posed of national armed forces selected from the best trained and equipped formations (Art.3, 4).

---

189 *See* P. Lewis, *Panel Sees Growing U.N. Intervention*, N.Y. Times, Feb. 27, 1993.

190 UN Charter, Article 47.

The number would be limited to strength sufficient to enable the Security Council to take prompt action "in any part of the world" to maintain or restore peace (Art.6).

All member nations would have the obligation to place armed forces and facilities at the disposal of the Security Council at its call, but initially the major contribution would come from the permanent members, as determined by the Security Council on advice of the Military Staff Committee (Art. 9, 10, 12).

No nation would be obliged to increase its armed forces to meet a UN call but could satisfy its obligation by providing facilities instead (Art.13, 14).

Armed forces made available to the Security Council could only be employed by decision of the Council and only for the period necessary; they could be kept ready to forestall or suppress promptly a breach of the peace or act of aggression (Art.18, 19, 23).

Replacements, reserves and logistical support should be provided by members from their respective forces (Art.29, 30).

Armed forces made available to the UN would be based, during the carrying out of enforcement measures, in areas designated by the Security Council and would be under the command of the respective contributing nations, "except when operating under the Security Council" (Art.35, 36).

The Military Staff Committee would be responsible, under the Security Council, for strategic direction of the forces but command of national contingents would be under commanders appointed by the respective Member Nations (Art.38, 39, 40).

All of the above provisions were acceptable to all members of the Military Staff Committee. The points of disagreement, which brought the negotiation for the UN Charter mandated agreement to a halt, seemed more quibble than substance: the U.S.S R. wanted the Council to call contingents from Permanent Members on an equal basis rather than subject to special negotiation (Art.7, 8, 11); China and France wanted to specify the right to recall their troops temporarily if needed for self-defence (Art.17); the Soviets wanted the date of troop withdrawal after completion of mission to be fixed at no more than 90 days; the others wanted the date fixed by the Security Council (Art.20).[191]

---

191 Security Council, Official Records, Second Year, Special Supp. No. 1, *Report of the Military Staff Committee*, 30 Apr. 1947, *reproduced in* FERENCZ, ENFORCING INT. L. vol.2 Doc. 46(a).

Whether the nations involved ever really wanted to reach an agreement, as required by the Charter, is doubtful - as indicated by the fact that, since 1947, they have not made any serious effort to complete their Charter assignment. During the past *46 years*, the Military Staff Committee of high-ranking officers has met regularly, twice a month, only to report that it has nothing of substance to report![192]

In 1965, a Special Committee on Peacekeeping was appointed by the General Assembly to develop guidelines and principles for future peacekeeping operations. By 1977, the Committee had reached consensus on certain principles, but no final agreement was ever reached. A major stumbling block was whether the Security Council or the Secretary-General should exercise authority under different circumstances. There seemed to be general agreement that ultimate authority had to rest with the Security Council - although the Council could create new subsidiary organs pursuant to Charter Article 29 and also delegate certain responsibilities to the moribund Military Staff Committee.[193]

Now that the political climate has changed, the Military Staff Committee should be told to do its job. It can begin by building on the agreed principles accepted in 1947, as outlined above. If it is unable to do so promptly, the Security Council should find someone else who can. A group of professional military experts, free of national bias, may prove to be the right medicine for the ailing patient. A new UN Police Agency could appoint a small group of experts to complete the job in a brief period of time.

The most fundamental policy problem relates to a system of checks-and-balances to insure that no UN military force can ever become a dictatorial power capable of threatening the interests of peaceful nations. How this is done - and it *must* be done - will require specialized planning as the world moves from its present system of international anarchy toward a rule of international law and order. Even with the best of intentions on all sides, it will take a considerable period of time before a UN Police Force will be in a position where it can maintain world peace. In the interim, while nations are disarming step-by-step, world security will have to make use of the tools it has on hand. Until its own force is created, the UN has no alternative but to rely on forces provided voluntarily by nations ready to assist in peace enforcement - as it has recently been doing.

---

192 *See* Report of the Security Council to the General Assembly, A/47/2 (1993) p. 263, and annual reports for prior years.
193 *See* J.P.BARATTA, INTERNATIONAL PEACEKEEPING: HISTORY AND STRENGTHENING, Center for UN Reform Education Monograph No. 6 (1989) pp.78-83.

The United States is the only remaining superpower. It has, together with a few other nations, made powerful military force available to repel aggression by Iraq against Kuwait. U.S. oil interests certainly played a major role in influencing the magnitude and speed of the U.S. response, but the fact remains that very few nations are both able and willing to help the UN enforce peace. It is also a fact that neither the world community nor its own citizens have agreed that the U.S. should be the policeman of the world. The world should not have to rely on hired Centurions to be conquering heros. What it needs is its own force to protect and preserve the peace and dignity of humankind. The safest force would be one drawn from many nations, preferably those of limited size, pledged and dedicated to the service of all humankind. The sooner such a force is put in place the better, and safer, it will be for everyone.

NATO forces, that were supposed to be able to halt Soviet aggression against western Europe, stood by while civil war ravaged former Yugoslavia. The mobilization of adequate force to maintain peace in Yugoslavia proved too much for the Security Council or the Secretary-General or anyone else. It was only with great difficult that the UN was able to mobilize a humanitarian and tiny military force from nations willing to try to squelch a relatively minor insurrection in Somalia.[194] The frustration and futility of the present situation underscores the urgent need for a better way to maintain peace. A new enforcement agency is needed - independent and dedicated UN Marshals to enforce world law in a disarmed world.

The need for more coordinated peacekeeping has been recognized at UN headquarters. For the first time in its history, a command and control center has been created where a small team keeps close track of UN peacekeeping operations in Somalia,former Yugoslavia and elsewhere. According to Kofi Annan of Ghana, the Under-Secretary General in charge of UN's Department of Peacekeeping Operations: " The days of gifted amateurism are over."[195] What is being here proposed is to institutionalize a more comprehensive new UN Police Agency to continue a process that is vitally needed and already under way.[196]

---

194 UN Operations in Somalia (UNOSOM), with less than 700 persons was established in April 1992.

195 Efforts have begun to develop a system of stand-by forces able to be deployed anywhere for UN duties mandated by the Security Council, but the lines of command and communication have not yet been clarified and the means to carry out the missions are still non-existent. *See* P. Lewis, *U.N. Is Developing Control Center to Coordinate Growing Peacekeeping Role*, N.Y. Times, Sunday Mar. 26, 1993 p. 10 L.

196 See M. Berdal, Whither UN PeaceKeeping? Adelphi Paper 281, Int. Institute for Strategic Studies (1993) .

In sum, what is wrong with current UN peacekeeping is that it underestimates its own authority, fails to uphold the Charter plan, does not know the size or nature of military forces required or available, covers a wide diversity of unrelated and uncoordinated obligations, has no comprehensive plan, lacks adequate or assured funding and needs professional planners and executors. What is required is a new organ of the Security Council that can handle all peace-maintenance problems in an orderly, planned, dispassionate and professional way - free of the shackles of national, regional or UN politics.[197]

DRAFT RESOLUTION CREATING A UN POLICE AGENCY

THE SECURITY COUNCIL, acting pursuant to its authority under the Charter of the United Nations, declares that all members of the organization are bound by the following resolution:

ARTICLE 1- The Secretary-General of the United Nations is instructed to establish a UN Police Agency (UNPA) as an organ of the Security Council to carry out all measures related to peacekeeping forces and other forces recruited or placed at its disposal pursuant to the Security Council Resolution for Ending the Arms Race.

ARTICLE 2- Pursuant to Article 6 of the Security Council Resolution Eliminating the Arms Race, UNPA shall serve as the agent of the Security Council in supervising the implementation of all programs involving peacekeeping forces or other forces as set forth in that resolution and in drawing up such rules as shall be necessary for that purpose.[198]

ARTICLE 3- The Secretary-General shall invite nominations for the position of Director of the UN Police Agency from the Military Staff Committee, members of all the Security Council Committees or Missions dealing with UN Peacekeeping functions, as well as from other competent organizations or agencies. The

---

197 *See* J. Mackinlay & J. Chopra, *Second Generation Multinational Operations*, The Washington Qtrly (Summer 1992) p.113; UN Fifth Committee Press Release GA/AB/2857, 18 Aug. 1993. See Statement by Austrian Ambassador Sucharipa, Sixth Comm. Mtg., 13 Oct, 1993.

198 See Chapter Eight, Section A.

list of nominees shall be screened by the UN Secretary-General and reduced to no more than 20 and no less than 10. The appointment shall be made by majority vote of the Security Council and require approval by a majority of the members of the General Assembly.

ARTICLE 4 - The Security Council will use all necessary means to enforce the provisions of the Resolution on Elimination of the Arms Race and the decisions and rules of UNPA whenever the Council decides that failure to do so would constitute a threat to the peace.

COMMENTARY:

The Resolution for a UN Police Agency follows the lines of the Resolution for Ending the Arms Race and the proposed Resolution for a UN Sanctions Agency. The three are linked as pre-requisites for acceptance of any system of universal and complete disarmament as outlined in the McCloy/Zorin Agreement.

Article 1 charges the Secretary-General to establish the UNPA. The insertion of the reference to forces "recruited" is intended to indicate that not only national units are covered but also new contingents that may be created by the UN directly.

Article 2 is intended to make clear that UNPA is an organ of the Security Council and hence backed by Security Council authority. It also seeks to limit the responsibility of UNPA to military sanctions and policing problems that may require the use of UN force rather than those related to disarmament or non-military sanctions that will be dealt with by the proposed UN Disarmament Enforcement Agency and the UN Sanctions Agency.

Article 3 is intended to provide a system of checks-and-balances in selecting the Director of UNPA. As in the proposals for the related UN Sanctions Agency, it follows general principles approved by the Security Council for designating judges for the new *ad hoc* International Criminal Court to deal with crimes in former Yugoslavia.[199]

Article 4 reinforces the authority of UNPA yet retains ultimate enforcement power in the hands of the Security Council - where the Charter put it.

---

199 See Chapter Two, Section D-4 and Chapter Eight, Section B (2).

The resolution creating a UN Police Agency completes the trilogy of related peace-enforcement organs: disarmament, sanctions and UN force. What still remains to be considered is an agency to enforce the minimum standards of social justice.

(4) *Creating A UN Social Justice Agency*

Over one billion people on this planet try to survive on less than one dollar per day.[200] The need for a new approach to social justice should be evident. We have approached the problem of enhancing world social justice by suggesting the adoption of two new Security Council resolutions. The first resolution, a Charter for Enhancing Social Justice, was designed to set forth and make legally binding and mandatory those few general principles of basic human rights - regarding trade, environment and human dignity - that seem to have found worldwide acceptance.[201] The second resolution, creating a World Tribunal for Social Justice, was intended to set up a judicial mechanism to handle legal disputes regarding interpretation or violation of the Social Justice Charter - whenever it appeared to the Council that peace was being threatened by such disputes.[202] In addition to the clarification of *law* in the first resolution and the creation of a new *court* in the second resolution, what is still needed to create a workable social justice system is a new structure for improved enforcement of the declared goals - a UN Social Justice Agency.

A new UN Social Justice Agency, created as an organ of the Security Council, can only deal with such violations of fundamental human rights that pose a threat to peace. Its focus and concentration is therefore limited. Since there are a host of agencies already in the field - national as well as regional - to cope with a wide assortment of human rights and social justice issues, the new agency will serve as a coordinator or facilitator for the carrying out of those recognized universal rights that fall within its purview.

Jan Eliasson, UN Under-Secretary-General for Humanitarian Affairs, explained that humanitarian crises such as those in Somalia and the former Yugoslavia raged dangerously out of control

> because tested international mechanisms do not yet exist to respond to the kind of complex emergencies that are now erupting globally.[203]

---

200 See The World Bank, Implementing the World Bank's Strategy to Reduce Poverty (1993).

201 See Chapter Eight, Section A.

202 See Chapter Eight, Section B.

203 *See* S. Lone, *Enlarging the UN's Humanitarian Mandate*, UN Dept. of Public Information, Dec. 1992.

By focusing on those basic rights essential for human dignity and peace, the Social Justice Agency can help the existing agencies attain the shared goals within a larger global framework. By alerting the Council to dangerous social injustices and oppression that may rise to a level that threatens world peace, a Social Justice Agency serves to prevent the outbreak of violence and bring to bear at an early stage the pressure of Security Council support. It reinforces the peace agenda of Secretary-General Boutros-Ghali calling for both preventive diplomacy as well as peace-building.

The proposed new Social Justice Agency would be neither a law-making nor a law-interpreting body. Those functions are assigned to the Security Council Resolution for Enhancing Social Justice and the resolution for creating a World Tribunal for Social Justice. The primary mission of the Social Justice Agency would be:

(a) To monitor those human rights objectives set down in the Security Council Resolution for Enhancing Social Justice to see to what extent they are being implemented and to report to the Council whenever their violation may pose a threat to peace.

(b) To coordinate the activities of the many existing agencies dealing with those basic human rights - economic, political, social and environmental - articulated in the Security Council resolution in order to maximize their implementation in an efficient and effective way, with the objective of avoiding crises that may threaten world security.

(c) To recommend and organize specific enforcement measures for Council approval whenever the Agency concludes that such action is required to maintain the peace.

The agency is not intended to replace other UN bodies that may already be fulfilling some of the human rights programs in an efficient way. Where such other programs may be ineffective, however, the Agency would be expected to make recommendations for improvement, consolidation or elimination of programs that are not achieving their declared goals. Greater coordination among the myriad UN and other organizations dealing with social problems would be a great step forward. The problem is not that there are not enough agencies; the problem is that there are too many talking too much and doing too little.[204]

---

204 *See Report of the Economic Committee* of ECOSOC on Regional Cooperation, E/1992/108, 30 July 1992.

When the UN was 40 years old, Professor Maurice Bertrand of Geneva, prepared a report for the United Nations after a Joint Inspection Unit had studied UN reform for some 17 years. Bertrand recognized that an improved political climate was a *sine qua non* before changes could be expected but he felt that it was "possible to explore other paths than those followed 40 years ago." What Bertrand suggested for the "third-generation World Organization" was quite similar to the organizational alterations we are proposing here.

In considering the world's economic problems, Bertrand called for replacement of the existing Economic and Social Council (ECOSOC) and the UN Conference on Trade and Development (UNCTAD) by a much smaller Council.[205] He recommended the creation of a new "Economic Security Council" to coordinate and render more effective the many inter-related or competitive UN efforts now carried on by ECOSOC, UNCTAD, IMF, the World Bank and other agencies trying to promote economic development. He calculated that if a new "Economic Security Council" of 23 members could be established,

> the main major States and the main regions of the world could be represented on it. It should be possible for the secretariats of the United Nations and the major agencies to be reorganized under the authority of one or more "Commissions" made up of independent persons of distinction.[206]

The thrust of Betrand's thinking was undoubtedly valid: decrease the size of the supervisory political group and rely more on qualified experts.

Van B. Weigel has looked into the future for a "Basic Needs Approach" to alleviate absolute poverty and provide the "core attributes of human life." The global mal-distribution of resources that exists in the world today is sharply criticized as he urges the creation of a new international resource management agency as both a political and moral imperative for the 21st century.[207] Plans for resource management, to assure minimum food, water and fuel supplies, would fall within the range of attention by a new Social Justice Agency.

In 1991, a very distinguished group of former world statesmen met in Stockholm and, after careful deliberation, issued a report on Global Security and Governance. This "Stockholm Initiative" built on the work of similar

---

205 UN Charter Art.61 enlarged ECOSOC membership from 18 to 27 on 31 Aug. 1965 and enlarged it again to 54 on 24 Sept. 1973.

206 M. Bertrand, *Some Reflections on Reform of the United Nations*, A/40/988, 6 Dec, 1985 at 68-69; M. BERTRAND, THE THIRD GENERATION WORLD ORGANIZATION (1989).

207 V.B. WEIGEL, A UNIFIED THEORY OF GLOBAL DEVELOPMENT (1989).

earlier groups such as the Brandt, Palme and Brundtland Commissions. The Stockholm report called for universality in world economic cooperation. Regional organizations were necessary and important but they were not considered good enough to meet global requirements. "The global character for world economic cooperation must be ensured," they said.[208]

In 1992, a group of very highly-regarded Americans, members of a Carnegie Endowment Commission, put the same conclusion another way:

> Over time we should move toward an even more inclusive global system of economic and financial cooperation. A central concern must be the interests of developing countries, whose futures will have much to say about our own.[209]

Recently fifty thinkers from countries throughout the world, considering the political, economic and social problems of our time, led to the conclusion that the promotion of peace and security, of economic and social development, and of democracy are all indivisible.[210]

The UN, pushed by increasing public pressure, is already moving toward a more rational and pragmatic approach to major social problems. Following the Rio Conference on Environment and Development that took place in 1992, the General Assembly requested ECOSOC to set up a high-level Commission on Sustainable Development to help implement Agenda 21. The Assembly recommended that the Commission consist of 53 representatives elected with due regard to equitable geographical distribution. The Secretary-General was asked to propose the rules of procedure. Related UN organizations were asked to coordinate and cooperate with the new Commission. The Assembly endorsed the view of the Secretary-General that there should be a small High-Level Advisory Board consisting of eminent persons with recognized expertise and drawn from scientific and non-governmental constituencies - giving due account to gender balance.[211] It called upon the Secretary-General to establish a new Department for Policy Coordination and Sustainable Development to serve as a support structure for the new Commission.[212]

Former President Jimmy Carter, as well as President Bill Clinton have joined the parade of those calling for a High Commissioner of Human Rights.[213] Elliot Richardson, former head of the U.S. delegation to the Law

---

208 The Prime Minister's Office, Stockholm, Sweden, *Common Responsibility in the 1990's* (1991) at 40.

209 *Report of the Carnegie Endowment National Commission on America and the New World*, (Washington DC, 1992) at 36.

210 U. KIRDAR & L. SILK Eds., A WORLD FIT FOR PEOPLE (1994) p. xiii, xv.

211 GA Res. 47/191 Dec. 22, 1992; *reproduced in* 32 ILM 236 (1993) at 254.

212 *Id.* at 261.

213 J. Carter, *Get Tough on Rights*, N.Y. Times Op-Ed, Sept. 21, 1993, at B-3; President Clinton's address to the General Assembly, Sept. 27, 1993.

of the Sea Conference, called for the creation of a new global Environmental Protection Agency.[214] A Preparatory Committee for the World Summit for Social Development, planning a world conference in 1995 to address major issues of human poverty, called for participation of non-governmental organizations and requested the Secretary-General to appoint internationally acknowledged experts in their personal capacities to offer professional guidance.[215] Von Peter Leuprecht, Human Rights Director of the Council of Europe, made similar recommendations regarding more effective human rights protection in the European Community. [216]

Various UN agencies were being mobilized to coordinate their efforts for enhanced social justice but what seemed lacking was Security Council involvement to give teeth to the many Assembly recommendations. Without a Security Council mandate, ECOSOC or Assembly recommendations may - and often do - remain ineffective. Backed by the Security Council exercising its enforcement powers under Charter Chapter VII, vital recommendations acquire the force of law.

The proposed new Security Council resolutions for improved *laws*, *courts* and *enforcement* help to fill the gap in the prevailing structure for peace. The "Guiding Principles" to govern the adoption and implementation of Security Council resolutions, designed to insure a gradual and coordinated approach, apply to the creation of every new Security Council structure for peace enforcement, including the proposed new UN Social Justice Agency.[217]

DRAFT RESOLUTION CREATING A UN SOCIAL JUSTICE AGENCY

THE SECURITY COUNCIL, acting pursuant to its authority under the Charter of the United Nations, declares that all members of the organization are bound by the following resolution:

ARTICLE 1- The Secretary-General of the United Nations is instructed to establish a UN Social Justice Agency (UNSJA) as an

---

214 See *World Federalist,* **spring 1990 at 5.**

215 *Report of the Preparatory Committee for the World Summit for Social Development,* GAOR Forty-eight Sess., Supp. No. 24 (A/48/24) 5 May 1993.

216 V.P. Leuprecht,*Der Schütz der socialen Rechte im Rahmen des Europarats, (Schriftenreihe der Hochschule Speyer, Band 109)* 1993.

217 See Chapter Seven, Section D.

organ of the Security Council to help implement and carry out the Security Council Resolution for Enhancing Social Justice.

ARTICLE 2- UNSJA shall serve as the agent of the Security Council in observing and reporting on the implementation of all UN activities related to the implementation of programs and goals referred to in the Resolution for Enhancing Social Justice, and shall advise, coordinate and assist in achieving such programs and goals in every feasible way. Subject to Security Council and Secretary-General approval, it may set up such subsidiary organs as it deems necessary for the fulfillment of its mission.

ARTICLE 3- The Secretary-General shall invite nominations for the position of Director of the UN Social Justice Agency from members of all the UN Committees or Commission or other agencies dealing with social justice functions, as well as from other competent organizations or agencies. The list of nominees shall be screened by the UN Secretary-General and reduced to no more than 20 and no less than 10. The appointment shall be made by majority vote of the Security Council and shall also require approval by a majority of the members of the United Nations Economic and Social Council.

ARTICLE 4 - The Security Council will use all necessary means to enforce the recommendation of UNSJA whenever the Council decides that failure to do so would constitute a threat to the peace.

COMMENTARY:

Article 1 charges the Secretary-General to establish the UNSJA, thereby reinforcing a system of checks-and-balances.

Article 2 is intended to make clear that UNSJA is an organ of the Security Council, with observing, reporting, advising and coordinating functions. Its recommendations will be backed by Security Council enforcement action only when the Council decides that such enforcement action is needed to avert or halt a threat to peace, as provided in Article 4. Subsidiary organs of UNSJA, necessary to cope with the varied economic, social and environmental goals, require Secretary-General approval as well as the vote of nine members of the Security Council, without veto, since it is a procedural matter under Charter Article 27.

Article 3 is intended to reinforce the system of checks-and-balances in selecting the Director of UNSJA. Nominees may come from an almost unlimited variety of sources. The Secretary-General, through his power to limit the final list, plays a key role. Requiring majority approval from both General Assembly and ECOSOC gives both of those organs a significant voice in the selection and diminishes the risk of domineering control by the Security Council.

Article 4 reinforces the authority of the United Nations Social Justice Agency (UNSJA) yet retains ultimate enforcement power in the hands of the Security Council - where the Charter put it.

D - *Evaluation*

The twelve proposed resolutions seek to strengthen international *laws,* international *courts* and international law *enforcement* by asserting the Security Council's primary responsibility and authority to maintain or restore international peace and security.

(a) International *laws* are strengthened by five resolutions:

(1) Mandating peaceful settlement and the non-use of force for the settlement of international disputes - without exceptions;

(2) Clarifying, without ambiguity or evasion, what is meant by international aggression;

(3) Stopping crimes against humanity by defining the scope of the offence and prohibiting it without equivocation;

(4) Requiring, as a matter of binding law, that all nations disarm under effective international controls in a manner that does not jeopardIze the security of anyone.

(5) Stipulating the minimum standards of human dignity and environmental protection to which all peoples are legally entitled.

(b) International Courts are strengthened by three resolutions:

(1) Increasing the authority of the International Court of Justice by having the Security Council request advisory opinions and by the Council ordering parties to turn to the court where legal disputes are not resolved by other peaceful means and continue to pose a threat to peace.

(2) Creating a permanent International Criminal Court to hold personally accountable - after fair trial - any individuals who defy international criminal law or who threaten peace by their violations of international law.

(3) Establishing a World Tribunal for Social Justice that can judicially determine whether universally accepted norms of international behavior regarding human rights, including economic rights and environmental rights, are being violated to such an extent that they constitute a threat to peace.

(c) International law *enforcement* is strengthened by four resolutions:

(1) Creating a Disarmament Enforcement Agency to help implement and supervise the Security Council mandate requiring all nations to disarm under effective international controls.

(2) Creating a Sanctions Agency to help organize and implement the Security Council mandate that economic and other peaceful sanctions will replace national military force as a means of peace enforcement.

(3) Creating a UN military force to replace national armed forces as the means for enforcing international law should peaceful methods fail to maintain peace and security.

(4) Creating a new Social Justice Agency to help monitor and correct universally recognized human rights and environmental abuses that threaten peace.

We come thus to the conclusion of recommendations for the creation of 12 new peace-enforcement measures or structures designed to enable the Security Council to carry out its primary responsibility under the UN Charter. By combining the twelve resolutions, adding a brief preamble and omitting repetitive clauses, a possible new regime for peace may become more clearly visible. To enable the reader to see the complete picture in its totality as one integrated and comprehensive plan for peace, a consolidated omnibus resolution -incorporating all the others - is hereby presented.

E - A SINGLE CONSOLIDATED RESOLUTION FOR PEACE

THE SECURITY COUNCIL,

RECALLING that, pursuant to Article 24 of the United Nations Charter, all Members of the United Nations have conferred on the Security Council "primary responsibility for the maintenance of international peace and security" and they have all agreed that "in carrying out its duties under this responsibility the Security Council acts on their behalf",

RECALLING that, pursuant to Article 25 of the United Nations Charter: "The Members of the United Nations agree to accept and carry out the decisions of the Security Council",

RECALLING that, pursuant to Article 26 of the United Nations Charter, the Security Council: "In order to promote the establishment and maintenance of international peace and security with the least diversion for armaments of the world's human and economic resources.. shall be responsible for... the establishment of a system for the regulation of armaments",

RECALLING that, pursuant to Article 29 of the United Nations Charter: "The Security Council may establish such subsidiary organs as it deems necessary for the performance of its functions",

RECALLING that, pursuant to Article 33 of the United Nations Charter: "The parties to any dispute, the continuation of which is likely to endanger the maintenance of international peace and security" are required to settle their dispute by "peaceful means of their own choice",

RECALLING that, pursuant to Articles 36 and 37 of the United Nations Charter, the Security Council may at any stage of a dispute which is likely to endanger the maintenance of international peace and security, "recommend appropriate procedures or methods of adjustment," or "such terms of settlement as it may consider appropriate",

RECALLING that, pursuant to Article 39 of the United Nations Charter, the Security Council is mandated to "determine the existence of any threat to the peace, breach of the peace , or act of aggression" and authorized to "decide what measures shall be taken in accordance with Article 41 and 42, to maintain or restore international peace and security",

RECALLING that, pursuant to Articles 41 and 42 of the United Nations Charter, the Security Council, to give effect to its decisions, is authorized to call upon the Members of the United Nations for complete interruption of economic relations, communications and diplomatic relations, and is also authorized to take action "by air, sea or land forces as may be necessary to maintain or restore international peace and security," including "operations by air, sea, or land forces of Members of the United Nations",

RECALLING that, pursuant to Article 43 of the United Nations Charter, agreements regarding the forces to be made available to the Security Council for the maintenance of international peace and security "shall be negotiated as soon as possible on the initiative of the Security Council",

NOTING with regret that, despite the provisions contained in Articles 33 through 38 of the United Nations Charter, requiring nations to settle disputes only by peaceful means, nations have continued to use armed force in violation of the Charter,

NOTING with regret that, despite the provisions contained in Article 25 of the United Nations Charter, requiring the Members to carry out the decisions of the Security Council, some Members have violated their agreement and failed to carry out Security Council decisions - as they were legally obliged to do.

NOTING with regret that, despite the provisions of Article 26 of the United Nations Charter, calling for the establishment of a system for the regulation of armaments with the least diversion of the world's human and economic resources, it has not been possible to establish such a system and the arms race continues to drain resources vitally needed for human betterment,

NOTING with regret that, despite Articles 42 through 50 of the United Nations Charter, requiring all Members to cooperate and comply with Security Council mandates for the creation of military forces to be made available to the Security Council for the purpose of maintaining international peace and security, it has not been possible to create such a system as envisaged by the Charter.

ACKNOWLEDGING with regret that, despite the primary responsibility vested in it by the United Nations Charter and agreed to by all the Members, it has not been possible for the Security Council to maintain international peace and security.

ACKNOWLEDGING with regret that, despite the fundamental purpose set forth in the opening paragraph of Article 1 of the United Nations Charter, to maintain peace "in conformity with the principles of justice and international law," it has not been possible for the Security Council to maintain peace in accordance with justice and international law.

ACKNOWLEDGING with regret that aggression has never been clearly defined, nor has it been possible to reach a common agreement on the definition of terrorism and other crimes against humanity that may threaten peace.

ACKNOWLEDGING with regret that gross disparities in economic and social conditions in various parts of the world threaten world security and that environmental hazards pose a threat to future generations.

MINDFUL of the opening sentence of the Preamble to the United Nations Charter, which expresses the determination of The Peoples of the United Nations, "to save succeeding generations from the scourge of war" and to reaffirm "the dignity and worth of the human person",

DESIROUS of enhancing the effectiveness of the Security Council in maintaining international peace and security for the benefit of all nations, peoples and individuals, and in conformity with the fundamental purposes and principles of the United Nations Charter,

DECIDES to adopt this omnibus single consolidated resolution to: A- clarify and strengthen international laws of peace, B- strengthen the International Court of Justice and create new international courts for peace and C-strengthen the means and methods for more effective international law enforcement on behalf of peace.

TO THAT END the Security Council affirms and declares that all Members of the United Nations are bound by the following twelve resolutions:

A - Five Resolutions to Strengthen International Laws of Peace:

RESOLUTION MANDATING PEACEFUL SETTLEMENT

ARTICLE 1- All states, groups or individuals are legally prohibited from using armed force for the settlement of controversies of any kind, or for any purpose not specifically authorized by the Security Council of the United Nations.

ARTICLE 2- All states, groups or individuals are legally bound to settle all disputes or conflicts of whatever nature or origin by peaceful means in accordance with Chapter VI of the UN Charter.

ARTICLE 3- There may be no exceptions whatsoever, under any circumstances, to the mandates of Articles 1 and 2.

RESOLUTION CLEARLY DEFINING AGGRESSION

ARTICLE 1- The use of armed force in violation of the above Security Council Resolution Mandating Peaceful Settlement is a breach of the peace. It shall also constitute an act of aggression if it includes:

(a) Invasion or attack by armed forces.

(b) Bombardment from land, sea or air, using nuclear, chemical, bacteriological or any other weapons capable of destroying human life directly or indirectly.

(c) Blockade of ports, coasts, cities or regions.

(d) Sending armed bands, groups or mercenaries to carry out acts of armed force in violation of Security Council prohibitions.

ARTICLE 2- No consideration of whatever nature, whether political, economic, military or otherwise, may serve as a justification for aggression.

ARTICLE 3- An act of aggression is a crime against international peace. No territorial acquisition or special advantage resulting from aggression shall be recognized as lawful. No nation, group or individual shall be allowed to benefit from any act of aggression.

RESOLUTION PROHIBITING CRIMES AGAINST HUMANITY

ARTICLE 1- The following acts, when determined by the Security Council to constitute a threat to the peace, are absolutely prohibited as Crimes Against Humanity:

(a) Genocide, by which is meant any act committed with intent to destroy, in whole or in substantial part, any racial, national, linguistic, religious or political group of human beings. Such acts shall include: killing or causing serious physical harm or inflicting conditions calculated to bring about the destruction of the group.

(b) Terrorism, by which is meant any threat or illegal act of violence intended to coerce, intimidate or cause a state of panic, fear, insecurity or terror among a civilian population. Such acts shall include political assassinations, hostage taking, dangerous interference with civilian aircraft, destruction of public buildings, systematic kidnaping, massive physical abuse or torture and similar acts of illegal violence designed to terrorize the public.

(c) Apartheid, by which is meant the practice of racial discrimination and segregation on a scale to constitute a threat to international peace and security, including acts for the purpose of establishing and maintaining domination of one racial group of persons over any other racial group of persons and systematically oppressing them.

ARTICLE 2- No consideration of whatever nature, whether political, economic, military or otherwise, may serve as a justification for crimes against humanity.

RESOLUTION ENDING THE ARMS RACE

ARTICLE 1: All states shall have at their disposal only those
non-nuclear armaments, forces, facilities, and establishments as
are agreed by the Security Council to be necessary to maintain
internal order and protect the personal security of its citizens.

ARTICLE 2: States shall support and provide manpower for a
United Nations Police Force when called for by the Security
Council.

ARTICLE 3: The Security Council shall establish rules to implement the program for general and complete disarmament, including:

(a) Disbanding of armed forces, dismantling of military establishments, including bases, cessation of the production of armaments as well as their liquidation or conversion to peaceful uses;

(b) Elimination of all stockpiles of nuclear, chemical, bacteriological, and other weapons of mass destruction and cessation of
the production of such weapons;

(c) Elimination of all means of delivery of weapons of mass
destruction;

(d) Abolishment of the organization and institutions designed to
organize the military effort of states or other entities, cessation
of military training, and closing of all military training institutions;

(e) Discontinuance of military expenditures.

ARTICLE 4: The disarmament program mandated above shall be implemented in a sequence until it is completed, with each measure and stage carried out within specified time-limits after verification by the Security Council that there has been compliance, that no military advantage has been gained and that security is ensured equally for all.

ARTICLE 5: All disarmament measures will be implemented from beginning to end under such strict and effective international control as will provide firm assurance that all parties are honoring the obligations set forth herein. Any organ created by the Security Council to implement control over and inspection of disarmament shall be assured unrestricted access, without veto, to all places as necessary for the purpose of effective verification.

ARTICLE 6: During and after the implementation of general and complete disarmament, the Security Council shall take the necessary measures to maintain international peace and security, including the use of economic and other sanctions, UN peacekeeping forces, other forces placed at its disposal pursuant to Article 2 above, and all other means it may consider necessary to deter or suppress any threat or use of arms in violation of the purposes and principles of the United Nations.

ARTICLE 7: In carrying out the program of comprehensive and complete disarmament, the Security Council, and whatever organs it may create to implement the program of disarmament, sanctions or policing, shall consult with the General Assembly and with existing agencies dealing with similar problems with a view to making implementation effective in the widest possible area at the earliest possible date with the minimum possible economic hardship to persons and industries affected by the transformation.

RESOLUTION ENHANCING SOCIAL JUSTICE

ARTICLE 1- Every state has the duty to cooperate in promoting a steady and increasing expansion and liberalization of world trade and improvement in the welfare and living standards of all peoples, in particular those of developing countries.

ARTICLE 2- The protection, preservation and enhancement of the environment for the present and future generations is the responsibility of all states. All states have the responsibility to ensure that activities within their jurisdiction or control do not cause damage to the environment of other states or of areas beyond the limits of national jurisdiction.

ARTICLE 3- All human beings are entitled to a minimum standard of human dignity, including: clean air and water, food, shelter, medical care, education, gainful employment and religious and political freedom.

B - Three Resolutions to Strengthen International Courts:

RESOLUTION ENHANCING THE WORLD COURT

ARTICLE 1: Any legal dispute which the parties have not settled by peaceful means, and the continuation of which the Security Council determines is likely to endanger the maintenance of international peace and security, must be submitted to the International Court of Justice for binding decision.

ARTICLE 2: In all cases where the Security Council determines that failure of any of the parties to honor a decision of the International Court of Justice poses a threat to the peace, the Security Council will use all necessary means to see that the decision is enforced.

ARTICLE 3: No national of a party to a dispute which is the subject of an opinion or decision by the International Court of Justice may vote on such decision or on any Security Council measures in enforcement thereof.

RESOLUTION CREATING AN INTERNATIONAL CRIMINAL COURT

ARTICLE 1- The Secretary-General of the United Nations is instructed to establish an International Criminal Court as an organ of the Security Council.

ARTICLE 2- The International Criminal Court shall be competent to deal with all crimes that the Security Council determines constitute a threat to the peace, breach of the peace or act of aggression. Such crimes shall include violations of any of the twelve Security Council resolutions referred to herein.

ARTICLE 3- Judges of the International Criminal Court shall be elected in accordance with the procedures laid down in the UN Charter for the election of judges for the International Court of Justice. Nominees may also be submitted by non-governmental organizations, universities or other qualified sources. The judges shall create their own rules of procedure consistent with the requirements of fair trial and the most efficient methods for carrying out the Court's assignment.

RESOLUTION CREATING A WORLD TRIBUNAL FOR SOCIAL JUSTICE

ARTICLE 1- The Secretary-General of the United Nations is instructed to establish a World Tribunal for Social Justice as an organ of the Security Council. It may sit on an *ad hoc* or permanent basis, as may be necessary to discharge its responsibilities.

ARTICLE 2- The World Tribunal for Social Justice shall be competent to decide all legal questions concerning the interpretation of the Security Council Resolution Enhancing Social Justice, or any other human rights violation that the Security Council determines constitutes a threat to peace.

ARTICLE 3- Judges of the World Tribunal for Social Justice shall be elected by the Economic and Social Council in accordance with procedures laid down for the election of judges for the International Court of Justice. Nominees may be submitted by non-governmental organizations, universities or other qualified sources. The judges shall create their own rules of procedure consistent with the requirements of fair trial and the most efficient methods for carrying out the Court's assignment.

C - Four Resolutions to Strengthen Peace Enforcement:

RESOLUTION CREATING A
UN DISARMAMENT ENFORCEMENT AGENCY

ARTICLE 1- The Secretary-General of the United Nations is instructed to establish a UN Disarmament Enforcement Agency (UNDEA) as an organ of the Security Council to carry out the disarmament objectives of Security Council **Resolution Ending the Arms Race.**

ARTICLE 2- Pursuant to Article 3 of the Security Council Resolution Ending the Arms Race, UNDEA shall serve as the agent of the Security Council in supervising the implementation of the program of general and complete disarmament as set forth in that resolution and in drawing up such rules as shall be necessary for that purpose.

ARTICLE 3- The Secretary-General shall invite nominations for the position of Director of the UN Disarmament Enforcement Agency from members of the UN Disarmament Commission as well as other competent organizations or agencies. The list of nominees shall be screened by the UN Secretary-General and reduced to no more than 20 and no less than 10. The appointment shall be made by majority vote of the Security Council and require approval by a majority of the members of the General Assembly.

RESOLUTION CREATING A UN SANCTIONS AGENCY

ARTICLE 1- The Secretary-General of the United Nations is instructed to establish a UN Sanctions Agency (UNSA) as an organ of the Security Council to carry out the sanctions objectives of the Security Council Resolution for Ending the Arms Race.

ARTICLE 2- Pursuant to Article 6 of Security Council Resolution for Ending the Arms Race, UNSA shall serve as the agent of the Security Council in supervising the implementation of the program of economic and other sanctions as set forth in that resolution and in drawing up such rules as shall be necessary for that purpose.

ARTICLE 3- The Secretary-General shall invite nominations for the position of Director of the UN Sanctions Agency from members of the Special Security Council Committees dealing with sanctions, as well as from other competent organizations or agencies. The list of nominees shall be screened by the UN Secretary-General and reduced to no more than 20 and no less than 10. The appointment shall be made by majority vote of the Security Council and require approval by a majority of the members of the General Assembly.

RESOLUTION CREATING A UN POLICE AGENCY

ARTICLE 1- The Secretary-General of the United Nations is instructed to establish a UN Police Agency (UNPA) as an organ of the Security Council to carry out all measures related to peacekeeping forces and other forces recruited or placed at its disposal pursuant to the Security Council Resolution for Ending the Arms Race.

ARTICLE 2- Pursuant to Article 6 of the Security Council Resolution Ending the Arms Race, UNPA shall serve as the agent of the Security Council in supervising the implementation of all programs involving peacekeeping forces or other forces as set forth in that resolution and in drawing up such rules as shall be necessary for that purpose.

ARTICLE 3- The Secretary-General shall invite nominations for the position of Director of the UN Police Agency from members of all the Security Council Committees or Missions dealing with UN Peacekeeping functions, as well as from other competent organizations or agencies. The list of nominees shall be screened by the UN Secretary-General and reduced to no more than 20 and no less than 10. The appointment shall be made by majority vote of the Security Council and require approval by a majority of the members of the General Assembly.

RESOLUTION CREATING A UN SOCIAL JUSTICE AGENCY

ARTICLE 1- The Secretary-General of the United Nations is instructed to establish a UN Social Justice Agency (UNSJA) as an organ of the Security Council to help implement and carry out the Security Council Resolution for Enhancing Social Justice.

ARTICLE 2- UNSJA shall serve as the agent of the Security Council in observing and reporting on the implementation of all UN activities related to the implementation of programs and goals referred to in the Resolution for Enhancing Social Justice, and shall advise, coordinate and assist in achieving such programs and goals in every feasible way. Subject to Security Council and Secretary-General approval, it may set up such subsidiary organs as it deems necessary for the fulfillment of its mission.

ARTICLE 3- The Secretary-General shall invite nominations for the position of Director of the UN Social Justice Agency from members of all the UN Committees or Commissions or other agencies dealing with social justice functions, as well as from other competent organizations or agencies. The list of nominees shall be screened by the UN Secretary-General and reduced to no more than 20 and no less than 10. The appointment shall be made by majority vote of the Security Council and shall also require approval by a majority of the members of the United Nations Economic and Social Council.

GENERAL PROVISIONS

ARTICLE 1- Violators of any of the provisions of this Single Consolidated Resolution for Peace are subject to individual criminal punishment. Leaders, organizers, instigators, and accomplices participating in the formulation or execution of a common plan or conspiracy to violate this resolution shall be held criminally responsible. Those who aid and abet persons accused of violating these rules, either before or after the commission of the crime, will share criminal responsibility.

ARTICLE 2- The interpretation of these rules and their implementation and enforcement shall be the responsibility of the Security Council or such organs as it may designate for that purpose.

ARTICLE 3- The Security Council will use all necessary means to enforce the provisions of this resolution when it determines that their violation poses a threat to the peace.

COMMENTARY

The Preamble has been added to the omnibus resolution (although no preamble was suggested for each individual resolution) to establish the general frame of reference by citing the specific Charter provisions that authorize Council action and which have not been fulfilled. The acknowledgement of shortcomings indicates the reason why the resolution is needed. The consolidation of all twelve resolutions in one omnibus resolution is similar to the approach adopted effectively by the Security Council in Resolution 687, of 3 April 1991 imposing an assorted variety of obligations on Iraq in response to its war against Kuwait.

The Articles of each Resolution are commented upon as each separate resolution was considered. No additional comments are deemed necessary, particularly since the articles are intended as suggestions rather than definitive texts.

Even if it is recognized that the proposed new Security Council Regime for Peace would be a much better, easier and faster way to move toward a world of human dignity and security than any other pending proposal, one must still find the way to have such a plan accepted by the world community. It is to that problem that we now turn our attention.

CHAPTER NINE
WHERE DO WE GO FROM HERE?

> Out of sheer necessity, the peoples of the world must marshal
> unprecedented cooperative efforts to create a climate for lasting
> peace. It requires renewed respect for the moral constraints on
> violence, deceit and lawlessness. These constraints, acknow-
> ledged in every religious and moral tradition, are indispensable
> for maintaining cooperation in any community. Too often, how-
> ever, they are seen as inessential in politics.
>
> Sissela Bok, Christmas 1989.[1]

War is not inevitable, peace is not inevitable and human survival is not
inevitable. Whether we kill each other or help each other depends on us.
The assumption on which this book is based is that persons everywhere
share a common interest in peace and human dignity. If it can be demonstrated that the peace system herein proposed is much more likely to
enhance human rights and global survival than the current international
chaos and cruelty, presumably human reason will prevail and the needed
changes will be supported and eventually accepted. But it's not that simple.

The historical record hardly justifies the conclusion that humans will
behave rationally. It should always have been obvious that peace is better
than war and yet the war system still dominates and terrorizes humankind.
More than a simple appeal to reason is required to bring about the changes
needed to enhance human security and well-being. The Security Council is
already legally bound under the UN Charter to maintain international
peace and security. What does it take to generate the wisdom and the
political will for the Council to fulfill its existing obligation to create a more
peaceful world order?

A - Changing Entrenched Perceptions

If Security Council members are not responsive to human needs perhaps they will be more responsive to human demands. Before the public can
assert itself, it must know what it wants. Almost every adult already has a
pre-conceived mind-set regarding the problems of world peace. Except
among the young, most people are indifferent, skeptical or even cynical
about their capacity to influence the future. Many existing perceptions will
have to be altered if the power of the public is to be realized and brought to

---

1   N.Y.Times Op-Ed, Dec. 25, 1989. Sissela Bok teaches philosophy at Brandeis University
     and is the author of "A Strategy for Peace" (1989).

bear on national leaders who now hold the reins of political decision in their hands.

There are those who firmly believe that war is inevitable as part of man's nature - nothing can be done to change it. Others are convinced that not only is war an expression of Divine will, but indeed war is necessary to bring out the finest qualities of man's character - nothing *should* be done about it. Others suggest that the war system is so obviously obsolete that it will atrophy and disappear by itself. Besides, recent Security Council action in opposing aggression and inhumanity indicates that there is no need to rock a UN boat that is finally sailing in the right direction - nothing more needs to be done. Still others are convinced that something *must* be done - and done soon - to avert the worldwide catastrophe that looms on the horizon. Let us consider the merit of each position.

(1) The View That Nothing Can Be Done:

Those who throw up their hands in despair argue that humans have always killed humans - which proves that there is something inherently brutal in human nature and that will never change. The logic is, of course, fallacious. The fact that something has not happened in the past is certainly no proof that it can not happen in the future. If that pervasive and pessimistic theory were true, slavery, that existed for centuries (justified by the false notion that some humans are by nature born to work for a superior race) would still be acceptable. Women would still be regarded as inferior to males. Duelling would still be considered the most honorable response of a gentleman to an insult. No persuasive evidence leads to the Hobbesian conclusions that man is inherently brutish and that a dog-eat-dog mentality condemns humanity to a man-eat-man existence forever.

The fact that an opinion is widely held does not establish its validity. A few centuries ago, practically everyone believed that the earth was the center of the universe. Failure to accept that scientifically false dogma (devoutly believed by millions of the faithful) led to excommunication, torture or burning at the stake. Ridiculed and intimidated "star-gazers" were the ones who finally dared to liberate humanity from entrenched misperceptions. It took the knowledge, determination, and persuasion of a few dedicated and courageous people - often at peril to their lives - to alter the course of history.

The Polish astronomer Copernicus, the Danish astronomer Tycho Brahe, the German Kepler and the Italian Galileo were among leading "stargazers" of the 16th century. Today, in the corridor leading to the library at the United Nations, a stone bust of Copernicus honors this courageous and pioneering thinker who dared to speak the truth when universal opinion held the contrary to be immutable. Everyone believed the world was flat - until a few daring sailors circumnavigated the globe. Until the Wright brothers invented the airplane, no one believed that man could fly

- let alone land on the moon and explore extraterrestrial space. The examples are countless to show that what is considered impossible, and what is blindly accepted as inevitable or unchallengeable truth, can be altered when people learn to think for themselves, and dare to stand up for what they know is right.

(2) *The View That Nothing Should Be Done:*

One of the fundamental difficulties of getting a new peace system accepted may be exemplified by an interesting exchange of letters that took place in 1880 between a distinguished Professor at the University of Heidelberg, Dr. Johan Caspar Bluntschli (originally of Switzerland) and the celebrated Prussian Field Marshal Count von Moltke in Berlin. Bluntschli had drawn up a code setting forth the laws of peace and had proposed a Federation of European States to eliminate war and maintain permanent peace in Europe. The Professor asked the hero of the Franco-Prussian War for his views. Von Moltke, the highest ranking German army officer, replied with some disdain:

> Permanent peace is a dream, and not even a nice one, and war is a link in God's world order. Within it are embraced the noblest virtues of mankind: courage, sacrifice, loyalty to duty, and willingness to risk one's life. Without war, the world would sink into materialism.[2]

Von Moltke was credited with Germany's victory over France in 1871 but his glorification of war would eventually cost Germany and the world dearly. The philosophy of the great German Field Marshal led to his country's devastation and produced two world wars that killed over 60 million people.

Views similar to von Moltke's still prevail in many parts of the world today. There is probably little that can be done to change rigid and entrenched perceptions about the desirability and glory of war. Fortunately not all military leaders believe that war is glory rather than gory. Quite the contrary - those who have fought the battles of modern warfare share the view of General Sherman that "War is Hell."[3] General Douglas MacArthur wrote in his memoirs: "For years I have believed that war should be abolished as an outmoded means of settling disputes between nations."[4] On 26 Jan. 1955, he told the American Legion: " The next great advance in the

---

2   J.C.BLUNTSCHLI, *GESAMMELTE KLEINE SCHRIFTEN* (1881) at 271 (Translation of citation by B. Ferencz); *See* FERENCZ, ENFORCING INT. L. vol.1 pp.30-31.

3   Attributed to U.S. Civil War hero General William T. Sherman; *see* C.HURD, TREASURY OF GREAT AMERICAN QUOTATIONS (1964) at 155.

4   D.A MacARTHUR, REMINISCENCES (1964) at 303.

evolution of civilization cannot take place until war is abolished.[5] General Eisenhower's farewell address, as he left the U.S. presidency, referred to the malignant power of "the military-industrial complex" and warned the nation:

> Disarmament with mutual honor and confidence is a continuing imperative. Together we must learn to compose differences, not with arms, but with intellect and decent purpose...another war could utterly destroy this civilization.[6]

A host of modern military men - concerned for the lives of their troops and the safety of their country - have joined hands to support only peaceful solutions to future world problems.[7] An American organization of war veterans (whose membership is increasing) has called for the abolition of war.[8]

Those who still adhere to the antiquated notion that power comes only from the muzzle of a gun are entitled to their opinion - as long as they don't act on it. In a democratic world, hopefully, those who wish to rule by force can be reduced to a small minority without power of political decision. No people - and no nation - can be secure until everyone is secure. Those who place their faith in arms must come to realize that the only real victor in war is Death.

(3) The View That Nothing More Needs to be Done:

There are those who are inclined to do nothing because they are convinced that combat is such an archaic method of resolving disputes that it must fall of its own dead weight. They note that there have been no wars between nuclear powers, democracies don't go to war against each other, and the UN and Security Council have begun to do their job of deterring aggression. According to Political Scientist Anatol Rapoport, the modern war system is an unscientific "superstition" and "peace is an idea whose time has come."[9]

---

5   Cited in M. Sommer, *An Emerging Consensus: Common Security Through Qualitative Disarmament*, published by the Fund for Peace (1988) at 1.

6   Eisenhower's speech of Jan. 17, 1961 is reprinted in *U.S. News and World Report*, Jan. 30, 1961 at 68-71.

7   Admiral Gene R. La Rocque, Director of the Center for Defense Information in Washington D.C. has been in the forefront of former military leaders seeking to end the war system. *See* J. KIDD (retired Major General U.S. Air Force) THE STRATEGIC COOPERATION INITIATIVE (1988).

8   *See Abolish War, The Last Campaign*, published by Veterans for Peace, Portland Maine, (1992).

9   A.RAPOPORT, PEACE, AN IDEA WHOSE TIME HAS COME (1992) at 199.

Every thinking person must comprehend that the moral, legal or political justifications for war, that may have been valid centuries ago, are now obsolete. No medieval theologian could possibly have anticipated today's technological capacity to annihilate all living things, or modern warfare's inability to avoid victimizing large numbers of innocent non-combatants. No scholar of antiquity could have foreseen the financial and social cost and enormous environmental damage caused by modern warfare. Today's "total war" - directed at civilian and economic targets - can not possibly be "proportionate" or "just" on any moral, theological or traditional legal basis.[10]

Just because the arguments against modern warfare are sound does not mean that their validity will be universally accepted - or even considered. The cynically indifferent suffer from a form of mental paralysis that may be incurable. (Hopefully, that potentially fatal disease is not too widespread and a cure can be found.) It can not be denied that relatively few persons give much thought to the issues of war and peace on which the duration and quality of their lives and those of their children actually depend. The future seems as uncontrollable as it is unpredictable and most people are engrossed in more immediate problems of their daily lives. They take the easy road of leaving difficult political decisions to the politicians. They have not learned the lesson of history that blind reliance on entrenched bureaucrats who seek no change is a path that leads straight over the precipice.

(4) *The View That Something New Must Be Done:*

There are those who see the carnage and insecurity all around them and remember the adage: "All that is necessary for evil to triumph is for good people to do nothing." Persons who are not prepared to accept the world as it is, insist that something new must be done to change the way in which global problems that threaten peace and human dignity are now managed. They note the hesitation of the Security Council to intervene in crisis situations until public demand is overwhelming. They point to unalterable political machinations that still encumber United Nations decisions and the absence of clear vision and direction that - despite some progress - continues to confound effective international action for peace.

Those who feel that corrective measures are imperative are convinced that failure to respond promptly to eliminate perils can be fatal to large segments of human society. Even though no one can predict the source of future conflicts - whether between regions, religions, economic blocs or (as Samuel P. Huntington of Harvard suggests) between civilizations, those

---

10 *See* J.T. JOHNSON, JUST WAR TRADITION AND THE RESTRAINT OF WAR (1982); M. WALZER, JUST AND UNJUST WARS (1977).

who demand reform conclude that - to survive - people will have to learn to coexist with each other better than they have in the past, or than they do today, if they expect to be here tomorrow.[11]

It is our theme that if we are to master the future, we must replace politics and passion by reason and decide issues on the pragmatic basis of what best serves not only the temporary personal or national interest but also the permanent human interest. Morton Deutsch of Yale wrote:

> ...[T]he old notion of 'national security' must be replaced by the new notion of 'mutual security'...It is difficult to give up old, well established beliefs even when they have become dysfunctional until the new beliefs have been implemented and seen to work. We must begin to implement the idea of mutual security and give it a chance to work.[12]

The only viable option is to build a new order for a peaceful world.

The United States, a rich country, born in response to the human demand for freedom, yet having created the atom bomb and being the only nation ever to have used it to destroy other human beings, has a special responsibility to help maintain peace in the world. Jim Leach, Republican Congressman from Iowa, referred to the theologian Rheinhold Niebuhr's 1950 observation that the price of our survival was our ability to give leadership to the free world. Leach went on to say:

> Today, the price of the prosperity of the free world still depends on our ability and willingness to lead. No other society has the capacity or inclination to light freedom's lamp in quite the same way; nor is any other as capable of combining self-interest with a genuine historically-rooted concern for others. For the United States to deny its transnational responsibilities and thwart the development of internationalist approaches to problem-solving is to jeopardize a future of peace and prosperity for the planet.[13]

A new global agenda for the 1990's has been advanced by Gareth Evans, Australia's perceptive Foreign Minister, a distinguished lawyer and editor of books on foreign affairs. He assigned a team of highly qualified experts to analyze how the UN might best achieve its goals and to make specific proposals for improving the structures and processes of the UN

---

11 *See* S.P. Huntington, *The Coming Clash of Civilizations, or the West against the Rest*, N.Y. Times op-ed. June 6, 1991 p.19.

12 M. DEUTSCH, DISTRIBUTIVE JUSTICE (1985) at 282.

13 Final Report of the US Commission on Improving the Effectiveness of the UN (1993) at 15.

system. His excellent book, published after September 1993, merits worlwide support.[14]

B - *Mobilizing Public Opinion for Peace*

In the last analysis, war or peace is a choice of personal values. Individuals everywhere must decide which values are more important to them, nationalism or survival. People should be willing to surrender their hatreds rather than their lives - the choice is theirs. They must decide whether the rule of law and order is in everyone's long-term interest or whether they prefer the present "wild-west" system that allows each sovereign state to grab whatever it can to further its own short-term political goals. The uninformed or misguided public must be re-educated to recognize that their own self-interest requires a new world order that enables all to live with at least a minimum standard of human dignity. The time has come for the people to wake up and make up their minds.

As Abdelkader Abbadi has noted:

> A state of peace can only derive from a state of mind, fueled by a higher consciousness, which places a premium on the development of new norms of international life, including international responsibility and new forms of human solidarity. It is the task of the family, the school teacher, the community leaders and the statesman. Together, they can today begin to sow the seeds which would enable future generations to aspire tomorrow to a state of peace.[15]

Blind traditions that have led to major disasters in the past must be replaced by policies and practices capable of reconciling the discords of today. If the public is to be awakened from its lethargy, extraordinary re-educational efforts by many individuals and groups over a sustained period of time will be essential. All of the new techniques of persuasion must be used to mobilize public action in support of the promised new international system capable of maintaining world peace.

Robert Johansen, President of the Institute for World Order, has concluded:

> In a world where system change is desirable and necessary but where dominant institutions resist change, an extraordinary

---

14   G. EEVNAS, COOPERATING FOR PEACE - The Global Agenda for the 1990's and Beyond (1993).

15   A. Abbadi, Prospects for Enhancing international Peace-making at the United Nations, Collected Papers of the University of Zagreb Law School, p.725 (1992).

responsibility falls upon the individual citizen, religious communities, and other non-governmental agencies to bring about the required changes...achieving peace...depends upon a popular movement fueled by our own imagination and willingness to act.[16]

Professor Lung-chu Chen, of Yale and New York Law School, has come to a similar conclusion:

It is largely within the power of people to make choices to shape the constellation of factors and to affect future development in preferred ways...What is required is a grand strategy of simultaneity that would mobilize all participants - groups and individuals - to the common task of human survival and human fulfillment...the common interest of all humanity toward a world community of human dignity calls for ingenuity, goodwill, vigilant endeavor and boundless creativity...[17]

A grand strategy for human survival and fulfillment in a world community of human dignity has been here outlined. It is certainly not intended as the last word - all improvements will be eagerly welcomed. What is called for now is greater awareness, knowledge and agreement about what needs to be done, courage to think independently, a burning desire for a better world and a determined program of positive action that will lead to the desired goals. Fortunately, new educational techniques enhance the possibility that what was not possible in the past may yet prove attainable in the foreseeable future.

(1) The Goals of Peace Education:

The Constitution of the UN Educational, Scientific and Cultural Organization (UNESCO) reminds us: "Since wars begin in the minds of men it is in the minds of men that the defenses of peace must be constructed."[18] The mind can not be changed until the heart is changed. Moderation and tolerance must find a home in the hearts and minds of people everywhere for peace to survive. A society filled with intolerance and hate can not be saved.

---

16 R.C.JOHANSEN, THE NATIONAL INTEREST AND THE HUMAN INTEREST (1980) at 407.See R.J.GLOSSOP, CONFRONTING WAR, (2d ed. 1983) and WORLD FEDERATION? A CRITICAL ANALYSIS OF FEDERAL WORLD GOVERNMENT (1993).

17 L.CHEN, AN INTRODUCTION TO CONTEMPORARY INTERNATIONAL LAW (1989) at 444, 448, 449; See D.V.JONES, CODE OF PEACE - Ethics and Security in the World of the Warlord States (1991).

18 4 UNTS 275, 16 Nov. 1945.

Educating for peace must go beyond the simple dissemination of information or the presentation of new Security Council resolutions. Ervin Staub, Professor of Psychology and a survivor of the Nazi Holocaust, has described what is required for individuals to overcome the feeling of personal helplessness and to be willing to join in efforts aimed at improving the human condition: they must become aware of the intensity and urgency of the needs of others in an interdependent world; they must distinguish long-range from intermediate goals so they can measure and appreciate progress and be less dependent for encouragement upon visible results but continue to persevere because they are convinced their action is necessary and right. According to Professor Staub:

> The improvement of the world must not become an abstraction;
> it must be grounded in the welfare of individual human beings.
> In that framework the future of children, the shared humanity
> of all people, the satisfaction of connection and of helping others
> in need, the ideals of peace and justice, can appeal to many.[19]

Esteemed television journalist Bill Moyers, encourages every community and individual to adopt the philosophy of "live and *help* live" and not just "live and *let* live."[20]

Enlightened self-interest can only be recognized by the enlightened. Those who, through indolence, incapacity or malevolence, remain in the dark can not be expected to support what they can not see or understand. Betty Reardon of Columbia University Teachers College, a leading peace educator, has written:

> Stated most succinctly, the general purpose of peace educa-
> tion...is to promote the development of an authentic planetary
> consciousness that will enable us to function as global citizens
> and to transform the present human condition by changing the
> social structures and the patterns of thought that have created
> it."[21]

Another important goal of peace education is to teach people - and nations - to show greater respect for the rule of law. The UN has proclaimed the 1990's to be "The Decade of International Law" when wider appreciation of international law will be fostered and encouraged by a program of public activities.[22] The public must be taught that the Charter vested them with

---

19 E. Staub, *Transforming the Bystanders: Altruism, Caring and Social Responsibility,* in H.FEIN, Ed., GENOCIDE WATCH (1992) at 180.

20 *Healing the World,* The Stanley Foundation *Courier,* Spring 1993, at 12.

21 B.A REARDON, COMPREHENSIVE   PEACE EDUCATION (1988) at x. *See* A.M. STOMFAY-STITZ, PEACE EDUCATION IN AMERICA, 1828-1990 (1993).

22 *Draft Report of the Working Group,* UN *Decade of International Law,* A/C.6/48/WG/DEC/CRP.1, 28 Oct. 1993.

certain legal rights. National leaders who refuse to accept or support a new legal regime for enforcing peace in accordance with Security Council resolutions should be exposed as lawbreakers who refuse to honor the legal obligations they have freely accepted to abide by and assist Security Council peace enforcement measures. Public condemnation should be the only reward to those who subvert the effort to create a new legal structure designed to enable everyone to live in peace and dignity.

Professor Frowein of Heidleberg has pointed out that although the present system of international law is still weak and depends upon support by the most important and powerful nations, the international community, as such, has developed its own legal rights which places limits on arbitrary action by individual nation states. International lawyers and the media have an obligation to enlighten public opinion that absolute sovereignty is being curbed by the emerging legal entitlement of the human community as a whole.[23]

International lawyers need not fear to stray from the worn-out amorphous paths that led to war and turn instead to "the road less travelled" of true humanity and binding law.[24] They may find inspiration in the teachings of that wise scholar and Judge of the International Court of Justice, Manfred Lachs, who noted the growing importance of law as he called for less parochialism and for people to "do wise things together rather than foolish things separately." In his last book, he concluded:

> It is within the reach of the Teacher of international law -armed with imagination and reason - while relying on true social humanism, to move across new frontiers, to help and inspire, to make the study of international law more humane, and law itself a meaningful part of our culture, an effective instrument of a lawful world, and an important agency for the betterment of mankind.[25]

The ultimate goal of peace education is to persuade the decisionmakers - those who hold political power - that change is necessary. Since very few public leaders have time for detailed study of complicated new proposals, they must rely on experts, civil servants, friends, supporters and voters - who must also be re-educated to think along new lines. Learning peacemaking is everybody's business.

---

23 J.A. Frowein, *Die Staatengemeinschaft als Rechtsbegriff im Völkerrecht*, LJZ (4/1991).

24 *See* M.SCOTT PECK, THE ROAD LESS TRAVELLED (1983).

25 M.LACHS, THE TEACHER IN INTERNATIONAL LAW (1982) at 209. Judge Lachs died in 1993. He was eulogized by leading international lawyers. 87 AJIL 414 (1993).

(2) *The Teaching Institutions:*

Education will require increased efforts in homes, schools, organizations of concerned citizens, the media and all agencies and groups concerned with the betterment of humankind. The process is already under way. Young people throughout the world are learning more about the calamities of war and the advantages of settling conflicts of all kinds in non-violent ways.[26] Public and private schools - secular and religious - national and local civic organizations and many others offer an expanding array of courses, conferences, public events and seminars to enhance public awareness of the problems of war and peace.[27] Harvard University has established a Center for International Affairs, which receives important private funding and includes a Program on Non-violent Sanctions in Conflict and Defense.[28] Peace education is slowly coming of age.[29]

Although many wars have been fought in the name of religion, the overwhelming sentiment of all great religions - Christian, Muslim, Hebraic, Hindu and others - favors a humane society of tolerance and human compassion. Religious institutions of all denominations try to educate their congregations and others about the advantages of peace. Soka Gakkai International, the largest organization of Buddhist lay believers in Japan, has advocated that "Peace Ministries" be included in all national governments.[30] The spiritual Baha'i community of some five million souls calls for a world order founded on the oneness of humankind, in which racism is viewed as a major barrier to peace and unbridled nationalism as a sentiment to be subdued to a wider loyalty to humanity as a whole.[31] The Unitarian Universalist Association, the United Church Board for World Ministries, the United Church of Christ, the United Methodist Church, the U.S. Catholic Mission, the United Synagogue of America and many other religious groups participate in UN peace activities as accredited non-governmental organizations. As a wise old friend of mine, Professor Norman Bentwich of London, wrote many years ago:

---

26 *See* G.RABOW, PEACE THROUGH AGREEMENT (1990).

27 *See* D.THOMAS & M.T.KLARE Eds., PEACE AND WORLD ORDER STUDIES (1989), containing extracts from about 1000 syllabi received from faculties across the United States; D.P.BARASH, INTRODUCTION TO PEACE STUDIES (1991); P.DUNGEN, Ed.,IN SEARCH OF PEACE RESEARCH - Essays by Charles Boasson (1991); T.WOODHOUSE, Ed.,PEACEMAKING IN A TROUBLED WORLD (1991).

28 *See* Harvard Center for International Affairs publication, *TRANSFORMING STRUGGLE*, Strategy and the Global Experience of Nonviolent Direct Action (1992).

29 *See* I.HARRIS, PEACE EDUCATION (1988).

30 *See Proposals on Peace and Disarmament,* submitted to the Third UN Special Session on Disarmament, May 31, 1988; D.IKEDA, A LASTING PEACE (1981).

31 C.LERCHE, Ed., EMERGENCE: DIMENSIONS OF A NEW WORLD ORDER (1991); *See The Promise of World Peace to the Peoples of the World* (1985) also Qtrly *Newsletter* of the Baha'i International Community.

The cooperation of the religions of the world must help to bring about the fulfillment of the prophetic conception of the reign of moral law in the affairs of States, which alone can be a firm foundation of the peace of nations.[32]

(3) Peace Publications:

The publications offered to the public on various facets of peace themes - disarmament, environment, development, human rights, etc. - is overwhelming. Countless books, pamphlets, brochures, articles, flyers, audio and visual tapes flood the mails and markets. They advocate one or another step toward a peaceful world - most of them quite valid and important. But the peace proposals are seldom comprehensive and details of just how a new regime is to be legally structured and put in place is usually unspecified, unclear or unconvincing. Gradually a new vision is forming - but it is a very slow process. Exhortation without explanation is not education.

According to William Harmon, President of the Institute of Noetic Sciences:

Much of the public seems disinterested, apathetic, and resigned or feels powerless to take effective action. ...Slowly but surely people are building up opposition to continuing the same perilous trends...a new vision has been forming: a vision of a world with nuclear disarmament and global security, appreciation of the diversity of Earth's many cultures, wholesome relationships between humans and the planet, elimination of subtle and not-so-subtle oppression of minorities and women, fundamental rights that are guaranteed by universal agreement - a vision of a world at peace.[33]

Johan Galtung, for many years the Director of the International Peace Research Institute in Oslo, published five volumes of his edited essays in peace research and methodology. His search was for a non-exploitive structure for world peace.[34] After much profound study, Galtung expressed his fears about possible abuse of power by centralized authority as the appropriate medium for world peace. His preferred alternatives looked instead to people's organizations rather than governments and to conflict resolution, non-military defence, inner strength and "outer usefulness"

---

32   N.BENTWICH, THE RELIGIOUS FOUNDATIONS OF THE LAW OF NATIONS (1932). See J.KELSAY & J.T.JOHNSON, Eds. JUST WAR AND JIHAD (1991).

33   R.SMOKE & W.HARMAN, PATHS TO PEACE (1987) ix, xiii. See International Peace Research Newsletter, issued quarterly by International Peace Research Association (IPRA) Jan. 1993. R.A.IRWIN, BUILDING A PEACE SYSTEM (1988).

34   J.GALTUNG, ESSAYS IN PEACE RESEARCH (1980).

through non-governmental cooperation.[35] But all of these solutions required greater understanding and acceptance by a public most of whose members remained uninformed and thus unaccepting of new peace proposals. The average person remained untouched or inadequately moved by the flow of peace publications.

(4) *The Power of the Media:*

We live by symbols and slogans. War evokes images of glory, bravery, heroism, "old glory" flying over a battlefield and martial music to churn the blood and stir the spirit. War memorials throughout the world invariably glorify those who perished in pursuit of the goal of peace. No one should denigrate or minimize the heroic sacrifices of brave young people "who gave their last full measure of devotion." But their memory is better served and hallowed by abolishing the institution of war that cost them their lives. The chief purpose of military establishments was formerly to fight wars and to win them. If the memory of those who were killed in wars is to be honored, and their lives not sacrificed in vain, the chief purpose and goal of military establishments in future must be to *avoid* wars.[36]

It is no longer tolerable that the young will be betrayed by old worn-out slogans of a by-gone age. To replace the existing war ethic by a peace ethic will not be easy. Modifying public opinion has become a highly skilled and specialized profession. In popular perception today, being for peace is to invite ridicule and the risk of being regarded as naive, unpatriotic, cowardly or worse - a traitor. Being for peace is mistakenly perceived by many as being disloyal to one's country. But - as loyal Germans learned in following Hitler into World War II, "my country right or wrong" is a sure recipe for national disaster. True patriotism is to support your country when it is right and help it find its way when it has gone astray - even if you are denounced as an agitator or a "Peacenik."

Comprehensive peace education will require the skillful application of all of the techniques of mass persuasion. As live broadcasts of the Gulf War and atrocities in former Yugoslavia vividly demonstrated, television newscasts - now more than ever before - can evoke moral outrage throughout the world by bringing into homes everywhere graphic pictures showing the human suffering of warfare. Nothing on this scale was possible in the past.

In addition to films and television, special events and programs designed to attract public support for the Security Council Resolution for Peace proposed herein might be part of a worldwide publicity campaign. A slogan

---

35   J. GALTUNG, THERE ARE ALTERNATIVES (1984).

36   *See* R.A.HINDE,Ed., THE INSTITUTION OF WAR (1991) at 244.

that captures the mind and fires the imagination may carry more impact than a ton of scholarly tomes that gather dust on university library shelves. "Rock" concerts, youth rallies, marches, runs, and a host of similar public relations events are among modern opinion-forming techniques. If distinguished personalities and celebrities of outstanding integrity and popularity can be recruited to provide leadership to campaigns for peace, the impact can be very powerful. Experience shows that persons with the charisma and dedication of a Woodrow Wilson, Mahatma Gandhi, Eleanor Roosevelt, Martin Luther King Jr., Archbishop Desmond Tutu or a Nelson Mandela can attract and stimulate world support for causes that may have seemed hopeless.[37]

An electronic information revolution is taking place and it can be marshalled to lead a peace revolution. A new electronic educational network has already been established and is rapidly expanding all over the world. In 1972, Dr. Takeshi Utsumi of Japan created "a virtual global-scale electronic lecture hall" which by 1986 encompassed 14 sites ranging from the U.S. east coast to Korea and Australia, spanning 14 time zones.[38] The Peace Studies Association at the University of Colorado has been developing an Electronic Library and Discussion Group for better communication on peace themes.[39] International law networks offer informational access never previously possible and can be a powerful new tool for peace[40]

Public opinion polling is another professional device that can be used to demonstrate to political leaders that the public supports specific peace proposals. The Americans Talk Security Foundation, a public opinion survey organization in Washington D.C., specializing in bi-partisan high-quality telephone surveys covering international security issues, found recently that a 62% majority of American voters support U.S. participation in a world conference to review the UN Charter. 80% favor the UN becoming responsible for world security and 83% favor an international criminal court to try individuals for gross violation of human rights.[41]

An example of an enlightening town-hall meeting can be found in the report of an assemblage in Alberta, Canada in 1989. We are told that "something magical happened" when over 1500 thoughtful people from the

---

37   It may be recalled that the U.S. Constitutional Convention in Philadelphia had George Washington and Benjamin Franklin to help focus national attention on the problem of federation.

38   T. Utsumi & P. Rossman, *Global Education for Fostering Global Citizenship: Proposal for a Global (Electronic) University Consortium*, 15 Transnational Perspectives (1989) 23.

39   PSA *The Peace Studies Bulletin*, Winter 1992-93.

40   See P. Zarins, What's On Line in International Law, ASIL Newsletter, Sept.- Oct. 1993 p. 24.

41   *See* World Federalist Quarterly Newsletter, Summer 1993, p.1.

Northern Hemisphere came together to listen to about two dozen informed experts and to share ideas about the best way to maintain peace and security in the Arctic region.[42]

Political "lobbying" is another effective tool that can be employed to gain support for specific peace proposals. The Baha'i community succeeded in deflecting persecution of its followers in Iran by employing the services of a leading public relations firm in the United States to advertise their plight and appeal to world public opinion for protection.[43] Inexpensive approaches are followed by many local organizations that encourage members to phone or write to their political leaders on important social issues.[44] In the last analysis, whether the world community will accept a new legal foundation for world survival by insisting that the Security Council do its job will be a test of the will and the power of the people.

C - The Power of the People

Ultimately, power lies with the people. Those millions who now demand a more rational and humane world order under law can no longer be brushed aside as unrealistic dreamers. The reality can not be concealed that self-styled "realists," who depicted the future as an unending feud between two irreconcilable superpowers locked in escalating armed competition for world domination, turned out to be completely *un*realistic. Nuclear weaponry, costing hundreds of billions of dollars and capable of destroying everything and everyone, proved to be totally unnecessary and totally unusable. Massive NATO military forces, assembled, armed, financed and trained to defeat an onslaught by Soviet nuclear armies, turned out to be unneeded paper tigers that proved incapable of stomping out relatively minor brush fires that erupted in Europe after the internal collapse of the Soviet empire. The "realists" and "militarists" - with their credibility severely tarnished - have a lot of explaining to do to the public and to the maligned "idealists." David Cortright, President of the Fourth Freedom Forum, has convincingly demonstrated:

> Credit for ending the cold war belongs to those who struggled for freedom from within, not those who brandished weapons from without. Peace was achieved in spite of, and not because of, the arms buildup.[45]

---

42   THE ARCTIC, CHOICES FOR PEACE AND SECURITY (1989), Proceedings.

43   K.R. Bigelow, A Campaign to Deter Genocide: The Baha'i Experience, in H. FEIN, GENOCIDE WATCH (1992) Chap.12.

44   A group called 20/20 Vision in Amherst, Massachusetts, sends out draft post-cards encouraging its members to write to their legislators. Peace letters and reports are distributed by thousands of groups and organizations, too numerous to mention.

45   D. CORTRIGHT, PEACE WORKS, The Citizen's Role in Ending the Cold War (1993) at 2.

(1) The Peace Movement:

A large peace movement involving millions of citizens all around the globe is already demanding the abolition of war, disarmament, protection of human rights and the preservation of the natural environment. Hunger for change to a more peaceful world order exists on a very large scale - without even counting "the silent majority." But the power of the people has not yet been sufficiently concentrated and unified - their message is not getting through clearly enough to move overly-cautious decsionmakers. Security Council diplomats who have the power to maintain peace, but fail to exercise their authority in the common interest, should not misjudge the explosive potential of the aroused passions of those who may reach the conclusion that the UN has lost its legitimacy.[46]

Young people in America, and elsewhere, have already demonstrated their aversion to wars that appear unjustified to many. Conscientious objectors fled the country or went to jail rather than face the choice of kill or be killed in Vietnam. Young students carrying placards saying: "Hell No, We Won't Go!" toppled a U.S. President and brought the Vietnam war to a halt. The massive assembly of Chinese youth in Tiananmen Square demonstrated the power of an unarmed public to halt armed tanks in their tracks. Apartheid in South Africa was dismantled by economic sanctions, peaceful protests and public opinion. Unarmed people pounding at the gates tore down the Berlin Wall, sent tyrants in flight and opened the floodgates to oppressed humanity demanding freedom.

Women - the wives and mothers of those who die in wars - have always been in the forefront of the struggle for a more peaceful world. As the women's liberation movement has demonstrated, women-power can be a most effective barrier against discrimination and the tides of violence that have drenched the world in brutal anarchy. An attempted military coup against a liberalized Soviet government was stopped by unarmed patriots led by mothers carrying banners saying: "Soldiers, Don't Shoot Your Mothers!" If women remain united in their idealism, clear in their goals and determined to attain a peaceful world, there is no government that can prevail against them.[47]

"Greenpeace" activists, at risk of their lives, confronted armed French flotillas to stop nuclear testing and - with the help of law - won. In August 1993, millions of Nigerians stayed away from work in the country's largest

---

46   *See* L.S.WITTNER, REBELS AGAINST WAR - The American Peace Movement 1933-1983 (1984).

47   According to Nobel Prize laureate Alfonso Garcia Robles: "...the mobilization of world public opinion has become essential for the achievement of disarmament." A. Robles, *The United Nations and Disarmament*, VIII *Disarmament* No.2 (Summer, 1985) at 57.

cities at the start of a three-day campaign of civil disobedience to protest the military Government decision to annul a Presidential election. Two weeks later, the New York Times headline reported: "Nigerian Ruler Cedes Power to Civilian."[48] As Gene Sharp of Harvard and many others have argued and demonstrated, mobilized civilian resistance can be an unstoppable force.[49]

(2) *Role of Non-Governmental Organizations:*

The UN Charter provides that the Economic and Social Council *may* make suitable arrangements for *consultation* with non-governmental organizations concerned with matters within ECOSOC's competence.[50] Over 500 international associations are accredited to ECOSOC and an even greater number are associated with the UN Department of Public Information. Most NGO's are special interest groups primarily concerned with protecting their own particular domain. Many, including church and educational associations with branches or affiliates throughout the world, are dedicated to supporting the UN Charter and the interests of world peace. They speak for millions of their members or followers all around the globe.[51]

As part of the observance of the International Year of Human Rights in 1968, René Cassin, who won the Nobel Prize for his work on the Universal Declaration of Human Rights, lauded the NGO's, saying:

> As disseminators of information they are truly irreplaceable...the non-governmental organizations play an important part in education for citizenship...they are the means of making the rights of human beings known and respected...It is impossible to say how many problems involving human rights would never have got on the agendas of these [official] bodies but for the initiative or indirect action of non-governmental organizations.[52]

NGO's have played a vital role in advancing the protection of human rights everywhere.[53] Human Rights Watch, with headquarters in New York, conducts systematic investigations of human rights abuses in some sixty

---

48   *See* K.B. Noble, *Millions of Nigerians Stay Home in Protest Campaign*, N.Y. Times, Aug. 13, 1993 p. A6; K.B. Noble, Nigerian Ruler Cedes Power to Civilian, N.Y. Times, Aug. 27, 1993 p. A-3.

49   *See* The Albert Einstein Institution, *Biennial Report 1990-1992*.

50   UN Charter, Article Art.71 (Italics added).

51   *See* DPI, *Non-Governmental Organizations Associated with the Department of Public Information*, Directory (1992).

52   Cited in UN publication THE UN AND HUMAN RIGHTS (1984) at 22-23.

53   *See* C.M. Eya Nchama, *The Role of the Non-Governmental Organizations in the Protection of Human Rights*, Bull. of Human Rights 90/1 (1991) 50.

countries.[54] A leading NGO, Amnesty International, won a Nobel Prize in 1977 for its work in protecting human rights around the world.

NGO's of many kinds have demanded a halt to nuclear testing or proliferation. They have fought for disarmament and environmental protection and economic development of the Third World. Not only do NGO's relieve the UN of financial burdens by not waiting for UN relief subsidies but such NGOs as Caritas, International Alert, the International Committee of the Red Cross and many others serve as an early warning signal of trouble brewing and thereby create a foundation for the preventive diplomacy that may prevent conflicts. Soon after taking office, Secretary-General Boutros-Ghali expressed his appreciation for the important work done by non-governmental organizations and the support which they rendered to the UN. On 8 November 1993 he noted:

> There were 200 non-governmental organizations at the start of this century. There are over 18000 today. They link groups to Governments and peoples around the world. They are a powerful force for education, cooperation and conflict prevention. [55]

But, as with so many other things at the UN, appearance and reality are not always identical. Although the work of the NGO's is publicly lauded, NGO's enjoy no privileges or immunities at the UN. They are grudgingly given a limited right to enter the building and receive documents available for public distribution. Some states would be happier if NGO's just went away and disappeared. No sovereign likes to have someone looking over his shoulder to judge the legality or propriety of his conduct and particularly how he treats his subjects. It should not be too surprising if some governments inclined to suppress human rights oppose the work or status of NGO's. Civic groups are granted UN NGO status by sufferance. ECOSOC has worked out a system of classifying those NGOs that it chooses to consult according to categories that determine whether such "consultants" can submit papers of up to 2000 words, 500 words, or none at all.[56]

NGOs are at the complete mercy of a UN Committee that has the power arbitrarily to silence an NGO by altering its status whenever it suits a nation

54   *See* HUMAN RIGHTS WATCH WORLD REPORT (1933). An International Human Rights Law Group of Washington D.C. champions human rights causes everywhere.*See The Law Group Docket* (1993).

55   Secretary-General Stresses Growing Role of Non-Governmental Organizations in Helping UN Meet Challenges Ahead, SG/SM/4754 20 May 1992 and Press Release SG/SM/5152, 8 Nov. 1993.

56   ECOSOC Resolution 1296 (XLIV), 23 May 1968. See C.J.Dias, *The UN World Conference on Human Rights, A Plentitude of Wrongs*, International Observer, July 1993 p. 13; Press Release, *Secretary-General calls for Greater UN-NGO Cooperation in Field of Social Development*, SG/SM/5706, 8 Sept. 1993.

represented on the Committee to do so. Since the NGO Committee acts by consensus, the discriminatory whim of any member can have a chilling effect on the freedom of speech of an organization which can find itself out of UN action without having any semblance of a hearing or due process of law. It is an unfair and unwise situation that calls for correction.[57]

In writing of NGO's, Professor Bowett confirms that the value of NGO's contribution to the work of ECOSOC is often regarded with skepticism, but he acknowledges that:

> If the UN is to be regarded as an organization representing 'We, the peoples...', as the Preamble states, then in principle the development of this consultative process is a worthy aim.[58]

The potential power of non-governmental organizations dedicated to the cause of peace and justice should not be underestimated. Despite the fact that NGO's are threatened by expulsion, retaliation, threats and all sorts of attacks directed against NGO activists, their participation in the activities of the UN Commission on Human Rights has more than tripled in the last two decades.[59] When the United Nations Conference on Environment and Development (UNCED) was being planned, it was officially recognized that:

> The Earth Summit will be a conference of leaders of Governments, but its success will largely depend on the interest and support of peoples and their active participation in NGO's and citizens groups which are contributing to its preparations.[60]

In the summer of 1992, nearly 30,000 people - men and women, young and old - from 171 countries assembled on the outskirts of Rio de Janeiro to let it be known that they expected solutions to the world's environmental problems. Shridath Ramphal, Guyana's former Foreign Minister, called the Earth Summit "the enlightened global community of people" aware that there was a crisis that humanity had to face and conquer.[61] Despite public relations indications to the contrary, the truth was that governments wished to - and did - exclude the NGO's from the official deliberations at UNCED.

Not willing to stand aside silently, the unofficial gathering of NGO's (in what they called the '92 Global Forum) took place about 30 miles from

---

57   *See* Report on Committee of NGO's, NGO/228, 1 April 1993.

58   D.W.BOWETT, THE LAW OF INTERNATIONAL INSTITUTIONS (2d Ed.) at 63.

59   It grew from 33 interventions in 1970 to 62 in 1980 and 119 in 1988; *Bulletin of Human Rights* 90/1 (1991) at 32, 72.

60   UN DPI Brochure, *In Our hands - Earth Summit*, Rio de Janeiro, 1-12 June 1992.

61   *See* I.S.RAMPHAL, OUR COUNTRY, THE PLANET: FORGING A PARTNERSHIP FOR SURVIVAL (1992).

the official governmental meetings. It brought together about 9000 regis-
tered journalists and attracted nearly half a million visitors. There were 700
exhibition booths presenting information from some 500 organizations. 350
scheduled meetings in tents and corridors produced 32 unofficial alternative
draft treaties for UNCED in about two weeks time. Former world leaders
and celebrities made pledges to act for a better world and were backed by
the signatures of over a million people from around the globe. The "ama-
teurs" were sending a message to the professional diplomats.[62]

President George Bush said he would not go to Rio, but - under
mounting public pressure - changed his mind at the last minute. His indecision and lack of enthusiasm may have cost him his Presidency. Democratic
candidate Clinton and his Vice-Presidential candidate Al Gore, an enthusi-
astic supporter of environmental reform, were elected. When 1500 NGO's
assembled in Vienna at the World Conference on Human Rights in June
1993, they were treated condescendingly and excluded from the drafting of
the final declarations. Nevertheless they succeeded in persuading the U.S.
government and the conference to support a proposal for the creation of a
new post of High Commissioner on Human Rights. The issue was referred
back to the General Assembly for consideration.[63]

Clive Archer's comprehensive study of international organizations led
him to conclude:

> With this power to mould people's minds and strengthen their
> willpower, the international non-governmental organizations
> have the potential to transform that which seems unlikely into
> a programme that governments and IGOs [International Gov-
> ernmental Organizations] can accept as possible. The history of
> international organizations, with its modest beginnings in the
> nineteenth century, might then enter a Golden Age.[64]

This latent power of the people and their organizations is not merely a potent
tool to push bureaucracies forward but it also represents a safeguard against
tyranny by politicians, diplomats, nations and even the Security Council.

---

62 *See Network '92*, the journal of the independent sectors at Rio published by the Centre for
Our Common Future, Geneva.

63 See M.H. Posner, Reflections on the Vienna Conference, ASIL Newsletter Sept. - Oct. 1993
p. 19. *See* A. Riding, *Rights Forum Ends in Call for a Greater Role by U.N.*, N.Y. Times, June
26, 1993, p. 2L. When the official organizers for the UN (fearful of antagonizing China)
decided to ban the Dalai Lama of Tibet from addressing the conference, twelve winners
of the Nobel Peace Prize boycotted the opening in protest. *See* E. Sciolino, *U.S. Rejects
Notion that Human Rights Vary with Culture*, N.Y. Times June 15, 1993 at A18.

64 C.ARCHER, INTERNATIONAL ORGANIZATIONS (2d ed.1992) at 187.

(3) Who Pays the Bill?

In addition to power of the people there is power of the purse - which may be even more powerful. A worldwide public relations campaign in support of a transformation of the present world legal order is a major - and expensive - undertaking. Mass media are often controlled by those primarily concerned with expanding their own economic or political power. Arms producers and others who benefit from the present war system are not eager to change it - and their profits may be very considerable. Being a prophet of peace is very unprofitable. How can this enormous inequity between the wealth of those who oppose change and the poverty of those who seek it be balanced?

At practically no cost, enlightened viewers, by whatever means they can muster, should repudiate the demeaning assumption of many TV producers that the public is interested only in bland entertainment, violence or tasteless pap. The viewing public should applaud and support programs and advertisers that seek a more tranquil world order. There are, of course, many TV shows worldwide that devote considerable time to serious peace and cultural themes, and these should be encouraged.

Fund raising for peace, as every peace organization - including the UN - can attest, is a very difficult process. Most Foundations or individuals support a specific cause and seldom contribute to others. Throwing money at major universities for additional colloquia, fellowships and seminars where old ideas are rehashed among old professors is not always the best way to support world peace. Donations to uphold world law are hard to come by, but there may be arising a new awareness of the relationship between law and peace.[65] Many governments have recognized the utility of peace studies and have allocated funds for such purposes. An office in Bonn, collaborates to distribute the work of several German Peace Institutes generously funded by state governments.[66]

The U.S. government has begun to move very slowly in a similar direction - as a result of public pressure. Around 1977, a group of private American citizens formed a non-profit organization - The National Peace Academy Campaign - to establish a federally sponsored graduate institution for training and research in peacemaking and conflict resolution. The idea was to create an official "Peace Academy" to balance the militarism being taught at the US Military Academy, US Naval Academy, U.S.Air Force

---

65   The Ford Foundation increased its funding for "international organizations and law" from
     $840,000 in 1985 to about $6.2 million in 1990; *International Organizations and Law*, A
     program paper of the Ford Foundation (1990).

66   *See* Reports of the *Hessische Stiftung Friedens und Konfliktforschung*, Frankfurt/Main,
     Germany.

Academy and similar institutions training young people for war. After skillful lobbying by proponents of the idea, Congress created a Commission to study the matter.[67] The Commission heard about 300 expert witnesses and unanimously recommended that a U.S Academy of Peace be created, that by helping to avoid conflicts, "could potentially save American citizens billions of dollars, directly and indirectly, each year."[68]

Both the State Department and Pentagon considered the bill an unwelcome incursion into their turf. Some conservative lawmakers considered it a "liberal scheme, insulting to the military services trained and armed to preserve the peace." The Reagan administration opposed the whole idea. But a long list of Congressional sponsors and the backing of a vigorous group of 45,000 private citizens finally forced a small amendment to the Defense Departments multi-billion dollar budget and allocated $16 million (over a two-year period) to establish a US Institute of Peace (USIP). To gain acceptance, the bill had to stipulate that the U.S. Institute of Peace would not be a teaching institute, as originally proposed, and that the Reagan administration would control who was appointed its Directors.[69]

Since its creation in 1984, as a result of public pressure, the USIP - not unmindful of the political climate in which it operates - has made many grants amounting to millions of dollars annually for peace studies and other peace-related activities.[70] It may not yet have lived up to the hopes of some of its sponsors, but the existence of the Institute is another illustration of the power of the people - even to override the will of the Executive Branch of the U.S. Government.

If one compares the amount of money spent on "defense" - even against invisible enemies - and the amount available to educate for peace, the disparity is shocking. According to a reliable report, the world spent close to 900 *billion* dollars on public military expenditures in the year 1987.[71] The United States spent over $23 *billion* in 1992 only to cover the budgets of thirteen different U.S. intelligence agencies that presumably were primarily engaged in spying on communists.[72] The nation's five <u>trillion</u> dollar military

---

67   Peace Academy Commission Bill (S.469) became part of the Elementary and Secondary Education Act (ESEA) that passed the Senate on Oct. 13, 1978 and the House on Oct. 15, 1978.

68   96th Congress, 2d Sess, *Interim Report of the U.S. Commission on Proposals for the National Academy of Peace and Conflict Resolution*, Public Law 95-561, Oct. 1980, at p.2.*See* C. McCarthy, *Doing Battle for Peace*, The Washington Post, June 15, 1980.

69   Public Law 98-525 - Oct. 19, 1984, *Dept. of Defense Authorization Act, 1985*, Title XVII. *See* B. Knickerbocker, *Congress Approves $16 million to Establish US Peace Institute*, Christian Science Monitor, Sept. 27, 1984.

70   *See* Biennial Reports of the USIP, and USIP monthly *Journal*.

71   R.L.SIVARD, WORLD MILITARY AND SOCIAL EXPENDITURES 1989 (1989) at 46.

72   *See* Article, based on figures from the Department of Defense Five Year defense Plan, *The Task: Rethink Spy Agencies for the New World Order*, N.Y. Times, Sunday May 10, 1991 p. E-5.

investment in the Cold War was diverted from public education, health, the environment and similar local problems, while the lethal technologies pioneered by the United States were leaking out in ways that posed new risks to the American public.[73]

Less than one-half of one percent of current world military expenditures (about four billion dollars per *day*) for a single day would be more than enough to mount a massive worldwide re-educational and publicity campaign for peace. The Security Council Consolidated Resolution for Peace, herein proposed, with its plan for worldwide disarmament under effective international controls would start to save nations hundreds of billions of dollars almost immediately. The cost of one single B-2 nuclear attack bomber - twenty of which are under construction - is about two billion dollars.[74] Would U.S. security be seriously jeopardized if we had *one* less? It is not unreasonable for the public to demand that national defense budgets divert a tiny fraction of the costs of preparing to kill people to the costs of teaching them how to live in peace.

D - Everybody Gains

Everybody gains from acceptance of the proposals put forth herein. The time may finally be "ripe" for change.

(1) Self Interest as Catalyst for Peace:

Roger Morris, who served on the National Security Council staff of Presidents Lyndon Johnson and Richard Nixon, in an Op-Ed piece, advised incoming President Bill Clinton to beware of the stale cadres of the establishment and to develop a coherent view of a transformed world and of America's new international interest, role and purpose. He noted the unprecedented opportunity for cooperation and peace in the face of unparalleled challenges posed by weapons proliferation, ecological damage, festering poverty, mass migrations and separatist violence. He wrote:

> National security dictates a sustained commitment to a genuinely cooperative, collective international security system...a peacekeeping force drawn proportionally from U.N. member states...the reconversion of its economy to a long-earned peace

---

73   See Editorial, The defense challenge, The Boston Globe, Oct. 16, 1992; R. Forsberg, Defense Cuts and Cooperative Security in the Post-Cold War World, Boston Review, May-July 1992.

74   *See* T. Weiner, *Military Accused of Lies Over Arms*, N.Y. Times June 26, 1993, p. A10, reporting that twenty B-2 bombers are under construction at a cost of more than $2 billion each and that military officials have misled Congress about the cost, performance and necessity of many of the most expensive military systems ever built.

and nonmilitary prosperity...tragedies such as Bosnia and Somalia are the real Munichs, the ominous dominoes, of our
era...the U.S. should immediately work to forge a system of
collective action to redress such outrages...a truly peaceful
planet must outlaw aggression within borders as well as across
them...He must reach for a fresh generation of thinkers and
doers...[75]

No one suggests that it will be easy to reverse an ancient tradition that
glorified killing "For God and Country." Nor will it be easy to eradicate
ethnic hatreds and fears or to persuade those who profit from armaments,
and hostilities to consider the general welfare or their own long-term
advantage before their own immediate gain. Entrenched bureaucrats fear
nothing more than change. But the effort to bring about needed changes
must be made - as an act of patriotism, morality and self-interest as well.
The proposed system of enforcing peace via the drafted new Security
Council resolutions is so much better, safer and cheaper than the existing
world disorder that the alteration must redound to everyone's ultimate
benefit.

(2) *Peace is Good Business:*

Peace is good for everybody - it is good for the world, good for the
United States and good for business. Nothing disrupts trade more than the
hazards of war. The World Bank has noted that war (international or civil)
makes its heaviest claims on the most productive workers. Each side strikes
at the economic jugular vein of the other. Economic disruption and the cost
in lost output and economic opportunity that results from war is almost
incalculable. Instead of expanded economic development, war breeds expanded human misery and impoverishment. [76]

Ambassador Madeleine K. Albright, U.S. Permanent Representative to
the United Nations and a member of the National Security Council, affirmed
that a system of effective collective security to cope with weapons of mass
destruction, refugee flows, economic dislocations and the "senseless killing
and maiming of millions of civilians" was clearly necessary and in the
interest of the United States:

Unless we face up to it and create the institutions and resources
necessary to share the burden of restoring international order,
the United States will stand exposed to an endless raid on its
resources, its goodwill, its soldiers, and finally its territorial

---

75   R. Morris, *A New Foreign Policy for a New Era*, N.Y. Times Op-Ed. Dec. 9, 1992.
76   *See* World Bank Information Briefs #L.01.8-92

integrity or the territorial integrity of its allies....When you start to add up the loss of on-going and potential business, trading, and investment opportunities for Americans because of proliferating armed struggles in this decade, the cost must be colossal...[T]he United Nations needs us and we need it to reach and then implement multilateral strategies. There simply is no other way.[77]

If there is some human urge to go to war, let it be a war against poverty, hunger, disease, environmental degradation, drug abuse, crime and the biggest crime of all - war itself. If there must be competition, let nations compete with each other to see which can be most helpful to the underprivileged and those less fortunate. Businesses that now seem to depend upon war preparation can be retooled - as they have been after every war -to help satisfy urgent social needs. Sure, there will be periods of hardship for both companies and individuals, but these can, if necessary, be helped by tax benefits and assistance programs to tide them over until they are reestablished. If subsidies can be given to farmers not to grow food that feeds people, why can't there be a program of temporary support to those who need it as a result of not producing weapons to kill people?

Self-interest is probably the principle catalyst driving human behavior. Every person called upon to act for peace must ask whether the insecure world in which we live today is better for him or her or future generations than the system outlined herein. The peace system that has been here formulated is based on new ways of thinking and improved international legal formulations and mechanisms designed to create an enhanced sense of social justice in a climate of safety which renders the present dangerous war system obsolete. It is a new approach that is attainable if there is enough public determination to insist upon it. It meets the test of what Mark Sommer has called

> a synthesis of mutually reinforcing elements blended into an integrated system in which the machinery of war is gradually supplanted by the coordinated mechanisms of international peacekeeping and a complex web of less formal arrangements. The formal mechanisms would center around constitutionally established global organizations vested with the necessary authority and capacity to inspect and enforce international law

---

77   M.K. Albright, *Statement before the Committee on Foreign Affairs, U.S. House of Representatives, Subcommittees on Europe and the Middle East and on International Security, International Organizations and Human Rights*, May 3. 1993, UN Press Release USUN 68-(93). *See* E.C. Luck, *The Collective Security Debate, Making Peace*, 89 Foreign Policy (Winter 1992-93) 137 at 155.

and to settle disputes without resort to armed force. Before relinquishing the unlimited right to possess and develop the hardware of unilateral defense, governments and peoples will both need to feel fully assured that their security can be better guaranteed by other means.[78]

(3) *Making it Happen:*

The first step in achieving any goal is to *believe* that it can be done. The next step is to make it happen! The fiftieth anniversary of the United Nations will be celebrated in the summer of 1995. The Secretary-General's proposed theme for the celebration is "We the Peoples".[79] It would be highly appropriate if *We*, the Peoples, did not depend upon *them*, the failed diplomats, to continue to determine the fate of the world.

The UN commemoration must pass from the hands of states, that have a vested interest in applauding and entrenching themselves, to the hands of people whose only concern is better protection of the public interest in the future. Pompous phrases and the heavy hand of hypocritical bureaucracy can not be allowed to smother common sense and human hope. What we need to really celebrate the event is to improve the workings of the United Nations; that can best be done by raising the united voice of millions of angry men and women from all around the globe who feel betrayed by the broken promises of the past.

The public will not remain indifferent forever. The sight of unendurable suffering all over the world that appears on the nightly television screen is provoking a reaction. The time is here for the people to speak out - **LOUD AND CLEAR!** The fact that nations have not yet been confronted with an overpowering public demanding change away from the existing war system should not be misinterpreted as chronic or incurable intimidation or paralysis. New York's senior Senator Daniel Patrick Moynihan, surveying the inability of states to curb the ongoing brutality of ethnicity in international politics, warned:

> The horror does not go away, and an international community will in fact ask itself just how much horror can be looked upon with indifference. To which the answer, of course, is plenty. But a large capacity to tolerate atrocity does not imply an unlimited

---

78   M.SOMMER, BEYOND THE BOMB (1985) at 91; *See* M.SHUMAN & J. SWEIG, Eds., CONDITIONS OF PEACE (1991); D.MITRANY, A WORKING PEACE SYSTEM (1966); H. Kelman, *Reflections on the History and Status of Peace Research*, 5 Conflict Management and Peace Science (1981) p. 108.

79   Preparatory Committee for the Fiftieth Anniversary of UN, ANV/178, 16 March 1993.

capacity. Civilizations with claims to universal values, do, in general, try to uphold them, if only after a point.[80]

Silence is not necessarily golden - a time comes when it is necessary to stop dreaming and **START SCREAMING!**[81]

The 50th anniversary of the United Nations should be organized by *We the Peoples* in every capital of the world. The citizens of China, India, Africa and the Middle-East yearn for peace and human security just as do those in all other parts of the globe. They are all beginning to feel the stirring of democracy and the yearning for a normal human life. Today they aspirations can be reinforced and they can all be linked by satellite communication systems for a massive demonstration of human solidarity. The theme should be to review the old prototype UN Charter to see what is needed to save future generations from the scourge of war and to promote the human justice and dignity under law that was paid for in the blood of sixty million people and never delivered by those who promised to make the world safe.

Local Heads of State can be invited to appear at massive citizens convocations in leading cities of their home countries. There is no need to wait for the UN or the Heads of State to convene a distant summit - as they did in Rio and Vienna - from which their citizens and the citizens of the world are effectively excluded. Since political leaders usually will not act until they are confident that they have the support of their constituencies, and nations will not act unless they believe that other states are with them, let the message from the people be delivered:

WE THE PEOPLES DEMAND A NEW PEACE SYSTEM *NOW!*.

If the leaders won't lead, let the people lead, and the leaders will surely follow.[82]

E - Evaluation

World security can only be guaranteed when a comprehensive new security system is in place. There is no assurance that the proposals herein contained will prove attainable. The public must know in which direction it wishes to go and start going there. The journey toward a new world of peace must be started now.

---

80   D.P.MOYNIHAN, PANDEMONIUM (1993) at 173.

81   The World Government Organization Coalition, based in San Francisco, is planning a conference of peace organizations to commemorate UN Charter Day in 1995 with debates regarding a *Citizen's Agenda for the 21st Century* that calls for re-examination of the UN Charter. WGOC News, Summer 1993.

82   *See* D.CORTRIGHT, PEACE WORKS, THE CITIZEN'S ROLE IN ENDING THE COLD WAR (Sept. 1993).

If our present structure of international society is not changed so that it can cope effectively with problems that can only be resolved globally, the existing global institutions will become irrelevant anachronisms. Humankind will either seek and find new pragmatic solutions and working modalities which will, of necessity, be invented to resolve regional and global problems - or it will destroy itself. The problem of world peace is too important to be left to the diplomats.

The Security Council has between now and 1995 to report to the people of the world how it intends to carry out its mandate for maintaining peace. If the report is not persuasive, it is up to the people of the world to find a better way to save themselves from the future. All of the plans for Charter reform, Charter amendment or Charter abandonment can be reviewed. There is no need to wait for the next world war before deciding that an improved world organization is needed to manage global problems -there may be no one left to make the decisions.

Those torch bearers who have the courage to strive for peace today may never see their prize but their reward shall be in knowing that they participated in the race to save the human race.

> In the time to come...perhaps a hundred years,
> Perhaps a thousand, when our poor names
> Are quite forgotten and our kingdom dust,
> On one sure certain day, the torch bearers
> Will, at some point of contact, see a light
> Moving upon this chaos.
> Though our eyes be shut forever in an iron sleep,
> Their eyes shall see the kingdom of the law...[83]

---

[83] From the poem "Tycho Brahe" by Alfred Noyes in WATCHERS OF THE SKY - The Torch Bearers (1922).